Propaganda and Neutrality

Propaganda and Neutrality

Global Case Studies in the Twentieth Century

Edited by
Edward Corse and Marta García Cabrera

BLOOMSBURY ACADEMIC
LONDON • NEW YORK • OXFORD • NEW DELHI • SYDNEY

BLOOMSBURY ACADEMIC

Bloomsbury Publishing Plc, 50 Bedford Square, London, WC1B 3DP, UK
Bloomsbury Publishing Inc, 1385 Broadway, New York, NY 10018, USA
Bloomsbury Publishing Ireland, 29 Earlsfort Terrace, Dublin 2, D02 AY28, Ireland

BLOOMSBURY, BLOOMSBURY ACADEMIC and the Diana logo are trademarks of Bloomsbury Publishing Plc

First published in Great Britain 2024
Paperback edition published 2025

Copyright © Edward Corse and Marta García Cabrera 2024

Edward Corse and Marta García Cabrera have asserted their right under the Copyright, Designs and Patents Act, 1988, to be identified as Editor of this work.

Cover Image © Uncle Sam Cartoon (1915), Chronicle / Alamy

This work is published open access subject to a Creative Commons Attribution-NoDerivatives 4.0 International licence (CC BY-ND 4.0, https://creativecommons.org/licenses/by-nd/4.0/). You may re-use, distribute, and reproduce this work in any medium, including for commercial purposes, provided you give attribution to the copyright holder and the publisher and provide a link to the Creative Commons licence.

All rights reserved. No part of this publication may be: i) reproduced or transmitted in any form, electronic or mechanical, including photocopying, recording or by means of any information storage or retrieval system without prior permission in writing from the publishers; or ii) used or reproduced in any way for the training, development or operation of artificial intelligence (AI) technologies, including generative AI technologies. The rights holders expressly reserve this publication from the text and data mining exception as per Article 4(3) of the Digital Single Market Directive (EU) 2019/790.

Bloomsbury Publishing Plc does not have any control over, or responsibility for, any third-party websites referred to or in this book. All internet addresses given in this book were correct at the time of going to press. The author and publisher regret any inconvenience caused if addresses have changed or sites have ceased to exist, but can accept no responsibility for any such changes.

Every effort has been made to trace the copyright holders and obtain permission to reproduce the copyright material. Please do get in touch with any enquiries or any information relating to such material or the rights holder. We would be pleased to rectify any omissions in subsequent editions of this publication should they be drawn to our attention.

A catalogue record for this book is available from the British Library.

A catalog record for this book is available from the Library of Congress.

ISBN: HB: 978-1-3503-2553-1
PB: 978-1-3503-2552-4
ePDF: 978-1-3503-2554-8
eBook: 978-1-3503-2555-5

Typeset by Deanta Global Publishing Services, Chennai, India

For product safety related questions contact productsafety@bloomsbury.com.

To find out more about our authors and books visit www.bloomsbury.com and sign up for our newsletters.

Contents

List of illustrations	vii
Notes on contributors	ix
Foreword *Jo Fox*	xiv
Acknowledgements	xviii
List of abbreviations	xxi

Alternative battlegrounds: An introduction to propaganda and neutrality
Edward Corse and Marta García Cabrera 1

Part I Propaganda and neutrality in the First World War

1 American neutrality and belligerent propaganda: Contested histories
    Stephen Badsey 23
2 First World War propaganda in neutral Argentina *María Inés Tato* 35
3 Legacies of neutrality: The propaganda battle and the Greek 'National Schism' at the local level *Georgios Giannakopoulos and Zinovia Lialiouti* 48
4 The Great War at sea and Portuguese propaganda *Miguel Brandão* 61
5 Propaganda and *Pistolerismo*: Barcelona as an alternative battleground of the First World War *Florian Grafl* 75

Part II Propaganda and neutrality in the Second World War

6 American propaganda challenging Irish neutrality *Karen Garner* 91
7 An 'irregular intellectual': Elizabeth Wiskemann in Berne *Guy Woodward* 103
8 Propaganda and Vichy France's 'neutrality': The impossible challenge
    Richard Carswell 116
9 Turkey's struggle for neutrality and the surveillance of Nazi propaganda
    Yasemin Türkkan Tunalı and Yasemin Doğaner 132
10 Beyond neutrality: Italian cultural propaganda in Portugal *Simone Muraca* 144
11 British propaganda and contingency planning for Spain
    Marta García Cabrera 157
12 Censorship and private shows: Mapping British film propaganda in Sweden *Emil Stjernholm* 169
13 Neutrality and (anti-)Imperialism: Multinational propaganda competition in neutral Macau *Helena F. S. Lopes* 181

14 Magazine propaganda: Influencing readership in neutral and occupied countries *João Arthur Ciciliato Franzolin* — 195

Part III Propaganda and neutrality in the Cold War and beyond

15 'Operation Mrs Partington': The British Council and the emergence of the Non-Aligned Movement *Edward Corse* — 213
16 Neutrality and Maoist propaganda in 1960s Switzerland *Cyril Cordoba* — 227
17 Diverging ideas in a tragic effort for the neutrality of Laos *P. Mike Rattanasengchanh* — 239
18 The global anti-Apartheid campaign as counter-neutrality propaganda: The US and the UK cases compared *Nicholas J. Cull* — 250

Epilogue: The Russo-Ukrainian war, propaganda and the end of neutrality? *Pascal Lottaz* — 263
Select Bibliography — 277
Index — 288

Illustrations

Figures

0.1	'Remember Belgium: Enlist to-day', British First World War recruitment poster, *c.* 1914	10
0.2	'Journey's End', Irish Taoiseach, Éamon de Valera, depicted by the Canadian cartoonist John Collins in *The Gazette*, April 1941	12
0.3	'*Spillinget Blod: Nej till NATO*' [Spilled blood: no to NATO], a protest against Sweden's application to join NATO, 16 May 2022, following the Russian invasion of Ukraine	15
4.1	Illustration of Kaiser Wilhelm II 'sowing' mines in the North Sea in the Portuguese magazine *O Zé*, 13 April 1915	68
4.2	The magazine *Ilustração Portuguesa*, 1 November 1915, showing the alleged German attack on the Portuguese ship *Douro*	70
5.1	Cartoon depicting the downfall of the (former) Spanish Prime Minister, Count Romanones, in *La Acción*, 21 April 1917, using the title of the article attributed to him '*Neutralidades que matan*' [Fatal Neutralities] two and a half years previously	77
8.1	'*N'oubliez pas Oran!*' [Don't forget Oran!], Vichy French poster, *c.* 1940	119
8.2	'Dakar-Mers El-Kébir', Vichy French poster, October 1940	121
8.3	Pétain and Hitler shaking hands at Montoire, 24 October 1940	123
8.4	'*L'Europe en marche contre le bolshevisme*' [Europe on the march against Bolshevism], Vichy French poster, *c.* 1942	125
13.1	Macau and Hong Kong. Royal Navy Intelligence Map, 1945	182
13.2	The *Dundee Courier* report on the *Sai-On* case, reproducing the exaggerated information from the Chinese Central News Agency in Chongqing, 30 August 1943	188
13.3	The Ferreira do Amaral statue in Macau, undated	189
14.1	'*O mundo livre*' [The Free World], *Em Guarda*, Ano 1, No. 8 (1942), page 24	203
14.2	'*O mundo escravizado*' [The Enslaved World], *Em Guarda*, Ano 1, No. 8 (1942), page 25	204
14.3	'*Capturado pelos americanos, esse general alemão contempla o seu mísero futuro, completamente vazio des grandes conquistas*' [Captured by the Americans, this German general contemplates his miserable future, completely empty of great conquests], *Em Guarda*, Ano 4, No. 1 (1944/5), page 6	205
15.1	Gamal Abdel Nasser of Egypt, Jawaharlal Nehru of India and Josip Broz Tito of Yugoslavia at the Brioni Summit, July 1956	216

15.2 Sir Laurence Olivier and Vivien Leigh meeting Josip Broz Tito and Jovanka Broz after a performance of Shakespeare's *Titus Andronicus* at the National Theatre in Belgrade, June 1957   219
15.3 An extract from a letter from Benjamin Britten and Peter Pears to Mary Potter, recording their meeting with Nehru in December 1955, in the handwriting of Britten   221
18.1 Anti-Apartheid demonstrators picketing Barclays Bank near Trafalgar Square in London, March 1978   259
19.1 Protestors outside the Swiss Parliament in Berne, demonstrating against the Russian invasion of Ukraine, March 2022   269

Table

16.1 Chinese Periodicals Seized by Swiss Customs (Number of Copies)   230

Contributors

Stephen Badsey is Professor of Conflict Studies and Co-Director of the First World War Research Group at the University of Wolverhampton, UK. His books include: *Modern Military Operations and the Media* (1994); *The Media and International Security* (2000); *Britain, NATO, and the Lessons of the Balkan Conflicts 1991–1999* (2004), with Paul Latawski; *Doctrine and Reform in the British Cavalry 1880–1918* (2008); *The British Army in Battle and Its Image 1914–1918* (2009); and *The German Corpse Factory: A Study in First World War Propaganda* (2019). He is also the series editor of the *Wolverhampton Military Studies Series* for Helion publishers.

Miguel Brandão is a PhD student at the University of Porto and a researcher of the Portuguese Navy Centre, Portugal. He graduated in history at the Faculty of Arts in Porto and he concluded his Master's degree in the same institution. He is the author of many articles on Portuguese naval and military history, the most recent being 'War at Sea – Portugal, Navigation and Maritime Commerce during World War One' in *Essays in Economic & Business History* (2021).

Richard Carswell is an independent researcher in European history of the mid-twentieth century. His book *The Fall of France in the Second World War: History and Memory* was published in 2019. His translation from Spanish of Javier Rodrigo's *Fascist Italy in the Spanish Civil War, 1936–1939* was published in 2021. He is a regular book reviewer for the journals *French History* and *Modern & Contemporary France*. He has acted as an adviser to the combined Museums of the Liberation of Paris/General Leclerc/Jean Moulin.

Cyril Cordoba is a Postdoctoral Researcher at the Department of Contemporary History at the University of Fribourg, Switzerland. His doctoral thesis analysed the Sino-Swiss cultural and political relationships during the Cold War and Beijing's propaganda networks in the West. It has recently been published under the title 'Au-delà du Rideau de Bambou [Beyond the Bamboo Curtain]' and will soon be published in English as *China-Swiss Relations during the Cold War* (2022). He contributed to the collective books *Europe and China in the Cold War* (2019) and *Transnational History of Switzerland* (2020) and co-edited a special issue of the historical journal *Traverse about Switzerland and East Asia* (2020). He is currently working on the political history of the International Locarno Film Festival.

Edward Corse is an Honorary Research Fellow at the Centre for the History of War, Media and Society at the University of Kent, UK and at the Centre for the Study of Health, Ethics and Society at the University of Hamburg, Germany. He published *A*

Battle for Neutral Europe: British Cultural Propaganda during the Second World War (2013), which examined the role of the British Council in four neutral European countries during this period. He has also researched separately on different aspects of British propaganda in Ireland, Sweden and Poland. He is currently researching British propaganda policy and practice more generally in neutral Turkey during the Second World War.

Nicholas J. Cull is Professor of Public Diplomacy at the Annenberg School for Communication and Journalism at the University of Southern California, USA. He is a pioneer scholar and educator in the field of public diplomacy, and a historian of the role of mass communication in foreign policy. Cull served as President of the International Association for Media and History from 2004 to 2019. His many books include *Selling War: The British Propaganda Campaign against American 'Neutrality' in World War II* (1996) and *Public Diplomacy: Foundations for Global Engagement in the Digital Age* (2019).

Yasemin Doğaner is Professor of History at Hacettepe University, Ankara, Turkey. She has examined the role of the founder of Modern Turkey, Mustafa Kemal Atatürk, and the effect of his revolution on Ankara's society. She is the author of two research books, *Cumhuriyet Döneminde Sansür (1923–1973)* [Censorship in the Republican Era (1923–1973)] (with Mustafa Yılmaz) and *Türk Demokrasi Tarihinde Vatan Cephesi* [Vatan Cephesi (Homeland Front) in the History of Turkish Democracy].

Jo Fox is Pro Vice Chancellor (Research and Engagement) and Dean, School of Advanced Study, University of London, UK. She is a specialist in the history of propaganda and psychological warfare in twentieth-century Europe. She has published on propaganda in Britain and Germany during the First and Second World Wars, in particular exploring the connections between propaganda and popular opinion, and on mis- and disinformation in contemporary society. She is currently working on a four-year Leverhulme-funded project with James Smith (Durham) and Pat Waugh (Durham) on 'The Political Warfare Executive, Covert Propaganda and British Culture' and on an AHRC Covid-19 rapid response project on 'Covid-19 rumours in historical context'.

João Arthur Ciciliato Franzolin is a Postdoctoral Research Student and Assistant at the State University of São Paulo (UNESP), Brazil. His doctor's degree on German war magazine *Die Wehrmacht* was obtained at the Europa-Universität Flensburg, Germany (2014–17). He is the author of the book *Uma aposta arriscada: O Jornal Meio-Dia e o Nazismo (1939–1942)* [A Risky Bet: The Newspaper *Meio-Dia* and Nazism] (2013).

Marta García Cabrera is a Postdoctoral Researcher at the University of Las Palmas de Gran Canaria (ULPGC), Spain, and Honorary Research Fellow at the University of Kent, UK. Her doctoral thesis analysed British propaganda in Spain during the First and the Second World Wars, but her research interests also include foreign intelligence in Spain during the twentieth century. She has been carrying out her research as a visiting researcher at the Freie Universitat in Berlin (Germany) through the funding of the Ministry of Universities of the Spanish Government and the European Union - Next Generation Funds. García Cabrera has published numerous book chapters and articles, and her first book was *Bajo las zarpas del león: la persuasión británica en España durante las guerras mundiales* [Under the Lion's Paw: British persuasion in Spain during the world wars] (2022).

Karen Garner is Professor of Historical Studies at SUNY Empire State College in upstate New York and a Fulbright Scholar. She is the author of several book chapters and four academic books focusing on how gender power operates in twentieth- and twenty-first-century international politics and governance including most recently *Women and Gender in International History: Theory and Practice* (2018) and *Friends and Enemies: The Allies and Neutral Ireland during the Second World War* (2021).

Georgios Giannakopoulos is Lecturer in Modern History at City, University of London, UK. He has held research and teaching posts at New York University, Durham University, LSE, KCL, the Academy of Athens and the University of the Peloponnese. He is currently completing a monograph titled *The Interpreters: British Intellectuals and Imperial Order in Southeastern Europe*. His published works include articles in the *History of European Ideas*, *Global Intellectual History*, *Modern European History* and the *Journal for Modern Greek Studies*. Part of this research project has been supported by a postdoctoral grant from the Greek States Scholarship Foundation.

Florian Grafl is a research coordinator at the University of Heidelberg, Germany. His PhD entitled 'Terroristas, Pistoleros, Atracadores. Collective Violence in Barcelona during the Interwar Period (1918–1936): Urban Space, Practices and Protagonists' was defended in February 2017. His research interests include the history of urban violence in twentieth-century Europe, media history with a special focus on transnational media in modern times and the global history of knowledge in the nineteenth century.

Zinovia Lialiouti is Assistant Professor of Modern and Contemporary European History at the Department of Political Science and Public Administration, National and Kapodistrian University of Athens, Greece. She is also Director of the Institute for the Study of Greek-German Relations at the same department. She is the author of the books *Anti-Americanism in Greece 1947–1989* (2016) and *The 'Other' Cold War: American Cultural Diplomacy in Greece 1953–1973* (2019). Her research interests involve the history of ideas and propaganda in the twentieth century, cultural diplomacy and the formulation of national identities. She is currently the scientific academic responsible for the project 'Images of Germany in Greece during the First World War: Propaganda and Public Discourse, 1914–1918', funded by the German Federal Foreign Office through the Greek-German Future Fund.

Helena F. S. Lopes is Lecturer in Modern Asian History at Cardiff University, UK. She was previously a Leverhulme Early Career Research Fellow at the University of Bristol, UK. She holds a DPhil in History from St Antony's College, Oxford, and has taught modern Chinese history and global history at both Oxford and Bristol. Her research focuses on the international, political and social history of the Second World War and the early post-war period in South China. She is the author of *Neutrality and Collaboration in South China: Macau during the Second World War*.

Pascal Lottaz is Adjunct Professor at Temple University Japan Campus and Adjunct Researcher at the Waseda Institute for Advanced Study, Tokyo. His research focuses on neutral actors in international relations, especially on neutrality during the two world wars and during the Cold War. His publications include a monograph on *Sweden, Japan, and the Long Second World War 1931–1945* (2022), several edited books of which the most recent is *Neutral Beyond the Cold: Neutral States and the Post-Cold War International System* (2022) and several articles like 'The Politics and Diplomacy of Neutrality' (2022) and 'Neutrality Studies' (2022).

Simone Muraca obtained his PhD in Historical Studies from the University of Padua, Italy, with a comparative and transnational study on Italian fascist cultural diplomacy in Spain and Portugal during the decade of Italian wars (1935–45). He holds a BA in Philosophy and an MA in History from the University of Milan, Italy. His main research interests lie in practices and theories of cultural diplomacy, transnational fascism, intellectual history and cultural mobilities in the twentieth century.

P. Mike Rattanasengchanh is Assistant Professor of Asian and US History at Midwestern State University, USA. He focuses his research and teaching on Southeast and East Asia, Cold War in the global south, public diplomacy/propaganda, political social media and nationalism, US foreign relations, counterinsurgency and Asian American studies. He is currently working on a book project on US–Thai relations during the Cold War, examining the role of public diplomacy/public relations programmes in nation-building.

Emil Stjernholm is Assistant Professor in Media and Communication Studies at the Department of Communication and Media, Lund University, Sweden. His areas of research include documentary film, propaganda studies and Swedish television history. Together with Fredrik Norén and Claire C. Thomson, he has edited *Nordic Media Histories of Propaganda and Persuasion* (2022).

María Inés Tato is a Researcher of the National Scientific and Technical Research Council, Argentina (CONICET) at the Institute of Argentine and American History 'Dr Emilio Ravignani', University of Buenos Aires (UBA), Argentina. She is Founder and Coordinator of the Group of Historical War Studies (GEHiGue) at that institute. She is Professor at UBA and the Master in War History at the Superior War College, Army Faculty, at the National Defense University (UNDEF). Her current research area is the impact of the First World War in Argentina and the Falklands/Malvinas War. She is the author of *La Trinchera Austral. La sociedad Argentina ante la Primera Guerra Mundial* [The Southern Trench: Argentine society before the First World War] (2017) and co-editor of *Las Grandes Guerras del Siglo XX y la Comunidad Española de*

Buenos Aires [The Great Wars of the Twentieth Century, and the Spanish Community of Buenos Aires] (2015), and most recently *La Cuestión Malvinas en la Argentina del Siglo XX. Una historia social y cultural* [The Malvinas Issue in Argentina during the Twentieth Century: a social and cultural history] (2020) and *The Global First World War: African, East Asian, Latin American and Iberian Mediators* (2021).

Yasemin Türkkan Tunalı is Assistant Researcher at Hacettepe University, Ankara, Turkey. Her work has primarily focused on the First World War, with studies into the Romanian Prisoners of War in the Ottoman territories and the perception of the Armenian Question from Spanish diplomatic records. More recently she has considered the transition to multiparty political life in the Turkish Republic. She is the author of the research book, *Cumhuriyet'in Yeni Adam'ı* [*Yeni Adam* (The New Man) of the Republic].

Guy Woodward is a Postdoctoral Research Associate at the Department of English Studies, Durham University, UK, where he works on the project 'The Political Warfare Executive, Covert Propaganda and British Culture', funded by the Leverhulme Trust. His research interests lie in the intersections of literature, politics and international relations, with a particular focus on culture in Ireland and Britain during the mid-twentieth century and the Second World War. His book *Culture, Northern Ireland, and the Second World War* was published in 2015, and he has contributed articles to the *Irish University Review*, *Literature and History*, *Modern Fiction Studies* and the *Review of English Studies*. He also co-edited *Irish Culture and Wartime Europe, 1938–48* (2015).

Foreword

Jo Fox

What is the relationship between neutrality and propaganda? The complexity of the question is compounded by the collision of two highly contested and flexible concepts, with definitions and meanings that often say as much about the historical context in which those definitions were created and deployed as they do the concepts themselves.

There are differences between permanent or perpetual states of neutrality, ad hoc neutrality, elected or imposed neutrality and non-belligerency, where there is the opportunity to favour one side over the other. Neutrality can apply to military situations where there may be clear points of reference (such as Article 15 of the 1907 Fifth Hague Convention or the UN charter) or the more inscrutable concepts of political or attitudinal neutrality. And there is, of course, the gulf between the theory of neutrality and its operation in practice. History reveals that 'neutrality' can be anything but, either a guise for implicit and hidden support or using neutral status to play one side off against the other for a particular gain.

Equally, propaganda operates across a broad spectrum of activity – from the more subversive, clandestine acts of psychological and political warfare through to the soft power of cultural interaction. Propaganda emerges as a complex confluence of ideas, messages and themes, emerging from formal and informal sources, designed to appeal to individual and collective belief systems.

It is perhaps because of this mutability and adaptability that neutral spaces are interesting places for the propagandist to operate: where what is permissible is open to a degree of interpretation, or can certainly be flexed, and boundaries pushed (although there are obvious risks in doing so). Neutral spaces are sites for the interaction between the longer, slower burn of softer cultural diplomacy and the sharp, hotter interventions that characterize political warfare.

There is the obvious tension between the purpose of propaganda – to elicit behaviours or a particular mindset conducive to the desires of the propagandist – and the state of being neutral, unless, of course, the desire is the continued state of neutrality, in which case they can be mutually reinforcing. Local circumstance – the extent to which a state is 'collaboratively' or 'oppositionally' neutral – determines just how sharp those tensions will be. Many of the chapters in this volume are a case in point.

Let's take one example to show the complexities of the interplay between propaganda and neutrality: the Second World War. Neutral states (e.g. Ireland, Portugal or Spain) became prime sites of propagandistic activity, arenas where belligerents entered a cultural and political 'face-off' and where there were complex layers of disinformation, at the tougher end, and persuasion, at the other. Obviously, different types of intervention served different ends and could work in concert, in parallel or even in tension.

Edward Corse's work on the British Council during the Second World War clearly demonstrates that cultural propaganda was primarily about generating broad sympathy sufficient to prevent intervention on the side of the Axis powers, by encouraging an understanding of the British way of life and establishing common ground for cooperation or parity of experience. This kind of propaganda, as Corse has observed, is marked by its seemingly benign and subtle nature, often performed at a remove and without overt reference to any particular propagandistic messaging.[1]

The soft power of cultural affinity or shared reference points was often deployed in neutral contexts to subtle effect. Historical bonds, for example, could also be used more directly. The Portuguese decision in 1943 to permit Allied airbases on the Azores (thus preventing the proposed seizure of the islands under the codename Alacrity) was presented by Winston Churchill simply as the honouring of a treaty, 'signed in 1373 between ... King Edward III and King Ferdinand and Queen Eleanor of Portugal'. Churchill went to great lengths to point out that this treaty had been 'reinforced in various forms by the Treaties of 1386, 1642, 1654, 1660, 1661, 1703, 1815 and a secret declaration of 1899. In more modern times, the validity of old Treaties was recognized in the Treaties of Arbitration concluded with Portugal in 1904 and 1914'. Although this act gave a clear advantage to the Allies in a strategically significant area, propagandists were at pains to stress that 'nothing should be said which would imply that Portugal has abandoned her neutrality or which would give the Germans any further excuse for exerting increased pressure on the Salazar Government'. Indeed Salazar was to be praised for honouring a treaty that was over six hundred years old, 'an engagement', stated Churchill, that was surely 'without parallel in world history', a further affirmation of, in the words of Article 1 of the 1373 treaty, 'true, faithful, constant, mutual and perpetual friendships'.[2] Elsewhere religion provided the connective tissue. Nazism's threat to organized religion and established belief systems could be effectively mobilized by propagandists operating in the neutral Mediterranean states.

'Softer', culturally informed and focused propaganda operated alongside the more subversive work of organizations such as the Political Warfare Executive. For 'black' propagandists, neutral nations served as an important operational space, where propaganda could operate under the radar of official censorship, where international interactions were less scrutinized and where networks for onward transmission to enemy and enemy-occupied territories could be cultivated. Neutral nations could also be the target of such activity, particularly in generating scepticism or mistrust and sometimes (as in the case of the First World War) advocating active intervention. This work involved a high degree of risk – to be found to be undertaking active disinformation campaigns on the ground in a neutral state jeopardized relations, created diplomatic tension and undermined 'white' or cultural propaganda.

But there were circumstances under which such interventions could be more controllable and where soft cultural propaganda and subversive political warfare could coexist comfortably, and indeed merge, with a neutral nation. Sir John Betjeman's tenure as press attaché to neutral Eire was undoubtedly a success in the sense that his more subversive activities were disguised by his appearance as simply an eccentric, exceptional host and raconteur.[3]

Of course, neutral states are not only the site of propaganda, they are also the subject of it. It was the violation of Belgian neutrality, formalized in the Treaty of London of 1839, by Germany that served as a propagandistic focus at the outbreak of the First World War. The German invasion of neutral Belgium was interpreted as a simultaneous assault on moral order, the rule of law, Christian values and civilization. Allied propagandists made much of German Chancellor Theobald von Bethmann Hollweg's denunciation of the Treaty of London as a mere 'scrap of paper'. This became the strapline for hard-hitting visual propaganda, while authors lost little time in condemning Bethmann Hollweg's pronouncement to the Reichstag that 'necessity knows no law'. That Germany could seemingly ignore international treaties, particularly those that enshrined a nation's right to declare its neutrality, was framed as a challenge to international order and to the foundations of society.

The relationship between neutrality and propaganda, then, is a fascinating subject for further investigation. Because of its particular status, the neutral space sees the full spectrum of propagandistic activities ranging from soft, cultural power through to the more subversive elements of psychological warfare. It is arguably the space where the lines between diplomacy and propaganda are more blurred, and it is a place where, historically, propagandists from belligerent nations directly engage, competing for attention, and where campaigns clash. Equally, it is a hazardous enterprise, since the consequences of not respecting neutrality are high and may jeopardize diplomatic relations or future campaigns.

In attempting to harness what is happening in these spaces, researchers face the challenge of locating the wide variety of propaganda sources in circulation, capturing the multiple forms propaganda took and understanding the dynamics created by the interaction between formal and informal propaganda, specifically how various strands of propaganda reinforced one another or indeed generated frictions. Historically such dynamics have been complex to track, map and explain.

But how does this translate into the digital age? Does the ability to undertake this task become more complex due to the scope and scale of propagandistic activity now, or does the ability to analyse computational propaganda at scale facilitate greater insight? What constitutes digital neutrality, and is it possible to curtail propagandistic activity within it? As psy-war becomes increasingly digital in nature, should international agreements seek to protect neutrality in these new spaces, or do current international agreement extend to cyber-warfare? Are such protections even possible? And what are the obligations of neutral states for preventing belligerent activities operating out of their territories? Certainly, clarification is needed on these matters; but we might expect, as the historical examples in this volume attest, that propaganda will morph and change according to the new circumstance, in subtle, sometimes undetectable and unpredictable ways, and that the propagandist will always get through – somehow.

Notes

1 Edward Corse, *A Battle for Neutral Europe: British Cultural Propaganda during the Second World War* (London: Bloomsbury, 2013).
2 The UK National Archives (TNA), Foreign Office files (FO) 898/1654 Statement by the Prime Minister.
3 Robert Cole, *Propaganda, Censorship and Irish neutrality in the Second World War* (Edinburgh: Edinburgh University Press, 2006); Ian S. Wood, *Britain, Ireland and the Second World War* (Edinburgh: Edinburgh University Press, 2010).

Acknowledgements

This volume was inspired by an international conference entitled 'Propaganda and Neutrality: Alternative Battlegrounds and Active Deflection', which took place in June 2021. The conference was hosted online by the University of Kent's Centre for the History of War, Media and Society in the UK,[1] in collaboration with the Institute of Historical Research (IHR) in London and the University of Las Palmas de Gran Canaria (ULPGC) in Spain.[2] The conference was held over two days with all but two of twenty-nine speakers joining live from sixteen different countries around the world. We had originally planned to hold the event in person in June 2020 at the IHR. The Covid-19 pandemic, of course, impacted our plans and turned the conference into a different sort of event: fully virtual via Zoom, but also with the benefit of allowing for people around the world to participate as speakers and audience members.

We organized the event to try to overcome the limitations of the existing historiography on propaganda and neutrality. We recognized that despite several important studies published to date, the role of neutral states in relation to propaganda struggles had not been subject to a comprehensive and comparative study across different time periods and geographies. The conference offered a space for debate in which neutrals and the role they have played regarding propaganda activities became the exclusive focus of analysis. This volume has also been partly designed as a companion to two previous books published by I.B. Tauris and Bloomsbury: *Propaganda, Power and Persuasion: From World War I to Wikileaks*, edited by David Welch and published in 2013; and *Propaganda and Conflict: War, Media and Shaping the Twentieth Century*, edited by Mark Connelly, Jo Fox, Stefan Goebel and Ulf Schmidt, published in 2019.[3]

Our keynote speaker at the conference was Jo Fox – Dean of the University of London's School of Advanced Study and a renowned expert in propaganda studies – who described the study of propaganda and neutrality together as 'a fantastic subject that illuminates the many faces of propaganda': a 'very revealing' subject that brought a fresh perspective to her field of study. We are very grateful to Jo for her participation in the conference and also for writing a foreword for this volume.

We would, of course, like to thank all the contributors to this volume for their time and effort in creating what we think is an excellent set of chapters outlining different case studies. Most of the contributors participated in the conference itself, but there is one exception – Pascal Lottaz – whom we invited to participate in the volume at a late stage, as we considered that Pascal would be able to provide an analysis of the propaganda and neutrality aspects relating to the war that started in February 2022 through Russia's invasion of Ukraine. We are very grateful for Pascal for writing his chapter quickly, reflecting fast-moving events. The main challenge of writing such a chapter about contemporary events is, of course, that it is impossible to know the outcome or the significance of things which are happening day by day – perhaps, by the time you are reading this book, you might know the outcome of that war – but we think Pascal's analysis is a very useful addition which sheds light upon the other case studies in this volume.

Other participants who provided papers for the conference but who were not able to take part in the book for various reasons, whom we would like to thank (in the order that they spoke), are: Maartje Abbenhuis, Mario Draper, Richard Dunley, Vincent Trott, Lior Tibet, Veronica Barry, Hillary Briffa and Steve Westlake. The conference benefited greatly from their participation and perspectives. In addition, we would like to thank the chairs of the panels for the conference: Michael Auwers, Mark Connelly, Stefan Goebel, Nick Cull, Gaynor Johnson, Mark Lawrence, Ulf Schmidt and Philip Boobbyer. All the chairs helped ensure we had a great couple of days and they adeptly took on the challenge of online chairing. Jacinta Mallon and Jenny Turner also helped us through their live tweeting on the day (@WMS_UniKent) and through social media support more generally. We would also like to thank Gemma Dormer at the IHR for her support while we were planning an in-person event (even though, in the end, that did not happen because of Covid-19) and also for helping us advertise the event for a wide participation. The following people: Chrissie Dixon at the BISA (British International Studies Association), Rogelia Pastor-Castro and James Ellison at BIHG (the British International History Group), Richard Smith of the FCDO (Foreign, Commonwealth and Development Office) Historians, Peter Johnston of the RAF Museum (then of the National Army Museum), Bill Hale (SOAS), Stephen Mitchell (British Institute at Ankara), Gareth Winrow (Turkish Area Studies Review), Neville Wylie (University of Stirling), Sofia Leitão (formerly of the British Council in Lisbon) and Thomas Meyer (H-Soz-Kult) also helped us advertise the conference through channels available to them, as well as the team at the Royal Historical Society. Events would not work without all the preparation and, indeed, the audiences who attend – and we are grateful to all of those around the world who joined us for those two days and for the questions they asked.

We are grateful particularly to Stefan Goebel as the Director of the Centre for the History of War, Media and Society at Kent for his encouragement and enthusiasm for the conference and this volume and his helpful advice throughout. He also took the time to read an early draft of our introduction and provided very useful comments and reassurance that we were along the right lines. We are grateful as well to David Welch, Ulf Schmidt, Gaynor Johnson and Jo Fox for their views on the introduction, which were particularly helpful as we completed the manuscript. Any deficiencies, of course, remain with us as editors. All Crown Copyright material from The National Archives in the UK (TNA) is displayed under the Open Government Licence version 3.0.[4] We, and the relevant chapter authors, and the publisher gratefully acknowledge the permission granted to reproduce copyrighted material in this book. All other third-party copyrighted material displayed in the pages of this book, unless otherwise stated, is done so on the basis of fair dealing for the purposes of criticism and review.

We would like to thank our families and friends who have encouraged us to continue to pursue our historical interests – it has been a lot of work, but their support has been very important in getting everything 'over the line'. Finally, we would also like to thank each other for being a great two-person team – we have both enjoyed the experience of putting together a conference and volume all the more for getting on so well – and happy to call each other 'amigos'.

Written virtually somewhere between Kent, Gran Canaria and Berlin, June 2022.
Edward Corse and Marta García Cabrera

Notes

1. The University of Kent's Centre for the History of War, Media and Society was established by Professor David Welch as the Centre for the Study of Propaganda in 1995 and has become known as a world leading centre for propaganda studies.
2. Recordings of the conference are available at: https://kent.cloud.panopto.eu/Panopto/Pages/Sessions/List.aspx?folderID=1961e036-9e1c-45b4-99f1-ad8e00bcb5a8 (or for easier typing http://bit.ly/PropNeutralConference which will take you to the same place) (accessed 20 March 2022).
3. David Welch (ed.), *Propaganda, Power and Persuasion: From World War I to Wikileaks* (London: I.B. Tauris, 2013); Mark Connelly, Jo Fox, Stefan Goebel and Ulf Schmidt (eds), *Propaganda and Conflict: War, Media and the Shaping of the Twentieth Century* (London: Bloomsbury, 2019).
4. See details of the Open Government Licence version 3.0 here https://www.nationalarchives.gov.uk/doc/open-government-licence/version/3/ (accessed 18 June 2022).

Abbreviations

ACS	Archivio Centrale dello Stato (Central State Archives), Rome, Italy
AFIN	American Friends of Irish Neutrality
AHD	Arquivo Histórico Diplomático (Historical Diplomatic Archives, Ministry of Foreign Affairs), Lisbon, Portugal
ANC	African National Congress, a political party in South Africa
ANTT	Arquivo Nacional Torre do Tombo (National Archives of Portugal), Lisbon, Portugal
AOS	Arquivo Oliveira Salazar (Oliveira Salazar Papers) (at ANTT)
AP	Affari Politici (Political Affairs) files (at ASMAE)
AS	Archivio Scuole (Schools Archive) files (at ASMAE)
ASA	Allmänna säkerhetstjänstens arkiv (Sweden's Civilian Security Service archive) (at RA)
ASEAN	Association of Southeast Asian Nations
ASMAE	Archivio Storico-diplomatico Ministero degli Affari Esteri (the Historical-Diplomatic Archives of the Italian Ministry of Foreign Affairs), Rome, Italy
BBC	British Broadcasting Corporation
BCA	Türkiye Cumhuriyeti Cumhurbaşkanlığı Devlet Arşivleri Başkanlığı, Cumhuriyet Arşivi (the Presidency of State Archives of the Republic of Turkey, Archives of the Republic) Ankara, Turkey
BCRR	British Council's Representative's Report (in BW)
BUPO	Bundespolizei (Swiss Federal Police)
BW	British Council files with classmark BW at TNA
CADLC	Centre des Archives Diplomatiques de La Courneuve (La Courneuve Diplomatic Archives Centre), Paris, France
CHP	Cumhuriyet Halk Partisi (the Turkish Republican People's Party)
CNT	Confederación Nacional del Trabajo (the Spanish National Labour Confederation)
DDI	Documenti diplomatici italiani (Italian diplomatic documents)
DFA	Department for Foreign Affairs papers (at NAI)
DGIE	Direzione Generale Italiani all'Estero (Directorate-General for Italians Abroad) files (at ASMAE)

DG Papers	David Gray Papers (at FDR Library)
DIRCO	Department of International Relations and Cooperation, South Africa
DNB	Deutsche Nachrichtenbüro (a German news agency during the Second World War)
EdV Papers	Éamon de Valera Papers (at UCD)
EH	Electra House (a secret British department of enemy propaganda during the Second World War)
EU	European Union
FA Papers	Frank Aiken Papers (at UCD)
FDJP	Federal Department of Justice and Police papers, Switzerland (in SFA)
FDR Library	Franklin Roosevelt Presidential Library, Hyde Park, New York, USA
FDR Papers	Franklin Roosevelt Papers (at FDR Library)
FLN	Front de Libération Nationale (National Liberation Front, a political party in Algeria)
FO	Foreign Office files (at TNA)
FPD	Federal Political Department papers, Switzerland (in SFA)
FRELIMO	Frente de Libertação de Moçambique (Liberation Front of Mozambique, a political party in Mozambique)
GM	General Motors (an American car manufacturer)
HKUL	Hong Kong University Library, Hong Kong, China
HPK Papers	Helen Paull Kirkpatrick papers (at Smith College, Northampton, MA, USA – Sophia Smith Collection)
IRA	Irish Republican Army (a paramilitary organization in Ireland)
IWM	Imperial War Museum, London, UK
JWT	Just War Theory
KV	The classmark of the UK's security service archive (at TNA)
LRS	*Lao Ruam Samphan* (a newspaper in Laos translating as 'National Union')
MEH	Milli Emniyet Hizmetleri Riyaseti (the Turkish Presidency, National Security Services – the Turkish government's security service from 1926 to 1965)
MNE	Ministério dos Negócios Estrangeiros (Portuguese Ministry of Foreign Affairs)
MoI	Ministry of Information (Britain's information ministry during the Second World War)
NAI	National Archives of Ireland, Dublin, Ireland

NAM	Non-Aligned Movement (a movement established during the Cold War by Egypt, India and Yugoslavia to play a neutral role between the two blocs led by the superpowers, the USA and the USSR)
NATO	North Atlantic Treaty Organization
NLF	National Liberation Front in Laos
NLHX	Neo Lao Hak Xat (the Lao name for the Pathet Lao, the Lao Communist Party or Lao People's Liberation Army)
NUP	National Union Party in Laos
OCIAA	Office of the Coordinator of Inter-American Affairs (a US government agency promoting inter-American cooperation during the Second World War)
OPC	Overseas Planning Committee (a British committee for planning propaganda abroad during the Second World War)
OWI	The US Office of War Information (a US government information agency created during the Second World War)
PAC	Pan Africanist Congress (a political party in South Africa)
PK	Propagandakompanien (the Propaganda Companies of the German Armed Forces during the Second World War)
PL	Pathet Lao (the Lao Communist Party – see also NLHX)
PoWs	Prisoners of War
PPS	People's Party of Switzerland
PRC	People's Republic of China
PWE	Political Warfare Executive (a secret British government department for disseminating clandestine propaganda during the Second World War)
RA	Riksarkivet (the National Archives of Sweden), Stockholm, Sweden.
RLG	Royal Lao Government
RMS	Royal Mail Ship
RMVP	Reichsministerium für Volksaufklärung und Propaganda (the German Reich Ministry for Public Enlightenment and Propaganda during the Second World War – Nazi Germany's propaganda ministry)
RNG	Reorganized National Government (a Chinese nationalist government that sought to collaborate with Japan during the Second World War)
RSI	Repubblica Sociale Italiana (Italian Social Republic, the puppet government led by Benito Mussolini in northern Italy 1943–5)
SFA	Swiss Federal Archives, Berne, Switzerland

SIS	Secret Intelligence Service (a secret British government intelligence service organization also known as MI6)
SOE	Special Operations Executive (a secret British government department for various clandestine activities including propaganda during the Second World War)
TNA	The National Archives, London, UK
UAR	The United Arab Republic (a short-lived union between Egypt and Syria between 1958 and 1961)
UCD	University College Dublin, Ireland
UK	United Kingdom of Great Britain and Northern Ireland
UN	United Nations
UNESCO	The United Nations Educational, Scientific and Cultural Organization
US or USA	United States of America
USIA	The US Information Agency (a US government information agency during the Cold War)
USSR	Union of Soviet Socialist Republics (also known as the Soviet Union)
VOKS	Vsesoiuznoe Obshchestvo Kul'turnoi Sviazi s zagranitsei (the Soviet All-Union Society for Cultural Ties – a Soviet cultural propaganda agency)
WHO	World Health Organization
WMDs	Weapons of Mass Destruction
WPr.	Wehrmacht Propaganda Department (the propaganda department of the German Armed Forces during the Second World War)

Alternative battlegrounds

An introduction to propaganda and neutrality

Edward Corse and Marta García Cabrera

'Even though Ireland is a militarily neutral country, let me be clear, we are not neutral on this war', said Irish Foreign Minister Simon Coveney on a visit to Kyiv on 14 April 2022.[1] Recent events following the Russian invasion of Ukraine have demonstrated that debates around neutrality – what it means and how it works – are as live now as they have ever been, with a wider propaganda war in many forms running alongside the war on the battlefield. This book highlights the role played by propaganda in neutral countries and relating to neutral positions from just prior to the First World War and just into the twenty-first century. The following chapters demonstrate that propaganda has always been a prominent component of neutrality in a variety of forms, whether that be as alternative battlegrounds for the belligerents carrying on war through other means or through neutral countries being protagonists in their own right. Indeed, the concept of neutrality has often become a propaganda instrument itself, capable of projecting predetermined diplomatic and political messages that have complemented the objectives established by the foreign policies of neutral states. Perhaps one might say that, just as David Welch has considered *propaganda* to be seen as an ethically *neutral* concept,[2] the concept of *neutrality* can also be conceived as a tool of *propaganda*.

What makes the study of propaganda and neutrality so fascinating – but also challenging – is that the definitions of both terms are contested, as Jo Fox points out in her foreword to this volume. Peter Pomerantsev, in his book *This Is Not Propaganda*, even goes as far to state that the term 'propaganda' was 'so fraught and fractured in its interpretation' that he chose to avoid using the word almost entirely.[3] Many people might claim to know its meaning, but identifying what is and what is not propaganda depends very much on who is defining it. The *Propaganda and Mass Persuasion: A Historical Encyclopaedia*, edited by Nicholas J. Cull, David Culbert and David Welch, explored a multitude of different types of propaganda and spent nearly five pages examining the definition of the word itself.[4] The word originates from the seventeenth-century Roman Catholic Commission of Cardinals, when it was set up by Pope Gregory XV for the propagation of the Catholic faith. However, as Philip M. Taylor demonstrates in his *Munitions of the Mind*, the concept of propaganda has been a core part of history since ancient times. It became especially prominent in the twentieth century when governments used propaganda as a state instrument in both war and peace, making use of modern mass communication technology.[5] The concept is often seen in a pejorative sense, commonly connected with the ideas of 'falsehood', 'deception' and 'brainwashing'.[6] Nevertheless, while it is often seen in this way, Welch, as indicated above, has maintained that propaganda itself – as a method of communication, influencing and persuasion – is 'an ethically neutral phenomenon': it is more the messages and ideas of disreputable propagandists that have given propaganda a bad name.[7]

Propaganda is generally seen as a persuasive instrument used by states, political groups, ideological organizations and individuals with the aim of achieving or maintaining a position of power through the orientation and alignment of opinions and attitudes. It is not a uniform or immutable concept, since its implications respond to a multitude of categories and variants. Propaganda can come in different forms (oral, printed, visual etc.) and through different means of dissemination (radio, pamphlets, newspapers, cinema, photography, cultural visits and events, diplomacy, social media, word-of-mouth and through the use of 'troll farms' and bots etc.). Propaganda can have a variety of different objectives (it can, for example, seek to legitimize, celebrate, justify, inveigle or cajole, evangelize, subvert, reinforce existing opinions, explain, distract, confuse or deceive). Propaganda can act in different circumstances – in war, peace and times of crisis, as well as being employed to form national identities over generations. Its source can be known (generally conceived as white propaganda), unclear (generally known as grey propaganda) or deliberately obfuscated (i.e. black propaganda).[8]

There is also debate around the meaning of the word 'neutrality'. The idea, defined as '[a]n intermediate state or condition, not clearly one thing or another' or 'abstention from taking any part in a war between other states', is as old as the concept of war and alliance. Just as with propaganda, early usage from the 1500s appears to be in the context of religion.[9] In his book *Neutrality and Small States*, Efraim Karsh argued that neutrality is an intrinsic component of humanity, as 'ever since human beings began to wage war upon one another, there have been individuals and groups that have sought to avoid their participation'.[10] Maartje Abbenhuis also explored the origins of the concept in some detail in *An Age of Neutrals*. She noted that neutrality was far from being a modern phenomenon and has been around since at least the time of Ancient Greece.[11] Neville Wylie also opened his edited volume about neutrality in the Second World War with the statement '[n]eutrality has been one of the most enduring features in the history of international relations', and persuasively argued that neutrality's impact has been 'profound'.[12] Neutrality has been an intrinsic component of conflicts, in all its aspects and dimensions such as through choices made in relation directly to armed conflict as well as diplomatic, ideological, political, religious and various other ways.

Neutrality has often been seen as something immoral – a position of weakness and lacking heroism – particularly by those who have decided to take sides in a conflict.[13] In fact, both Wylie and Abbenhuis quoted Niccolò Machiavelli, who described neutrality as a 'false policy for a Prince to undertake' as it means they 'will invariably fall prey to the conqueror'.[14] For example, Abbenhuis went on to show that Switzerland, which has been formally neutral since 1815, has often been seen as a state with 'supposed stifled creativity' precisely because of its long-term neutrality. However, as she has also shown, neutrality has not always been seen in this way. The Congress of Vienna in 1815 to the First World War was a 'golden age' for neutrality – a period in which it became 'a tool that helped globalisation and underpinned many free-trade liberal policies' – and balanced the great powers.[15] Indeed, neutrals have often seen themselves as taking a moral stance on particular issues – being above the political machinations and power conflicts that lead to war, as well as above the suffering caused by war itself. A number of organizations, such as the International Committee of the Red Cross, base themselves in neutral countries for this very reason. According to Pascal Lottaz and Herbert Reginbogin, neutrality is also a multifaceted concept, as it can be qualified as 'permanent, occasional, relative, differential, absolute, armed, ideological, political, moral, territorial, maritime, and others'.[16] Nasir Ahmad Andisha, in his *Neutrality and Vulnerable States*, has provided a similar view.[17] However, it is also true that neutrality, particularly in times of war, can lead to opportunities to gain concessions from, or sell goods (including weapons) to both warring sides.

How does 'neutrality' manifest itself? Often states declare their neutrality publicly, and usually as a legal position as neutrality was codified in the 1899 Hague conferences – a milestone that established our modern understanding of neutral rights and duties.[18] It developed into a permanent feature of the international system, referred by Abbenhuis as 'a much lauded, used and promoted policy by great and small powers alike'. She noted that it was used as an instrument to maintain the balance of forces, protect the hegemony of great powers and empires – such as Great Britain or the United States – and it also favoured the definition and institutionalization of key concepts such as globalization, internationalism and humanitarianism.[19] This political position usually relates to a particular war which has placed certain obligations on the warring sides, such as the respect of the territorial integrity of neutral states in that war – thus avoiding invasions – with varying degrees of success. There is also the concept of permanent neutrality, unconnected to any specific conflict – such as the position of perhaps the most famous neutral state, Switzerland. With the emergence of the Cold War, the concept accommodated a new form – known as 'neutralism', which is usually defined as a political and diplomatic position of non-alignment, particularly between the two superpowers, the United States of America and the Soviet Union, but also with reference to disconnecting association with the 'old imperialists', particularly Britain and France, in the context of decolonization.[20] A neutral position has also been assumed by states who do not wish to interfere in another country's internal conflicts or policies, from civil wars to abuses of human rights, while often seeking to further their own economic or other interests. In this context, maintaining neutrality can be met with counter-neutrality pressures, when non-intervention becomes increasingly unviable.[21] The example of the Red Cross shows also that the concept of neutrality does not have to be restricted to governments but also a range of other organizations, such as non-governmental organizations (NGOs), who claim to be impartial. This includes, for example, the British Broadcasting Corporation (BBC). However, full impartiality has not always been possible: in the Second World War, the BBC worked closely with the British government;[22] and Steve Westlake has argued, through a study of the BBC in the 1990s, the BBC's World Service has been 'an active, if largely autonomous agent of British overseas development and foreign policy'.[23]

As this volume will demonstrate, different states and groups can have different reasons for choosing the path of neutrality – from the pragmatic and opportunistic to the principled. They have played a diverse number of roles from the more passive – such as buffer zones between conflict – to the active, playing the role of mediators and pressure groups for change.[24] Neutrality does not necessarily imply immunity or aloofness from war or conflict – official non-belligerency can also mean providing ideological or financial support to one side or another of a particular conflict.[25] Neutrals can also choose to end their own neutrality or non-interventionist stance voluntarily as a result of opportunism, the effect of diplomatic and sociocultural pressure, the threat of war or an internal change of circumstances.[26]

The interrelationship between propaganda and neutrality

As the following chapters demonstrate, however the terms are defined, the concepts of propaganda and neutrality are intertwined. Propaganda is clearly often seen in the context of war and conflict – both hot and cold – and neutral states have also played a key role in wars in several different ways. Belligerent propaganda has often been directed towards neutral countries to try to guide the opinion of undecided populations, thus gaining new support or weakening the enemy position in both military and ideological conflicts – making neutral states alternative battlegrounds. This has perhaps been the main focus of most previous English-language studies. However, neutral states can also promote their neutrality through propaganda or actively deflect attempts to influence them through imposing censorship controls. Propaganda can also use the violation of neutrality as a rallying cry, with perhaps the most famous example used being that of the invasion of Belgium in 1914. As Abbenhuis demonstrates, 'the supposed naïveté and powerlessness of the Belgians stood both as a useful propaganda message for the Entente partners and their empires during the war and as a historical example of the weakness of neutrality after its conclusion'.[27]

Several historians have devoted efforts towards demonstrating the importance of how propaganda and neutrality have interacted in particular case studies. Michael Sanders and Philip M. Taylor, for example, dedicated part of their research to the analysis of British propaganda towards the neutrals throughout the Great War.[28] Chad R. Fulwider explored German propaganda with regard to the neutrality of the United States, while Evgeny Sergeev has highlighted Russian propaganda campaigns deployed in neutral countries during the First World War.[29] Robert Cole's *Britain and the War of Words in Neutral Europe* is often seen as a benchmark study for the role of propaganda in neutral Europe during the Second World War, to which he added later a study on neutral Ireland.[30] Cull also studied the role of Britain in persuading the neutral United States to join the Second World War in his seminal study *Selling War*.[31] J. R. Vaughan analysed the anti-communist and Cold War propaganda disseminated in the Arab Middle East, while Marek Fields considered the effects of Anglo-American persuasion efforts in Finland.[32] All of these works have highlighted the importance of neutral or non-aligned states in wider conflicts, propaganda battles and in specific circumstances. However, the benefit of this volume is to provide a diverse range of case studies in a variety of different scenarios – in different wars and geographies – allowing an opportunity to build upon these previous works and draw out common themes around how propaganda can interact with neutrality. Never before have these concepts been brought together in such a broad-ranging and comprehensive way.

In some sense, propaganda in a neutral context is no different to other scenarios. The methods of dissemination, for example, can be similar. Propaganda through magazines, newspapers, radio, television, speeches and other forms is common in all scenarios. However, neutral territories give an opportunity for propaganda to spread in different forms and ways. Propaganda from one source can be observed or experienced directly contrasting with propaganda from other sources with different aims – underlining more obviously and directly a competition for the attention of neutral audiences and a competition for power. For example, during both world wars, several neutral cities, particularly in Europe, were hotbeds of rumour-spreading often coupled with espionage and deployment of messaging in ways that were simply not available in enemy territory. As the chapters of María Inés Tato, Yasemin Türkkan Tunalı and Yasemin Doğaner, Marta García Cabrera, João Arthur Ciciliato Franzolin and Cyril Cordoba demonstrate, the bulk of propaganda – both foreign and national – in neutral territories was channelled through an avalanche of print productions in the form of books, periodicals and magazines, newspapers, pamphlets, posters, photographs and postcards; and, as Emil Stjernholm shows, film screenings were also an important tool in neutral countries.

The influencing and subsidizing of the neutral press by the belligerents was a key battleground. Of course, neutral states were not inactive in trying to control such propaganda, instituting censorship regimes to try at least to control belligerent influence and perhaps also to try to promote their own messaging. Therefore, belligerents have needed to be inventive to circumvent such censorship, and some methods of propaganda have been more prominent in a neutral space. Stjernholm's chapter demonstrates that private viewings of films, taking advantage of the popularity enjoyed by this resource as mass entertainment, helped get around Swedish censorship. Simone Muraca and Edward Corse show that cultural propaganda was used by Italy and Britain as a way of reaching audiences more directly and in a more subtle way than through the press or publications in countries such as Portugal, Yugoslavia and India. This volume shows that verbal communications have also been important in neutral states. This can be through clandestine means including through organizations such as the British Political Warfare Executive (PWE) and the spreading of rumours, as demonstrated in the chapters by Florian Grafl, Guy Woodward, Helena F. S. Lopes and García Cabrera, or through more open activity such as speech acts as shown by P. Mike Rattanasengchanh in the context of Laos in the Cold War. The propaganda machinery of the belligerents was often coordinated with other political, diplomatic and cultural entities, and it was reinforced with the collaboration of commercial agents, social clubs, bookstores, libraries, intellectual platforms and foreign communities. The willingness of local intellectuals and agents to promote messaging from foreign states was crucial in providing legitimacy to the messaging, but also ensured an adaptation to local conditions allowing for messages to be better understood and more influential. Understanding local circumstances, as Fox states in her foreword, was crucial for success. There are several key intellectuals whose names stand out in this volume who played prominent roles in propaganda in a neutral context – names such as

Francisco Barroetaveña, Ernesto Quesada, Elizabeth Wiskemann, David Gray, Gino Saviotti, Theo Pinkus, Nils Andersson – although not always successfully achieving their aims. Specific conditions in places like Buenos Aires, Barcelona, Lisbon and, as Giannakopoulos and Lialiouti demonstrate in their analysis of circumstances in Greece, particularly in Patras, were important to grasp in order to understand the role of propaganda and its potential effect.

In terms of the objectives of propaganda in a neutral context, these can be multifaceted, and clearly a lot of this depends on the specific context. There are some general themes, however, that are worth drawing out. Several chapters reveal that neutral audiences have often been targeted to achieve a particular outcome sought by belligerents, often aligned to their broader political and strategic objectives. The most extreme objective, of course, is persuading neutrals to participate in a war on their side. Stephen Badsey shows that despite prevailing views around the role of propaganda, British propaganda should be studied further to understand how and why the United States entered the First World War; Miguel Brandão shows that propaganda around the sinking of the *Douro* and *Cysne* ships helped bring Portugal into the same conflict. By contrast, Tato, Karen Garner and Türkkan Tunalı and Doğaner show that similar propaganda activity in different wars was not successful in Argentina (despite similar propaganda around the sinking of three ships, the *Monte Protegido*, the *Oriana* and the *Toro*), Ireland and Turkey (in the latter until very late in the Second World War), partly because of the local context and historical reasons, and partly because both of the opposing sides in the war were similar in strength in their propaganda campaigns.

Belligerent propaganda can, of course, have less obvious objectives in neutral countries than merely to break that neutrality. Belligerents can seek to gain influence in some way to achieve a less direct benefit (such as raw materials or safe passage), or perhaps see the neutral state as a convenient starting point for spreading ideas more broadly. Woodward and Cordoba demonstrate, for example, that Switzerland was seen by Britain in the Second World War and the People's Republic of China in the Cold War as a convenient hub for spreading their respective propaganda material into otherwise 'impenetrable' Western Europe. García Cabrera demonstrates that propaganda campaigns in neutral states can also facilitate the preparation for potential military operations; encourage an economic, cultural, political and even military mobilization; or complement diplomatic activities. This was the case in Spain, for example, in the Second World War, where Allied propaganda was designed as an operational instrument to encourage a potential need for Spanish resistance and laying the ground for Allied intervention as the solution for the ultimate freedom of Spain.

The messages conveyed in these alternative battlegrounds are clearly important and were a key factor in determining success. Common to much propaganda content directed at neutrals was the focus on war justifications, exaltations of belligerent virtues and negative descriptions of the enemy – 'the other'. Foreign propaganda in neutral Argentina and Spain, for example, reproduced a binary representation of the conflict as a struggle of civilization and order against enemy barbarism. Despite the fact that atrocity propaganda has been a prominent component of propaganda in other contexts of conflict, in neutral territories it is especially adapted to the immediate context of the neutrals. For example, as evidenced by Grafl, Brandão and

Franzolin, the stressing of violations of other neutralities as well as interference in commercial and naval matters such as through submarine warfare and blockades have been particularly important. Belligerents have often emphasized the post-war order too, making the point that neutrals should recognise that their interests are not just confined to the war itself.[33]

Propaganda themes have had to recognize a constantly changing context – the ebbs of flows of wars, both hot and cold. For instance, as shown in Muraca's chapter, Italian propaganda in Portugal during the Second World War was reshaped as Italy's position in the war changed from non-belligerence to joining the war alongside Germany, to changing sides to the Allies in 1943; Garner explores how American propaganda in Ireland during the Second World War evolved as a result of ending its own neutrality; while, according to García Cabrera, British propaganda also evolved alongside Franco's fluctuating neutrality. Corse shows that in the context of the Cold War's Non-Aligned Movement (NAM) the importance of the 'Khrushchev Thaw', the context of decolonization, the Suez Crisis and the Sino-Soviet Split all affected the characteristics and effectiveness of British cultural propaganda. Rattanasengchanh shows that Laos' representatives during the Cold War propagated their own different versions of neutralism, which led to what he calls a 'tragic effort' for neutrality which was ultimately engulfed by the Vietnam War.

Several chapters demonstrate that propagandists can build upon supranational identities and connections as prominent component of their claims – for struggle, resistance, neutrality or pacifism. Repeated exploitation of the concept of shared roots, manifested, for example, through notions such as Latinity, pan-Americanism and pan-Asian concepts. The common roots of the Latin language or Roman Catholic religion have been used to act as unifying, motivating and justifying element of war movements and stances not only in Iberia but also in South America, Italy and France as shown by Tato, García Cabrera and Muraca in particular. The relationship between imperialism and neutrality often appears in our case studies in different forms and is often connected to supranational identities. For example, propaganda can be employed to claim and defend colonial and imperial aspirations in both belligerent and neutral scenarios. As demonstrated by Richard Carswell, an important adjunct to Vichy propaganda during the Second World War was the theme of empire, conceived as France's trump card to the nation's survival and success. Lopes shows that imperialism and anti-imperialism concepts were also important components of the multinational propaganda competition in neutral Macau, from 1937 to 1945. While Chinese, Japanese and British representatives mobilized an intense propaganda campaign that aroused the complaints of the adversaries, Portuguese authorities used neutrality to promote its colonialism. Corse shows that the British Council work in non-aligned countries in the Cold War was directly affected by pre-existing views of Britain's historical imperialism. Meanwhile Cordoba demonstrates that the People's Republic of China claimed the position of 'natural ally' to colonized countries and positioned itself as an anti-imperialist spearhead, and this aided its attempts to use Switzerland to spread its propaganda.

Beyond the censorship regimes that neutral states often put in place, neutrals also, of course, create their own propaganda programmes with the aim of defending and maintaining their own neutrality, justifying their position in a conflict, fighting against a war, limiting foreign influence in the country or defending peace, and creating a vision for a nation. However, this has never been very straightforward, particularly where there has not been a homogenous view within the neutral country of what that national vision should be and these differing views have often been connected to or even fomented 'national struggles'. Carswell shows that Marshal Philippe Pétain tried unsuccessfully to forge a new vision for France through its National Revolution, but this was ultimately illusory. Rattanasengchanh demonstrates that Laos' neutralism during the Cold War faced opposition both in the international community and within Laos, which forced its defenders to promote the values of non-alignment. According to Giannakopoulos and Lialiouti, the Greek case in the First World War provides a particularly interesting example of how propaganda around neutrality had become intertwined with national identity. The so-called National Schism that emerged in 1915 over Greece's neutrality was essentially a crisis of national integration which also incorporated foreign propaganda as an instrument which could be utilized to help forge a vision of Greece. The case of Spain between 1917 and 1923 also serves as an example, in which propaganda favoured the conversion of Catalonia into an alternative battleground of the Great War. Grafl shows that the beginning of the social and regional conflict in Barcelona, referred to as *Pistolerismo*, was stimulated by the dissemination of journalistic messages which framed national political arguments with episodes from the international war.

Neutrality itself can be seen as a form of propaganda – when it is promoted as something moral and above conflict. A number of countries have promoted their position as a neutralist interlocutor and mediator in international relations. However, as Cull demonstrates, through his study of British and American attitudes towards the Apartheid regime in South Africa, propaganda campaigns can be particularly powerful where countries, which have previously taken a neutral status on a divisive internal conflict, shift their position to an interventionist one. They can make a decisive change to shift international perceptions, to help promote, maintain or avoid alignment with certain powers, ideologies, economic or socio-political systems. As Lottaz shows, recent events in Ukraine which have shifted positions of certain neutral countries in reaction to the Russian invasion have also taken place at rapid speed – the long-term effects, of course, are yet to be seen.

Chronological perspectives on propaganda and neutrality

This volume is structured into three main parts, in chronological order. The first part considers propaganda and neutrality in relation to the First World War, the second part considers the concepts relating to the Second World War and the third part explores propaganda and neutrality in the Cold War and beyond.

Propaganda and neutrality in the First World War

Propaganda and neutrality played an important role in international relations during the 'long' nineteenth century – from the Congress of Vienna to the First World War –

when they developed into highly useful diplomatic tools for both small and large states. With the aim of preventing the expansion of military and revolutionary movements in the continent – thus guaranteeing the much sought-after European stability and favouring economic-imperial interests – states sought to legally codify neutrality to set limits on war through the institutionalization, defence and propagation of neutral positions. In addition to limiting and preventing conflicts, neutrality favoured the creation of national identities that incorporated this diplomatic and military position into their collective self-identification – as in the case of Switzerland.[34] The road to the First World War was paved with mistrust which precipitated the formation of alliances between the major European powers. More generally, the 'Great Powers' no longer sought to try to preserve the international system, but instead moved towards aspiring to create competing new world orders.

The outbreak of 'the Great War' in 1914 marked the beginning of a new war concept, that of a 'total war' that radicalized the scope of the conflict and its propaganda campaigns.[35] Over the years, the initial predominant neutrality of countries was soon replaced by an increasing inclination of states towards belligerence. Neutrals still played a key role, however, as economic intermediaries, profiteers, suppliers and bankers. Their territories served as humanitarian or refugee havens, as strategic points against the enemy, as targets of secret movements and as active locations for propaganda campaigns, both national and foreign. The invasion of 'little Belgium' became a propaganda message in itself, a mythologized episode of war 'crusade' that inspired pamphlets, posters, magazines, reports and books through the detailed – but also exaggerated – description of German atrocities (Figure 0.1).[36]

Between 1915 and 1916, neutrals witnessed the spread of a war on an unprecedented scale, a conflict that increasingly radicalized violent actions on land, sea and air. The support of the neutrals was increasingly important, and so the belligerent powers therefore launched premeditated propaganda campaigns in strategic neutral territories. The United States would be the neutral country that occupied arguably the most prominent position as the target of foreign propaganda campaigns.[37] In his chapter, Badsey considers the neutrality of the United States and belligerent persuasion between 1914 and 1917. His contribution offers a fresh historiographical analysis on the influence of propaganda on American military involvement arguing that the study of propaganda needs to be more in the mainstream of First World War studies. Latin America was also a prominent location for propaganda battles, as the continent boasted a major number of neutral countries. Given the historical connections with Europe, Argentine society was also particularly shaken by the Great War, which led to a strong economic, cultural, political and even military mobilization. Tato analyses Allied and German propaganda campaigns disseminated in Argentina, considering their channels, arguments and strategies, as well as the immediate and emotional connections established.

The maintenance of a long and seemingly indefinite war – also affecting neutral countries through commercial and naval blockades, submarine warfare, national shortages, and so on – spread a wave of political unrest and revolution in many countries. The situation in states such as Greece was exacerbated since the outbreak of conflict, when they became progressively dragged into the war by the pressure of the

Figure 0.1 'Remember Belgium: Enlist to-day', British First World War recruitment poster, c. 1914. Courtesy Getty Images.

combatants. This produced an intense political fracture between the supporters of the war intervention, on the side of the Entente and those who defended the maintenance of neutrality, generally favourable to the Central Empires. Giannakopoulos and Lialiouti analyse the interrelationship between the propaganda battle and the Greek 'National Schism' from 1915 to 1918. They consider the role played by foreign propaganda to negotiate Greek identity. There were other alternative battles taking place on the Iberian

Peninsula because of its strategic location. Traditionally allied to the UK, Portugal tried to comply with British requests for aid while protecting its own colonies in Africa. Despite its initial neutrality, Portugal soon broke off its relations with Germany, which led to formal declarations of war in 1916.[38] Brandão analyses Portuguese 'neutrality' between 1914 and 1916, through a case study that links the concept of the war at sea and the role of propaganda in bringing Portugal into the war. Neutral Spain not only became the target of foreign propaganda campaigns but also the epicentre of an intense popular debate on war and neutrality.[39] Grafl considers the propaganda coverage of 'The *Pistolerismo*' (1917–23) – a political and social struggle in Catalonia, which could be also considered as an alternative and national battleground of the First World War. The *Pistolerismo* was partially a reaction to the Russian Revolution and the ideological battle between left- and right-wing politics, and it also foreshadowed, in some ways, the Spanish Civil War (1936–9).

The distortion, manipulation or exaggeration of propaganda messages of the First World War became the subject of debate for a large part of European public opinion during the interwar period, which questioned the morality of propaganda.[40] This situation produced a wave of protests across the continent and notably influenced the decision of many democratic countries to question the stories of atrocities in the immediate aftermath. In the meantime, fascist, totalitarian or communist governments spread anti-liberal propaganda that democratic nations found difficult to counter. The international involvement in the Spanish Civil War, with many nations taking one side or the other, made staying neutral a real challenge, especially from the point of view of propaganda and information.[41] These examples show that neutrality in relation to the First World War and the interwar period hardly meant a lack of tension and conflict. There were wider ramifications to choices made which continued towards the next world war, although the ideal of neutrality was still maintained by many nations.

Propaganda and neutrality in the Second World War

With the outbreak of the Second World War, the world was once again witnessing a total war: a conflict that reinforced its radicalism, multiplied its fronts and protagonists, expanded the scope of its effects and involved, more than ever, neutral countries. The United States maintained a position of neutrality until the Japanese attack on Pearl Harbor in December 1941. During its period as a neutral state, the country was once again the subject and object of incisive propaganda campaigns, which has parallels to the subject analysed by Badsey in relation to the First World War.[42] As Garner explains, the United States also played a role throughout the Second World War in neutral Eire, where there were competing American and Irish propaganda campaigns to either denigrate or defend Ireland's wartime neutrality (See Figure 0.2 for a contemporary Canadian perspective on de Valera's position).

As Efraim Karsh argues elsewhere, the German invasion of France and the Italian dictator Benito Mussolini's participation in the war in the spring and summer of 1940 encouraged other nations, which had remained neutral in the First World War, such as Sweden, Switzerland and Spain, to adopt a closer position to the Axis, through self-imposed censorship and active propaganda campaigns.[43] Sweden and

Figure 0.2 'Journey's End', Irish Taoiseach, Éamon de Valera, depicted by the Canadian cartoonist John Collins in *The Gazette*, April 1941. Image from the McCord Stewart Museum, Montreal, Canada. Object number: M965.199.3091.

Switzerland shed their apparent initial support for democracies to ensure their own survival after the early Axis victories. This situation reinforced the potential for propaganda activities – especially Allied – which were deployed officially and diplomatically, but also secretly.[44] Thus, for example, Woodward opens up a new understanding of the intelligence and propaganda networks established by the PWE in neutral territories, through the wartime role played by the historian Elizabeth Wiskemann in Switzerland. The German invasion of France also directly affected France's relationship with war and persuasion. The Vichy regime maintained a supposed neutrality until the liberation of France by the Allied forces, but it became a form of puppet state of Nazi Germany that, as Carswell demonstrates, found its role as a neutral ultimately impossible to perform.

Turkey joined the Allies late in the war, in February 1945, when the defeat of Germany was all but certain. Nevertheless, it was able to keep neutral for the vast majority of the war, precisely because it was strategically placed between key theatres of the conflict. This strategic position meant that it was also a propaganda battleground for the Allied and Axis powers. Türkkan Tunalı and Doğaner focus on Turkey's foreign policy and the Nazi propaganda campaign, revealing to what extent the German activities affected Turkish public opinion. Portugal, too, just as it had started the First World War, chose to be neutral in the Second World War.[45] Muraca considers the impact of fascist cultural propaganda in Portugal between 1939 and 1945, describing the different actors that were involved – both official and informally. The Spanish government of Francisco Franco leaned towards Germany and stretched its neutral condition, indebted to Axis help during the Spanish Civil War. Its neutrality was stretched not only because it negotiated its potential participation in the war in the summer of 1940 but also because it adopted a position of 'non-belligerence' rather than 'neutrality'. This allowed for an open-door policy towards German propaganda.[46] García Cabrera shows that Spain was also the scene of an intense British diplomatic and soft propaganda campaign that sought to counteract Germany's persuasive advantage. The country was also part of the secret planning of the PWE which, between 1941 and 1943, designed much more active and subversive operational propaganda aimed to combat the potential belligerence of Franco. Both Nazi Germany and the Allies invested heavily in propaganda in neutral Sweden. The battle for hearts and minds did not only involve widespread dissemination of propaganda, but Stockholm became a veritable hotbed of espionage as well as intelligence gathering on the propaganda efforts of others. Stjernholm studies the media production of the British Legation in Stockholm, mapping the circulation of British film propaganda in Sweden, a country that was not easily accessible from Britain.

The survival of the imperialism of the Allied powers and the territorial extension of Japan considerably reduced the number of countries that remained neutral in Asia. Nevertheless, the Asian colonial territories were not always synonymous with belligerence. As Lopes demonstrates in her chapter, the Portuguese colony of Macau was one genuinely neutral territory that survived the war, although diplomats, spies and merchants of all belligerent nations intermingled until the very end of the conflict. Her chapter considers practices of Chinese, Japanese and British propaganda in Macau from 1937 to 1945, including the use of rumours, newspapers and visual and performative arts. To complete the chapters on the Second World War, Franzolin compares the characteristics, objectives and achievements of the German magazine *Signal* and the United States' *Em Guarda/On Guard* and *Victory*, which were printed in different languages and distributed throughout neutral and occupied countries. Magazines were often the most visible element of belligerent propaganda in neutral countries where the propaganda of one side could be directly compared side by side with the propaganda of the other.

Propaganda and neutrality in the Cold War and beyond

Although the end of the Second World War once again reinforced the search for collective security, it did not result in a reduction of international conflict and belligerence. The world was witnessing a new international order, dominated mainly by two superpowers – the United States and the Soviet Union – that vied with each other to reinforce their influence across the world. The decolonization process (primarily meaning the end of the British and French empires) favoured the formation of new independent states over which the superpowers tried to exert their influence, with the aim of aligning themselves with their respective blocs and thus avoiding reinforcing the power of the other. This was complicated by the Sino-Soviet Split over ideological differences which divided the communist world itself broadly into two camps.[47]

However, some strategic countries tried to stay out of this global positioning – as in the case of Finland, Austria, Yugoslavia, Egypt and Switzerland, among others.[48] The Cold War therefore favoured the extension of a new type of neutrality – referred to as 'neutralism' or 'non-alignment' – that survived after the fall of the Soviet Union in 1991 and that continues to exist in the world today in the form of the NAM.[49] Despite their desire not to align themselves with any of the opposing sides they continued to witness the arrival of well-defined foreign propaganda campaigns and sociocultural activities. Corse compares the way in which the cultural diplomacy agency of one of the old imperialists – the British Council – operated in the founding countries of the NAM (Egypt, India and Yugoslavia), with the objective of exerting British soft power.

In this period, Switzerland continued to reassert its traditional neutralism, as a continuation of its historic positioning in international affairs. However, European neutral states did not escape either the propaganda of capitalism or communism, which reached their countries through various forms and channels. For example, as is demonstrated by Cordoba, the Swiss capital Berne became Beijing's most important diplomatic mission for the spread of Maoism in Western Europe until the 1970s – despite the efforts of the Swiss authorities to prevent it. As neutralism took root in some parts of Europe, the dissolution of Europe's colonial empires in Africa and Asia gave rise to newly independent nations. Although many of these countries adopted a policy of non-alignment, they had to deal with new national conflicts that were also caught up in the nets of the Cold War. For instance, Rattanasengchanh analyses the efforts and disagreements of Lao neutralists in pushing for non-alignment between 1957 and 1960, which ultimately favoured the growth of communism. The rejection of war and violence was a prominent component of the 1960s and was not just confined to the ideological bipolarization of the Cold War. Global audiences also witnessed important sociocultural movements that challenged the world's passivity and demanded a more active position in situations of generalized injustice – such as the Civil Rights movement in the United States and against the Apartheid regime in South Africa. Although the initial reaction of the Western world to the system of racial segregation in South Africa was one of strict neutrality, the Sharpeville massacre in 1960 intensified calls for action and interventionist propaganda campaigns. Thus,

Cull analyses the propaganda campaign that tried to end British and US government neutrality over Apartheid alongside other examples of persuasion to undermine a non-interventionist stance.

Lastly, Lottaz explores in the Epilogue the role of propaganda and neutrality in the twenty-first century more generally, particularly in relation to the Russian invasion of Ukraine in 2022 which has again raised the role of neutrality in debates. Here, traditionally neutral countries, such as Finland, Sweden, Switzerland and Ireland, have acted against Russia, alongside their neighbours, with the imposition of sanctions and bans of use of their airspace. This might suggest that neutrality in the twenty-first century on such an issue is impossible, and that long-standing neutral positions may appear to have crumbled almost overnight. Appearances might be deceptive, however. Other views certainly exist – there is a Russian view put forward that Ukraine should be neutral and not aligned with or a member of NATO, and Russia has issued threats to Finland and Sweden if they were to choose NATO membership. There have also been some protests within those countries too against NATO membership (see Figure 0.3). Some states such as India and some African countries have continued to maintain their neutrality or non-alignment despite Russia's actions, demonstrating neutralism is not dead. Lottaz explores the propaganda surrounding the events in Ukraine, but also puts this in a broader context considering how the issues have morphed and developed in the world we are living in today, as we complete this volume.

Figure 0.3 *'Spillinget Blod: Nej till NATO'* [Spilled blood: no to NATO], a protest against Sweden's application to join NATO, 16 May 2022, following the Russian invasion of Ukraine. Courtesy Getty Images.

Notes

1. 'Ukraine War: Coveney Visits Kyiv to Meet Ukrainian Government', *BBC News Website*, 14 April 2022. https://www.bbc.co.uk/news/world-europe-61105160 (accessed 12 June 2022).
2. Mark Connelly, Jo Fox, Stefan Goebel and Ulf Schmidt, 'Prologue: "Power and Persuasion": Propaganda into the Twenty-First Century', in *Propaganda and Conflict: War, Media and the Shaping of the Twentieth Century*, ed. Mark Connelly, Jo Fox, Stefan Goebel and Ulf Schmidt (London: Bloomsbury, 2019), 5, who are commenting on David Welch's contribution to the study of propaganda.
3. Peter Pomerantsev, *This Is Not Propaganda: Adventures in the War against Reality* (London: Faber, 2019), 5.
4. Nicholas J. Cull, David Culbert and David Welch (eds), *Propaganda and Mass Persuasion: A Historical Encyclopedia, 1500 to the Present* (Santa Barbara: ABC-CLIO, 2003), 317–23.
5. Philip M. Taylor, *Munitions of the Mind: A History of Propaganda from the Ancient World to the Present Day* (Manchester: Manchester University Press, 2003).
6. David Welch, *Propaganda: Power and Persuasion* (London: British Library, 2013), 1–13.
7. Connelly, Fox, Goebel and Schmidt, 'Prologue: "Power and Persuasion"', 5. For other definitions of propaganda, see Harold D. Lasswell, 'The Person: Subject and Object of Propaganda', *Annals of the American Academy of Political and Social Science* 179, no. 1 (1927): 189; Terrence H. Qualter, *Propaganda and Psychological Warfare* (New York: Random House, 1965), 27; 'Government, Propaganda and Public Relations', in *The Oxford Companion to American Military History*, ed. John Whiteclay Chambers (New York: Oxford, 1999), 571–2; David Welch, 'Powers of Persuasion', *History Today* 49, no. 8 (1999): 24–6.
8. Garth S. Jowett and Victoria O'Donnell, *Propaganda and Persuasion* (Los Angeles: Sage, 2019), 11–21.
9. 'Neutrality, n.', *Oxford English Dictionary* (OED) (Oxford: Oxford University Press, March 2022).
10. Efraim Karsh, *Neutrality and Small States* (London: Routledge, 1988, reprinted 2012), 13; see also Karsh in relation to Finland in Efraim Karsh, 'Geographical Determinism: Finnish Neutrality Revisited. Cooperation and Conflict', *Cooperation and Conflict* 21, no. 1 (1986): 43–57.
11. Maartje Abbenhuis, *An Age of Neutrals: Great Power Politics, 1815–1914* (Cambridge: Cambridge University Press, 2014), 1–3. See also Robert A. Bauslaugh, *The Concept of Neutrality in Classical Greece* (Los Angeles: University of California Press, 1991) and Nasir Ahmad Andisha, *Neutrality and Vulnerable States: An Analysis of Afghanistan's Permanent Neutrality* (London: Routledge, 2020), 1–3.
12. Neville Wylie, 'Introduction: Victims or Actors? European Neutrals and Non-belligerents, 1939–1945', in *European Neutrals and Non-Belligerents during the Second World War*, ed. Neville Wylie (Cambridge: Cambridge University Press, 2001), 1.
13. Abbenhuis, *An Age of Neutrals*, 1–2; Pascal Lottaz and Herbert R. Reginbogin, *Notions of Neutralities* (London: Lexington Books, 2018), xi.
14. Abbenhuis, *An Age of Neutrals*, 1; Wylie, 'Introduction', 1.
15. Abbenhuis, *An Age of Neutrals*, 2.
16. Lottaz and Reginbogin, *Notions of Neutralities*, xi.

17 Andisha, *Neutrality and Vulnerable States*, 11. See also Christine Agius and Karen Devine, 'Neutrality: A Really Dead Concept? A Reprise', *Cooperation and Conflict* 46, no. 3 (2011): 273.
18 The concept of neutrality is widely analysed by scholars of international law. See, for example, Lassa F. L. Oppenheim, *International Law: A Treatise – War and Neutrality*, Vol. II (London: Longmans Green, 1912), 6 and 655; Abbenhuis, *An Age of Neutrals*, 2.
19 Abbenhuis, *An Age of Neutrals*, 2.
20 Andisha, *Neutrality and Vulnerable States*, 12. See also Cyril E. Black and Richard A. Falk, *Neutralization and World Politics* (Princeton: Princeton University Press, 2016), XI; Peter Lyon, 'Neutrality and Emergence of the Concept of Neutralism', *The Review of Politics* 22, no. 2 (1960): 267 and Nataša Mišković, Harald Fischer-Tiné and Nada Boškovska (eds), *The Non-Aligned Movement and the Cold War: Delhi-Bandung-Belgrade* (London: Routledge, 2017).
21 See, for example, Chapter 18 of this volume on the anti-Apartheid campaign as counter-neutrality propaganda.
22 See, for example, Edward Stourton, *Auntie's War: The BBC during the Second World War I* (London: Doubleday, 2017), 87–101, 248–50.
23 Steve Westlake, 'Building the BBC-Branded NGO: Overseas Development, the World Service, and the Marshall Plan of the Mind, c.1965–99', *Twentieth Century British History* 33, no. 1 (2022): 51.
24 See, for example, Isak Svensson, 'Who Brings Which Peace?: Neutral versus Biased Mediation and Institutional Peace Arrangements in Civil Wars', *Journal of Conflict Resolution* 53, no. 3 (2009): 446–69; Melanie C. Greenburg et al., *Words Over War: Mediation and Arbitration to Prevent Deadly Conflict* (New York: Carnegie Corporation of New York, 2000); Fernando Ramos Fernández and David Caldevilla Domínguez, 'Dos caras de España en la I Guerra Mundial: De la mediación humanitaria de Alfonso XIII al suministro logístico a ambos bandos', *Historia y Comunicación Social* 18 (2013): 223–44; W. Mueller and M. Graf, 'An Austrian Mediation in Vietnam?: The Superpowers, Neutrality and Kurt Waldheim's Good Offices', in *Neutrality and Neutralism in the Global Cold War: Between or within the Blocs?*, ed. Sandra Bott, Jussi M. Hanhimaki, Janick Schaufelbuehl and Marco Wyss (London: Routledge, 2017), 127–43 and Hillary Briffa, 'Neutrality and Shelter Seeking: The Case of Malta', in *Small States and the New Security Environment. The World of Small States*, ed. A. M. Brady and B. Thorhallsson (Cham: Springer, 2021).
25 For example, the role of Italy and Spain in the early part of the Second World War is analysed by Robert R. Wilson, '"Non-Belligerency" in Relation to the Terminology of Neutrality', *American Journal of International Law* 35, no. 1 (1941): 121–3; Emanuele Sica and Richard Carrier, *Italy and the Second World War: Alternative Perspectives* (Leiden: Brill, 2018); Neville Wylie, *European Neutrals and Non-belligerents during the Second World War* (Cambridge: Cambridge University Press, 2002). Also see Natalino Ronzitti, 'Italy's Non-belligerency during the Iraqi War', in *International Responsibility Today*, ed. Oscar Schachter and Maurizio Ragazzi (Leiden: Brill, 2005), 197–207.
26 For example, the role of the United States in both world wars, see Jennifer D. Keene, *The United States and the First World War* (London: Routledge, 2021) and Martin Folly, *The United States and World War II* (Edinburgh: Edinburgh University Press, 2002).
27 Abbenhuis, *An Age of Neutrals*, 2–8.

28 Michael Sanders, 'Official British Propaganda in Allied and Neutral Countries during the First World War, with Particular Reference to Organization and Methods' (Thesis, London School of Economics and Political Science, 1972); Michael Sanders and Philip M. Taylor, *British Propaganda during the First World War, 1914–18* (London: Macmillan, 1982).

29 Chad R. Fulwider, *German Propaganda and U.S. Neutrality in World War I* (Missouri: University of Missouri Press, 2017) and Evgeny Sergeev, 'The Influence of Russian Official Propaganda upon Neutral Countries During the First World War', in *War and Propaganda in the XXth Century*, ed. María Fernanda Rollo, Ana Paula Pires and Noémia Malva Novais (Lisbon: Universidad Nova de Lisboa, 2013), 34–9. Stefan Rinke and María Inés Tato – who has also provided a contribution to this book – published on the propaganda campaigns deployed in Latin American, while Javier Ponce Marrero considered the foreign propaganda efforts in neutral Spain. See Stefan Rinke, *Latin America and the First World War* (Cambridge: Cambridge University Press, 2017), 80–159; María Inés Tato, 'Luring Neutrals: Allied and German Propaganda in Argentina during the First World War', in *World War I and propaganda*, ed. Troy Paddock (Leiden: Brill, 2014), 322–44 and Javier Ponce Marrero, 'Propaganda and Politics: Germany and Spanish Opinion in World War I', in *World War I and Propaganda*, ed. Paddock, 292–321.

30 Robert Cole, *Britain and the War of Words in Neutral Europe, 1939-45: The Art of the Possible* (New York: Macmillan, 1990); Robert Cole, *Propaganda, Censorship and Irish Neutrality in the Second World War* (Edinburgh: Edinburgh University Press, 2006). Also see Edward Corse, *A Battle for Neutral Europe: British Cultural Propaganda during the Second World War* (London: Bloomsbury, 2013) and 'British Propaganda in Neutral Eire after the Fall of France, 1940', *Contemporary British History* 22, no. 2 (2008): 163–80.

31 Nicholas J. Cull, *Selling War: The British Propaganda Campaign against American 'Neutrality' in World War II* (New York: Oxford University Press, 1995). Also see Martin Andreas Lutz, *Britische Propaganda in der Schweiz während des Zweiten Weltkriegs 1939-1945* (doctoral thesis, Luzern: Luzern University, 2019) and Alejandro Pizarroso Quintero, *Diplomáticos, propagandistas y espías: Estados Unidos y España en la Segunda Guerra Mundial: información y propaganda* (Madrid: CSIC Press, 2009), among others.

32 James R. Vaughan, *The Failure of American and British Propaganda in the Arab Middle East, 1945-57* (New York: Palgrave Macmillan, 2005); Marek Fields, 'Balancing Between Neutral Country Promotion and Cold War Propaganda: British and American Informational and Cultural Operations in Finland', in *Regime Changes in 20th Century Europe: Reassessed, Anticipated and in the Making*, ed. Marja Vuorinen, Tuomas Kuronen and Aki Huhtinen (Cambridge: Cambridge Scholars Publishing, 2016).

33 See, for example, Carolina García Sanz, 'British Propaganda Dilemma over Neutrals during the Great War: More Business than Usual?', in *War and Propaganda*, ed. Fernanda Rollo, Paula Pires and Malva Novais.

34 Abbenhuis, *An Age of Neutrals*.

35 See, for example, Eberhard Demm's recent work: Eberhard Demm, *Censorship and Propaganda in World War I: a Comprehensive History* (London: Bloomsbury, 2021).

36 Leanne Green, 'Advertising War: Picturing Belgium in First World War Publicity', *Media, War and Conflict* 7, no. 3 (2014): 309–25; Lisa M. Todd, 'The Hun and the Home: Gender, Sexuality and Propaganda in First World War Europe', in *World War

I and Propaganda, ed. Paddock, 137–54; John Horne and Alan Kramer, *German Atrocities, 1914: A History of Denial* (New Haven: Yale University Press, 2001).
37 Sanders and Taylor, *British Propaganda during the First World War*, 54–5 and 213–19; 166–205 and Fulwider, *German Propaganda and U.S. Neutrality in World War I*.
38 John Vincent Smith, 'Britain, Portugal, and the First World War, 1914–16', *European Studies Review* 4, no. 3 (1974): 207–38.
39 Maximiliano Fuentes Codera, *España en la Primera Guerra Mundial: una movilización cultural* (Madrid: Akal, 2014) and Marta García Cabrera, *Filias y Fobias en Acción: Propaganda británica en España durante la Primera y la Segunda Guerra Mundial* (Doctoral thesis, Las Palmas de Gran Canaria, Universidad de Las Palmas de Gran Canaria, 2021).
40 The person responsible for revealing the exaggeration of British propaganda during the Great War was Arthur Ponsonby who, in his book *Falsehood in War-Time*, condemned the lies fabricated during the conflict. See Arthur Ponsonby, *Falsehood in War-Time: Containing an Assortment of Lies Circulated throughout the Nations during the Great War* (London: Allen and Unwin, 1928); Connelly, Fox, Goebel and Schmidt, *Propaganda and conflict*, 270–82; Cull, Culbert and Welch, *Propaganda and Mass Persuasion*, 30–40.
41 Enrique Moradiellos García, 'Una guerra civil de tinta: la propaganda republicana y nacionalista en Gran Bretaña durante el conflicto español', *Sitema: revista de ciencias sociales* 164 (2001): 69–97; Alejandro Pizarroso Quintero, 'La Guerra Civil española, un hito en la historia de la propaganda', *El Argonauta español*, no. 2 (2005); Alejandro Pizarroso Quintero, 'Intervención extranjera y propaganda. La propaganda exterior de las dos Españas', *Historia y comunicación social*, no. 6 (2001): 63–96.
42 Cull, *Selling War*.
43 Karsh, *Neutrality and Small States*, 43–4.
44 Neville Wylie, *Britain, Switzerland, and the Second World War* (Oxford: Oxford University Press, 2003), 48–58 and 201–42; Pia Molander, 'Intelligence, Diplomacy and the Swedish Dilemma: The Special Operations Executive in Neutral Sweden, 1939–45', *Intelligence and National Security* 22, no. 5 (2007): 722–44.
45 António José Telo, *Propaganda e Guerra Secreta Em Portugal: 1939–45* (Lisboa: Perspectivas e realidades, 1990).
46 García Cabrera, *Filias y Fobias en Acción*, 219–41 and Mercedes Peñalba-Sotorrío, 'Beyond the War: Nazi Propaganda Aims in Spain during the Second World War', *Journal of Contemporary History* 54, no. 4 (2019): 902–4.
47 Cull, Culbert and Welch, *Propaganda and Mass Persuasion*, 92–6.
48 Andrew Cottey, 'Introduction: The European Neutral States', in *The European Neutrals and NATO*, ed. Andrew Cottey (London: Palgrave Macmillan, 2018), 1–20 and Bott et al., *Neutrality and Neutralism*, 1–15.
49 Bott et al., *Neutrality and Neutralism*, 1–15 and 213–16; Samir N. Anabtawi, 'Neutralists and Neutralism', *The Journal of Politics* 27, no. 2 (1965): 351–61; Dietmar Rothermund, 'The Era of Non-alignment', in *The Non-Aligned Movement*, ed. Mišković, Fischer-Tiné and Boškovska, 21–3.

Part I

Propaganda and neutrality in the First World War

1

American neutrality and belligerent propaganda

Contested histories

Stephen Badsey

In his war memoirs, written immediately after the end of the First World War, General Erich Ludendorff, First Quartermaster General of the German General Staff from 1916 to 1918, gave two main reasons for Germany's defeat: 'The blockade of extermination and starvation and the enemy propaganda'.[1] Ludendorff's assertion was part of the *Dolchstosslegende* (stab-in-the-back myth), the claim that neither on the Western Front nor at sea had Germany's armed forces been defeated, and that the war had been lost through the Allied naval blockade and the influence of enemy propaganda, which together had led to the collapse of the German home front. Although the *Dolchstosslegende* has long been discredited by historians, it was heavily influential in the war's immediate aftermath.[2] It was made more credible by being part of a much wider acceptance that propaganda had played a significant and sometimes decisive role in all aspects of the war, including in the entry of the previously neutral United States on the side of the Allies in April 1917.

The Allied naval blockade has remained of continuing interest to historians, both as part of the war at sea and as part of the war's political and economic conduct. This interest experienced some rejuvenation as part of the war's centenary of 2014–18, with bold new claims being made about the blockade's nature, importance and consequences, including the impact of the often neglected blockade of Austria-Hungary through the Mediterranean and Adriatic.[3] In contrast, the role of propaganda in the First World War, although well studied and documented by specialist historians, has failed to win a comparable place in the modern mainstream understanding of the war and remains at best an eccentric outlier, a fact lamented by historians of propaganda.[4] This marginalization of the study of propaganda is particularly surprising, given the twenty-first century's concerns about the role of propaganda and the media in more recent wars up to the present day.

The failure of propaganda to find its place in the wider history of the war has not been for lack of evidence or scholarship, and substantial developments have been made in the field over recent decades. The most widely shared conclusion among First World

War historians is that propaganda was an important part of the relationship between belligerent governments and their own domestic populations, and a valuable way of discovering what domestic working class popular opinion might have been. Several researchers also acknowledge that propaganda grew in increasing importance as a battlefield weapon (known at the time as 'front propaganda') as the war progressed. Just as importantly, from the war's start propaganda was an integral part of grand strategy, diplomacy and international politics, particularly propaganda targeted at elites rather than mass society. As the British wartime propagandist Sir Peter Chalmers Mitchell wrote in his 1922 *Encyclopaedia Britannica* entry on propaganda, 'Neutral countries were the battle-ground in which contending propagandas met'.[5] Despite this, not even the comprehensive three-volume *Cambridge History* of the war, published in 2014 to identify the main themes of the war for future historians, thought it worthwhile to include a chapter on propaganda.[6] At the end of the war's centenary commemorations, the landmark 2019 International Society for First World War Studies conference on the 'Legacies' of the war also found no room for any paper or discussion on propaganda.[7] The only prominent exception to this comparative disregard of propaganda is the *1914–1918 Online: International Encyclopedia of the First World War*, hosted by the Free University of Berlin, which provides an important international platform for refereed scholarly articles on propaganda's many significant roles.

This neglect of propaganda in the wider history of the war is due to a phenomenon that has many precedents and is commonly known as stovepiping or siloing. The pieces of the First World War propaganda story are scattered between the historiographical traditions and practices of different countries, and of different approaches and specialisms, so that historians working in one field are largely unaware of developments in others. Given what may legitimately be described as the tsunami of publications that has accompanied the centenary of the war, it is a difficult task to estimate the present extent of this neglect in the case of propaganda. But the proposition that the overwhelming focus for First World War propaganda studies in recent years has been on the social and cultural history of the belligerent home fronts is unlikely to be challenged. This has been particularly true in France, where the study of propaganda and censorship has been increasingly limited to what is described as domestic 'war culture' and to a sometimes angry debate over the extent to which French popular support for the war depended on a general consensus of approval or on government coercion. Those few – mainly British – historians who are interested in front propaganda as an aspect of battles have had their focus almost entirely on the Western Front and the last year of the war, including the mechanisms by which the *Dolchstosslegende* was created.[8] Propaganda as an instrument of wartime international diplomacy and the influencing of elites, seen for parts of the war as its most important function, is presently a seriously neglected field.

Belligerent Propaganda in the United States

This present neglect of wartime propaganda provides a context for why, in explaining the entry of the United States into the war in April 1917, nothing has so far replaced the one-chapter case study on British propaganda and American neutrality in Michael Sanders' and Philip M. Taylor's book *British Propaganda during the First World War 1914–18*, now almost forty years old.[9] It is also a feature of the way in which these rival propaganda campaigns have been understood that they are almost always described in terms of an exclusively Anglo-German conflict, fought – as the German ambassador to Washington DC in Spring 1917 expressed it – for the American soul. French wartime propaganda within the neutral United States gets almost no mention in English-language historical writings. The only recent study of French propaganda aimed at the United States, Robert Young's *Marketing Marianne*, devotes only a chapter to the First World War.[10] Possible explanations for this are that pro-French Americans originally produced propaganda in their native American English rather than French; and that France, of all the major belligerents, placed the heaviest wartime emphasis on domestic censorship, which became the main French topic for debate and investigation in the interwar years through the writings of critical authors such as Georges Demartial.[11] In fact, a significant French propaganda campaign against American neutrality did exist, very similar to that mounted by the British in working through sympathetic American elites, although with more of an emphasis on cultural rather than political propaganda, a calculation perhaps based on the belief that for elite Americans it was almost the definition of being cultured to be pro-French. The American volunteers who served with the French on the Western Front before April 1917 were only the most visible manifestation of this propaganda campaign, whether they knew it or not.

It was also established as orthodoxy during the war, and has continued largely unchallenged by historians, that the Allied propaganda campaigns benefited greatly from the clumsiness of German propaganda, coupled with the negative impact on American elite and public opinion of the scale of German war crimes, whether committed on American soil or elsewhere at sea and on land, including in occupied countries. It is not that the Allies did not commit war crimes or actions contrary to American wishes, but that they had a much better sense of how to limit, conduct and portray their actions for American elite and popular understanding; whereas the Germans failed repeatedly to coordinate their propaganda with their political and military actions. Unlike the French propaganda campaign, the significance of the German propaganda campaign in the United States is usually acknowledged, together with its failure through being misconceived and mismanaged. But it is only very recently that a full-length study, by Chad Fulwider, has been published. Even so, although Fulwider's book is very welcome as covering a gap in the literature, it presents an interpretation of Allied propaganda which is now seen as out of date, including a belief that much of the wartime antagonism towards German-Americans in the United States was 'provoked by the anti-German propaganda created by the Allies'.[12] The view that the Germans lost the propaganda war for the support of the United States, just as much as the Allies – predominantly the British – won it, has prevailed since the war itself.

Two problems that historians have always had with understanding British propaganda during the war are the complexity of its organizations and the subtlety and indirect nature of many of its methods. Many of those who worked to bring neutral America into the war did not consider themselves propagandists, but simply British patriots – or even American patriots – supporting their country's war effort. There were many British and pro-British propagandists who had no connection at all with official propaganda, but who the British government saw no reason to discourage. There were also many people who worked with the official propaganda organizations but never held an official position, perhaps the most prominent at the time being Rudyard Kipling. In common with many other British wartime institutions, their propaganda evolved throughout the war in an often chaotic way in response to immediate threats and circumstances. There were repeated cases of overlapping authority and of propaganda institutions ignorant of each other's work. Government ministries, notably the War Office (the Army) and the Admiralty (the Royal Navy), developed their own independent propaganda arms during the war, and some of their activities were kept secret from the rest of the government. Even while the war was being fought, most British government officials and parliamentarians did not understand the nature or organization of propaganda, and few official records were left after the war.

The central arm of British official propaganda was created a month after the war's outbreak as the War Propaganda Bureau, always known in practice as Wellington House from its location, under the junior minister Charles Masterman. Wellington House's initial propaganda target was elite opinion in the United States and to oversee this Masterman recruited Sir Gilbert Parker. In February 1917, a much expanded Wellington House was absorbed into the new Department of Information, created to bring greater order to the organization of propaganda, under the famous novelist John Buchan. The nature of British propaganda was further complicated by the influential London press, which occupied a unique role in politics in comparison to other countries. Among the many ambitions of the powerful newspaper owner Lord Northcliffe was to head or direct British propaganda, an ambition he shared with his fellow newspaper owner, Lord Beaverbrook. In February 1918, Northcliffe became head of the new Directorate of Propaganda in Enemy Countries, while Beaverbrook became head of the Ministry of Information, an expanded version of the Department of Information. However, several other propaganda institutions remained in existence, and British official propaganda policy was always a matter of dispute and negotiation, while remaining true to a few broad objectives, one of which was the importance of the United States.[13]

This account of British propaganda in the war is familiar to historians of war propaganda, but it contrasts strongly with claims and assumptions made about British propaganda between 1914 and 1941, particularly by Anglophobe and isolationist Americans. These writers portrayed British propaganda as the product of a large and sinister apparatus with a pre-war existence, that had played an important part in creating the conditions for the outbreak of the war; and portrayed its stock in trade as orchestrated, relentless and cynical lying, directed at its own people, at neutrals, at Allies and at enemies. The entry of the United States into the war was claimed to be the personal achievement of either Northcliffe or sometimes of Sir Gilbert Parker. In reality, Wellington House's propaganda campaign chiefly aimed to influence American elites and opinion-formers, as an extension of British foreign policy; it placed a high value on selective use of factual information and avoided falsehood on principle; and it was carried out through multiple official, semi-official and informal methods and channels, something not significantly changed by the creation of the Department of Information. Some of these British channels of propaganda remain very obscure to historians, the best identified being the work of Captain Guy Gaunt, the Royal Navy attaché in Washington DC, for Captain Reginald 'Blinker' Hall, the Director of Naval Intelligence at the Admiralty. The potential for confusion because of these overlaps has appeared in a recent account in Keith Jeffrey's invaluable *1916: A Global History*, who writing from the perspective of a historian of government Intelligence portrays the British propaganda campaign in the United States as run principally by Captain Gaunt, while failing to mention either Masterman or Parker.[14]

The exact role of Sir Gilbert Parker in leading the British propaganda campaign from Wellington House has probably been overstated, although he was certainly more than a figurehead. Most claims about Parker's importance rest on just three paragraphs of his own article, 'The United States and the War', published in *Harper's Monthly Magazine* in March 1918, together with his Wellington House reports.[15] The Conservative Member of Parliament (MP) for Gravesend since 1900, Parker had been born in Canada and was the author of several successful novels with a Canadian theme. His second home was in New York society, where he had a web of influential contacts partly through his wife, a New York heiress. In June 1915, Parker reported to Wellington House that 'we have an organization that does not know it is an organization' in the United States, a classic example of Wellington House's style.[16] But in the critical year of 1916, Parker was convalescent on the French Riviera for the early months, and thereafter spent time at various British country retreats, although he was not so ill as to stop writing his novels. By early 1917, he had a staff of more than fifty who functioned well without him. Shortly after having travelled to New York, he resigned his post with Wellington House on the day that the United States broke off diplomatic relations with Germany, 3 February 1917.[17]

The often prickly relationship of Lord Northcliffe as owner of *The Times* and the *Daily Mail* to official British propaganda was subject, at the time and later, to numerous inaccurate claims and assumptions, some of which still persist. Both during the war and through the interwar period, it was widely believed in the United States, in Germany, and to some extent in Britain, that from the start of the war Northcliffe had a central role in the official government propaganda campaign or even that he was in charge of it. The isolationist Senator William J. Stone (Democrat of Missouri) told the Senate in March 1917 that 'the news, so called, which comes to the United States from Europe is filtered, as we all know, through the London news bureau presided over and managed by Lord Northcliffe'.[18] In reality, Northcliffe found the Official Press Bureau, which oversaw press censorship in London, so obstructive to his views and ambitions that in the same month he complained to the War Office that it was full of 'pro-Germans'. The view of Northcliffe as the mastermind of British propaganda was strengthened for many Americans immediately after the country's entry into the war by Northcliffe's arrival to run the British War Mission in the United States (the chief role of which was to sort out the many contracts and orders for American goods and munitions placed by the British) and by a personal propaganda campaign of speeches and articles on which he embarked in Autumn 1917, chiefly in the Midwest, having failed to convince Prime Minister David Lloyd George to come over and carry this out himself.

The British government under Lloyd George tolerated this personal propaganda campaign of Northcliffe's rather than officially sanctioning it. While Northcliffe is undoubtedly important to the story of British propaganda, and the recent writings of J. Lee Thompson in particular have thrown a helpful light on his role, the extent of his contributions to propaganda in the United States remains a matter of debate.[19]

Allied Propaganda and American Neutrality

The description of the complex story of British propaganda given above is very familiar to British and American historians who specialize in this field. But there is a marked gap between this and an equally strong consensus among American and British political and diplomatic historians, who have found little or no place for belligerent propaganda in their thinking on American neutrality and entry into the war. The presently dominant view holds that the critical decision path was the second unrestricted U-Boat campaign from 1 February onwards, and that the United States was 'torpedoed into the war'. The release to the American public by its government on 1 March of the Zimmermann Telegram, showing that Germany had offered an alliance to Mexico in a possible war with the United States, is accepted as an important factor by some historians, while being downplayed by others. The main disagreements within this consensus are over the internal politics of the United States and the wisdom and motives of American politicians, especially President Wilson.[20] The financial and economic links between the United States and the Western Allies are often accepted as contributory factors; the sinking of RMS *Lusitania* in May 1915, in which 123 American civilians drowned, is sometimes included as a long-term factor, and more rarely some weight is given to the German campaign of sabotage and subversion conducted on the United States mainland.[21] The very few of these books which also discuss belligerent propaganda in this context maintain the tradition that the British relied on deliberate and systematic lying, that overturning American neutrality was the sole objective of British propaganda before April 1917, and even in some cases that Sir Gilbert Parker rather than Masterman was in charge of Wellington House, or the later Ministry of Information.[22]

This present neglect or misinterpretation of the role of belligerent propaganda in the American entry into the First World War stands in complete contrast to the view that prevailed in the United States in the years immediately following the war, among writers on what was then much less history and more current affairs. From the mid-1920s onwards, the most prevalent critical narrative among American authors was that the United States was drawn into the war by unscrupulous capitalists, notably arms manufacturers on both sides of the Atlantic. As part of this, it was taken for granted that British propaganda played a critical role. Serious academic studies of wartime belligerent propaganda and its impact on the United States effectively began in 1927 with the book *Propaganda Technique in the World War* by Harold Lasswell of the Chicago School of sociologists.[23] The increasingly Anglophobe and isolationist context in which this work appeared is well expressed by a comment from the famous American novelist Upton Sinclair in the same year, 'I am one of a hundred and ten million suckers who swallowed the hook of the British official propaganda, conducted by an eminent bourgeois novelist, Gilbert Parker, who was afterwards knighted for what he did to me' during the war, 'now he grins at me from behind the shelter of his title'[24] (Parker was in fact knighted in 1902). Between 1927 and 1941, up to the entry of the United States into the Second World War, Lasswell's book was followed by three more analytical books on the belligerent propaganda campaigns, plus in 1935 the best-selling *Road to War* by the distinguished journalist Walter Millis, who borrowed heavily from Lasswell's conclusions regarding propaganda, and from George Sylvester Viereck, an outspoken pro-German propagandist both during and after the war.[25] Although varying in emphasis and detail, all these interwar American books told essentially the same story: of the triumph of British lying propaganda over their own home front population, over American neutrality and over their German enemy. H. C. Peterson's book *Propaganda for War*, published in 1939, took the firmest stance, concluding that 'the most important of the reasons for the American action' in 1917 was 'the attitude of mind in this country – the product of British propaganda'.[26] The influence of these early political studies, with their characterization of Allied propaganda as baseless and deceitful lying, persisted in American histories of the war almost to the end of the twentieth century.[27] As with several other aspects of the history of the First World War, recent historians who have established the scale and nature of German war crimes, in occupied France and Belgium and in the conduct of the war at sea, had to begin by explaining the context in which such distorted and inaccurate beliefs could have persisted for so long.[28] But although long discredited or modified, the position taken by these interwar authors continues into the present day in a small number of books that stand outside the mainstream American interpretation. For illustration, Stewart Halsey Ross's recent book, titled *Propaganda for War* as a homage to Peterson, asserts that 'When lies were called for, [Sir Gilbert] Parker lied glibly; when atrocities were found to play well in the press, Parker created enormous German barbarities'.[29]

It is not suggested that the work of Lasswell and other interwar American writers represented bad scholarship. But they were severely limited by a lack of hard documented evidence and the lack of any equivalent scholarly books or interest in wartime propaganda from Great Britain itself. The official British wartime propaganda archive seemed to have disappeared; indeed its partial reconstruction over decades since the 1970s has been critical to the changes that have led to present-day views. The few memoirs by British propagandists revealed little about propaganda policy, with the exception of works in praise of Northcliffe by his former employees, chiefly Sir Campbell Stuart's *Secrets of Crewe House* in 1920, and Chalmers Mitchell's *Encyclopaedia Britannica* article in 1922, the year that Northcliffe died.[30] Despite their aspirations to scholarship and a 'scientific' approach (a characteristic claim of the Chicago School), interwar American authors had little choice but to draw heavily on openly polemical post-war writers with the strongest political motives. The most bizarre of these was *Spreading Germs of Hate* of 1931 by George Viereck, a book laden with imagined statements and easily disprovable claims about Allied propaganda that is still occasionally taken as a reputable source. Equally and intentionally polemical was the best-selling denouncement of all British newspapers and propaganda organizations by Arthur Ponsonby MP, *Falsehood in War-Time* of 1928, which is still in print and is often quoted or cited in general studies of propaganda. The former Kaiser, in exile, was so delighted by Ponsonby's book on publication that he requested a further twenty-four copies. Modern assessments of Ponsonby are that he was closer to a propagandist for his own anti-war and anti-establishment causes than an impartial investigator. James Duane Squires in particular, in his 1935 book *British Propaganda at Home and in the United States from 1914 to 1917*, praised Ponsonby for his information and advice.[31] The same reliance on Ponsonby appeared in the two-volume *The Origins of the World War* of 1928 by the influential American historian Sidney Bradshaw Fay, which is also still in print. Fay's book included, and may have introduced, the now clichéd and disputed list of the deep and underlying causes of the war: militarism, alliances, imperialism and nationalism. But Fay added a fifth deep cause that he judged equally important: 'The newspaper press', which in his analysis had poisoned European public opinion in favour of war before 1914, and which together with Allied propaganda had progressively turned the United States against Germany.[32]

This belief in a ubiquitous and pernicious Allied – chiefly British – propaganda linked to the press, pre-dating the war and from which all its evils flowed, was a deeply held conviction among the Central Powers during the war which would eventually lead to the *Dolchstosslegende*. In addition to many claims such as Ludendorff's, a remarkable non-German illustration of this appears in a desperate offer of peace sent to President Wilson from Emperor Karl in Vienna in late February 1917, stipulating only two conditions: that Austria-Hungary should remain intact, and 'the cessation of the propaganda [that] led to Sarajevo', and which from their perspective was still continuing.[33] Fay himself was quite open about the contemporary political purpose of his book: that in his view the position taken in the Treaty of Versailles, that Germany and the Central Powers held the sole guilt for the war, was wrong; that the treaty should be opened to negotiation and revised in Germany's favour; and that 'There must first come a further revision by historical scholars, and through them of public opinion'.[34] This fitted admirably with the position of the post-war German Weimar government, which distributed copies of Fay's book as gifts through its embassies, and paid for translations into both German and French. Ponsonby's book was also translated into both languages within a year of publication.

An important recent book on propaganda and the United States in the First World War, *Manipulating the Masses* by John Maxwell Hamilton, draws on the same interwar tradition regarding propaganda, as well as on present American orthodoxy on the factors leading to American entry into the war. Hamilton's book is also representative of a further tradition among journalist-historians, which emerged among journalists after the First World War (and was almost certainly influenced by the war itself), but did not reach its full development until much later. This tradition, which was brought to prominence by Philip Knightley's very influential *The First Casualty* of 1975,[35] may be summarized as a conviction that the role of reporters is to challenge all government behaviour on principle, that all government engagement with the mass media or the public is propaganda or censorship appropriate only for a police state and that wartime propagandists who thought otherwise only deluded themselves. The main concern of Hamilton's book is President Wilson's creation in April 1917 of the Committee on Public Information (known as the Creel Committee from its chairman George Creel), which was influenced by British and French propaganda institutions and which he describes as being the start of 'a profound and enduring threat to American democracy that rose out of the Great War – the establishment of pervasive systematic propaganda as an instrument of state' and that has continued in peace as well as war to the present day.[36] In explaining American entry into the war, Hamilton also focuses on domestic politics and on the behaviour of President Wilson, drawing attention to his views on controlling public opinion, while taking unrestricted submarine warfare and the Zimmermann Telegram as the inevitable cause of the end of American neutrality. Understandably, since belligerent propaganda up to April 1917 is less important to Hamilton, his understanding of the organization and function of British propaganda is vague, although he pays reluctantly ironic tribute to the British 'cunning of juijitsu fighters' in outsmarting the Germans.[37]

Conclusion

To summarize this brief survey: thanks to the work of many historians of propaganda in recent years, both the nature and function of British propaganda aimed at the neutral United States are much better understood among specialists in the field, although no equivalent studies exist for French propaganda. Thanks to the work of other historians, the nature of German war crimes and atrocities during the war is also better understood, giving the British and French propaganda response to them a significantly different perspective to that which prevailed in the interwar years. But, and almost completely separate from these discoveries, the idea that British propaganda played a major part in the entry of the United States into the war, which was a dominant theme during the interwar years, has dropped almost completely from modern thinking among historians of wartime politics and diplomacy, except among a few historians who continue to repeat the interwar Anglophobe and isolationist position. To paraphrase Sidney Bradshaw Fay, before any further investigation can be made, first the idea that belligerent propaganda played a role in the United States' entry into the war that is worth investigating needs to re-enter our wider thinking.

Notes

The author wishes to thank Dr David Monger for many helpful conversations which have contributed to the writing of this chapter.

1 Erich von Ludendorff, *Ludendorff's Own Story: August 1914–November 1918*, vol. I (New York and London: Harper & Brothers, 1919), 427. Despite his name on the title page of this book, Ludendorff in fact had no claim to the title of 'von'; see also George S. Vascik and Mark R. Sadler (eds), *The Stab-in-the-Back Myth and the Fall of the Weimar Republic* (London: Bloomsbury, 2016).
2 For a recent exception, maintaining that the German Army was undefeated on the Western Front, see Jörn Leonhard, *Pandora's Box: A History of the First World War* (Cambridge and London: Belknap Press, 2018), 759.

3   For example, see Nicholas A. Lambert, *Planning Armageddon: British Economic Warfare and the First World War* (Cambridge, MA: Harvard University Press, 2012); Lawrence Sonhaus, *The Great War at Sea: A Naval History of the First World War* (Cambridge: Cambridge University Press, 2014); Greg Kennedy (ed.), *Britain's War at Sea 1914–1918: The War They Thought and the War They Fought* (London: Routledge, 2016); Eric W. Osborne, *Britain's Economic Blockade of Germany 1914–1919* (Abingdon: Frank Cass, [2004] 2013); Nicholas Mulder, *The Economic Weapon: The Rise of Sanctions as a Tool of Modern War* (New Haven: Yale University Press, 2022).

4   Eberhard Demm, *Censorship and Propaganda in World War I: A Comprehensive History* (London: Bloomsbury Academic, 2019), ix–xi; Stephen Badsey, *The German Corpse Factory: A Study in First World War Propaganda* (Warwick: Helion, 2019), 38–9; Pierre Purseigle, 'Controversy: War Culture', 1914–1918 Online: International Encyclopedia of the First World War, at https://encyclopedia.1914-1918-online.net/article/controversy_war_culture?version=1.0 (accessed 11 June 2022).

5   Peter Chalmers Mitchell, 'Propaganda', in *The Encyclopaedia Britannica 12th Edition*, ed. Hugh Chisholm (London: The Encyclopaedia Britannica Company, 1922). The 12th edition consisted of new volumes to supplement the twenty-nine volumes of the 11th edition of 1911.

6   Jay Winter (ed.) *The Cambridge History of the First World War*, 3 vols (Cambridge: Cambridge University Press, 2014); this work does include a chapter on film propaganda.

7   See the programme for the 2019 'Legacies' Conference of the International Society of First World War Studies at https://www.firstworldwarstudies.org/perch/resources/legacies-2019-final-programme.pdf (accessed 11 June 2022).

8   For example, see Alexander Watson, *Ring of Steel: Germany and Austria-Hungary at War 1914–1918* (London: Allen Lane, 2014), 529–33; David Stevenson, *Cataclysm: The First World War as Political Tragedy* (New York: Basic, 2004), 376–7. For a rare attempt to place front propaganda in a wider context, see Bernard Wilkin, *Aerial Propaganda and the Wartime Occupation of France, 1914–1918* (London: Routledge, 2017).

9   Michael Sanders and Philip M. Taylor, *British Propaganda during the First World War, 1914–18* (London: Macmillan, 1982), 167–207.

10 Robert Young, *Marketing Marianne: French Propaganda in America 1900–1940* (New Brunswick: Rutgers, 2004), 42–70; see also Justin Quinn Olmstead, *The United States' Entry Into the First World War: The Role of British and German Diplomacy* (Woodbridge: Boydell, 2018), 112 and for the paucity of studies of the French propaganda campaign, see John Maxwell Hamilton, *Manipulating the Masses: Woodrow Wilson and the Birth of American Propaganda* (Baton Rouge: Louisiana State University Press, 2020), 37n.

11 Georges Demartial, *Patriotism and Responsibility for the War* (New York: B.W. Huebsch, 1920); Harold D. Lasswell, *Propaganda Technique in the World War* (New York: Alfred A. Knopf, 1927), 1–2.

12 Chad R. Fulwider, *German Propaganda and U.S. Neutrality in World War I* (Missouri: University of Missouri Press, 2017), 2.

13 While it would be impractical to list every historian of propaganda, for examples of authors based in the United States who study the general history of war propaganda and who concur with this accepted view, see Susan A. Brewer, *Why America Fights: Patriotism and Propaganda from the Philippines to Iraq* (Oxford: Oxford University Press, 2009), 46–86 and Susan L. Carruthers, *The Media at War* (London: MacMillan,

2000), 28–9 and 54–73; see also David Welch, *Germany and Propaganda in World War I: Pacifism, Mobilization and Total War* (London: I.B. Tauris, 2014), 135–40.
14 Keith Jeffrey, *1916: A Global History* (London: Bloomsbury, 2015), 330–5.
15 Sir Gilbert Parker, 'The United States and the War', *Harper's Monthly Magazine* CXXXVI, no. 814 (March 1918): 521–31. Parker's reports are part of the INF 4 Series of documents in The National Archives, Kew, the main source of documents on British First World War propaganda.
16 Quoted in Lucy Masterman, *C. F. G. Masterman: A Biography* (London: Frank Cass, [1939] 1968), 277.
17 Badsey, *The German Corpse Factory*, 125–7.
18 Quoted in Thomas Boghardt, *The Zimmermann Telegram: Intelligence, Diplomacy, and America's Entry into World War I* (Annapolis: Naval Institute Press, 2012), 131.
19 J. Lee Thompson, *Politicians, The Press and Propaganda: Lord Northcliffe and the Great War 1914–1919* (Kent: Kent State University, 1999), 123–218 and J. Lee Thompson, *Northcliffe: Press Baron in Politics 1865–1922* (London: John Murray, 2000), 266–313.
20 These are the only factors listed on the webpage 'U.S. Enters the War – Why Did the U.S. Fight in World War I?', National World War I Museum and Memorial, at https://www.theworldwar.org/us-enters-war (accessed 11 June 2022). For the general acceptance of this view, see Watson, *Ring of Steel*, 443–9; Holger H. Herwig, *The First World War: Germany and Austria-Hungary 1914–1918* (London: Arnold, 1997), 312–25; Lawrence V. Moyer, *Victory Must Be Ours: Germany in the Great War 1914–1918* (London: Leo Cooper, 1995), 186–8; Niall Ferguson, *The Pity of War* (London: Allen Lane, 1998), 282–4; Leonhard, *Pandora's Box*, 586–7.
21 For American views, see Jennifer D. Keene, 'Finding a Place for World War I in American History: 1914–2018', in *Writing the Great War: The Historiography of World War I from 1918 to the Present*, ed. Christoph Cornelissen and Arndt Weinrich (New York: Berghahn, 2021), 459–60; this useful assessment also makes no mention of belligerent propaganda's impact on American neutrality. See also Michael S. Neiberg, *The Path to War: How the First World War Created Modern America* (Oxford: Oxford University Press, 2016), 66–94 and 206–30; Richard F. Hamilton and Holger H. Herwig, *Decisions for War 1914–1917* (Cambridge: Cambridge University Press, 2004), 202–24; Olmstead, *The United States' Entry Into the First World War* and for the longevity of this interpretation, Ross Gregory, *The Origins of American Intervention in the First World War* (New York: Norton, 1971), 131–9. For the British, see Daniel Larsen, *Plotting for Peace: American Peacemakers, British Codebreakers, and Britain at War, 1914–1917* (Cambridge: Cambridge University Press, 2021), 246–306; David Stevenson, *1917: War, Peace and Revolution* (Oxford: Oxford University Press, [2017] 2019), 13–66.
22 Fulwider, *German Propaganda and U.S. Neutrality in World War I*, 168–9; Justus D. Doenecke, *Nothing Less Than War: A New History of America's Entry into World War I* (Lexington: The University Press of Kentucky, 2011), 18.
23 Lasswell, *Propaganda Technique in the World War*; see also Martin Bulmer, *The Chicago School of Sociology* (Chicago: University of Chicago Press, 1987), 193–9.
24 Upton Sinclair, *Money Writes!* (New York: Albert and Charles Bonie, 1927), 25–6; see also John Coldwell Adams, *Seated with the Mighty: A Biography of Sir Gilbert Parker* (Ottawa: Borealis Press, 1979), 174 and John E. Moser, *Twisting the Lion's Tale: Anglophobia in the United States 1921–48* (London: MacMillan, 1999), 17–67.
25 Walter Millis, *Road to War: America 1914–1917* (Boston: Houghton Mifflin, 1935), viii–ix.

26 H. C. Peterson, *Propaganda for War: The Campaign against American Neutrality, 1914–1917* (Norman: University of Oklahoma Press, 1939), 326. See also George G. Brunz, *Allied Propaganda and the Collapse of the German Empire in 1918* (Stanford: Stanford University Press, 1938); J. M. Read, *Atrocity Propaganda 1914–1919* (New Haven: Yale University Press). For recent analysis of these interwar books, see Badsey, *The German Corpse Factory*, 44–7.
27 For example, see Moyer, *Victory Must Be Ours*, 95–101 and 192–6.
28 John Horne and Alan Kramer, *German Atrocities 1914: A History of Denial* (New York: Yale University Press, 2001); Jeff Lipkes, *Rehearsals: The German Army in Belgium, August 1914* (Leuven: Leuven University Press, 2007); Larry Zuckerman, *The Rape of Belgium: The Untold Story of World War I* (New York: New York University Press, 2004); Sophie de Schaepdrijver (ed.), *Military Occupation in First World War Europe* (London: Routledge, 2015); Isabel V. Hull, *A Scrap of Paper: Breaking and Making International Law During the Great War* (New York: Cornell University Press, 2014). For the wider phenomenon, see Dan Todman, *The Great War: Myth and Memory* (London: Hambledon and London, 2005); David Reynolds, *The Long Shadow: The Great War and the Twentieth Century* (London: W.W. Norton, 2014).
29 Stewart Halsey Ross, *Propaganda for War: How the United States was Conditioned to Fight the Great War of 1914–1918* (Joshua Tree: Progressive, 2009), 18; see also Fulwider, *German Propaganda and U.S. Neutrality in World War I*, 25–6; Alan Axelrod, *Selling the Great War: The Making of American Propaganda* (New York: Palgrave Macmillan, 2009), 56–62.
30 Campbell Stuart, *Secrets of Crewe House: The Story of a Famous Campaign* (London: Hodder & Stoughton, 1920); see also Peter Chalmers Mitchell, *My Fill of Days* (London: Faber and Faber, 1937), 278–98.
31 James Duane Squires, *British Propaganda at Home and in the United States from 1914 to 1917* (Cambridge, MA: Harvard University Press, 1935), x; George Sylvester Viereck, *Spreading Germs of Hate* (London: Duckworth, 1931); Arthur Ponsonby, *Falsehood in War-Time: Containing an Assortment of Lies Circulated Throughout the Nations During the Great War* (London: George Allen and Unwin, 1928); for modern assessments of Ponsonby, see Adrian Gregory, *The Last Great War: British Society and the First World War* (Oxford: Oxford University Press, 2008), 41–4; Todman, *The Great War*, 156–83 and Badsey, *The German Corpse Factory*, 28–31.
32 Sidney Bradshaw Fay, *The Origins of the World War*, 2 vols, vol. I (New York: Macmillan, [1928] 1930), 47–9.
33 Larsen, *Plotting for Peace*, 297–8.
34 Fay, *The Origins of the World War*, vol. II, 556–8.
35 Philip Knightley, *The First Casualty: From the Crimea to Vietnam – The War Correspondent as Hero, Propagandist, and Myth Maker* (London: Harcourt, 1975) and revised and updated editions.
36 Hamilton, *Manipulating the Masses*, 4.
37 Ibid., 41 and 355.

2

First World War propaganda in neutral Argentina

María Inés Tato

As a global conflict, the First World War was fought *in* and *from* different world locations and at different levels, including through the realms of symbolism. To mobilize human and material resources, justify the war and maintain or extend commercial, geopolitical and cultural influence, the belligerent states (the Allies or Entente Powers of Britain, France and later the United States on the one hand, and the Central Powers of Germany and Austria-Hungary on the other) appealed to the cooperation of their Allies but also to neutral nations. Thus, propaganda turned out to be a fundamental strategy for economic, military and cultural war mobilization and neutrals became battlefields where the warring nations competed for support to the war effort. This chapter aims to analyse war propaganda disseminated in Argentina during the conflict and its reference to neutrality. It argues that although both sides distributed content suitable for any audience in a variety of formats, they also produced more specific materials alluding – directly or indirectly – to the country's neutral status. Besides, it reveals that European communities residing in the country and Argentine intellectuals played a crucial role in producing propaganda according to local cultural codes and history, thus contributing to its effectiveness.

The relevance of the Argentine case study lies in several factors. First, since the mid-nineteenth century, it became an important destination for migration to the Americas, second only to the United States.[1] On the eve of the First World War, 27 per cent of the country's population came from Europe, which gave the conflict a broad impact, leading to an intense mobilization around the arguments relating to the war.[2] Second, Argentina was a fulcrum for disseminating news and propaganda in South America more generally.[3] Finally, the active engagement of local intellectuals in war propaganda activities increased the conflict's social impact and provided new arguments and materials to the belligerents' propaganda effort.

After a brief overview of the attitude of the Argentine government and society towards the 'Great War', this chapter will examine the different propaganda resources distributed in Argentina, the main arguments put forward by both sides and their reference to neutrality.

Neutral state, belligerent society

The Argentine government remained neutral throughout the First World War. During the conflict, two presidents of opposing political tendencies governed Argentina: Victorino de la Plaza (1914–16) and Hipólito Yrigoyen (1916–22). However, despite some nuances, both maintained a neutralist foreign policy. The policy of neutrality responded to several factors: the lack of direct interest in the conflict or links with the system of international alliances associated with the war; the prioritization of uninterrupted trade with both sides; the awareness of Argentine economic and military weakness, which made the country's participation in the war unfeasible; and the interest in preserving social harmony given the importance of foreign origin within the population demographics.[4] In the first year of the war, the Argentine government faced two serious incidents involving the two warring sides that challenged its neutrality. However, its foreign policy seemed to give the impression of maintaining equidistance from both sides, ignoring events that could compromise the diplomatic position that Argentina had adopted. Although this passive neutrality aroused vehement complaints in Argentine National Congress [Congreso de la Nación Argentina] and provoked some spontaneous protest demonstrations, social pressure did not alter the official stance adopted regarding the conflict.[5]

The year 1917 drastically changed the situation. The entry of the United States into the war on the side of the Entente stimulated the abandonment of neutrality by most Latin American countries, encouraged by a campaign of diplomatic and economic pressure under the slogan of pan-Americanism.[6] On the other hand, German unrestricted submarine warfare led to the sinking of three Argentine ships – the *Monte Protegido*, the *Oriana* and the *Toro* – between April and June. The United States exploited these incidents disclosing confidential telegrams sent by the German Minister in Argentina – Count Karl von Luxburg – which were intercepted and decrypted by the British intelligence services. They not only revealed the recommendation made by the Minister to continue with the sinking operations 'without a trace', but referred in offensive terms to the Argentine Minister of Foreign Affairs, Honorio Pueyrredón, and hinted at the existence of a verbal agreement with President Yrigoyen to prevent the entry of Argentine ships into the exclusion zone established by Germany.[7]

Despite the internal repercussions unleashed by the so-called Luxburg affair and the intense external and internal pressures, Yrigoyen kept a neutralist policy. However, the pan-American campaign promoted by the United States induced him to promote an approach to neutral Spain and, consequently, to encourage pan-Hispanism. In that vein, he decreed that 12 October was *Día de la Raza* [The Day of the Race], explicitly extolling the Spanish discovery, conquest and colonization of the Americas.[8] Although this pan-Hispanism was promoted publicly as an alternative to pan-Americanism, it was still the case that the Argentine government tempered its strict neutrality and adopted a benevolent stance towards the Allies. Thus, Argentina was able to formally maintain its neutrality during its most serious wartime diplomatic crises and avoid being forced into belligerence.[9]

In contrast with this cautious diplomatic position, civil society revealed early on that there was an intense cultural divide between supporting one or another warring side.[10] That support adopted various expressions: fervent debates in the public space, mass street demonstrations, humanitarian contributions and the enrolment of military and medical volunteers to serve in the European armies. Public opinion was also polarized. Until 1917, opinion was split between the so-called *Aliadófilos* (i.e. supporters of the Allies) and *Germanófilos* (i.e. supporters of the Central Powers, especially Germany), expressing cultural affinities and, at the same time, backing Argentine neutrality.[11] Pro-Allies predominated in the Argentine cultural field – especially in literary and artistic circles – as a result of a deep-rooted devotion for France. Since the beginning of the nineteenth century, France had become a republican model for the continent's new states and a cultural reference for the intellectual and political elites. French cultural diplomacy took advantage of this affinity affirming the existence of a cultural and spiritual unity between France and the new Latin American states. This transnational identity – usually referred to as pan-Latinism (or Latinity) – was grounded on the common origin of their languages.[12] On the other hand, German influence prevailed in the spheres of law, medicine, the military and the natural sciences, which had less resonance in public opinion. The inclination towards one side or the other reflected elective affinities related to a certain professional origin. However, many counterexamples show that the polarization between *Aliadófilos* and *Germanófilos* existed within various professional fields and civil associations. Both sectors of public opinion differed regarding the country proposed as a model for Argentina. *Aliadófilos* praised France and Britain for their political values (democracy, freedom) and industrial capitalism (in the British case). *Germanófilos* presented Germany as a model for being an industrial power with a progressive social policy and a democratic parliament. In this sense, there was no opposition between traditionalism and modernization.[13]

From 1917, following the entry of the United States into the war, that antagonism mutated into 'rupturists' (i.e. those who promoted a severance of relations with Germany) and 'neutralists'. Although neutralism was a complex field, contemporaries tended to equate those who defended the official foreign policy with being pro-German. Both antagonists considered the policy they promoted as the more accurate to defend Argentine sovereignty, preserve its international status in South America and a prominent position in the post-war international order.[14]

The belligerents' propaganda operated in this local cultural and social mobilization framework. It facilitated the dissemination of propaganda produced in Europe and also provided narratives that were deeply rooted in Argentine history and values, contributing to the local appropriation of the conflict.

Propaganda arsenals

As the conflict prolonged beyond expectations, belligerents centralized the production of information and propaganda.[15] The information about the Great War arriving in Argentina had faced the censorship of the belligerents, as well as the selection made by the international news agencies and the telegraphic services. The French agency Havas distributed the news in Latin America through two British telegraph companies – the *Western Telegraph Company* and the *Central and South American Company*.[16] When, on 4 August 1914, Britain cut the transatlantic submarine cables that telegraphically linked Germany with the American continent, the Allies obtained a virtual monopoly of the information and propaganda disseminated through the press.[17] Official belligerent propaganda coexisted with that spontaneously created by civil society actors supporting their states' war effort. Propaganda therefore took on a dual character that combined vertical and horizontal initiatives.[18] In the case of Argentina, European immigrant communities and local intellectuals, linked by cultural affinities to one or another belligerent side, played a leading role in distributing European propaganda and devising other materials sensitive to the predominant local cultural codes. This sensitivity was a key factor in determining the effectiveness of the propaganda.

The British government led the distribution of Allied propaganda in Argentina. It is possible that its predominance was due to the geopolitical influence of Britain, the principal commercial partner of Argentina at that time. In the case of the Central Powers, German propaganda hegemony was indisputable. The bulk of foreign propaganda was channelled through an avalanche of printed productions, both textual and iconographic – in the form of books, periodicals, brochures, pamphlets, flyers, posters, photographs and postcards. In addition, publications often reflected other activities that were ongoing at the time such as the speeches and lectures of political leaders and intellectuals which were usually compiled in writing, contributing to forming a vast corpus of war literature that was widely circulated. This literature included: official documentation about the causes and responsibilities of the war; works by prestigious European intellectuals defending their country's cause; writings by authors both of other nationalities and political affiliations as well as from other neutral countries; texts aimed at specific audiences (children, workers etc.); accounts of war battles; and opinions of local intellectuals.[19]

Belligerent powers also made extensive use of photography and cinema. These new resources acquired increasing importance for influencing public opinion, as they were seen to represent the reality truthfully and objectively.[20] The warring states distributed photographs to newspapers and illustrated magazines extolling the combat epic, displaying their arsenals and showing the enemy's violence. However, they also resorted to exhibitions of war pictures. For instance, the British government set up a travelling photo exhibition which visited many places in Argentina and, from there, other Latin American cities.[21] The Allied powers also organized a war exhibition similar to those carried out by the belligerents in their capital cities to show their military potential.[22] Thus, for example, between May and August 1917, the French-Argentine Committee organized in Buenos Aires the 'Allied Exhibition' – sponsored by the French, Belgian and British governments. It displayed uniforms and weapons used in various battles. One of the main attractions was the small-scale replica of the trench system and the aeroplane used by the multi-decorated pilot Vicente Almandos Almonacid, an Argentine volunteer in the French Air Force.[23] In Argentina, French and British propaganda films had been exhibited since August 1916, while US and German films started to be projected only towards the end of the war.[24]

Propagandists also resorted to the traditional strategy of verbal communication through speeches. After returning from Europe, several direct witnesses of the European war – volunteer doctors, military personnel and war correspondents – talked about their own experiences. Besides, pro-Allied and pro-German Argentine intellectuals also made speeches in public meetings to support their respective cause.[25] Among the first ones, it is worth mentioning Leopoldo Lugones, Ricardo Rojas, Alberto Gerchunoff and Francisco Barroetaveña. On the other hand, Ernesto Quesada and Juan P. Ramos were the principal representatives of the pro-German side.

Usually, the embassies and, in particular, military attachés distributed in Argentina the propaganda produced in Europe, which was sent to the local press and the foreign communities established in the country. The British community provides a case in point. The British Patriotic Committee – created after the outbreak of the war to centralize the community's war effort – created a specific branch in charge of the distribution of propaganda called the Pro-Allied Propaganda Commission. It established offices in the main railway stations which was straightforward as most of the railway companies in Argentina were British. This commission also had 204 distribution centres across Argentina outside of Buenos Aires. The commission's average distribution of propaganda was around 68,000 copies per month.[26]

During the course of the war, the British Patriotic Committee was able to distribute about three million copies of eighty-four propaganda publications in the form of pamphlets and flyers funded by the local community. Among those publications, it is worth mentioning the book *Alemania contra el mundo* [translating as 'Germany against the world'], created by the politician and intellectual Francisco Barroetaveña, which reached four successively corrected and expanded editions.[27] The German community, on the other hand – with some support from the German Legation – launched a daily newspaper in Spanish called *La Unión* ['The Unity'], published throughout the war and its aftermath. *La Unión* aimed to counterbalance the Allied narrative about the war.[28] According to Stefan Rinke, the newspaper was the most important German propaganda newspaper in South America.[29]

The local elaboration of propaganda counted on the active contribution of Argentine intellectuals who sympathized with the cause of the nations at war. The role of these intellectuals was decisive, as they adapted and connected the general and universal themes produced by the European propaganda services to Argentina's history and idiosyncrasy so that it would be understood according to the local cultural codes. In this way, the accuracy and efficacy of propaganda were reinforced.[30] The diplomatic representatives of the warring nations and their community institutions were also attentive to the effectiveness of propaganda. They recommended corrections to adapt them to the local interests and facilitate their impact. They assessed the social mood through the analysis of the local press, the orientations of the government and the stance in relation to the war of several sectors of Argentine society. The British plenipotentiary minister, Sir Reginald Tower, and his French counterpart, Henri Jullemier, periodically judged the practicality of the propaganda received from Europe and frequently suggested changes or new themes. On its part, the 'British Society', one of the leading associations of the British community in Argentina, advocated the projection of documentaries on King Edward's cavalry – where many Anglo-

Argentines enrolled – or views of the *River Plate 1* and *2* – aeroplanes donated by this Society to the British government. Thus, it sought to establish more immediate connections with the local audience.[31]

Some of the materials produced in Argentina expanded the foreign propaganda catalogue. Some publications that were the work of authors from this neutral country gave these writings a supposed objectivity to their cause. That is to say, the neutral status of the sender of the message was used as a principle of authority. For instance, this was the case of the book *La significación de Alemania en la guerra europea* ['Germany's significance in the European war'], by Juan P. Ramos, later published in German, or the eight volumes of *El enigma de la guerra* ['The war enigma'], by Néstor Carrico, sent from Buenos Aires to Spain.[32]

Propaganda arguments

Propaganda implemented in Argentina by both warring sides appealed to the same ideas and stereotypes used in other latitudes, reproducing the binary representation of the conflict that dominated in the more general imaginaries used during the war: the clash of civilization and barbarism, according to the Allies,[33] or the renewed confrontation between the Germanic culture and Western civilization, according to the Germans.[34]

Allied propaganda emphasized Germany's militarism and expansionism, considered responsible for the outbreak of the war. In Barroetaveña's words, 'German peril is the worst enemy of our contemporary civilization'[35] due to its 'praetorianism' – the excessive influence of the armed forces in politics – and 'the ambitious dream of universal domination'.[36] The accusations made about German imperialist pretensions were based on some pan-Germanist writings which advocated world conquest, such as Otto Richard Tannenberg's *Gross Deutschland* ['Greater Germany']. A world map published in the Argentine magazine *Alma Latina* ['Latin Soul'] marked in red the regions coveted by Germany – among them, South America. It included quotations from German intellectuals like Friedrich Lange, who considered Argentina a 'decrepit state' which deserved absorption by the German Reich.[37]

The violation of Belgium's neutrality reinforced the propaganda that denounced Germany's unlimited and greedy expansionism. Allied propaganda presented the invasion and occupation of the neutral country to the other neutral nations as a warning of the German threat. The atrocities against civilians attributed to the German troops constituted one of the central topics of Allied propaganda and stimulated the mobilization of Argentine public opinion.[38] Among the different materials circulating in Argentina reporting the violence imposed on the civilian population, it is worth mentioning the pamphlet *Pedazos de papel: proclamas alemanas en Bélgica y Francia* ['Scraps of paper: German proclamations in Belgium and France'].[39] This large and colour booklet contained facsimiles of advertisements issued by the German occupation authorities and their translations into Spanish, accompanied by brief explanatory comments.[40] The placards illustrated Germany's infringement of international conventions: violence against civilians, in the form of shootings and burning of settlements; requisitions of money or in kind; deportations to prison camps; and restrictions of the freedom of movement and assembly. In addition to highlighting German barbarism, these documents operated as a tacit forewarning of other neutral nations' possible fate: the German advance could lead to the violation of their neutrality and the perpetration of war crimes against their civilians.

Allied propaganda also appealed to the aforementioned Argentine society's Francophile inclination. It recalled the role exerted by the 1789 French Revolution in the Latin American independence processes, presenting France as the mother of revolutions.[41] In the context of the Great War, pan-Latinism was used to gather support for the Allied cause, as the magazine *América-Latina* ['Latin America'] – a joint initiative of British and French propaganda services – constantly pointed out.[42] Although publicists also recognized other European economic, demographic and cultural contributions to modern Argentina, the primordial allegiance was aimed at France.

The obverse of the Francophilia on which Argentine public opinion's Aliadophilism was founded was a profound Germanophobia. The hyperbolic poem *Apostrophe*, by Almafuerte (the sobriquet of Pedro Bonifacio Palacios), offers a complete synthesis of these anti-German manifestations and a personalized form of criticism against of German militarism, a widespread global trend in pro-Allied propaganda stereotypes.[43] Its author attributed harsh epithets to Kaiser Wilhelm II, whom he compared to the Roman Emperor Nero; Attila 'the Hun'; Alaric the Visigoth who sacked Rome and King Herod, the instigator of massacre of the innocents. He characterized the Kaiser as 'the dictator of a tame people', 'a parasite and octopus', 'the crowned murderer, with his hands soaked in the blood of millions of innocents', 'mythological demon', 'indifferent invader' and 'the antichrist'.[44] The year 1917 – with the entry of the United States into the war, the Luxburg affair and the German unrestricted submarine warfare campaign – boosted the dualist interpretation of the war, the pan-Latinism and Germanophobia which had been disseminated by Allied propaganda since 1914. However, it also gave impetus to a campaign based on pan-Americanism to encourage Argentine society's mobilization. Although a deep-rooted distrust of the United States limited its appeal, some Argentine intellectuals urged a rapprochement with that country and stressed the similarities that would indicate both nations' common destiny.[45] According to the poet Leopoldo Lugones, the critical international juncture revealed the impossibility of neutrality and the need to align the country with the Allies.[46] As another renowned Argentine writer – Ricardo Rojas – pointed out: 'it is no longer a question of choosing between France's allies and Germany's allies. Submarine warfare transformed us from spectators into actors of tragedy. What was once sporting emotion or philosophical polemic, abruptly became – by the will of Germany – a moral conflict and an episode of our own history'.[47]

Persisting with neutrality would mask a latent Germanophile position that would be impossible to be recognized openly. Rojas went on: 'I denounce, gentlemen, that neutrality is today the covert form of Germanism! Since the honourable defence of Teutonic militarism is already impossible, they dare to propose resigned abstention.'[48] Despite these passionate declarations, which showed the end of the neutralist consensus regarding international relations, the Argentine government maintained an unaltered foreign affairs policy until the end of the war.

For its part, German propaganda had a mainly defensive character, aiming to disprove the accusations against Germany. To this end, Germany highlighted the advanced nature of German society that made it a world power, denying its supposed barbaric character. Among the works devoted to exhibiting German achievements, it is worth mentioning the book *Alemania y la guerra europea* ['Germany and the European war'], written by prestigious German intellectuals from different disciplines, like Otto Hintze, Friedrich Meinecke and Ernst Troeltsch, and also those authored by two Argentine intellectuals, Ernesto Quesada[49] and Juan P. Ramos.[50]

Likewise, following a strategy similar to the Allied one, German propaganda tended to stigmatize as 'barbaric' some practices of its enemies, such as using colonial troops and alleged ill treatment of their prisoners of war. The latter was the core theme of the book *Los bárbaros* ['The barbarians'] by the war correspondent Alfredo Luis Beltrame, who recounted his experience in the French prisons where he was detained on charges of spying for Germany. In the same vein, the book *Diario de un argentino soldado en la guerra actual* ['Diary of an Argentine soldier in the current war'] – which was written by Juan B. Homet, an Argentine volunteer in the Foreign Legion, criticized French military life and the lack of recognition of their efforts – enjoyed a wide distribution.[51]

Another theme of German propaganda's arguments was the rejection of the image of the German Empire as an imperialist power and a threat to Latin American countries' sovereignty. As Quesada asserted:

Germany has never pretended to play a political role in America: on the contrary, England has taken possession, during the nineteenth century, of various American territories, such as, for example, current British Honduras, the Malvinas [Falkland] Islands, etc., vainly tried to conquer Argentina itself in 1806 and 1807 and has exerted diplomatic and military pressure in various Latin American states.[52]

Thus, German propaganda reversed the accusation and transferred the qualification of imperialism to Britain as part of its global strategy of fostering Anglophobia.[53] Consequently, it emphasized Britain's disputes with other states and its character as an aggressor throughout history. Put forward by German propaganda literature at a general level, these themes were quickly adapted to the Argentine context. Consequently, it persistently insisted on evoking episodes perpetrated by the British Empire which were harmful to the Argentine interests, such as the invasions around the Rio de la Plata [River Plate] in 1806 and 1807 and the disputed sovereignty over the Falklands/Malvinas Islands in 1833. The diplomatic conflict over the Falklands/Malvinas was fuelled to underline the disparity of interests that separated the two states and reprove the support that being pro-Allied gave to Britain, the very country that, according to Argentina, had seized a territory considered its own. German propaganda also suggested the rapprochement of the Argentine government with Germany to recover the islands in case the latter won the war, presenting the empire as a potential ally.[54] It also highlighted some British policies that harmed Argentine interests in different areas as part of the economic war – such as the naval blockade's implementation, and the 'blacklists' against German companies based in the country and their local partners.[55]

After the United States entered the conflict, it tried to align the Latin American countries behind its own cause. Therefore, German propaganda included the United States in its anti-imperialist discourse. It denounced US expansionism and pan-Americanism as a tool to establish its domination over the whole of the Americas, including Latin America.[56] It also attributed to the United States the intention to erode Argentina's influence in South America. For instance, this was the principal argument of the book *Nuestra guerra: la coalición contra la Argentina* ['Our war: the coalition against Argentina'], written by Gonzalo de Reparaz under the pen name Pedro de Córdoba.[57] According to the author, the 'Colossus of the North' encouraged the ambitions and misgivings of Argentina's neighbours (Brazil, Uruguay and Chile) to lead it towards an armed conflict against its will. In sum, German propaganda propagated the disparity of interests between the Allied powers and Argentina, which led to the incongruity of eventually supporting them in the war.

Conclusion

By analysing the Argentine case, this chapter has revealed the potential of war propaganda as a global phenomenon. Its examination provides several conclusions.

In the first place, propaganda exhibited a bidirectional nature. Far from being a passive, one-way process, the dissemination of war propaganda involved active local appropriations, adaptations and resignifications. Thus, the global arguments of the belligerents were decoded and interpreted according to the local particularities. As a result, they acquired greater efficacy. In the same way, there were cultural transfers in reverse, as the diffusion in Europe of physical manifestations of propaganda, such as magazines and pamphlets produced in Argentina demonstrates. Undoubtedly, the circulation of propaganda was favoured by a context of intense social mobilization and polarization around the war. The presence of European immigrant communities was vital, as were the historical, cultural and economic ties with Europe. In contrast to the official diplomatic neutrality, the society's cultural belligerence explains the receptivity to the propaganda campaigns. Likewise, Argentine intellectuals acted as cultural mediators whose actions were fundamental for the appropriation and decoding of war propaganda. Consequently, the belligerents counted on the additional contribution of other agents to elaborate and distribute propaganda: their emigrants and the local Argentine intellectuals who supported their cause.

In the second place, Allied propaganda mainly appealed to emotional factors: the sentimental connection between Argentina and France, and the compassion for the Belgian civilian victims. On the contrary, German propaganda was more versatile, argumentative and rational. It denied the accusations of barbarism, reversed the burden of proof, highlighted the ambiguities and contradictions of its enemies and exposed how their policies were harmful to the Argentine national interests, appealing to a widespread nationalist sensibility. However, despite its persuasive potential, German propaganda developed in a cultural field that was dominated since the nineteenth century by French hegemony, which conditioned its deployment and naturally reduced its effectiveness. The Allied control of news and cable agencies – which limited the ability of German perspectives on the conflict reaching the press and public opinion – and the demographic supremacy of the population from the Allied countries reinforced solidarity with the Allies, which was already strong due to the French cultural influence.

Finally, both belligerents emphasized the confluence of values and/or interests that united the country with them. The Allies mainly underlined the 'filial bond' between France and Argentina and the common belonging to the field of 'civilization'. The Germans emphasized the divergence of interests between Argentina and the Allies more than the convergences that would bring it closer to Germany. However, they also positioned Argentina as a potential ally facing against the advances of the imperialism of Britain and the United States in South America. In fact, none of them – except probably the United States – wanted Argentina to abandon neutrality. The Allies aspired to preferential treatment vis-à-vis their enemy during the war and to improve their post-war trade position. Germany, for its part, was aware that the dominant pro-Allied tendencies in Argentine society made neutrality the policy most favourable to its own interests. Ultimately, both sides defended the status quo: to reinforce their dominant position in the case of the Allies or to avoid a formal alignment in favour of its enemy in the German case. In a total war that lasted longer than expected, propaganda became a crucial persuasive tool to obtain neutral support.

Notes

1. Fernando Devoto, *Historia de la inmigración en la Argentina* (Buenos Aires: Sudamericana, 2003), 247.
2. *Tercer Censo Nacional levantado el 1º de junio de 1914* (Buenos Aires: Talleres Gráficos L. J. Rosso & Cía., 1916), 395–6.
3. Centre des Archives Diplomatiques de La Courneuve (CADLC), Paris, Fond Maison de la Presse et Services d'Information et de Presse 1914–1940, Dossier 3, 'La transmission des Communiqués Officiels de guerre à l'étranger', 23 December 1915; Stefan Rinke, *Latin America and the First World War* (Cambridge: Cambridge University Press, 2017), 99.
4. María Inés Tato, *La trinchera austral. La sociedad argentina ante la Primera Guerra Mundial* (Rosario: Prohistoria Ediciones, 2017), 120.
5. Juan Archibaldo Lanús, *Aquel apogeo. Política internacional argentina, 1910–1939* (Buenos Aires: Emecé, 2001), 65–72.
6. Olivier Compagnon, 'Entrer en guerre? Neutralité et engagement de l'Amérique latine entre 1914 et 1918', *Relations Internationales* 1, no. 137 (2009): 31–43.
7. Ricardo Weinmann, *Argentina en la Primera Guerra Mundial: neutralidad, transición política y continuismo económico* (Buenos Aires: Biblos, 1994), 129–30. See also Chapter 4 in relation to the sinking of the Portuguese ships *Douro* and *Cysne* and Chapter 5 in relation to the sinking of the Spanish ship *Joaquín Mumbrú*.
8. Hipólito Yrigoyen, 'Decreto instituyendo la Fiesta de la Raza', in *Documentos de Hipólito Yrigoyen. Apostolado Cívico – Obra de Gobierno – Defensa ante la Corte*

(Buenos Aires: Talleres Gráficos de la Dirección General de Institutos Penales, 1949), 115.
9   Weinmann, *Argentina en la Primera Guerra Mundial*, 125–8, 138–9 and 141–4.
10 We follow Olivier Compagnon and Pierre Purseigle's distinction between the concept 'belligerency' (state of war) from 'belligerence' (the social experience of the conflict). Consequently, official neutrality coexisted with social and cultural belligerence. See Olivier Compagnon and Pierre Purseigle, 'Geographies of Mobilization and Territories of Belligerence during the First World War', *Annales HSS* 71, no. 1 (2016): 49.
11 A similar polarization occurred in neutral Spain. See Gerald H. Meaker, 'A Civil War of Words: The Ideological Impact of the First World War on Spain, 1914–1918', in *Neutral Europe between War and Revolution, 1917–23*, ed. Hans A. Schmitt (Charlottesville: University of Virginia Press, 1988), 1–65. See also Chapter 5 of this volume.
12 See also Chapter 10 of this volume which considers Latinity in the context of Italian-Portuguese relations in the Second World War.
13 Tato, *La trinchera austral*, 95–118.
14 Ibid., 119–39.
15 On British propaganda services, Michael Sanders and Philip M. Taylor, *British Propaganda during the First World War 1914–1918* (London: Macmillan, 1982). On the French ones, Sophie Horvat, *De la naissance du B.E.P.E. a la Maison de la Presse: les ambiguïtés de l'information en temps de guerre, aout 1914–mars 1916* (Paris: Institut d´Études Politiques de Paris, 1998). On the German case, David Welch, *Germany, Propaganda and Total War, 1914–1918* (New Brunswick: Rutgers University Press, 2000).
16 Eberhard Demm, 'Censorship', in *1914–1918 Online. International Encyclopedia of the First World War*, ed. Ute Daniel et al., 1–7, available online: http://encyclopedia.1914-1918-online.net/article/censorship (accessed 8 March 2022); Rhoda Desbordes-Vela, 'L'information internationale en Amérique du Sud: les agences et les réseaux, circa 1874–1919', *Le Temps des medias* 1, no. 20 (2013/1): 126–7.
17 H. C. Peterson, *Propaganda for War. The Campaign against American Neutrality, 1914–1917* (Norman: University of Oklahoma Press, 1939), 12–14.
18 John Horne, 'Introduction: Mobilizing for "total war", 1914–1918', in *State, Society and Mobilization in Europe during the First World War*, ed. John Horne (Cambridge: Cambridge University Press, 1997), 5–7; Jay Winter, 'Propaganda and the Mobilization of Consent', in *The Oxford Illustrated History of the First World War*, ed. Hew Strachan (Oxford: Oxford University Press, 2014), 217.
19 On Allied and German written propaganda in Argentina, see María Inés Tato, 'Luring Neutrals. Allied and German Propaganda in Argentina during the First World War', in *World War I and Propaganda*, ed. Troy R. E. Paddock (Leiden: Brill Academic Publishers, 2014), 322–44.
20 Christian Delporte, 'Préface', in *Photographier la Grande Guerre. France-Allemagne. L'heroïsme et la violence dans les magazines*, ed. Joëlle Beurier (Rennes: Presses Universitaires de Rennes, 2016), 9.
21 According to the report, only in Buenos Aires 47,000 persons attended the eighteen days exhibition of 178 photographs. See the UK National Archives (hereafter TNA), London, UK, Foreign Office files (hereafter FO) 118/428, 'From Sir. R. Tower to Mr Balfour', 22 August 1917.
22 Stefan Goebel, 'Cities', in *The Cambridge History of the First World War*, ed. Jay Winter (Cambridge: Cambridge University Press, 2014), 370–1.

23. *Exposición Aliada Guerra y Arte* (Buenos Aires: Comité Franco-Argentino, 1917), 32.
24. Centre des Archives Diplomatiques de Nantes (CADN), Nantes, France, Dossier 106, 'Comité Patriotique Française a Monsieur A. Petijean, Délégué à la Propagande en Amérique Latine, Ministère des Affaires Etrangères', 3 April 1918; TNA, FO 118/387, 'Press report n° 66 from Sir R. Tower to Foreign Office', 10 September 1916; *Complete Report of the Chairman of the Committee on Public Information, 1917–1918–1919* (Washington DC: Government Printing Office, 1920), 283.
25. Tato, *La trinchera austral*, 30.
26. TNA, FO 118/427, 'Despatch from Sir Reginald Tower to Mr. Balfour', 13 February 1917 and 'Press report n° 74, from Sir Reginald Tower to Mr Balfour', 2 March 1917.
27. Arthur L. Holder (ed.), *Activities of the British community in Argentina during the Great War 1914–1919* (Buenos Aires: The Buenos Aires Herald, 1920), 242, 376–9.
28. On this newspaper, María Inés Tato, 'Fighting for a Lost Cause? The Germanophile Newspaper *La Unión* in Neutral Argentina, 1914–1918', *War in History* 25, no. 4 (2018): 464–84.
29. Rinke, *Latin America and the First World War*, 99.
30. On Argentine intellectuals and their activism around the war, see Tato, *La trinchera austral*.
31. TNA, FO 118/429, 'Press Report no. 104 from Sir R. Tower to Mr Balfour', 10 December 1917.
32. Ibid.
33. Christophe Prochasson and Anne Rasmussen, *Au nom de la patrie. Les intellectuels et la Première Guerre Mondiale 1910–1919* (Paris: Éditions La Découverte, 1996), 131.
34. Anne Rasmussen, 'Mobilising Minds', in *The Cambridge History of the First World War*, ed. Winter, 395–6.
35. Francisco Barroetaveña, *Alemania contra el mundo* (Buenos Aires: Otero y Co., 1915), 219. Translations from the Spanish here and in later quotations by the author.
36. Ibid., 22.
37. 'Lo que quiere Alemania. Demostración gráfica de sus pretensiones según los dirigentes del pensamiento alemán', *Alma Latina*, no. 5 (15 September 1917).
38. Rasmussen, 'Mobilising Minds', 399–400.
39. *Pedazos de papel: proclamas alemanas en Bélgica y Francia* (New York: Hodder and Stoughton, 1917).
40. On this booklet, see Maurice Rickards and Michael Twyman, *Encyclopedia of Ephemera. A Guide to the Fragmentary Documents of Everyday Life for the Collector, Curator and Historian* (London: Routledge, 2000).
41. *Razones para amar a Francia en guerra* (Paris: Diéval, 1917).
42. María Inés Tato, 'Propaganda de guerra para el Nuevo Mundo. El caso de la revista *América-Latina* (1915–1918)', *Revista Historia y Comunicación Social* 18 (2013): 63–74.
43. Eberhard Demm, 'Caricatures', in *1914–1918-online*. Available online: http://encyclopedia.1914-1918-online.net/article/caricatures (accessed 8 March 2022), 8.
44. Almafuerte, 'Apóstrofe', in *Almafuerte y la guerra* (Buenos Aires: Otero & Cía., 1916), 26–9, 33–5.
45. Ricardo Rojas, 'Profesión de fe de la nueva generación', in *La guerra de las naciones*, ed. Ricardo Rojas (Buenos Aires: La Facultad, 1924), 279–81.
46. Leopoldo Lugones, 'Neutralidad Imposible', in *Mi beligerancia*, ed. Leopoldo Lugones (Buenos Aires: Otero y García, 1917), 156.
47. Ricardo Rojas, 'La voz del atalaya', in *La guerra de las naciones*, ed. Rojas, 38.

48 Ricardo Rojas, 'La hora del destino', in *La guerra de las naciones*, ed. Rojas, 21.
49 *La actual civilización germánica y la presente guerra* (Buenos Aires: n.p., 1914), and *El 'peligro alemán' en Sud América* (Buenos Aires: Talleres Gráficos de Selin Suárez, 1915).
50 *La significación de Alemania en la guerra europea* (Buenos Aires: n.p., 1915) and *Alemania ante la guerra* (Buenos Aires: Selín Suárez, 1915).
51 Juan B. Homet, *Diario de un argentino soldado en la guerra actual* (Buenos Aires: Martín Schneider, 1918).
52 Quesada, *El 'peligro alemán'*, 53.
53 Matthew Stibbe, *German Anglophobia and the Great War, 1914–1918* (Cambridge: Cambridge University Press, 2006).
54 María Inés Tato, 'La cuestión Malvinas y las batallas por la neutralidad argentina durante la Gran Guerra', in *La cuestión Malvinas en la Argentina del siglo XX. Una historia social y cultural*, ed. María Inés Tato and Luis Esteban Dalla Fontana (Rosario: Prohistoria Ediciones, 2020).
55 Néstor E. Carrico, *El enigma de la guerra* (Buenos Aires: n.p., 1918), 87–148.
56 José María Vargas Vila, *Ante los bárbaros. Los Estados Unidos y la guerra: el yanki, he ahí el enemigo* (Maucci: Barcelona, 1917); Ernesto Vergara Biedma, *Guerra de mentiras: el discurso de Wilson y el peligro yanqui* (Buenos Aires: Talleres Gráficos de L. J. Rosso, 1917).
57 Pedro de Córdoba, *Nuestra guerra: la coalición contra la Argentina* (Buenos Aires: La Gaceta de España, 1917).

3

Legacies of neutrality

The propaganda battle and the Greek 'National Schism' at the local level

Georgios Giannakopoulos and Zinovia Lialiouti

The outbreak of the First World War turned Greece into one of the key hot spots of the Eastern Front. The question of neutrality became a contested concept in the Greek political debate and ruptured the country's political system. In the Council of Ministers session on 6 August 1914 the royalist Minister of Foreign Affairs, Georgios Streit, favoured a 'lasting' neutrality for Greece, while Prime Minister Eleftherios Venizelos opted for a 'temporary' neutrality. Venizelos believed that Greek neutrality should be terminated if Bulgaria entered the war or in the case of advantageous proposals by the Entente which would lead to the territorial expansion of the Greek state.[1] The seeds of a lasting division between the country's royalist camp and the anti-royalist opposition led by Venizelos had been sown. In the following days, Venizelos offered Greece's alliance to the Entente without the consensus of the King or the country's Foreign Minister. But the offer was rejected. At the time the Entente favoured Greek neutrality prioritizing a delicate balance with Bulgaria and Romania in the Balkan front.[2]

In the early stages of the conflict the Greek press praised neutrality as the best available course of action. Greek newspapers regarded the conflict as a 'European War' – a conflict reserved only for the 'Great Nations'.[3] A section of the press argued that neutrality as a concept and a political goal was multilayered and should be perceived through the prism of Greece's national interests and territorial aspirations. This line of reasoning also reveals how parts of the Greek elite understood the country's relationship to the so-called 'great powers', namely Great Britain, France and the German Empire. For instance, the Venizelist newspaper *Patris* [translating as 'Homeland'] associated Greek neutrality with the actions of Greece's neighbours, while also warning that the 'claims of third parties' – implying the Central Powers – on a lasting neutrality for Greece should not 'transcend the boundaries of reason and justice'. The papers' editorial offered a lengthy account of the transformation of the concept of neutrality after the outbreak of war. According to *Patris*, neutrality was no longer 'a holy and inviolable condition'; as the conflict transformed into a 'general war', lasting neutrality seemed utopian. *Patris* concluded that 'it would be absurd and unfair if any claim from any of the belligerent nations asked Greece to suffer damage related to her interests, just because it is in their interests to demand Greece remains neutral as if she were a Hestia Virgin'.[4]

The debate on neutrality was also interwoven with cultural predispositions and representations of the great powers and their imagined or perceived historical links to Greece. In this respect, the idea of neutrality comprised a rather complex web of ideological and cultural features. In August 1914, the royalist newspaper *Scrip* argued that although the forces of the Entente pursued a just cause, the war was 'a punishment for the mighty European nations' caused by their indifference to the sufferings of the Christian nations in the Orient. *Scrip* also emphasized the German emperor's family ties to Greek King Constantine and expressed the 'gratitude' of the Greek nation for the Kaiser's protective stance towards Greece. The newspaper concluded that 'small Greece' should not 'violate' its 'reasoned equality' towards the fighting 'colossi'.[5]

The banner of neutrality held together different and contradictory visions of Greece's place in a world immersed into conflict. And as the hopes for a short war started fading by 1915, the Allied attempt to lure Greece into the Entente in exchange for territorial concessions instilled in the country a long-lasting political divide. The rupture brought the country to the brink of civil war and gave rise to two rival camps, the Venizelist (liberal) and the so-called anti-Venizelist, royalist camp.[6] The two faces of the division were the King and liberal Prime Minister Venizelos. The royalist camp sought to maintain a pro-German neutrality, a policy option that after Bulgaria's entry to the war in 1915 became even more unattainable.[7] The situation was further complicated by Venizelos' invitation (in September 1915) to the French and the British governments to have troops stationed in Thessaloniki as a move to strengthen Serbia's position. In the following months, the presence of Entente troops in Greece and their control over strategic infrastructure evolved into a powerful pressure mechanism against the King and triggered negative attitudes towards the Entente in Greek society; the conduct of Entente troops on Greek territory was perceived by many as undermining Greek sovereignty.[8]

Beyond the fractured world of Greek politics, there is evidence to suggest that the policy of neutrality retained its popularity in the eyes of the Greek public.[9] This is due to several factors beyond the 'Germano-philia' of a considerable section of the Greek military and political elite. Prominent among them was a widespread feeling of war fatigue as Greece had been engaged in wars in the Balkans since 1912 and a widespread feeling of puzzlement regarding the great powers involved.[10] In any event, the so-called 'National Schism' that emerged in 1915 over Greece's neutrality was essentially a crisis of national ideology and national integration.[11] It reflected a wider strategic question about Greece's role in the world which in turn connected with competing varieties of Greek nationalism and expansionist visions. The pressure and interventions from the belligerent countries touched on the issue of Greece's sovereignty and the country's subservience to its so-called Protective Powers – a vague political term that had designated Greece's relation to Great Britain and France since the emergence of an independent Greek state during the nineteenth century.[12]

While the 'Great War' was turning global in 1916, Greece was increasingly becoming a propaganda battleground for Britain, France and Germany.[13] The British writer and intelligence officer stationed in Greece at the time, Compton Mackenzie, described the situation as one of 'armed neutrality'.[14] Following regional developments such as Bulgaria's military advances and Romania's entry in the war on the side of the Entente, the political ruptures in Greece crystallized into two rival state formations: a pro-Entente breakaway entity under Venizelos in northern Greece with Thessaloniki as its capital, and a pro-neutrality royalist government in Athens.[15] By the autumn of 1916 the deterioration of the relations between the Athens-based government and the Entente laid the ground for an Anglo-French intervention. This took the form of a military intervention in Athens followed by a naval blockade. The blockade created an acute humanitarian crisis. Although the blockade was designed to undermine popular support for the King, it reinforced sentiments of hostility towards the Entente and created fertile ground for anti-war and royalist propaganda.[16]

The idea of neutrality became the main question in the design of foreign competing propagandas. The means employed by Germany, France and Britain were far-reaching and controversial. For instance, in the autumn of 1916 French intelligence officers staged an attack at the French Embassy in Athens designed to appear as an act of royalist retribution.[17] This episode, in turn, triggered violent conflicts in the Greek capital between the Entente military forces and the Greek royalist army.[18] On the other hand, the German authorities lavishly funded a network of journalists and politicians coordinated by Baron Karl Freiherr von Schenck and high-rank officials in the German Embassy.[19] Schenck had settled in Greece under the official capacity of the representative of the Krupp firm; in essence he was in charge of German propaganda in the country. He had been most successful in the recruitment of several Athens-based and local newspapers to disseminate pro-German propaganda.[20]

As far as British propaganda is concerned, existing scholarship has explored the role of diplomats and prominent intellectuals, such as Joannes Gennadius and Ronald Burrows. The focus has been on the creation of a range of Anglo-Hellenic (i.e. Anglo-Greek) networks which provided political support for Venizelos and contributed to the crafting of his reputation as a leading international statesman.[21] Scholars have also partially examined the role of the British Archaeological School as a site for intelligence and propaganda activities in close collaboration with members of the British intelligence services.[22] Finally, cases of influential individuals invested in British propaganda, such as the industrialist and arms dealer Basil Zaharoff, have been brought to light.[23]

Despite the instructive questions that these studies raise, the full scope of British anti-German propaganda and, crucially, its day-to-day implementation has not yet been fully explored. This is attributed in part to the scarcity of records and the disorderly nature of existing archival entries. This chapter is part of a larger research project which aspires to cover a gap in the study of British First World War propaganda in Greece by exploring the mid-level of bureaucracy as well as the interaction between general propaganda themes and goals, and those which had a more general focus. It should be stressed that the regional dimensions of the propaganda battle are important when it comes to states in flux, such as Greece which involved territorial expansion in the early twentieth century. During the two Balkan wars (1912–13) Greece almost doubled its territory and increased its population by approximately 80 per cent.[24] The

'National Schism' further complicated the challenge of integrating heterogeneous populations into a singular state. The new cleavages that emerged in this context gave rise to a regional political divide between 'Old' and 'New Greece'. 'Old Greece' involved the regions which belonged to the Greek state before 1912 (Attica, Peloponnese, etc.) while the term 'New Greece' referred to the newly acquired territories (Macedonia, Epirus, Crete and islands in the Northern and Eastern Aegean Sea such as Lemnos, Lesvos, Thasos, Samothraki, Chios, Samos and Ikaria). Crucially, the 'Old' versus 'New Greece' divide served as an interpretive key for the shaping of British propaganda in the country.

The ensuing analysis uses the Greek city of Patras in the Peloponnese as a case study in the evolution of British propaganda, its function and working assumptions. It is argued that for sections of the Greek public the idea of neutrality challenged the main tenets of British propaganda. This prompted the British authorities to prioritize anti-German propaganda content and to differentiate regionally the British propaganda aims depending on the political and sociocultural profile of each region. Our analysis focuses on propaganda shaped by government institutions and officials. In this chapter, propaganda has been defined in line with Philip M. Taylor's definition, as 'the deliberate attempt to persuade people to think and behave in a desired way'. This conceptualization of propaganda is oriented to 'the conscious, methodical and planned decisions to employ techniques of persuasion designed to achieve specific goals that are intended to benefit those organizing the process'.[25]

The 'German Enemy' and the legacy of the 'National Schism'

In June 1917, King Constantine fled from Greece to Italy and ultimately Switzerland, after submitting to an ultimatum by France and Great Britain which demanded the King's abdication as precondition for the termination of the blockade. Even though Constantine was succeeded to the throne by his second son Alexander, he never officially abdicated.[26] In the weeks that followed the King's forced exile from the country and Venizelos' return to the capital, the British Foreign Office opted for a 'better organization' of British propaganda across mainland and island Greece.[27] What becomes clear when digging into the British propaganda records is an acute sense of urgency and insecurity regarding the popularity of the Entente cause in the country. Even after the King's departure and the country's formal entry to war in the summer of 1917, British officials were worried about the reach of German propaganda. Greek society would remain throughout the war as a 'divided' nation, while the lasting economic and social crisis aggravated the situation and nurtured anti-war sentiments. The Venizelos government was unable to contain pro-German or pro-neutrality propaganda, which grew after the end of the Allied blockade.[28] Failure in the government's recruitment campaign and the rise of desertions in 1917 and early 1918 became a measure for the strength of pro-neutrality sentiments and of the success of anti-Venizelist and anti-Entente propaganda. In this context, the Venizelos government was forced to proclaim 'partial mobilization' in January 1918.[29]

Anti-Venizelist and anti-Entente propaganda was particularly strong in the region of the Peloponnese in southwestern mainland Greece. The port city of Patras was the most important commercial centre of the region. The city had significant economic ties with Germany since the mid-nineteenth century and was home to a German community. During the war British officials recast the city's German population as an 'enemy alien' community. This attitude was in line with anti-German campaigns targeted at the civilian population which had been in practice in the British state during the war and involved, among other measures, the incarceration of 'enemy aliens'.[30] In the case of Patras, British intelligence regarded pre-existing economic and cultural ties between Greece and the German Empire as potential security threats. Crucially, the city was believed to be a royalist stronghold and it was the hometown of Dimitrios Gounaris, leader of the anti-Venizelist camp. The presence of a sizeable group of 'Reservists' [*Epistratoi*] was also alarming. The Reservists were a royalist paramilitary group which had been formed in the summer of 1916 after the Greek government fulfilled the Entente's demand for demobilization of the Greek army.[31] More than 1,400 people were reported to have been present at the Reservists' inaugural meeting in Patras.[32] Moreover, Patras' distance from Athens rendered it a critical outpost for the dissemination of pro-German propaganda. Taking all the above into consideration, British intelligence agents in Patras were increasingly wary of the 'the quantity of false news' circulating in the city. A report stated: 'German propaganda had everything in its favour, and as a result there are hundreds of Greeks, who having been thoroughly contaminated by the pernicious activities of German propagandists are today ardent Germano-philes.'[33]

The perceptions of the 'German enemy' presence in Patras and in the Peloponnese area were interwoven with cultural stereotypes involving Greece as an 'incomplete state'. These stereotypes were reinforced by the implications of the 'National Schism' and the problems arising in the reconstruction of the Greek state mechanism. The following security concerns raised by British officials can also be seen under this prism. Thus, towards the end of 1917 British intelligence repeatedly criticized 'the incapacity of Police authorities' to curb German propaganda as well as the 'absence of any special legislation, in the nature of our Defence of the Realm Act, which is particularly necessary in this country'.[34] On the other hand, the British were satisfied by the actions of the so-called National Defence Armed Forces [Stratevmata Ethnikis Amynis] – voluntary military corps who were loyal to Venizelos. Nevertheless, they feared that German propaganda had taken action to target this group and undermine its loyalty. In essence, the assessment of the British intelligence agents on the ground was that '[t]he Hellenic [i.e. Greek] authorities can only act energetically if properly directed by us but left to themselves are no better than ordinary amateurs'.[35]

Turning to the local public sphere of Patras, an analysis of the editorials of the local press in the beginning of 1917 showcases the extent of the pro-neutrality discourse. One of the leading regional newspapers, *Neologos* [translating roughly as 'New Discourse'] covered British Prime Minister David Lloyd George's speech at the Guildhall in London on 11 January 1917,[36] where he had argued that Britain had secured the 'increasing trust' of the Allies and predicted victory in the following terms:

What we previously noted on the intimate mood in England [sic] and on her motivations in the present war, has been manifested in the most official way in the last speech delivered by her new Prime Minister. Whether in the midst of an intoxication of lyricism, which characterized that speech, or caught in his overweening arrogance, Mr. Lloyd George went as far as to state that only the star of England [sic] is high in the Allies' sky and that her benign friends, financially – and perhaps even morally – weakened, are no more than offshoots in the great stem that gives them life. This verifies what we had already predicted: that England [sic] has set out not only to ruin Germany, but also to turn her Allied into vassals.[37]

The coverage of US President Woodrow Wilson's speech to Congress on 22 January 1917 (The 'A World League for Peace' Speech or 'Peace without Victory' Speech)[38] was more positive, though regarded as 'overly optimistic'. The newspaper argued that Wilson's post-war vision was destined to fail due to the irreconcilable nature of British and German interests.[39] At the same time, the newspaper's front pages often featured articles emphasizing the German military achievements and innovations, while raising the question whether Britain should be still considered the only major naval power. In this context, German submarine warfare was presented as a proof of German effectiveness and decisiveness: 'Germans do not just say things. They speak with their acts.'[40] This stood in contrast to the anti-German propagandist framing of submarine warfare as a proof of Germany's barbarism.[41]

The Greek national and regional press became a key mechanism in consolidating the new lines of political division[42] and an important asset for the organization of foreign propaganda.[43] Although in principle the British were reluctant to imitate the German propaganda methods, research has shown that in the Greek case – as well as in other neutral countries – British propaganda decided to subsidize Greek newspapers for the dissemination of its arguments.[44] In parallel, the extent of German cultural influence was a principal area of concern for British intelligence. This question prompted more ambitious and long-term plans to gradually substitute propaganda activities with a comprehensive cultural diplomacy effort that would serve Britain's commercial and economic aspirations in south-eastern Europe.[45] However, during the war the priority lay with countering German cultural influence, especially when the latter was associated with pro-German propaganda.

In the case of the Peloponnese, apart from the existing German communities in the area, the British were concerned about the 'excess of liberty' given to German, Austrian and Ottoman prisoners of war. This created a situation, the British intelligence officers noted, where 'the better educated amongst these prisoners have been giving lessons to many Greeks, and indoctrinating them no doubt, with the "Kultur" theories of their Fatherland'.[46] From the British perspective, the solution to this problem would be the Greek authorities to hand the prisoners over to the French or the British themselves or to have them deported to an island 'away from the district which they have thoroughly contaminated'.[47] It is worth commenting on the discourse employed by British officials in relation to German cultural influence; the metaphor of an infectious disease underlies the argumentation.

The case of Patras serves to illustrate the role of British consulates as propaganda agents in their interaction with the local press and networks of individuals. British consulates were nodes for counterintelligence and propaganda activities in neutral countries – and Greece was no exception in this respect.[48] Key in this process was the identification of selected individuals as propaganda agents of the enemy and undermining their activities. In Patras, the British Consulate had a particularly active role in this respect. In March 1916, two Germans had been arrested by Entente soldiers on the accusation of espionage. In 1917, as the country shifted from neutral to belligerent, consular authorities repeatedly raised the issue of pro-German propaganda activities by foreign and Greek citizens in Patras. Their suspicions revolved mainly around people with ties to the consulates of neutral countries and were either Germans or originating from friendly countries to the German Empire, such as Austria-Hungary, Bulgaria or the Ottoman Empire.

A number of cases are worth mentioning in detail. Firstly, Herman Stoltenhoff, Vice-Consul of Norway, but of German origin, was among many Germans and Austrians who avoided expulsion by obtaining Greek citizenship. Nevertheless, according to British intelligence reports in July 1917, he was regarded as the 'most dangerous man' in Patras and the 'centre of the German propagandist movement'. He was affiliated with the Stoltenhoff and Lucas Company, a firm placed on the Statutory Black List, and was believed to be gathering intelligence on the French fleet sailing in the Greek seas and to having developed 'some means of communicating with enemy submarines'.[49] Emma Müller, daughter of the consul of Switzerland, and also of German origin, was similarly described as a 'most dangerous and unscrupulous individual'. The British were alarmed by her purported capability to conduct anti-Entente and pro-German propaganda among the upper social strata of Patras.[50] The British Consul's character analysis of Müller is an instructive case study of how nationality, class and gender can be mobilized to construct an enemy:

> Being a clever and attractive young woman and constantly seen in the company of the Prefect and the General in Command, these rumours (spread by Emma Müller) carry a considerable weight. I think that some action should be taken in this matter, as many of the upper circles in Patras have Royalist sympathies and are carrying an active propaganda of which Miss Emma Müller is one of the principal agitators.[51]

Another group of individuals that raised British eyebrows were local Greek commentators or traders with pro-German commercial interests. Such was the case of Aristides Stavropoulos, a naval agent and editor of the local newspaper *Ethniki* ['National']. Stavropoulos was described as one of the worst enemies – a 'German spy'. The author of the intelligence report expressed the wish that Stavropoulos together with other anti-Venizelist agitators ought to be 'hanged as they are no Greek but pure Germans'.[52]

A final case worth highlighting is that of George Diamantopoulos, which showcases the lack of British trust in the Greek security mechanisms. Diamantopoulos had been employed as secretary and translator at the Austrian Consulate in Patras and was believed to be a high-ranking member of the Austro-German propaganda network. Even more, Diamantopoulos was, according to British intelligence, a leading member of the 'Reservists' movement and he was able to provide significant financial support to them. Following Venizelos' return to political power in Athens (in June 1917), Diamantopoulos had been exiled. However, following the intervention of 'influential political friends' he was set free and returned to Patras a few months later. British intelligence was convinced that Diamantopoulos returned to 'work in favour of his former protectors' and that he had significant economic resources at his disposal drawing from his affiliation with the insurance company Reunione Adriatica of Trieste. This prompted the British intelligence officers to attempt tracing the flow of money between Reunione Adriatica and other companies of German or Austrian ownership.[53] They appeared confident that the 'funds accumulated' by Reunione Adriatica and two Austrian insurance companies 'have been used for pro-German and reactionary propaganda'.[54]

The extent of British propaganda in Patras is not only reducible from intelligence reports. Since the autumn of 1917 British officials were actively promoting cinematographic propaganda across the Greek territory. Local conditions were an important factor in this endeavour as available facilities, resources, distribution system and audience size varied greatly between the capital and other regions. Patras had two active cinema theatres and the British Consul, C. B. Wood, ensured the screening of pro-Entente propaganda films. Wood was quick to realize that the initial plan to have the films rented directly to the cinema owners at a fixed price imposed on the latter undue burdens. Instead, he argued that the British Legation should use central distributing agencies in Athens who would in turn make the necessary arrangements for the distribution of films in other regions at much lower cost.[55]

As far as the geographical distribution of film propaganda is concerned, setting apart the capital area – which was of obvious importance – Patras was prioritized alongside with Ioannina (Epirus), Volos and Larissa (Thessaly), as target regions based on the 'old' versus 'new Greece' divide. British officials felt that 'old Greece, and more especially the Peloponnese has more need for propaganda'.[56] Even though some economic turnover was considered desirable, British officials were willing to accept that the distribution of propaganda films in certain parts of Greece would necessarily have to be cost-free. Among the factors that had to be accounted for, British officials included 'competition from French and Italian propaganda' who distributed propaganda war films entirely without fee.[57] The consuls were encouraged to secure the following ratio as a fee for the films distributed: 2.5 cents per metre for Larissa, 4 cents for Patras, 3 cents for Ioannina and gratis for Volos. By comparison, it is worth mentioning that the ratio for the Athens cinema was fixed at sixty cents per metre.[58] The variation in the fee charges can be seen as an index for the different prospects for the promotion of British film propaganda between the capital area and the periphery.

The British Consulate managed to have two British propaganda films displayed in Patras in January 1918, the *Battle of Peronne* and the *Capture of Messines*.[59] Although the Vice-Consul reported that the films had a 'very good reception', he suggested that future films selected for distribution 'should be of more interest to the Greeks' and suggested the 'taking of prisoners' and 'movements of naval life' as possible themes. The turnover from the exhibition of these films was meagre: 29.40 drachmas in contrast to the 1,320 drachmas that was the turnover from their exhibition in Athens. Following their exhibition in Patras, the consulate was to distribute the propaganda films in Corfu.[60] Moreover, the Consulate exploited the competition between the city's two theatre cinemas as one of them changed ownership status in 1918 and was controlled by Pathé Brothers. The Consulate supplied film material without charge to the Idéal Pathé cinema and the latter organized a lavish 'soirée de gala' for Greek and Allied officials in February 1918. This special event featured the French 1916 melodrama *Mme Tallien*, the propaganda films *The British Tanks in Action* and *Mr Venizelos' Reception* in Paris as well as a concert by the city's military band.[61]

In the following weeks, the British Consulate arranged for the exhibition of the films *Sons of the Empire* and *German Prisoners at Dorchester*.[62] According to British perceptions, these films were more appealing to audiences than the previous ones. The *German Prisoners*, in particular, was thought to be an 'interesting clear film proving good treatment of prisoners'.[63] The exhibition, however, proved somewhat controversial. Both the British Consulate and the French intelligence officers found particularly disturbing the negative comments made by the Prefect of Patras on the *German Prisoners* film. The Prefect expressed the view that it was 'bad taste to exhibit so many German prisoners' and he argued that 'there were many people in Patras who objected to this exhibition'. The report also noted that the Prefect was in the company of Emma Müller at the film exhibition.[64] The last propaganda films received by the British Consulate were the *Battle of Arras, Drifters, British Facts and German Fiction* in June 1918, but they were unable to be exhibited as there were no open-air cinema facilities in the city, and the indoor cinemas were unsuitable in the hot Greek summer.[65]

Conclusion

The study of the regional evolution of propaganda in Patras sheds light on a persistent inconsistency regarding the overall aims of British wartime propaganda. The general direction of British propaganda in neutral countries during the First World War rested on the existence of unified national identities. The task that laid upon the British was to manipulate those identities by either inciting support and mobilization for the Entente by fostering positive self-images or to provoking negative reactions against the perceived enemy by employing negative cultural stereotypes. However, this model did not work in a deeply divided country like Greece where regional and ideological identities were in competition with the state-sponsored national ideology. This feature made the shaping and implementation of foreign propaganda in Greece a particularly challenging enterprise.

By bringing to light new archival material, the chapter has offered an overview of British anti-German activities in Greece while the First World War reached its most dramatic moment. It has shown how the idea of neutrality and the responses to it not only cast a long shadow on Greece's politics but also shaped the efforts of foreign propaganda in the country. Despite the existence of overarching studies of Allied and 'enemy' propaganda, the regional dimension of propaganda activities remains relatively understudied. To address this gap, this chapter discussed intelligence reports and consular correspondence from one of the important regional sites of propaganda – the port city of Patras in southern Greece.

When the news of the Allied victory reached Greece, the reaction did not mirror the unperturbed enthusiasm witnessed across the Allied countries. Foreign observers remarked that no popular celebrations took place in 'Old Greece'; 'general apathy' seemed to be the prevailing mood.[66] For all the success of the Allies in pushing Greece from neutrality to active participation in the war, Allied and British propaganda was not able to win the hearts and minds of the peoples of a divided and heterogeneous state like Greece. The case study presented here highlights the legacy of neutrality; the latter was inextricably linked to the ideological cleavage produced by the 'National Schism' and to the formulation of Greek national identity in the context of the anti-Venizelist, royalist camp. British propaganda proved unable to contain the widespread pro-neutrality sentiments in the country. It nonetheless succeeded in amplifying the beliefs of the Venizelist, pro-Entente group. Thus, British propagandists were mistaken in arguing that it is 'not of much propagandist value to show films to those already friendly, except as a means of drawing others, the point being to get at waverers, neutrals and actual enemies'.[67] As scholarship in propaganda and communication research has shown since the early 1950s, a principal function of propaganda is not to alter opinions, attitudes or behaviours, but to reinforce pre-existing trends by providing people with information and narratives to sustain their existing ideas.[68]

Notes

This chapter 'Legacies of Neutrality: The Propaganda Battle and the Greek "National Schism" at the Local Level' was funded by the Germany Federal Foreign Office through the German-Greek Future Fund.

1 George B. Leon, *Greece and the Great Powers 1914-1917* (Thessaloniki: Institute for Balkan Studies, 1974), 32.
2 Ibid., 35–8.
3 *Anagennisis* [translating as 'Rebirth'], 25 June 1916, 1 [8 July on the Gregorian calendar hereafter 'GC'. Greece used the Julian calendar until 1923].
4 *Patris*, 22 July 1914, 1 [4 August GC]. Translation from the Greek here and for later quotations by the authors.
5 *Scrip*, 2 August 1914, 1 [15 August GC]. The newspaper name 'Scrip' was short for 'subscription' and it was meant as a sarcastic reference to much despised – in Greece – public loan of 1893.
6 Leon, *Greece and the Great Powers 1914-1917*, 98–132.
7 Georgios Mavrogordatos, *1915. O Ethnikos Dichasmos* (Athens: Patakis, 2015); Sotiris Rizas, *Venizelismos ke antivenizelimos* (Athens: Psychogios, 2019).
8 Mavrogordatos, *1915. O Ethnikos Dichasmos*, 62–4.
9 Leon, *Greece and the Great Powers 1914-1917*; Rizas, *Venizelismos ke antivenizelimos*.
10 Rizas, *Venizelismos ke antivenizelimos*, 54–5.
11 Mavrogordatos, *1915. O Ethnikos Dichasmos*, 189–233.

12 Katerina Gardika, *Prostasia kai eggiyseis: Stadia kai mythoi tes hellenikes ethnikes olokleroses (1821–1920)* (Thessaloniki: Vanias, 1999).
13 Elli Lemonidou, 'Propaganda and Mobilizations in Greece during the First World War', in *Propaganda and the First World War*, ed. Troy Paddock (Leiden: Brill, 2014), 273–91.
14 Compton Mackenzie, *Greek Memories* (London: Chatto and Windus, 939), xxii.
15 Leon, *Greece and the Great Powers 1914–1917*, 384–437.
16 Mavrogordatos, *1915. O Ethnikos Dichasmos*, 103–7; Georgios B. Leontaritis, *He Ellada ston A Pagkosmio Polemo 1917–1918* (Athens: National Bank of Greece Cultural Foundation, 2005), 172–6.
17 Leon, *Greece and the Great Powers 1914–1917*, 394. See also Mackenzie, *Greek Memories*, 364–5.
18 Giannis Mourelos, *Ta 'Noemvriana' tou 1916. Apo to Archeio tis Mektes Epitropes Apozimioseon ton Thymaton* (Athens: Patakis, 2007).
19 Stratos Dordanas, *'Argyronitoi'. He Germaneke Propaganda stin Ellada kata ton A Pagkosmio Polemo* (Athens: Alexandreia, 2020).
20 Elli Lemonidou, 'La Grèce vue de France pendant la Première guerre mondiale; entre censure et propagandes' (Doctoral thesis, Universite Paris IV, Sorbonne, 2007), 41–5; Mavrogordatos, *1915. O Ethnikos Dichasmos*, 39.
21 Slobodan Markovich, 'Eleftherios Venizelos, British Public Opinion and the Climax of Anglo-Hellenism (1915–1920)', *Balcanica* XLIX (2018): 125–55.
22 Richard Clogg, 'Academics at War: The British School at Athens during the First World War', *British School at Athens Studies* 17 (2009): 163–77.
23 Joseph Maiolo and Tony Insall, 'Sir Basil Zacharoff and Sir Vincent Caillard as Instruments of British Policy towards Greece and the Ottoman Empire during the Asquith and Lloyd George Administrations, 1915–9', *International History Review* 34, no. 4 (2012): 819–39.
24 Mavrogordatos, *1915. O Ethnikos Dichasmos*, 191.
25 Philip M. Taylor, *Munitions of the Mind: A History of Propaganda from the Ancient World to the Present Day* (Manchester: Manchester University Press, 2003), 6.
26 Leon, *Greece and the Great Powers 1914–1917*, 486–7.
27 The UK National Archives (hereafter TNA), Foreign Office files (hereafter FO) 286/650/113, Foreign Office to Crackanthorpe, 'British Propaganda in Greece', 25 August 1917.
28 Leontaritis, *He Ellada ston A Pagkosmio Polemo*, 90 and 151–2.
29 Ibid., 209–13.
30 Panikos Panayi, 'A Marginalized Subject? The Historiography of Enemy Alien Internment in Britain', in *Totally un-English?: Britain's Internment of 'Enemy Aliens' in Two World Wars* (The Yearbook of the Research Centre for German and Austrian Exile Studies 7), ed. Richard Dove (New York: Editions Rodopi B.V.), 17–26.
31 Georgios Mavrogordatos, *Ethnikos Dichasmos ke Maziki Organosi. He Epistratoi tou 1916* (Athens: Alexandreia 1996).
32 Calliope Calpodimou and Georgios Kondys, 'O antiktypos tou Ethnikou Dichasmou stin perifereia. H periptosi tis Argolidas', conference presentation, 7–8 November 1915. Available online: https://argolikoslibrary.files.wordpress.com/2018/07/cebf-ceb 1cebdcf84ceafcebacf84cf85cf80cebfcf82-cf84cebfcf85-ceb5ceb8cebdcebcf85cf8d -ceb4ceb9cf87ceb1cf83cebccebfcf8d-1915-1917-cf83.pdf (accessed 6 March 2022).
33 TNA FO 286/665/327, 'Intelligence Work in Patras', 26 November 1917.
34 Ibid.

35 Ibid.
36 'Lloyd George Speaks Again; Full Text of Guildhall Address', *The New York Times*, 12 January 1917, 1.
37 'England and the Allies', *Neologos*, 5 January 1917 (18 January 1917 GC), 1.
38 Woodrow Wilson, Address to the Senate of the United States: 'A World League for Peace', 22 January 2017. Available online: https://www.presidency.ucsb.edu/documents/address-the-senate-the-united-states-world-league-for-peace (accessed 15 March 2022).
39 'Wilson's Message', *Neologos*, 12 January 1917 (25 January GC), 1.
40 'Torpedoing', *Neologos*, 11 January 1917 (24 January GC), 1.
41 Michael Sanders and Philip M. Taylor, *British Propaganda during the First World War, 1914–1918* (London: Macmillan, 1982), 131–3, 173–7.
42 Despina Papadimitiou, 'O Typos ke o Dichasmos 1914–1917' (Doctoral thesis, National and Kapodistrian University of Athens, 1990).
43 Maiolo and Insall, 'Sir Basil Zacharoff and Sir Vincent Caillard', 819–39; Rizas, *Venizelismos ke antivenizelismos*, 78–9; Mavrogordatos, *1915. O Ethnikos Dichasmos*, 39.
44 Sanders and Taylor, *British Propaganda*, 117.
45 TNA FO 268/672/518, 'Memorandum by Astley Shute', 8 December 1917.
46 TNA FO 286/665/327, 'Intelligence Work in Patras', 26 November 1917.
47 Ibid.
48 Sanders and Taylor, *British Propaganda*, 34–6.
49 TNA FO 286/672/529, British Consulate Patras, 'Austro-German Propaganda in Patras: Neutral Consuls of German Origin', 27 July 1917.
50 Ibid.
51 TNA FO 286/682, British Consulate Patras, 31 January 1918.
52 TNA FO 286/665/1, 'List of Current Merchants and Exporters of Aeghion Who also do Currant Shipping Agency business', 21 December 1917.
53 TNA FO 286/665/327, 'Intelligence Work in Patras', 26 November 1917.
54 TNA FO 286/665/327, 'German Propaganda, Patras', 1 August 1917.
55 TNA FO 286/650/113, British Consulate Patras (Wood) to British Legation Athens (chargé d' affaires Crackanthorpe), 21 September 1917.
56 TNA FO 286/650/113, memorandum by Gerald Talbot, January 1918.
57 TNA FO 286/650/113, memorandum on Film propaganda in Greece by Gerald Talbot, undated.
58 TNA FO 286/650/113, British Legation Athens, 3 January 1918.
59 TNA FO 286/650/113, British Consulate Patras to British Legation Athens, 12 January 1918.
60 TNA FO 286/650/113, British Consulate Patras to British Legation Athens, 27 February 1918.
61 Ibid.
62 TNA FO 286/650/113, British Consulate Patras to British Legation Athens, 9 March 1918.
63 TNA FO 286/650/113, British Legation Athens, memorandum 'Cinematograph Propaganda in Greece' (undated).
64 Ibid.
65 TNA FO 286/650/113, British Consulate Patras to British Legation Athens, 6 June 1918.
66 Leontaritis, *He Ellada ston A Pagkosmio Polemo*, 232.

67 TNA FO 286/650/113, British Legation Athens, Memorandum 'Cinematograph Propaganda in Athens', 20 November 1917.
68 The starting point for this shift in the study of propaganda was the article published by Leo Bogart, 'Measuring the Effectiveness of an Overseas Information Campaign: A Case History', *Public Opinion Quarterly* 21, no. 4 (1957–58): 475–98.

4

The Great War at sea and Portuguese propaganda

Miguel Brandão

In the beginning of the twentieth century – and especially in the lead up to the First World War – the world was obsessed with naval affairs. The concept of 'navalism', the idea of promoting the navy as an extension of political power, conceived warships as symbols of national pride and the size of each nation's fleet was seen as proportional to its power and prestige. The citizens of the so-called 'great powers' were fascinated by the latest technological advances at sea, and they greatly admired its nation's ships and dreadnoughts; these huge castles of steel idealized collective nationhood and technological sophistication. It was not just about the navy in a military sense, the opulence of the ocean liners that crossed the seas – not least the *Titanic* – was seen as the height of luxury. According to Paul G. Halpern, perhaps never before or since have naval affairs been of such interest to the citizens of the great powers as it was during the first half of the century;[1] naval affairs were indeed central in public life. The press had a very important role in bringing navalism to the core of social discussion. Newspapers at the time contained a lot of information about the human relationship with the sea; news about the construction of new warships was received with much enthusiasm and the naval rivalry between the great powers was discussed on a daily basis.

Following the outbreak of the war in 1914, navalism was reinforced by each nation's war propaganda. Belligerent and neutral nations both foresaw gargantuan sea battles that would decide the war in a very short time frame – something like a modern Trafalgar was expected; after all, it was believed that Admiral Jellicoe, First Sea Lord of the British Royal Navy, could 'lose the war in an afternoon'.[2] Nevertheless, the First World War at sea would not be as imagined. The new technological advances such as the torpedo, the submarine, the wireless telegraphy and the aircraft made belligerent admiralties much more cautious; some historians even believe that fighting navies played a secondary role throughout the war.[3] For Norman Friedman, in contrast, the First World War was above all a maritime conflict, not necessarily for the action taken at sea, but rather for the maritime realities that shaped it.[4] The 'Great War' dissipated the perfume of navalism from the pre-war era – although war propaganda would hide the various miscalculations of the belligerent admiralties.

In this chapter, the focus of the analysis is on naval propaganda during the Portuguese 'non-belligerent' period between 28 July 1914 and 9 March 1916. To enhance our understanding of naval propaganda in the Portuguese society during this time, this chapter includes a detailed analysis of the national press. The most important Portuguese newspapers at the time gave the audience a broad perspective of the war at sea, but also propagandistic content related to this matter. Newspapers, such as *A Capital* [translating as 'The Capital'], *O Século* ['The Century'] and *O Comércio do Porto* ['The Commerce of Porto'], as well as the illustrated magazines *O Século Cómico* ['The Comic Century'], *Miau!* and *Ilustração Portuguesa* ['Portuguese Illustration'] portrayed relevant information on this topic.

The emphasis placed on newspapers and magazines in this chapter is the result of their role as main channels of communication in Portugal during the First World War, regardless of the fact that 75 per cent of the population was in fact illiterate.[5] In the absence of radio or later television, newspapers were practically the only means of communication for many Portuguese communities and illustrated magazines actually had an impact in the illiterate sectors of the society due to its visual content. Brochures, books, postcards and flyers were also used for propagandistic purposes, but they encapsulated less references to navalism. In addition, pro-war propaganda was particularly present in these primary sources during the 'non-belligerent' period, mainly due to the sinking of the Portuguese vessels the *Cysne* and the *Douro* – the first Portuguese losses at sea – which had some impact in Portuguese society.

Portuguese 'non-belligerency'

Portugal had a unique diplomatic stance in the beginning of the war; it was indeed the only country which kept a non-declared neutrality between 1914 and 1916.[6] This peculiar and ambiguous position was indeed very much desired by its oldest formal ally – Great Britain. London soon endorsed this diplomatic stance towards Portugal via its Foreign Office, who advised the Portuguese government to 'refrain proclaiming neutrality'.[7] Portugal followed this advice. On 7 August 1914, the Bernardino Machado administration made a vague declaration in the Portuguese Chamber of Deputies, stating that Portugal would correspond to all demands of the Anglo-Portuguese alliance.[8] Despite Lisbon's friendship to Britain, Portugal was indeed a 'non-belligerent' nation in the context of the early days of the Great War.[9] The singularity of this position led João Chagas, Portuguese diplomatic representative in Paris, to write in his memoirs: 'what is Portugal doing and what is happening in Lisbon . . . ? All [non-belligerent] nations, including Haiti, have declared neutrality'.[10] For some Portuguese republicans this diplomatic position was far from ideal as they considered it resulted in a decline in the political status of Portugal among the Allied powers.[11]

However, from a British perspective, Portugal's ambiguity was beneficial. The British expected to benefit from various services performed from Portugal, without seriously compromising its resources or military forces in any inconvenient action; the Foreign Office was well aware of the poor state of the Portuguese military forces.[12] Portuguese 'non-belligerency' rather than 'neutrality' allowed for opportunities for further collaboration in the context of the war – and Portugal responded positively. In the early moments of the global conflict, Lisbon was indeed a 'collaborative ally':

it provided artillery units for the Allies; it allowed the passage of Allied troops; it provided Gibraltar with supplies and opened its ports to British cruisers.[13] Due to these facts, Germany had no illusions when it declared war on Portugal on 9 March 1916: Portugal had not acted as a neutral previously.[14] However, Britain pressed Lisbon to keep its operations punctual and supported the diplomatic démarches that came from France.

Portuguese subservience towards London was uncomfortable, despite its strategic advantages. It was a difficult alliance to manage. Britain was very condescending about republicanism in this peninsular country and the pre-war escape of the Portuguese royal family to England definitely created some animosity between London and Lisbon. Arthur Henry Hardinge – British Minister in Portugal (1911–13) – later declared that Britain should never have allowed King Manuel II to be dethroned.[15] After the 1910 revolution, Lisbon begged for British recognition and that happened only in September 1911 – almost a year later. In fact, diplomatic relations with Lisbon were always tense until the very end of the republican establishment.[16]

Nevertheless, it was obvious for some republican diplomats and politicians that this alignment with Britain could help preserve the Portuguese possessions in Africa, notably Angola and Mozambique, as well as a hypothetical diplomatic prestige gained from being a belligerent in the aftermath of the war. The republican regime was still isolated in the European political context and a cooperative stance with the Entente seemed to be a life insurance for the weak, inexperienced and troubled Portuguese republican elite. Furthermore, Portugal was highly dependent on British trade for food, coal and other commodities, due to the fact that most Portuguese external commerce was made by sea.[17] The Royal Navy secured the integrity of the Portuguese Empire and its social–economic stability. For many, Portugal should remain loyal to its insular ally; acting without Britain's consent and support would be suicidal for some political thinkers.[18] Notwithstanding, this pro-British approach was not seen as desirable for many in the first moments of the war. Machado had a dubious position towards the conflict and Portuguese Foreign Affairs Minister, Freire de Andrade, was firmly against any kind of Portuguese military adventurism. The interventionist side was made up of the Portuguese Socialist Party [Partido Socialista Português], the Democratic Party [Partido Democrático], the Evolutionist Party [Partido Evolucionista] and some sectors of the Portuguese intelligentsia.[19] On the other hand, the Unionist Party [Partido Unionista], monarchists and Germanophiles opted for a more cautious path – Portugal should stay out of the war.

Portuguese ambiguity and pro-Allied collaboration led Germany to challenge Portuguese sovereignty in Angola and Mozambique; the German-Portuguese colonial borders in Africa created significant tension.[20] On 24 August 1914, German colonial troops attacked the Portuguese outpost of Maziúa, in Mozambique, and killed the local chief. However, Portugal continued to promote its neutrality. After this incident, de Andrade wrote to Sidónio Pais, Portuguese Ambassador in Berlin, with the following statement:

> Portugal does not declare its neutrality because, as being an ally of Britain, it should firmly and loyally comply with the duties that derive from it, if it is requested. Our

desire is to put us aside from the conflict. We would not hesitate in taking part of it, under the invocation of the Alliance, when England requests us to do so, but outside this obligation of loyalty, we shall proceed as neutrals. We are bound by our commitments to England and by our own interests.[21]

Despite this non-declaration, Portuguese 'neutrality' continued to prevail. Therefore, German-Portuguese skirmishes in Africa started to be more common; the massacres of Cuangar, also in Mozambique (31 October 1914) and Naulila in Angola (18 December 1914), were particularly shocking in this regard. At the beginning of 1915, the Portuguese Minister of the Colonies ordered the sending of more troops to Africa; by January–February 1915, Portugal had already mobilized 4,200 men for this war theatre.[22] The Portuguese diplomatic position was becoming unsustainable and true belligerency was just a question of time.

The war at sea would change Lisbon's stance. In February 1915, the Germans embarked upon an unprecedented submarine war around the British Isles without restrictions; by November, the British had already lost 1,021,800 tons in shipping.[23] Britain desperately needed more shipping to aid the war effort and the sustainability of its empire. Portugal had something desirable in this regard. Since the beginning of the war, several German ships were anchored in Portugal in order to escape the Royal Navy. According to Halpern, many of these ships were far away from home and many anchored in neutral ports such as Manila, Lisbon, Genoa, Buenos Aires and New York.[24] Portugal, for instance, had seventy German ships laid up at its ports – the seizure of these German steamers started to become appealing to the British. On 30 December 1915, Britain requested that Portugal seize all the German ships that had taken refuge in its ports since the beginning of the war, in an exchange for a loan of £2 million – much needed by Lisbon.[25] Portugal responded positively to the British request and seized the ships. On 9 March 1916, Berlin declared war on Portugal, considering this act intolerable; consequently, the Portuguese republic entered the war alongside the Entente alliance.

Propaganda and the Portuguese press during the 'non-belligerency' period

Naval affairs were definitely followed on a day-to-day basis in most Portuguese newspapers before and during the Portuguese intervention in the war. The Portuguese Navy manoeuvres, the schedules of ocean liners, the homeward and outward routes of shipping, the arrival of British and French cruisers at the mouth of the Tagus, the boarding of colonial troops in Portuguese Africa and many other aspects of the maritime life were very present in the Portuguese press at the time. In fact, so much so that, according to Lancelot Carnegie, the British Minister (and later Ambassador) in Lisbon (1913–28), Portuguese newspapers were careless in publishing Allied shipping movements in the context of the war.[26] In the first days of the conflict, the Portuguese press covered extensively the first British manoeuvres at sea and the initial naval engagements were present in the news headings. From August 1914 to July 1915

Portuguese newspapers covered the movement of British ships in the Portuguese coast with great detail, interest and anxiety.[27] Navalism was still very much alive in this peninsular country; crowds gathered in the port of Lisbon and in other points of the Portuguese coast to admire the British ships that were passing by.[28] Maritime life was central for the Portuguese media and for the coastal communities, considering its political, economic and cultural dimensions.

Portugal – besides France and Switzerland – was one of the few republics in Europe by 1914. The October revolution of 1910 abolished Portuguese monarchy and created a new republican regime which aimed to democratize and liberalize the country's administration.[29] A good example of this new political view was its Press Law. In 1914, the Portuguese press was regulated by the Press Law of 28 October 1910, which was enacted by the provisional government during the early days of the republican revolution. The new regulations established freedom of speech in the Portuguese press and pledged for a free and independent journalistic sector. According to Noémia Novais, the Press Law of 1910 was the most permissive in Portugal since the liberal revolution of 1822.[30] Therefore, the press could legally criticize governmental diplomas, political acts, religious beliefs, corporations and everyone who worked as a civil servant.[31] The matters regarding the sea were also subject to public scrutiny until the beginning of the war.

The Great War would change the republican liberal spirit towards the press. Before the Portuguese participation in the war, the Machado's republican establishment tried to take control of the press, by approving the 1:117 Decree on 28 November 1914.[32] With this promulgation, Lisbon pretended to 'restrain the publication of news relating to the movement of military forces without the appropriate guarantee of authenticity and without the discretion that was necessary'.[33] Therefore, Portuguese newspapers and illustrated magazines could only disseminate official information from the war ministries, including military operations taken at sea.[34] In practice, the Ministries of War [Ministério da Guerra], Navy [Ministério da Marinha] and Colonies [Ministério das Colónias] were obliged to produce daily information to the national newspapers and to publish them in the *Diário de Governo* ['Government Diary']; this would allow a strict control of the war news by the Portuguese Public Ministry.[35] The liberal principles of the constitution of 1911 were now momentarily ignored, while caution and public order were a priority for Lisbon.

In 1914, there were several newspapers that had been suspended or seized, especially those who were promoting anti-war feelings. For the Portuguese government some newspapers promoted 'insecurity', 'disorder' and 'disquiet'.[36] For example, on 17 August 1914, the editorial chief of the newspaper *Diário da Manhã* ['Morning Diary'] was arrested and several of its editions were confiscated; and later, in December, a similar procedure occurred with the right-wing newspaper *A Lucta* ['The Fight'] for advocating arguments against the Portuguese participation in the war.[37] On the other hand, interventionist or pro-Allied newspapers like *O Mundo* ['The World'], *República* ['Republic'] and *O Século* were much tolerated by national authorities during the period of Portuguese 'neutrality'.[38]

The Portuguese republican establishment very quickly understood the power of words – interventionist and non-interventionist polarization was very much controlled since the very beginning of the war.[39] When the Machado administration published the decree of November 1914, censoring the Portuguese press, Portuguese troops were already fighting in Portuguese Africa against the Germans. Since August 1914, Portuguese-German skirmishes south of the equatorial line were becoming more frequent; the Battle of Naulila in Portuguese Angola on 18 December 1914 made Portuguese 'non-belligerency' even more ironic. Eventually, interventionism started to gain some ground in the national public opinion. However, in a rural, illiterate, poor and scarcely industrialized country like Portugal in 1914, the world conflict seemed a distant reality. Convincing the Portuguese people to subsequently support participation in this 'war for civilization' was a major challenge for interventionist administrations of António José de Almeida[40] and Afonso Costa[41] once the formal German declaration of war against Portugal had taken place in March 1916.

War propaganda was not consistent during the 'non-belligerent' period. The country was divided and there was no political consensus towards the war.[42] However, this did not mean the Portuguese public were not interested in the war. During the 'non-belligerent' period, illustrated magazines were very important in bringing the war to the masses, and they definitely had great success in highlighting the battles, particularly considering that during this period photojournalism lacked proficiency.[43] In fact, the perception of the war was changing. The images contained in these magazines fomented the consciousness of the world conflict and many civilians, soldiers and amateur photographers contributed to the spread of war imagery.[44] Portuguese magazines like *Ilustração Portuguesa*, *O Século Cómico*, *Miau!*, *O Espelho* ['The Mirror'], *O Occidente* ['The West'], *O Thalassa* and *O Zé* [translating roughly as 'The Joe'] were particularly important propagandistic vehicles. The *Ilustração Portuguesa* was probably the most important one in this context; it stood out in the national panorama, with a more elitist public.[45] *O Século Cómico*, *Miau!* and *O Zé* magazines had humoristic and political contents that coexisted in a propagandistic form. The content of these magazines satirized German militarism and German naval warfare.[46]

'Navalism' and propaganda relating to the war at sea were also present during the 'non-belligerency' period. The republican cult of the Portuguese Navy was visible in several magazines and newspapers – the Navy was in fact the Republic's praetorian guard. During the 1910 republican revolution, the insurgent forces counted upon the aid of several Navy barracks and three of the most important Portuguese warships at the time (*Adamastor*, *São Rafael* and *Don Carlos*) to remove the monarchist power in Lisbon.[47] As the Portuguese republican José Relvas observed in his political memoirs: 'the navy units were indispensable for the success of the revolution'.[48] Indeed, the Portuguese Navy was very supportive of the new regime and was linked to the most radical left-wing republican factions. Its strategic control of the capital, the deterrence effect of its warships in the Tagus and the social alliance between its crewmen and the working classes of the main industrial areas in Lisbon provided some solid support to the republican administration.[49] The republicans praised its Navy for its safety and for its prestige, in the era of 'navalism'. Despite its cult and prestige within borders, the Portuguese Navy forces were negligible in comparison with other major naval powers during the First World War.[50]

The castles of steel of the new regime were part of its aesthetic. The Portuguese naval units were presented in many propagandistic postcards related to the October 1910 revolution[51] and also the figure of the Portuguese mariner was appreciated in some important visual magazines like *Ilustração Portuguesa* and *O Zé*.[52] *Ilustração Portuguesa*, for instance, dedicated several pages to naval affairs and covered the major engagements and events at sea with unique photographs – a valuable source in this regard; 70 per cent of its content was indeed visual.[53] Also, the Navy's new additions were received with much eagerness. For example, on 28 September 1914, *Ilustração Portuguesa* covered the ceremonial launching of Portuguese Navy's new destroyer *Guadiana* with photos from the famous Portuguese photographer Joshua Benoliel and generously described its capabilities and design.[54] Also, regiments that went to Portuguese Africa on board of transport ship *Africa* in the summer of 1914 were highlighted with photos and patriotic descriptions; *Ilustração Portuguesa* stated that 'Portuguese forces should not just defend continental Portugal and impress the Allied Powers, they should also protect its large colonial heritage'.[55] During Portuguese 'neutrality', this magazine explored the cultural dimensions of navalism and republicanism, praising the strength, the prestige, the patriotism and the loyalty of its naval forces. Later, *Ilustração Portuguesa* changed its tone in the winter of 1915, when the German started to attack Portuguese shipping. The alleged sinking of the *Douro* earned the attention of Portuguese newspapers and since then, German submarine war was covered more frequently.[56]

Furthermore, there was also a great interest in Allied naval affairs in this phase. Several magazines covered the anchoring of foreign warships in Portuguese ports with much enthusiasm and the friendship with the Allied powers was much praised. The visit of the British cruiser *Argonaut*[57] and the French battleship *Dupetit Thouars*[58] to Lisbon, to celebrate the Republic's fourth anniversary, seemed to express social interest in cultural navalism and Portugal's role among the Allies. Illustrations of British, French and German ships, as well as vivid descriptions of major naval engagements, were also quite common (Figure 4.1).

The case of the *Douro* and the *Cysne*

As mentioned above, during the 'non-belligerency' period, Portuguese newspapers covered the war at sea with significant detail. German submarine attacks, Portuguese shipping losses and governmental measures regarding coastal defence were quite frequent in the magazines and newspaper's headings. Readers could easily find descriptions of German attacks, interviews of surviving crew members, Portuguese Navy manoeuvres, sunken ships and much more information related to the war at sea. Portuguese newspapers received information in this regard mainly by telegraph,[59] mail, witnesses and particularly by the official statements of the Portuguese ministries, which were frequently delivered to the press. The official news concerning the war at sea was given directly by the Ministério da Marinha e das Colónias [Navy and Colonies Ministry], which centralised and censored all the information in this regard under Article 2 of the 1:117 Decree – a governmental order that aimed to regulate

Figure 4.1 Illustration of Kaiser Wilhelm II 'sowing' mines in the North Sea in the Portuguese magazine *O Zé*, (13 April 1915, 7). Image reproduced by kind permission of BLX-Hemeroteca Municipal de Lisboa.

war information.⁶⁰ Nevertheless, despite the censorial nature of the regulations, there was some room for criticism and pro-belligerent propaganda regarding the matters at sea. During Portuguese 'non-belligerency', the national press propagated the war at sea and the Allied naval engagements through different instruments, such as illustrations, photos, cartoons, articles, texts and opinion columns. However, there are two actions that were consistently promoted by pro-interventionist propaganda: the sinking of the Portuguese ships the *Douro* and the *Cysne*, in 1915.

The *Douro* incident coincided with the first phase of the German submarine war, when Germany declared a War Zone on 4 February 1915 around the British Isles which lasted until September 1915. The schooner left Porto and headed to Cardiff in order to bring coal to its owner Companhia Marítima do Douro [Maritime Company of Douro], based in the same city. On 3 April 1915, at a distance of 45 miles from the Welsh coast, the schooner was allegedly scuttled by a German submarine, which was confirmed by London's Board of Trade.⁶¹ This incident created a serious diplomatic incident between Germany and Portugal, given the fact that, at this time, Portugal was still asserting its 'neutrality', although the Germans denied any responsibility.⁶² However, it was not clear if the *Douro* was sunk or not; *Douro*'s crewmen assured the ship was torpedoed but they did not see any submarine.⁶³ Whether the *Douro* was deliberately sunk or not, the point is that the incident was used for propaganda purposes, by both the José de Castro and Afonso Costa administrations, in a similar vein to the sinking of the *Lusitania* the following month which shifted American opinion against the Germans. The magazine *A Ilustração Portuguesa* illustrated the 'attack' by portraying a German submarine torpedoing the fragile Portuguese vessel with a clear anti-German propagandistic bias.⁶⁴ In addition, the newspaper *O Século* considered this German action as another blow to Portuguese-German relations, considering the early skirmishes in Angola and Mozambique;⁶⁵ and the newspaper *O Mundo*, linked to left-wing Partido Democrático [Democratic Party], called for justice.⁶⁶ *O Século* recalled this sinking in various moments throughout the war, as a valid argument to justify Portuguese participation in the war.⁶⁷ In fact, Portugal would list this ship for war reparations at Versailles peace conference.⁶⁸

After the *Douro* incident, the Portuguese vessel the *Cysne* was scuttled on 29 May 1915 by U-41, which was commanded by Klaus Hansen. This vessel was operated by *Glama & Marinho* from Porto and was carrying pine logs to Newport, in Wales. When the *Cysne* was 50 miles NW of the French island of Ouessant, the Germans stopped the ship to verify if it was carrying war contraband to Britain. After this procedure, German crewmen looted some goods on board and blew up the ship with dynamite.⁶⁹ Later, Klaus Hansen sank two British ships that were cruising nearby; the British steamers *Glenlee* and *Dixiana* met the same fate as the *Cysne*.⁷⁰ The Portuguese authorities protested to the Germans considering its 'neutral' status; nonetheless, Berlin argued that Portugal did not ratify the Naval Declaration of London,⁷¹ in 1909, which in fact it did not.⁷² Thus, Germany argued that Portugal could not prove irrefutably that the *Cysne* was not transporting war contraband, according to international law.⁷³

Figure 4.2 The magazine *Ilustração Portuguesa*, 1 November 1915, showing the alleged German attack on the Portuguese ship *Douro*. Image reproduced with kind permission of BLX-Hemeroteca Municipal de Lisboa.

German submarine activity during the period of Portuguese neutrality definitely had an important role in bringing the Portuguese nation towards the war in the period July 1914–March 1916. The alleged attack on the *Douro* (April 1915) and the sinking of the sailing vessel *Cysne* (May 1915) started to inflame feelings in the Portuguese public and even among Portuguese authorities.[74] In spite of no clear confirmation of the sinking of the *Douro*, Portuguese government and a significant part of the Portuguese public opinion considered these two attacks unacceptable and it escalated the already tense diplomatic relations between Berlin and Lisbon – considering the earlier skirmishes that had taken place in Maziua and Naulila, in Portuguese Africa. Leote do Rego, commander of the Portuguese Naval Division stationed in Lisbon, said in an interview that the *Douro* and *Cysne* sinkings were of great offence to the Portuguese republic[75] and later he took the matter to the Portuguese Chamber of Deputies.[76] The spectre of belligerency was becoming closer with the unrestricted German submarine war; propaganda relating to the war at sea started gaining shape with these two incidents (Figure 4.2).

Conclusion

The Portuguese memory of the war is very much linked to the Flanders fields and the disastrous defeat of the Portuguese Expeditionary Corps in the Battle of the Lys (also known as the Fourth Battle of Ypres) in April 1918; the photos of Arnaldo Garcez[77] and Joshua Benoliel were particularly important to show the war to the Portuguese public.[78] In this context, the war at sea perhaps seems to be a sideshow. In the Portuguese 'non-belligerent period', the war at sea was present with an already strong naval culture that admired its Navy and covered the major naval battles between the Allies and the Central Powers, in various newspapers, magazines, brochures and postcards; notwithstanding, 'naval topics' were clearly not its core subject in most cases.

Portuguese actions at sea seemed peripheral and uninteresting for most propagandists, during the 'non-belligerency' phase. The power of photography and the ubiquity of the press brought the trail of destruction created by German ships to the eyes of Portuguese society, as they travelled around the Mediterranean, the Atlantic and the North Sea, but it did not have the impact of the Western Front images and illustrations. Indeed, during the 'non-belligerency' period, Portuguese naval propaganda had no proper form or systematic guidelines. Also, censorship in Portugal did a good job in 'correcting' war information towards the public; the government filters soon promoted a subtle pro-British or pro-Allied vision of the war through its media channels. Propaganda and censorship helped shape the perception of reality at sea, during the last moments of 'navalism'.

There were obviously some attempts of creating propaganda as a result of the German submarine attacks on the *Douro* and the *Cysne*, but its impact in Portuguese society seemed to be residual. However, considering the latest research, it appears it was actually very unlikely that the *Douro* was indeed deliberately sunk.[79] Nevertheless the incident definitely had some diplomatic and propagandistic outcomes. In addition to these incidents, the skirmishes that had already taken place in Portuguese Africa started to shape the nation's pro-Allied sympathies that became more and more visible throughout the war.

Notes

1. Paul G. Halpern, *A Naval History of World War I* (Annapolis: United States Naval Institute 1994), 1.
2. Norman Friedman, *Fighting the Great War at Sea. Strategy, Tactics and Technology* (Barnsley: Seaforth Publishing, 2014), 9.
3. Paul Kennedy, 'The War at Sea', in *The Cambridge History of the First World War*, ed. Jay Winter (Cambridge: Cambridge Press, 2014), 231.
4. Friedman, *Fighting the Great War at Sea*, 12.
5. Nuno Mira Vaz, 'Opiniões Públicas', in *Portugal na 1.ª Guerra Mundial. Uma História Militar Concisa*, ed. Abílio Pires Lousada and Jorge Silva Rocha (Lisboa: Comissão Portuguesa de História Militar, 2018), 641.
6. Maria Fernanda Rollo and Ana Paula Pires, *A Grande Guerra no Parlamento* (Lisboa Assembleia da República. Divisão de Edições, 2018), 17.
7. Ministério dos Negócios Estrangeiros (MNE), *Portugal na Primeira Guerra Mundial (1914–1918) – As Negociações Diplomáticas até à Declaração de Guerra*, vol. 1 (Lisboa: Ministério dos Negócios Estrangeiros, 1995), 17. Translations from the Portuguese here and in later quotations by the author.
8. *Diário dos Câmara dos Deputados*, 7 August 1914, 3–4. Available online: https://debates.parlamento.pt/catalogo/r1/cd/01/01/04/137/1914-08-07 (accessed 24 April 2022). See also Chapter 10 of this volume which refers to the Anglo-Portuguese alliance in the context of Portugal's neutrality in the Second World War.
9. Ana Paula Pires, 'The Iberian Peninsula and the First World War: Between Neutrality and Non-belligerency (1914–1916)', *War in History* 28, no. 3 (2021): 553.
10. João Chagas, *Diário de João Chagas 1914* (Lisboa: Parceria António Maria Pereira, 1929), 147.
11. Pedro Aires Oliveira, 'Diplomacy (Portugal)', *1914–1918 Online* (2015). Available online: https://encyclopedia.1914-1918-online.net/article/diplomacy_portugal (accessed 27 April 2022).
12. John Vincent Smith, *As Relações Políticas Luso-Britânicas 1910–1926* (Lisboa: Livros Horizonte, 1975), 99.
13. Rollo and Pires, *A Grande Guerra no Parlamento*, 25.
14. Friedrich Rosen, *Declarei a Guerra que Não Queria. Memórias de Portugal do Embaixador Alemão nos 100 anos da Primeira Guerra Mundial* (Lisboa: Alêtheia Editores, 2018), 147.
15. Smith, *As Relações Políticas Luso-Britânicas 1910–1926*, 77.
16. Rui Ramos, *Aparências e realidades: os republicanos perante a Aliança Inglesa até à Primeira Guerra Mundial* (Lisboa: Edições Tinta da China, 2011), 95.
17. *O Século*, 31 May 1917, 1.
18. Filipe Ribeiro de Meneses, *Afonso Costa* (Lisboa Texto Editora, 2010), 48–9.
19. Filipe Ribeiro de Meneses, 'Intervencionistas e anti-intervencionistas', in *História da Primeira República Portuguesa*, ed. Fernando Rosas and Maria Fernada Rollo (Lisboa: Tinta-da-China, 2009), 269.

20 Portuguese Angola bordered German Namibia and Portuguese Mozambique bordered German East Africa (later Tanganyika) by this time.
21 Ana Paula Pires, 'Portugal, África e a Grande Guerra: entre a neutralidade e a não beligerância (1914–1916)', *Storicamente.Org – Laboratorio de Historia* 12 (2016): 9–10.
22 Filipe Ribeiro de Meneses, *A Grande Guerra de Afonso Costa* (Alfragide: D. Quixote, 2015), 85.
23 R. H. Gibson and Maurice Prendergast, *The German Submarine War 1914–1918* (London: Naval & Military Press, 2015), 381.
24 Halpern, *A Naval History of World War I*, 66.
25 Smith, *As Relações Políticas Luso-Britânicas 1910–1926*, 129–30.
26 António José Telo and Augusto Salgado, *A Grande Guerra no Atlântico Português*, vol. 2 (Porto: Fronteira do Caos, 2018), 111.
27 In the first days of the war, British presence off the Portuguese coast was very strong. British cruisers like the HMS *Highflyer* and HMS *Vindictive* were patrolling Portuguese waters by this time.
28 *A Capital*, 9 August 1914, 2; *O Século*, 10 August 1914, 2.
29 Fernando Rosas, *A Primeira República 1910–1926. Como se venceu e porque se perdeu* (Lisboa: Bertrand Editora, 2018), 48–9.
30 Noémia Malva Novais, *Imprensa e I Guerra Mundial: Censura e Propaganda 1914–1918* (Lisboa: Caleidoscópio, 2016), 662.
31 Ibid., 652.
32 *Diário de Governo*, 30 November 1914, no. 224. Available online: http://hemerotecadigital.cm-lisboa.pt/LeisdeImprensa/1914/N224/N224_master/Decreto1117.pdf (accessed 27 April 2022).
33 Ibid.
34 Noémia Novais, 'A Imprensa Portuguesa e a Guerra. 1914–1918. Os jornais intervencionistas e anti-intervencionistas. A acção da censura e da propaganda' (Doctoral thesis, Universidade Nova de Lisboa, 2013), 115.
35 Ibid.
36 Ibid.
37 Ibid., 116.
38 Ibid.
39 Ibid.
40 Almeida's government lasted from 16 March 1916 to 25 April 1917.
41 Costa's government lasted from 25 April 1917 to 8 December 1917.
42 Meneses, 'Intervencionistas e anti-intervencionistas', 268.
43 Helena Lima and Jorge Pedro Sousa, 'A Ilustração Portuguesa e Cobertura da Primeira Guerra Mundial (1914–1918): imagens da guerra em contextos de censura e propaganda', in *A Grande Guerra (1914–1918): Problemáticas e Representações*, ed. Gaspar Martins Pereira et al. (Porto: CITCEM, 2015), 283.
44 Ibid.
45 Júlio Joaquim Rodrigues da Silva, 'A Ilustração Portuguesa', in *Portugal na 1.ª Guerra Mundial. Uma História Militar Concisa*, ed. Abílio Pires Lousada and Jorge Silva Rocha (Lisboa: Comissão Portuguesa de História Militar, 2018), 697.
46 *Miau!*, 10 March 1916, 1; *O Zé*, 1 October 1914, 1; *O Zé*, 13 April 1914, 1.
47 Rosas, *A Primeira República 1910–1926*, 77.
48 José Relvas, *Memórias Políticas*, vol. 1 (Lisboa: Terra Livre, 1977), 109.
49 Rosas, *A Primeira República 1910–1926*, 76.

50 Robert Gardiner, *Conway's All the World's Fighting Ships 1906–1921* (London: Conway Maritime Press, 1997), 372–5.
51 António Ventura, *Os Postais da Primeira República* (Lisboa: Tinta da China, 2010), 60, 62, 63 and 84.
52 *A Ilustração Portuguesa*, 17 October 1910, 1; *O Zé*, 5 October 1914.
53 Silva, 'A Ilustração Portuguesa', 699.
54 *A Ilustração Portuguesa*, 28 September 1914, 390–1.
55 *A Ilustração Portuguesa*, 12 October 1914, 479.
56 *A Ilustração Portuguesa*, 1 November 1915, 1.
57 *A Ilustração Portuguesa*, 5 October 1914, 421.
58 *A Ilustração Portuguesa*, 12 October 1914, 453.
59 The main Portuguese newspapers had reporters in some parts of the country, including its Atlantic islands and empire. Some British and Spanish consulates cooperated in sharing information regarding the war at sea.
60 *Diário de Governo*, 30 November 1914, no. 224.
61 *A Capital*, 16 April 1915, 2.
62 Jorge Miguel Russo Ribeiro, 'Os navios portugueses afundados pela arma submarina alemã na Grande Guerra' (Doctoral thesis, Universidade de Lisboa, 2018), 62.
63 *A Capital*, 1 May 1915, 1.
64 *A Ilustração Portuguesa*, 1 November 1915, 1. See also Chapter 3 in relation to the sinking of the Argentine ships *Monte Protegido*, the *Oriana* and the *Toro* and Chapter 5 in relation to the sinking of the Spanish ship *Joaquín Mumbrú*.
65 *O Século*, 9 June 1915, 1.
66 *O Mundo*, 5 May 1915, 4.
67 *O Século*, 22 September 1917, 1; *O Século*, 27 January 1918, 1–2.
68 Egas Moniz, *Um Ano de Política* (Rio de Janeiro: Portugal-Brasil Limitada, 1919), 354.
69 *A Capital*, 15 February 1916, 1.
70 See 'Ships Hit by U 41'. Available online: https://uboat.net/wwi/boats/successes/u41.html (accessed 5 April 2022).
71 The Naval Declaration of London of 1909 regulated war contraband during the First World War and was accepted by the majority of the naval powers at the time.
72 Russo Ribeiro, 'Os navios portugueses afundados pela arma submarina alemã na Grande Guerra', 63.
73 Ibid.
74 Arquivo Histórico Diplomático do Ministério dos Negócios Estrangeiros, Portuguese Delegation in London, 3rd floor, cabinet 7, pack 29.
75 *O Século*, 10 February 1916, 1.
76 *Diário dos Câmara dos Deputados*, 14 August 1915, 41. Available online: https://debates.parlamento.pt/catalogo/r1/cd/01/02/01/042/1915-08-14/41?q=torpedeamento&from=1914&to=1916 (accessed 27 April 2022).
77 According to the author António Pedro Vicente, Arnaldo Garcez was the first Portuguese war journalist. The Portuguese war minister Norton de Matos invited him in 1916 to take pictures of the Portuguese Expeditionary Corp in the Western Front.
78 António Pedro Vicente, 'O Fotógrafo Arnaldo Garcez ao Serviço do Corpo Expedicionário Português', in *Portugal na 1.ª Guerra Mundial. Uma História Militar Concisa*, ed. Abílio Pires Lousada and Jorge Silva Rocha (Comissão Portuguesa de História Militar, 2018), 713.
79 Ibid., 85.

5

Propaganda and *Pistolerismo*

Barcelona as an alternative battleground of the First World War

Florian Grafl

On 19 August 1914, less than a month after the beginning of the First World War, the newspaper *El Diario Universal* [translating as 'The Universal Journal'], which was the mouthpiece of the Spanish Partido Liberal [Liberal Party], published a very controversial article with the title '*Neutralidades que matan*' ['Fatal Neutralities'].[1] The text heavily criticized the decision of the cabinet in Madrid to declare Spain's neutrality immediately after hostilities had started. The article, which was attributed to the leader of the Partido Liberal, Álvaro de Figueroa (the first Count of Romanones), argued that Spain should enter the war on the side of the Entente instead.[2]

Prime Minister Eduardo Dato's reasoning for declaring neutrality was based on a lack of resources, the lack of obligations to any of the belligerents as there were no treaties into which Spain had entered and perhaps a hope of one day playing a mediation role.[3] Spain was not economically advanced, with only the Basque country and Catalonia as industrial centres and since 1898 was no longer, with the exception of Morocco, an imperial power which had diminished Spain's power and international prestige relative to other European nations. The country remained on the sidelines of continental affairs with a political system based on a restored monarchy and rotation of parties which suffered from structural weaknesses, and limited armed forces that were engaged in an ongoing confrontation in Morocco. Dato's position avoided these issues becoming more significant and also helped to balance a range of political and sociocultural factions and points of view within Spain, and, for a while, Dato was successful.[4]

In the course of the war, however, Spanish society became more deeply divided into *Aliadófilos* (i.e. supporters of the Allies) and *Germanófilos* (i.e. supporters of the Central Powers, especially Germany).[5] Generally speaking, the latter group mainly consisted of the upper classes as well as the military and the Catholic church. The *Germanófilos* admired the German monarchy and militarism for its traditional values such as discipline and authority. In their view, traditionalism had to be defended through the war as well as within Spain itself. Instead, the academic elite and the leading figures of the workers' movements favoured the Allies. They considered France as a blueprint for the modern, liberal, anti-clerical and republican state that they were hoping Spain would become in the near future. The formation of these two polarized groups, which effectively created two parallel Spains, has already been studied in significant detail – they are a key theme of historiography of Spain during the period of the First World War and, of course, laid the basis of the conflict during the Spanish Civil War (1936–9).[6] This fragmentation of Spanish politics and society was mainly manifested through the press, the most important media at that time. Both the Allied and the Central Powers financed newspapers in order to influence Spanish public opinion in their favour.[7] In addition, another important component of cultural mobilization was the intellectual movements which mainly used platforms, manifestos and writings to exert pressure on foreign policies in Spain.[8] Spanish neutrality, and the tensions that it tried to paper over, made Spain a propaganda battleground between the belligerents.

The tensions between pro-German and pro-Allied forces had already become obvious in Spain in the first year of the war. However, the conflicts between these two groups intensified in 1917 in such a way that foreign observers began to notice.[9] Riots, strikes and political instability were becoming more widespread. German submarine warfare had resulted in the sinking of several Spanish ships, including the *San Fulgencio* in April 1917, and strained diplomatic relations between the two countries. The American entry into the war, of course, encouraged the *Aliadófilos*. Romanones, who had replaced Dato as Prime Minister in December 1915, continued to push his pro-Allied agenda. He almost accomplished his goal to put an end to Spain's neutrality and join the Allies, spurred on by the American decision and describing the sinking of the *San Fulgencio* as 'the final straw'.[10] Due to lack of support, he had to resign and Spain remained neutral until the end of the hostilities, with the German-backed Spanish newspaper *La Acción* ['The Action'] depicting him in a front-page cartoon using his phrase 'Neutralidades que matan' in the title, with his heart pierced by a sword named 'neutrality'.[11] Around this time, Spanish society was also influenced and complicated by the Russian Revolution, itself catalysed by the First World War. The Russian Revolution became a rallying cry for workers' movements around the world, yet a *bête noire* for traditionalists (Figure 5.1).

The impact of the First World War on Spain has already been thoroughly investigated. The works of Fernando Díaz Plaja and Gerald Meaker as well as studies by Francisco Romero Salvadó and Maximiliano Fuentes Codera stand out as important in this regard.[12] Furthermore, the 100th anniversary of the beginning of the First World War also led to a considerable increase in publications on the subject in Spain.[13]

This chapter examines the effects of the First World War in Spain from a micro-historical perspective by focusing on the Catalan metropolis Barcelona, which at that time was dominated by the *Pistolerismo* – a political and social struggle characterized by the use of violence against businessmen, workers, politicians, trade unionists and members of the security forces. By outlining biographical sketches of the protagonists to reveal how propaganda, rumour-spreading, espionage and the *Pistolerismo* were closely connected, the chapter argues that Barcelona could be also considered as an alternative and national battleground of the First World War, which was able to take place because of the fragile neutrality of Spain. Additionally, the chapter takes

Figure 5.1 Cartoon depicting the downfall of the (former) Spanish Prime Minister, Count Romanones, in *La Acción*, 21 April 1917, using the title of the article attributed to him '*Neutralidades que matan*' [Fatal Neutralities] two and a half years previously. Image from the collection of the Biblioteca Nacional de España, BNE.

Barcelona as a showcase to reveal the continued impact of the First World War in the interwar period on the Iberian Peninsula.

The impact of the First World War on Barcelona

'I will never forget the impressive sight of the Ramblas, full of people frightened by the sudden outbreak of the hostilities and worried from the unpredictable gravity of its consequences.' This is how the industrialist Pedro Gual Villalbí remembered the beginning of the First World War in Barcelona in his memoirs.[14] Due to their proximity to France, the Basque country and Catalonia were most affected by the First World War. This had already become obvious in the first few weeks, when ten thousand Spanish migrants who had been working in France arrived back in the country.[15] Throughout the conflict, economically speaking, Catalan industrialists made good use of Spain's neutrality and delivered goods to both sides of the armed conflict. By contrast, working class families in the region were seriously affected by growing inflation. As a result, the tensions between rich and poor were particularly intensified in Catalonia, and specifically in Barcelona.[16]

Simultaneously, the demands for Catalan autonomy became more radicalized. Until the turn of the century, Catalanism had been a purely cultural phenomenon.[17] However, during the First World War, political Catalanism had considerably grown. The wave of nationalism, which had affected all the countries that took part in the hostilities, also spilled over into Catalonia.[18] Similarly to supporters of the emerging Basque and Galician nationalist movements, most Catalanists favoured the Allies as they expected them to guarantee the liberty of the smaller nations. Already in September 1914, the Catalanists made good use of the fact that the French General Joseph Joffre had been born in Roussillon, addressing him as 'Northern Catalan'. In April 1915, with the financial support of the Entente, the journal *Iberia* was launched. Its main propagandistic impact was the creation of the myth of the 'Catalan volunteers'. It claimed that thousands of Catalans were fighting on the battlefield in France for the Allied cause, whereas in truth their participation was rather modest.[19] Both this myth and the concept of the self-determination of small nations by US President Woodrow Wilson nourished the Catalanists' hopes for more autonomy when the victory of the Entente became apparent.[20] But at the end of the war, the application for more autonomy brought in by the Mancomunitat, the local Catalan parliament, was refused by the Madrid government on 12 December 1918.[21] The Allies did not intervene in favour of the Catalans, as the Catalanists had hoped they might.[22] After the political negotiations in Madrid had finally come to a dead end, the demands for Catalan independence were taken to the streets. In December 1918 and January 1919, street fighting between radical Catalanists and the police became an almost daily occurrence in the Ramblas, already at that time Barcelona's most popular avenue.[23]

The class conflict in Barcelona became even more radicalized. The relations between workers and entrepreneurs in the city had been affected by mutual acts of violence ever since the beginning of the industrialization in Catalonia in the second half of the nineteenth century.[24] The conflict intensified at the beginning of the twentieth century: strikes became frequent and were accompanied with violence against entrepreneurs and strike breakers.[25] Until 1916, however, there were only isolated attacks on industrialists.[26] Towards the end of the First World War, the attacks took a much more deadly turn.[27] One of the reasons was that due to the circulation of firearms in the course of the war, there was an abundance of weaponry. More and more attacks were carried out with pistols.[28] Industrialists were attacked by gunmen from working class circles. To revenge these acts, they hired contract killers. It was difficult to convict the perpetrators because many witnesses did not show up at the trials out of fear for their own lives. Some policemen took justice in their own hands and in response became targets as well. According to Albert Balcells, in this tit-for-tat spiral of violence, between January 1917 and September 1923, nearly a thousand people were gunned down in the streets of Barcelona.[29] Similar incidents occurred in other Spanish cities at the same time but on a much lower frequency.[30] As the attacks used to be carried out by small groups of armed gunmen, so-called *pistoleros*, the years from 1917 to 1923 went down in the history of Barcelona as the *Pistolerismo*.

In order to demonstrate how propaganda, rumour-spreading, espionage and the *Pistolerismo* were closely connected, this chapter examines the biographical sketches of three main protagonists in order to reveal how their stories were not only a background of *Pistolerismo* but also an alternative battleground of the First World War and its propaganda messages. These people are the Barcelona-based industrialist Josep Albert Barret, who, according to rumours, produced goods for the Allied in his factory and was one of the first victims of the *Pistolerismo*; the police officer Manuel Bravo Portillo, who worked for the German secret service in Barcelona, a fact that caused a huge scandal in the Catalan society when it was revealed by the press; and Fritz Stallmann, who had come to Barcelona alongside many foreign adventurers in dubious circumstances attracted by the ambition to make easy money – he became a legend of the Barcelona underworld by his alias 'Baron von Koenig'.

The assassination of Josep Albert Barret

On 8 January 1918, the day Woodrow Wilson outlined the principles of his fourteen points in a speech at the US Congress, 52-year-old Josep Albert Barret was on his way to give a lecture at the Universidad Industrial ['The Industrial University'], in the Faculty of Engineering of the University of Barcelona. Barret had taught both mathematics and engineering as a professor in various academic institutions in Barcelona for almost three decades. Simultaneously, he directed the factory Industrias Mecánicas Consolidadas ['Consolidated Mechanical Industries'], which he owned together with his brother Josep Antoni. Furthermore, he presided the Sociedad de Industriales Mecánicos y Metalúrgicos ['Society of Mechanic and Metallurgic Industrialists'] and the Unión Española de Transformadores Metalúrgicos [the 'Spanish Union of Metallurgic Transformers'], two powerful employers' federations in the metal processing industry.[31] Stepping out of the tram, Barret went down in a hail of bullets. Although he was immediately taken to the hospital, he did not recover from his wounds and died the next day. According to eyewitnesses, the shots were fired by a large group of about twenty persons. This assassination caused a huge shock among Barcelona's citizens as the victim was an influential figure not only in academic circles but also among leading Catalan industrialists.

Solidaridad Obrera ['Solidarity of the Workers'], the mouth pipe of the anarchist trade union Confederación Nacional del Trabajo ['the National Labour Confederation', known by its initials CNT], reported the attack on Barret in the following terms: 'We have been informed that Barret was severely injured. This man . . . was one of the most tyrant entrepreneurs in this area. Because of him, many strikes in the metallurgic sector had failed and many of us are in prison. In consequence, we say "everybody gets his comeuppance in the end"'.[32] *La Vanguardia* ['The Vanguard'], the newspaper with the highest circulation in Catalonia, as well as *El Diluvio* ['The Deluge'] also attributed Barret's assassination to the existing labour conflicts in his factory.[33] These reports seem to indicate that Barret was one of the first people who lost their lives in what later became known as the *Pistolerismo* due to the direct reference to the wider social unrest in Catalonia and, of course, his assassination through the use of pistols.

However, there were also reports on the death of Barret which pointed in another direction. *El Noticiero Universal* ['Universal Newspaper'] in its report of the assassination of Josep Barret ambiguously stated that 'materials for one of the belligerent nations' had been produced.³⁴ *La Publicidad* ['The Publicity'] and *La Veu de Catalunya* ['The Voice of Catalonia'], two pro-Allied newspapers, openly stated that these 'materials' were ammunition for the Allied forces.³⁵ Later, this assumption was verified, for example, by the memoirs of Ángel Pestaña, at that time a well-informed figure in working class circles.³⁶ In other words, Barret's assassination, according to these opinions, was all about the First World War, rather than Catalan social unrest, and connected to the arguments around Spain's continued neutrality. Germany was accused of having paid a group of agent provocateurs to cause disturbances in the Catalan factories which produced goods for the Allied forces.

One of the suspects was former police officer Guillermo Bellés Moliner. Several witnesses testified that Bellés had tried to provoke unrest in the factory of the victim by various means. Nevertheless, he was released by the police.³⁷ Nearly two months after the assassination of Barret, the Madrid-based newspaper *El Parlamentario* ['The Parliamentarian'] was the first to allege that Bellés was a German spy, and therefore acting on orders from Berlin. In two articles published on 25 February and 2 March, Bellés was accused of having organized an anarchist group to kill Barret. Furthermore, it was claimed that Bellés was also behind the attacks on Jaume Casadevall and Avelino Trinchet, two influential figures of the textile industry, who had suffered assassination attempts in 1917.³⁸ In Barcelona, these accusations of German involvement, and propaganda surrounding them, were taken up in the course of the Bravo Portillo affair, which is the subject of the next section.

The Bravo Portillo affair

In the summer of 1918, when the German spring offensive on the Western Front had almost come to a standstill and the victory of the Allied forces seemed just a matter of time, the propaganda war in Barcelona reached its climax. On 9 June, *Solidaridad Obrera* launched its issue with the sensational headline '*El espionaje alemán en Barcelona – Documentos importantísimos*' ['German espionage in Barcelona – Documents of upmost importance']. On the front page, two letters written by police inspector Manuel Bravo Portillo were published.³⁹ Those documents seemed to prove that Bravo Portillo had provided the German secret service in Barcelona with information about the Spanish ship *Joaquín Mumbrú*.⁴⁰ The *Mumbrú* had suffered the same fate as several Spanish ships which were supposed to deliver goods to the Allied forces and therefore were sunk by German submarines.⁴¹

Manuel Bravo Portillo had been born in 1876 in Manila in the Philippines, which was one of the last remaining colonies of the former Spanish Empire at the time. He came to Barcelona in 1909 as a police officer, where he rapidly advanced in his police career.⁴² His repressive measures against trade unionists brought him considerable recognition and respect among Barcelona's ruling elites, but made him a hated figure in the workers' movement. He married the daughter of a high-ranking military officer and worked for General Valeriano Weyler, one of the most prominent figures in the Spanish military who was known for his pro-German sentiments.⁴³

In Barcelona, the German secret service was directed by Isaac Ezratty under the pseudonym 'Barón von Rolland'. He could count on about two hundred agents and a budget of more than five million pesetas.[44] In 1915, von Rolland offered Bravo Portillo 50 pesetas per day for his services, much more than a usual police officer's salary. At first, Bravo Portillo's task was to assist two of von Rolland's agents, Albert Honnermann and Frederick Rueggeberg, with spying in the port of Barcelona on ships destined for France and Italy. When Bravo Portillo became the leader of a special police unit for the repression of anarchism and socialism in 1917, he was supposed to make use of his new influential position to destabilize Barcelona's working class along similar lines to how Bellés had been utilized to assassinate Barret.[45]

The Allied forces also tried to make ties with the Barcelona police department by contracting two of its most prominent figures, Ramón Carbonell and Francisco Martorell, both ardent rivals of Bravo Portillo. Already in August 1916, Carbonell had been decorated with a medal by the Italian military for his services. Martorell had passed information to the Allied forces and tried to release spies or collaborators of the Allies who had been detained in Barcelona. However, with the help of the German intelligence, Bravo Portillo managed to get rid of them and became the most powerful police officer in Barcelona. In August 1917, Martorell was arrested and moved to a new post in Madrid. He had been blamed by Bravo Portillo for having allowed Alejandro Lerroux, one of the agitators of the 1917 general strike, to escape to France. Carbonell was also moved to Madrid in March 1918 after the pro-German and Barcelona-based newspaper *El Tiempo* ['The Time'] had successfully launched a press campaign against him.[46]

The article published in *Solidaridad Obrera* provided evidence that Bravo Portillo had informed a contact person of the German secret service about *Mumbrú*'s movements. The 2,703-tonne steamer bound for New York with general cargo had left Barcelona on 20 December 1917. It was torpedoed ten days later near the Portuguese island of Madeira by the German submarine *U-155*. There were rumours that the German captain of the *U-155* had told the shipwrecked crew of the *Mumbrú* that he was following orders from Barcelona.[47]

After an expert had verified that the letters published in *Solidaridad Obrera* had indeed been written by Bravo Portillo, the judge ordered his arrest. Whereas the pro-German press launched a campaign in defence of Bravo Portillo, pro-Allied newspapers such as *La Campana de Gracia* ['The Bell of Gracia'] openly called for the execution of the 'traitor'.[48] Bravo Portillo was also accused of having been involved in the assassination of Barret. The judicial proceedings and the extensive media coverage had such a huge impact that the Spanish government felt obliged to pass a law 'against espionage and in defence of neutrality'.[49]

The trial lasted several months and only came to an end on 6 December. Despite all evidence, Bravo Portillo was acquitted, a fact that put the fairness of the judicial system into serious question.[50] After his release, he was not, however, able to return to duty. Instead, he became the leader of a small auxiliary police unit which the local press depicted as Banda Negra ['Black Gang']. The Banda Negra was established and supported by the Federación Patronal ['Employers' Association'], founded in 1919 by Fèlix Graupera as an association of Catalonia's most powerful employers to combat the influence of the CNT.[51] According to Gerardo Doval, a well-known criminologist who was sent to Barcelona in March 1919 to take over the police department, Bravo Portillo was not the only policeman in this unit who had served the German secret service previously.[52] Clearly operating in such an environment was dangerous and Bravo Portillo was a target, and he was eventually, perhaps inevitably, assassinated by a group of trade union *pistoleros* in September 1919. After his assassination this 'alternative battleground' continued to be active despite the ending of the First World War and with it Spain's neutrality in that conflict. He was replaced as the leader of the Banda Negra by Fritz Stallmann, who had the alias of 'Baron von Koenig'. As described in the next section, Stallmann was one of many foreign adventurers who had arrived in Barcelona during the war and became a prominent figure of the Barcelona underworld.

The enigmatic life of 'Baron von Koenig'

Some years later, when Bernardo Armengol passed away on 19 May 1923 after having been gunned down in the Barcelona district of Barceloneta, local newspapers reported that he was not associated with trade unions, but rather a former member of 'Baron Koeni(n)g's gang'. Whereas according to *El Noticiero Universal*, Armengol owned an investigative agency, *El Diluvio* claimed that he was working for the British Consulate.[53] *La Vanguardia* had already stated in January 1922 that Mariano Sans Pau, who just had barely survived an attempted murder, was 'the only friend of Baron von Koenig who remained in Barcelona, whereas all the others have been either assassinated or had escaped the city'.[54] Nowadays, however, sources agree that Armengol was indeed the last victim of *Pistolerismo* in Barcelona who died because of his former service for the so-called Baron von Koenig.[55]

So who was this Baron von Koenig? Koenig's real name was Fritz Stallmann, who was born in Berlin in 1871. Due to his addiction to gambling, he was notoriously short of money. Consequently, he had to make ends meet through fraud. In this context, he started to pretend to be from aristocratic origin and took on the pseudonym 'Baron von Koenig'.[56] Even before the events in Barcelona he had had a criminal past. He was arrested in August 1912 and convicted by a German court to several months in prison.[57]

In the course of the First World War, Stallmann came to Spain where at first, he settled down to run a casino in Hondarribia, located in the Basque country, close to the French border. Because things did not go his way, he turned away from gambling to the world of espionage. As he was only interested in money, he immediately understood that he could make the most profit if he would provide both sides of the First World War with information. He followed this policy until, after having moved around in Spain several times, he finally came to Barcelona in September 1918. He got to know von Rolland and Bravo Portillo, but as it seems, he was also working for the French secret service whom he facilitated information on illegal police activities.[58]

When Bravo Portillo was assassinated in September 1919, Stallmann made contact with the Federación Patronal. After having come to terms with the chief of the Barcelona police, Miguel Arlegui, he became the new leader of the Banda Negra.[59] In contrast to Bravo Portillo, Stallmann mainly followed his own ambition as the leader of the gang in order to make as much money as possible.[60] Consequently, he soon lost the protection of the authorities and was expelled from Spain in June 1920.[61]

On 6 June 1920, *El Sol* ['The Sun'], one of Madrid's most influential newspapers, commented on Stallmann's expulsion on its front page by asserting that 'during the war, Koenig was one of the most audacious German spies acting in Spain and a man of illicit business' and that, while in Barcelona, Stallmann had been under the service of the Federación Patronal.[62] About two weeks later, *El Fructidor*, the local bulletin of the CNT in the province of Tarragona, published seemingly fake correspondence of Tomás Benet, a representative of the Federación Patronal and a person with the name 'Rud Koenig'.[63] In his letter, Koenig claimed that he had been the chief of a private police force (i.e. the Banda Negra, although he did not state this name) paid by the Federación Patronal until it had been dissolved two weeks previously. Curiously, he stated that he was no longer able to cooperate with the president of the Federación Patronal, Fèlix Graupera, because of Graupera's pro-German sentiments.[64]

It appears this letter was a frustrated swipe at Graupera for taking away his illegal, but lucrative livelihood. However, it also shows that the *Pistolerismo*, sometime after hostilities on the Western Front had concluded, was still connected to the battles between the *Aliadófilos* and the *Germanófilos* encapsulated by the First World War. It also had parallels to the events in Russia between the bourgeois and proletariat, which itself had been catalysed by the events of the First World War. The fact that the newspapers of the time were being utilized to promote different points of view, and perhaps confuse and obfuscate the reality, shows that the *Pistolerismo* was not just a battle of guns, but a battle of propaganda as well.

Little is known of what Stallmann was doing in the next two decades after having migrated to France but, at some point in the beginning of the 1930s, he started to work for the French secret service.[65] Under the codename *Rex*, the Latin word for 'King', he was involved in the turning of Hans-Thilo Schmidt, who sold secret information about the Germans' Enigma machine to the French.[66] After the Battle of France, Stallmann was arrested by the Gestapo and betrayed Schmidt as a French spy. Schmidt committed suicide in his prison cell, but Stallmann managed to come to terms with the Gestapo. In 1946, his most enigmatic life came to an end in a US prison camp in Bad Wildbad in Southern Germany. Aged seventy-five, he suffered a deadly haemoptysis.[67]

Until this very day, popular culture in Catalonia vividly portrays the figure of Fritz Stallmann. The most famous example is Eduardo Mendoza's début novel *La Verdad sobre el caso Savolta* ['The Truth about the Savolta Case'].[68] Whereas Josep Albert Barret served as a blueprint for the protagonist Enric Savolta, the fiancé of his daughter, Paul-André Lepprince, strongly resembles Fritz Stallmann.[69] Recently, the movie *La sombra de la ley* ['Gun City'], set in Barcelona in the time of *Pistolerismo*, featured a character with the name 'El Barón'.

Conclusion

'Neutralidades que matan' – this prediction of the liberal Spanish newspaper *El Diario Universal* from August 1914 turned out to be valid for Barcelona. When the First World War was about to come to an end in 1918, the gun war in Barcelona which later became known as *Pistolerismo* had just started. The biographical sketches presented in this chapter illustrate that rumours and accusations connected to propaganda ideas with the First World War – with Spain playing a neutral role between those two sides – had a huge impact on the radicalization of the social conflicts that took place in Barcelona: in the case of Barret, the alleged involvement of the German secret service or, at least, the use of this idea as a propaganda message by the Allied forces; in the case of Portillo, the link between the national context and the international cause; and in the case of Stallmann, the repercussion of the First World War in Spain between the wars and the link between the foreign and the local *Pistolerismo* in Barcelona. Furthermore, all of these cases illustrate the huge impact of propaganda and the press. With full access to all the available sources even today it is still very difficult or maybe even impossible to differentiate between facts and rumours. It seems likely that the sensational news spread by the newspapers led to the radicalization of the political and social climate in the city. To conclude, this chapter has shown that propaganda, Spain's neutrality and the *Pistolerismo* were closely connected. Consequently, Barcelona should be taken as an alternative battleground of the First World War that deserves further investigation.

Notes

1. 'Neutralidades que matan', *El Diario Universal*, 19 August 1914, 1.
2. Although the author of the text remained unknown, it seems reasonable to assume that the article was written by the leader of the Liberal Party, Count Romanones, himself or at least expressed his point of view, see Francisco Romero Salvadó, 'España y la I Guerra Mundial neutralidad oficial, terremoto socio-político', *XXI Coloquio de Historia Canario-Americana* XXI-101 (2014): 1–12.
3. Francisco Romero Salvadó, 'Spain and the First World War: The Logic of Neutrality', *War in History* 26, no. 1 (2019): 49.
4. Javier Ponce Marrero, 'La neutralidad española durante la Primera Guerra Mundial: nuevas perspectivas', in *Ayeres en discusión: temas clave de Historia Contemporánea hoy*, ed. María Encarna Nicolás Marín and Carmen González Martínez (Murcia: Servicio de Publicaciones de la Universidad de Murcia, 2008).
5. See also Chapter 2 in relation to the *Aliadófilos* and *Germanófilos* in Argentina.
6. See, for example, Fernando Díaz Plaja, *Francófilos y Germanófilos. Los españoles en la guerra Europea* (Barcelona: Dopesa, 1973) and Gerald Meaker, 'A Civil War of Words: The Ideological Impact of the First World War on Spain, 1914–1918', in *Neutral Europe between War and Revolution, 1917–1923*, ed. Hans Schmitt (Charlottesville: The University Press of Virginia, 1988), 1–65.
7. Cristina Barreiro Gordillo, 'España y la gran guerra a través de la prensa', *Aportes* 29, no. 84 (2014): 161–82.

8   Maximiliano Fuentes Codera, *España en la Primera Guerra Mundial: una movilización cultural* (Madrid: Akal, 2014), 135–42.
9   Meaker, 'Civil War', 1.
10 Romero Salvadó, 'Spain and the First World War', 55.
11 Francisco Romero Salvadó, *Spain 1914–1918. Between War and Revolution* (London: Routledge, 1999), 71, 87; Romero Salvadó, 'Spain and the First World War', 55 citing *La Acción*, 21 April 1917.
12 Romero Salvadó, *Spain* and Maximiliano Fuentes Codera, *España y Argentina en la Primera Guerra Mundial. Neutralidades transnacionales* (Madrid: Marcial Pons Historia, 2022).
13 Fernando García Sanz, *España en la Gran Guerra. Espías, diplomáticos y traficantes* (Barcelona: Galaxia Gutenberg, 2014); Eduardo González Calleja and Paul Aubert, *Nidos de Espías. España, Francia y la Primera Guerra Mundial 1914–1919* (Madrid: Alianza Editorial, 2014).
14 Pedro Gual Villalbí, *Memorias de un industrial de nuestro tiempo* (Barcelona: Sociedad General de Publicaciones, 1922), 103.
15 Fuentes Codera, *España y Argentina*, 51.
16 Klaus-Jürgen Nagel, *Arbeiterschaft und nationale Frage in Katalonien zwischen 1898 und 1923* (Saarbrücken: Verlag breitenbach, 1991), 20.
17 Angel Smith, *The Origins of Catalan Nationalism, 1770–1898* (New York: Palgrave Macmillan, 2014), 222.
18 Gerald Meaker, *The Revolutionary Left in Spain 1914–1923* (Stanford: Stanford University Press, 1974), 155.
19 Xosé Núñez Seixas, 'Catalonia and the "War of Nations": Catalan Nationalism and the First World War', *Journal of Modern European History* 16, no. 3 (2018): 381–7.
20 Josep Mariá Poblet, *El moviment autonomista a Catalunya dels anys 1918–1919* (Barcelona: Pòrtic, 1970), 7.
21 Angel Smith, 'Cataluña y la Gran Guerra. De la reforma democrática al conflicto social', *Hispania Nova. Revista de Historia Contemporánea* 15 (2007): 495–6.
22 Núñez Seixas, 'Catalonia', 390.
23 Florian Grafl, '"Visca Catalunya Lliure!" – Battles for Catalan Autonomy in the Ramblas in the Immediate Aftermath of World War One', *Studies on National Movements* 7, no. 1 (2021): 13.
24 Chris Ealham, *Anarchism and the City. Revolution and Counter-Revolution in Barcelona, 1898–1937* (Oakland: AK Press, 2010), 31.
25 Juan Cristóbal Marinello Bonnefoy, *Sindicalismo y violencia en Catalunya, 1902–1919* (Barcelona: Universitat Autònoma de Barcelona, 2014), 257.
26 Fernando del Rey, *Proprietarios y patronos. La Política de las organizaciones económicas en la España de la Restauración (1914–1923)* (Madrid: Ministerio de Trabajo y Seguridad Social, 1992), 471.
27 Albert Balcells, *El pistolerisme, Barcelona (1917–1923)* (Barcelona: Pòrtic, 2009), 80.
28 Eduardo González Calleja, *El máuser y el sufragio. Orden público, subversión y violencia política en la crisis de la Restauración 1917–1931* (Madrid: Consejo Superior de Investigaciones científicas, 1999), 233.
29 Balcells, *Pistolerisme*, 56.
30 González Calleja, *El máuser*, 57 and 247.
31 Soledad Begoechea, *Organització patronal i conflictivitat social a Catalunya* (Barcelona: Publicacions de l'Abadia de Montserrat, 1994), 328–9.
32 *Solidaridad Obrera*, 9 January 1918, 3. Translation from the Spanish by the author.

33 *El Diluvio*, 9 January 1918, 9; *La Vanguardia*, 9 January 1918, 4; Barreiro Gordillo, 'España', 165.
34 *El Noticiero Universal*, 9 January 1918, 1.
35 *La Publicidad*, 9 January 1918, 4; *La Veu de Catalunya*, 9 January 1918, 11; Fuentes Codera, *España*, 133 and Barreiro Gordillo, 'España', 170.
36 Ángel Pestaña, *El terrorismo en Barcelona* (Barcelona: Planeta, 1978 [1919]), 88.
37 Sanz, *España*, 211–12.
38 Francisco Romero Salvadó, *Quién mató a Eduardo Dato. Comedia política y tragedia social en España, 1892-1921* (Granada: Editorial Comares, 2020), 245.
39 In some references, his name is given as Manuel Brabo Portillo instead.
40 *La Solidaridad Obrera*, 9 June 1918, 1.
41 Romero Salvadó, *Spain*, 171. See also Chapters 2 and 4 in relation to the war at sea and the sinking of neutral ships.
42 Del Rey, *Proprietarios*, 479; González Calleja, *El Máuser*, 122–3.
43 Romero Salvadó, *Spain*, 168.
44 Josep Pich Mitjana and David Martínez Fiol, 'Manuel Brabo Portillo. Policía, espía y pistolero (1876–1919)', *Vínculos de Historia* 8 (2019): 393.
45 González Calleja and Aubert, *Nidos*, 336.
46 Sanz, *España*, 212–13.
47 Romero Salvadó, 'España', 168.
48 *La Campana de Gracia*, 28 June 1918, 4; Pich Mitjana and Martínez Fiol, *Brabo*, 399.
49 González Calleja and Aubert, *Nidos*, 344–5.
50 Del Rey, *Proprietarios*, 484.
51 González Calleja, *El Máuser*, 146.
52 Del Rey, *Proprietarios*, 489.
53 *El Diluvio*, 20 May 1923, 14; *El Noticiero Universal*, 21 May 1923, 12.
54 *La Vanguardia*, 6 January 1922, 6.
55 Balcells, *Pistolerisme*, 63. Jacinto Leon Ignacio, *Los años del pistolerismo. Ensayo para una Guerra Civil* (Barcelona: Planeta, 1981), 282–3.
56 The word Koenig, or König, in German means 'King'.
57 Hugo Friedländer, *Interessante Kriminal-Prozesse von kulturhistorischer Bedeutung*, vol. 10, ed. Günter Bäcker (Köln: Günter Bäcker, 2013), 103–10.
58 González Calleja and Aubert, *Nidos*, 352–4.
59 Del Rey, *Proprietarios*, 514.
60 Francisco Romero Salvadó, '"Si Vis Pacem Para Bellum": The Catalan Employer's Dirty War, 1919-23', in *The Agony of Spanish Liberalism. From Revolution to Dictatorship, 1913-23*, ed. Francisco Romero Salvadó and Angel Smith (Basingstoke: Palgrave Macmillan, 2010), 175–201.
61 Maria Amàlia Pradas Baena, *L'Anarquisme i les lluites socials a Barcelona 1918-1923. La repressió obrera i la violencia* (Publicacions de l'Abadia de Montserrat, 2003), 143.
62 *El Sol*, 6 June, 1920, 1.
63 *El Fructidor*, 19 June 1920, 2.
64 The correspondence between Koenig and Benet was published in *El Fructidor*, 19 June 1920, 2.
65 Philippe Beck and Etienne Verhoeyen, 'Agents secrets à la frontière belgo-allemande. Des services de renseignements belges, alliés et allemands entre 1920 et 1940 dans la région d'Eupen', *CHTP-BEG* 21 (2009): 93–134, 103.
66 David Kahn, *Seizing the Enigma. The Race to Break the German U-Boat Codes, 1939-1943* (London: Frontline Books, 2012), 67–8.

67 Paul Paillole, *The Spy in Hitler's Inner Circle. Hans-Thilo Schmidt and the Intelligence Network that Decoded Enigma* (Oxford: Casemate, 2016), 201–32.
68 Eduardo Mendoza, *La verdad sobre el caso Savolta* (Barcelona: Seix Barral, 1975).
69 Jacques Soubeyroux, 'De la historia al texto. Genésis de la Verdad sobre el Caso Savolta de Eduardo Mendoza', in *XI Actas de la Asociación Internacional de Hispanistas. Volumen V. Lecturas y relecturas de textos españolos, latinoamericanos y US latinos*, ed. Juan Villegas (Barcelona: Asociación de Hispanistas, 1994), 371.

Part II

Propaganda and neutrality in the Second World War

6

American propaganda challenging Irish neutrality

Karen Garner

Relations between Great Britain, the United States and the twenty-six counties of southern Ireland were highly personalized during the Second World War, marked by the distinctive personalities, outsized egos, fraternal friendships and enmities of the three government leaders: Prime Minister Winston Churchill, President Franklin D. Roosevelt and Taoiseach Éamon de Valera.[1] In the minds of their admirers, Churchill, Roosevelt and de Valera personified the nations they led.[2] They also exemplified the 'dominant, culturally glorified form of masculinity' or the hegemonic masculinities as defined by their specific historical moments in time.[3] To be sure, their closest advisers and their governments' wartime propaganda campaigns fed their manly egos and created the national myths that lionized them and delineated the exceptional and virile character traits that distinguished these men and their nations from their enemies. But Churchill, Roosevelt and de Valera fully participated in creating these gendered (and raced, classed and sexualized) myths as they acted out their parts as wartime 'Great Britain', 'America' and 'Ireland' in their personal relationships with one another, and through proxies, that is their close foreign policy advisers on the ground in London, Washington DC, and Dublin. They each aimed to establish popular support for their wartime policies that were designed to achieve their ultimate goals of victory over their enemies, as they each defined what 'victory' would entail and who their 'enemies' were throughout the long and brutal war.

Churchill's, Roosevelt's and de Valera's foreign policy advisers in Dublin loyally followed their leaders' diplomatic directives as they interacted with one another and pressed their nations' wartime agendas. In particular, US Minister David Gray, who gained his diplomatic post and Roosevelt's confidence because he was related by marriage to Roosevelt (his wife was Eleanor's aunt), also shared Roosevelt's strong support for Britain's fight against the fascist powers.[4] Gray took to heart Roosevelt's frustration with de Valera and the Irish government's neutrality policy that seemed both immoral and a dangerous security threat to Britain specifically and to the Western Allies in general, and made it his mission to undercut that policy. Gray was the most enthusiastic and active proponent of the Allies' anti-neutrality propaganda campaigns in Dublin from the time he was appointed in early 1940 and throughout his tenure as

US Minister that lasted until 1947. During the war, Gray also worked with the British Foreign Office representative in Dublin, Sir John Maffey, a seasoned career diplomat. Gray and Maffey shared intelligence and often applied overt and covert pressures in tandem on de Valera's government, trying to persuade the Irish to abandon neutrality and aid Britain.

Gray also shared stories to discredit de Valera's neutrality policy with American journalists, and most particularly with Helen Kirkpatrick, a foreign correspondent for the *Chicago Daily News* who was based in London. Kirkpatrick's anti-fascist reporting from the mid-1930s onwards had earned her an inside track with British and American government and military officials and solidified her political friendship with Gray, whom she met in Dublin in 1940. For their parts, de Valera's Minister for Coordination of Defensive Measures, Frank Aiken, and Secretary for External Affairs, Joseph Walshe, followed their 'chief' and defended the Taoiseach's neutrality policy with a fierce and unwavering nationalistic zeal. They also shared a deep personal dislike and mutual distrust of Gray with de Valera. While the national leaders and their diplomatic representatives personalized Anglo–American–Irish state-to-state relationships during the war, the contours of those relationships were highly predictable, given their nations' intertwined histories.

Anglo–American–Irish special relationships

In regard to Anglo-American relations, from the seventeenth-century colonial relationship up until the turn of the twentieth century, Britain's imperial government had challenged the United States' sovereignty and its sphere of influence in the Western hemisphere. But, as the United States' national wealth grew and its world power status was established by the late 1800s, a 'special relationship' developed as the governments of the two Great Powers 'reappraised their interests'.[5] White Anglo-American male leaders dominated their nations' political, economic and social realms. The Anglo-American leaders also developed related conceptions of their nations' 'exceptionalism' and asserted their hegemonic power and 'rights' to rule over all others. For British leaders, national exceptionalism led to assertions of their 'White Man's Burden' and global 'civilizing' and colonizing mission; for American leaders, exceptionalism led to the articulation of their 'divinely inspired' 'Manifest Destiny', to be a model for democratic societies to follow worldwide. According to historian Alan Dobson, 'Towards the end of the nineteenth century these ideas came together in the minds of those who advocated a form of Anglo-Saxonism' that encompassed a cultural, racial and gendered sense of superiority over all other peoples.[6]

In contrast to the Anglo-American special relationship, a long-running antipathy characterized Anglo-Irish relations in the early twentieth century, as a result of tensions built up during Britain's long rule over Ireland as one of the empire's Crown Colonies. An unsuccessful bid for Irish independence led by Catholic nationalist revolutionaries reached a boiling point during the First World War, culminating in the 1916 Easter Rising. Following Britain's brutal suppression of the Rising and the execution of nearly all of its leaders – revolutionary leader Éamon de Valera was the most notable exception among those few whose lives were spared – Ireland was split apart in 1920, literally and figuratively, into two separately governed entities and was further divided by a violent civil war that lasted until 1923.[7] In the aftermath of the wars, a predominantly Irish Catholic population governed the newly christened 'Irish Free State', nominally a dominion of the British Empire that continued to pursue national independence, in the twenty-six counties of southern Ireland. A predominantly Anglo-Irish Protestant population governed in the six counties of 'Unionist' Northern Ireland that remained a loyal member of the UK. Former revolutionary de Valera abandoned his militant bid for Irish independence in the mid-1920s in favour of evolution through political settlement. He established a nationalist political party, Fianna Fáil [translating as 'Soldiers of Destiny'], and formed a coalition to win the majority seats in the Dáil Éireann [Irish Assembly] in 1932. Thereafter he led the government of partitioned southern Ireland through to the end of the Second World War. Fianna Fáil's radical nationalist rivals, the militant revolutionary association Sinn Féin [Ourselves Alone] and its Irish Republican Army (IRA), continued a violent campaign for Irish independence on the far political left that went as far as declaring open 'war' on Britain in January 1939.[8] The IRA colluded with the German Abwehr (military intelligence) during the Second World War.[9] This long and contentious history impacted Anglo-Irish relations throughout the war, fuelling de Valera's unwavering decision to declare Irish neutrality when war broke out to assert Irish sovereignty and independence from Britain and to placate Germany and the IRA.

Ireland's historic relations with the United States also factored into the wartime relations between de Valera and Roosevelt and their governments. Irish immigrants to the United States had retained close ties with the Irish homeland, and their settlement patterns concentrating in primarily Irish-American neighbourhoods encouraged a cultural cohesiveness that led to a unified political voting bloc that could sway election outcomes. Dominant White Anglo-Saxon Protestant, so-called native American politicians, whose governing power was tied to success at the ballot box such as Roosevelt, were sensitive to Irish-American voting behaviours, especially during the first half of the twentieth century. Irish politicians, including de Valera and his close advisers, asserted their influence over the political attitudes of the Irish diaspora. During the Second World War, de Valera and his advisers often used threats of their ability to mobilize Irish-American political opinion and votes in warnings to Roosevelt to respect Ireland's sovereign rights as a neutral power.[10]

Wartime propaganda and competing nationalist agendas

This is where the role of wartime propaganda became so critical in relation to Anglo–American–Irish relations. Churchill, Roosevelt and de Valera had to rally their compatriots to either support or reject the most consequential of all political projects: to go to war. The Anglo-American leaders created the dominant gendered, racialized and moral narratives of the war as it was being fought to make sense of the catastrophic devastation that engulfed Europe, North Africa, Soviet Russia, East and South Asia and the Pacific Islands for their nations' peoples when the fascist Axis powers launched their empire-building crusades. They also aimed to legitimize the often-merciless retaliations that the Western Allies perpetrated against their enemies. They told stories of heroism, collective courage and resistance displayed by their nations' soldiers and citizens on and off the battlefields. They emphasized the 'manly' virtues of the Western powers as a brotherhood of 'civilized', 'democratic', yet 'muscular' Christian nations fighting to protect weak and vulnerable peoples of all races, religions and cultures[11] from enslavement and genocidal atrocities committed by the German Third Reich army, directed by its demonic Nazi Party leaders.

By forging and cultivating their personal fraternal friendship and together defining and redefining who was a 'friend' and who was an 'enemy' of their noble cause and just fight, Churchill and Roosevelt tried to persuade de Valera to join the Western alliance. Their efforts to define the dominant narratives of 'war and manhood' for de Valera, his wartime policy advisers, and for the Irish people were pursued throughout the war because, at crucial moments in the anti-fascist campaign, a formal alliance with southern Ireland was deemed critically necessary to Britain's survival, if not to the Western Allies' eventual triumph over the fascist powers. Churchill, Roosevelt and their Dublin-based advisers understood that 'triumph' over fascism must come in the form of an absolute military victory *and* in a deeply symbolic and moralistic propaganda victory in the hearts and minds of their friends and their vanquished enemies.

Nevertheless, de Valera and his advisers rejected Anglo-American overtures during the war, wary of representations of Britain as 'friend' to the Irish people or to their nationalist aspirations to reunite the partitioned Irish Isle and to fully restore Irish sovereignty.[12] During the 'Emergency' as the Irish referred to the war, de Valera privately promised the German government and publicly pledged to the Irish people that Ireland would remain neutral.[13] In the Emergency Powers Act, de Valera's government claimed the power to take any action it deemed 'necessary', including enforcement of a strict censorship law over the wartime press and over any public speech that expressed a 'preference' for any belligerent power. The government also monitored private correspondence passing into or out of the country.[14] Although there was plenty of evidence that de Valera's government provided 'unneutral' aid to Britain and to Germany at different points during the war,[15] Minister for the Coordination of Defensive Measures, Frank Aiken, publicly defended the necessity of the government's emergency powers. Aiken quickly shut down all challenges to the government's 'undemocratic' censorship policies, from the press or elsewhere, with the justification that 'neutrality' in the age of total warfare did not guarantee 'peace' to the neutral power. Neutrality in the modern sense was, in fact, a condition of 'limited warfare', and Ireland had to recognize that fact to defend and preserve it.[16]

When Gray began his tenure as US Minister in Ireland, he carried out Roosevelt's foreign policy as he understood it, that is, to give as much aid to Britain as possible to fortify Britain's fight against the Germans.[17] This included developing arguments and schemes to 'break the backbone' of Irish neutrality.[18] Persuading de Valera's government to join the anti-fascist alliance and to open up southern Ireland's naval ports and airfields to the British military were all elements in Gray's support-for-Britain campaign. Most of Gray's initial encounters with de Valera, Aiken and Walshe focused on his proposals to trade Irish 'unity', ending partition and eventually securing independence for the island nation, for a wartime alliance with Britain. This included expelling Axis diplomats from Dublin and granting the British immediate access to southern Irish ports. He was not an effective negotiator because he quickly changed tactics from persuasion to intimidation.[19] Gray never respected de Valera's 'moral' arguments for peace through neutrality or accepted de Valera's suspicions of British motives, and he never appreciated how threats of reprisals from Germany and the IRA also impacted de Valera's foreign policy.

Propaganda wars between the neutral states

The following episodes focus on competing US–Irish propaganda campaigns from November 1940 to December 1941, when the United States was still nominally a neutral power. During this time, the British and the Irish governments were both campaigning hard for the United States' friendship. To Britain, America's friendship would be demonstrated through greatly increased quantities of war aid, including more weapons, ships, planes, tanks and an extension of credit to pay for the materials. America's friendship also meant that the US government, personified by President Roosevelt, would condemn Britain's enemies and stand side by side with Britain, personified by Prime Minister Churchill, in principled solidarity, proclaiming that the fight against the fascist powers was a fight for 'civilization', 'human dignity', 'freedom' and 'democratic' values. To southern Ireland, America's friendship meant respect for the government's decision to stay out of the fight in what Taoiseach de Valera defined as an ongoing imperialist war. De Valera sought America's friendship in the form of US government pledges to defend Ireland's rights as a sovereign nation to remain neutral and to protect the Irish nation from an attack originating from any belligerent power, either Germany or Britain, Axis or Allied power, with equal strength and speed. De Valera sought US military aid and proclamations of moral support for Ireland's sovereign rights and its sincere desire for peace. Throughout 1940, the version of neutral America's friendship on offer from Roosevelt from behind the scenes was much more closely aligned with Churchill's vision. By the end of 1940, Roosevelt was ready to advocate openly and energetically with Congress and the American people for military aid and moral support for Britain in order 'to save the American way of life'.[20]

Roosevelt's victory in the November 1940 presidential election had emboldened him, and Churchill's heart-rending appeal for aid in December 1940,[21] coming at a near-low point in Britain's fight for survival, inspired Roosevelt's Lend-Lease aid plan. Roosevelt first announced his plan to aid Britain in a press conference in mid-December, expressed in innocuous language as 'lending a garden hose to the neighbour whose house is on fire'.[22] In his 29 December radio address, Roosevelt pledged that the United States would become the 'arsenal of democracy', producing the weapons and war materials to defeat the fascist powers in the coming year.[23] On 6 January 1941, Roosevelt called on the American people to make sacrifices to support the 'four essential human freedoms' that threatened the 'American way of life', 'Western civilization' and a righteous moral order.[24] In his third inaugural address to the nation on 20 January, Roosevelt called up the nation's mythical origin story, and the mission that America's premier 'founding father', President George Washington, had laid out for the nation with the reminder that: 'The preservation of the sacred fire of liberty and destiny of the republican model of government . . . [is] entrusted to the hands of the American people'. 'If you and I . . . lose that sacred fire – if we let it be smothered with doubt and fear – then we shall reject the destiny which Washington strove so valiantly and so triumphantly to establish.'[25]

De Valera, Aiken and Walshe, along with Ireland's Minister in Washington, Robert Brennan, waged their own counter-propaganda campaign in America following Roosevelt's re-election. A new organization, the American Friends of Irish Neutrality (AFIN), was formed in November 1940 that hosted mass rallies in major cities with large Irish-American populations throughout 1941.[26] The Irish leaders rejected British and American arguments that Allied access to the southern Irish naval ports was necessary to fight the German submarine menace in the North Atlantic. They argued that showing preference for Britain would only bring on a German attack on Ireland, and they were not wrong about that. When de Valera's government refused German appeals to expand its legation staff in Dublin, Germany bombed several cities in southern Ireland, including Dublin, in January 1941, killing a few and damaging Irish property.[27] In April 1941, de Valera sent Aiken as his emissary to Washington DC, to secure US weapons so that Ireland could defend itself against any attacks, from Germany or Britain. Aiken and Brennan appealed unsuccessfully to State Department officials and in a contentious Oval Office meeting with Roosevelt they refused to agree with the President's view that Germany was the only aggressor they needed to fear and that Britain was fighting for 'freedom' for the world.[28] After that meeting, Aiken remained in the United States for several months, speaking at AFIN rallies, giving interviews to sympathetic 'isolationist' news outlets[29] and generally irritating the Roosevelt administration that was trying to drum up support for Lend-Lease aid to Britain in Congress and among the American people.[30]

By the end of June, following Germany's attack on the Soviet Union, Aiken finally returned to Dublin but the damage to US–Irish relations was done. In July, the Roosevelt administration sent the US Army Corps of Engineers to Northern Ireland to expand British airports and naval ports in the north, in anticipation of America's eventual entry into the war.[31] De Valera, Walshe and Brennan protested to the State Department that any 'foreign troops' stationed on 'Irish soil' constituted a violation of Irish sovereignty, while Roosevelt asserted that the British government was employing 'American workmen' to build bases within the UK's domain, paid for with Lend-Lease funds.[32] In Dublin, US Minister Gray was supporting Anglo-Irish opposition politician James Dillon, who criticized de Valera's neutrality policy in the Irish Assembly. Dillon caused a 'sensation' and earned his own opposition party's censure when he gave a fiery speech calling on the Irish government to 'declare, in no uncertain way, on the side of liberty, decency and freedom. . . . I say we know, as between these parties, what truth is – that on the side of the Anglo-American alliance is right and justice and on the side of the Axis is evil and injustice'.[33]

After Roosevelt met with Churchill off the coast of Nova Scotia in August and articulated their common Anglo-American values and shared political goals to be pursued in the post-war world in the Atlantic Charter, Roosevelt wrote to Gray that he hoped 'it may make a few more people in Ireland see the light'.[34] In the meantime, Gray advanced his own propaganda campaign that focused on the 'dangerous' presence (in Gray's opinion) of German spies in Ireland, who were allowed to operate freely, or in collusion with, de Valera's government, including cabinet secretaries Aiken and Walshe.[35] Gray met with sympathetic American reporters and circulated a report on 'Axis Activities in Ireland'.[36] His report asserted that German agents were financing the IRA and anti-British sabotage operations in Northern Ireland and were radioing 'useful' information from the German Legation in Dublin back to Berlin, that is, weather reports for German bombing campaigns and other intelligence, and that Aiken and Walshe knew this was happening. Much of what Gray was spreading to pro-British reporters was speculation or exaggerated reports of Germany's covert operations, but in early August, Germany was drawing up plans for a possible invasion of Ireland in preparation for an invasion of England and was using a 'secret' transmitter to send reports back to the German Foreign Ministry.[37]

In particular, Gray fed information to American reporter Helen Kirkpatrick. Kirkpatrick had been reporting on the war from her pro-British, anti-fascist perspective from London and criticizing Irish neutrality since the war began.[38] After they met in 1940, Kirkpatrick and Gray recognized their common political affinities and shared information that they each gleaned from their various sources, in Ireland and in Britain. Kirkpatrick also shared Gray's report on 'Axis Activities in Ireland' with the American Ambassador in London, John Winant, and this report fell into Walshe's hands through David Gray's carelessness.[39] Gray 'mistakenly' sent the report along with another official communication to Walshe,[40] and if the Anglo-American governments' attentions had not been focused elsewhere, this might have caused a serious diplomatic incident. As it was, Kirkpatrick was already on the Irish government's radar because of reports she wrote for the *Chicago Daily News* that denigrated Irish neutrality policy and focused on the dangers posed by Nazi Germany to the Irish people, all against southern Ireland's news censorship policy. These reports circulated in Ireland through British newspapers and through letters Irish Americans wrote to their families at home.[41] Frank Gallagher, director of the Information Bureau for de Valera's government, berated Kirkpatrick for spreading false stories, portraying the government officers as 'anti-American', and for knowing 'nothing about Irish history'.[42] Meanwhile, Walshe went on the attack against Gray, accusing him of spreading baseless rumours about German espionage in Ireland and exaggerating the size of the IRA and the extent of its connections with the German government. Walshe wrote to Gray that he should consider whether he could continue in his diplomatic post, given that 'the whole character of your notes forces the conviction upon me that your prejudices make it impossible for you to be the instrument through which a proper balance of goodwill can be established between our two Governments'. Walshe claimed that Gray had 'fallen into the fatal error of believing that the interests of a small nation are less sacred than those of countries in great size and population [and] such a philosophy holds no future for the world, and I can't see how it can be made a basis for friendship and cooperation between us'.[43]

US–Irish relations continued to deteriorate from that point forward through to the end of the war. Soon after that episode, in December 1941, the United States became an active belligerent in the war and sent many of its European-bound troops to bases in Northern Ireland to train for military campaigns in North Africa and Italy. The propaganda wars between southern Ireland and America also continued, with Gray aided by Kirkpatrick's reporting, leading the war of words in Dublin against their adversaries de Valera, Aiken and Walshe. Gray and Kirkpatrick were convinced that with America's entry into the war de Valera's government would be forced by public opinion in Ireland and America to give up its neutral stance and join the now-named 'United Nations' alliance against the fascist powers.[44] But the two critics, along with most other Anglo-American officials, misjudged the intensity of de Valera's negative reaction to the presence of US troops in the north and his commitment to neutrality. Although the Unionist community in Northern Ireland may have enthusiastically welcomed the 37,000 American soldiers that disembarked in January according to Kirkpatrick and other observers,[45] de Valera and his government advisers in the south vigorously protested the violation of Irish sovereignty to Allied governments and made their case with the Irish people. In the immediate instance, the Irish government felt disrespected when de Valera was not consulted about the placement of US troops on Irish soil. In the longer term, Ireland suffered due to partition of the motherland, 'one of the cruellest wrongs that can be committed against a people'.[46]

Conclusion

Competing US–Irish propaganda campaigns represented an important front in the Second World War, and they did not abate after the United States joined the fight. Gray and Walshe disparaged each other throughout the war, aided by the animosities that were periodically exchanged between de Valera, Roosevelt and Churchill. US–Irish tensions flared up in a major public media battle in 1944, as the Anglo-American joint military command prepared for the invasion of France, Operation Overlord. Although they weren't privy to any of the details of military planning for the D-Day invasion, Gray and British foreign officer Maffey focused on reining in German activities in Ireland as they worried about sabotage of the Allied operation.[47] Their shared security concerns and Gray's belligerence led to the delivery of the 'American Note' issued by the US State Department and delivered to Taoiseach de Valera by US Minister Gray, 'requesting' that the Irish government expel the German and Japanese ministers and their legation staffs from Ireland.[48] When de Valera vehemently rejected the request and its implied ultimatum, the note was leaked to the press.[49] While the US press focused on the threats that the active Axis spy network operating in Ireland posed to the Allied troops' security, and even branded de Valera's government as a '"fascist-like" regime, one that was "blind" and "insulated" from the outside world',[50] Irish newspapers took the opposite tack. They supported de Valera's decision to reject American demands and reasserted Ireland's sovereign rights. De Valera's response 'went down extremely well' and effectively guaranteed that his party, Fianna Fáil, won a majority of seats in the 1944 national elections.[51]

De Valera maintained his government's strict neutrality policy, and the high moral ground according to Irish nationalists, through the end of the European war. Nonetheless, Irish neutrality caused some significant repercussions in the post-war period. Most notably, to this day the Irish Isle remains partitioned into two separately governed states. Once the war ended, neither Britain nor the United States were eager to facilitate a compromise between Northern Ireland and the southern Irish governments that would lead to reunification. Moreover, southern Ireland, which became the independent Republic of Ireland in 1948, was initially isolated from post-war global governance organizations, although it eventually entered the United Nations in 1955 and has had a formal relationship with the North Atlantic Treaty Organization since 1999.[52] In part, the Republic of Ireland's post-war economic status as a 'poor' country until the 1990s was also a consequence of its wartime isolation from the Anglo-American alliance.[53] During the Second World War, all belligerent powers used propaganda to justify their actions. As this chapter demonstrates, the governments of neutral states also employed their own propaganda campaigns and censorship organs to justify their nationalist objectives and to promote their national identities and national values. This was certainly true of the United States, a neutral power until December 1941, and of southern Ireland, which remained neutral in order to assert its sovereign status and to preserve the Irish homeland from destruction during the cataclysmic Second World War.

Notes

1 This chapter is based on research conducted for Karen Garner, *Friends and Enemies: The Allies and Neutral Ireland in the Second World War* (Manchester: Manchester University Press, 2021).
2 See, for example, Winston Churchill Archives online, The Chartwell Trust, CHAR: 9/167/206-207, 'Winston Churchill's tribute to Franklin Roosevelt', 17 April 1945; Dwight D. Eisenhower, *Eisenhower's Tribute to Churchill, Delivered at St. Paul's Cathedral, January 30, 1965* (London: The Marble Hill Press, 1965); The UK National Archives (TNA), KV/2/515/1, 'Eamon de Valera is Dead', *Irish Times* special issue (30 August 1975), 1.
3 Carol Cohn (ed.), *Women and Wars* (Malden: Polity Press, 2013), 10.
4 Bernadette Whelan, 'Biography of David Gray', in *A Yankee in De Valera's Ireland: The Memoir of David Gray*, ed. Paul Bew (Dublin: Royal Irish Academy, 2012), 305–8.
5 Alan P. Dobson, *Anglo-American Relations in the Twentieth Century: Of Friendship, Conflict and the Rise and Decline of Superpowers* (New York: Routledge, 1995), 14–15.
6 Ibid., 8.
7 Richard English, *Irish Freedom: The History of Nationalism in Ireland* (London: Pan Macmillan, 2007), 271, 317–18.
8 T. Ryle Dwyer, *Irish Neutrality and the USA, 1939–47* (Dublin: Gill & Macmillan, 1977), 13.
9 John P. Duggan, *Herr Hempel and the German Legation in Dublin, 1937–1945* (Dublin: Irish Academic Press, 2003), 80–1, 87–8, 138–9; Robert Fisk, *In Time of War: Ireland, Ulster and the Price of Neutrality, 1939–1945* (London: Andre Deutsch Ltd, 1983), 294–5.

10 For an early expression of this strategy, see University College Dublin Archives, Éamon de Valera Papers (hereafter EdV Papers, UCD), P150/2571, Joseph Walshe, Minister for External Affairs, Report on Visit to London 6–10, September 1939.
11 See Jean Bethke Elshtain, 'Sovereignty, Identity and Sacrifice', in *Gendered States: Feminist (Re)Visions of International Relations Theory*, ed. V. Spike Peterson (Boulder: Lynne Rienner Publishers, 1992), 145.
12 Brian Girvin, *The Emergency: Neutral Ireland 1939–45* (London: Pan Macmillan, 2007), 30.
13 University College Dublin, Frank Aiken Papers (hereafter FA Papers, UCD), P104/3808 (on microfilm), 'Neutrality Declared, September 2, 1939, de Valera's address to the Dáil', in *Being a Selection of the speeches of Eamon de Valera during the War, 1939–1945* (Dublin: McGill & Son, 1946).
14 Ronan Fanning, *Eamon de Valera: A Will to Power* (Cambridge, MA: Harvard University Press, 2016), 190–1; FA Papers, UCD, P104/3436, 'Re: Censorship of foreign periodicals, illustrated and otherwise', 27 October 1939.
15 See Dwyer, *Irish Neutrality and the USA*, 17–19. De Valera's government monitored and radioed information about German submarines that the British could intercept; British aircraft were allowed to fly over Irish airspace; Irish nationals were permitted to serve in the British Armed forces or to work in British war industries and 'civilian' travel to Britain was allowed throughout the war; the Irish Army and British military shared information on German movements collected by the Irish coastal watch stations and other intelligence agencies.
16 Fisk, *In Time of War*, 141–2.
17 Dwyer, *Irish Neutrality and the USA*, 48–9.
18 The reference to Anglo-American efforts to break the backbone of Irish neutrality refers to comments made by German Minister in Dublin: American Heritage Center, University of Wyoming, Laramie, Wyoming, box 7, David Gray Papers, 1857–1960, Coll. 03082, Eduard Hempel, Typescript Translation of Intercepted message from Dublin (Hempel) via Berne to Berlin Foreign Ministry (Under Secretary of State Woermann) Dublin no. 168, sent 27 March, arrived 13 April 1942.
19 Whelan, 'Biography of David Gray', 305–8.
20 Robert Dallek, *Franklin D. Roosevelt: A Political Life* (New York: Penguin, 2018), 409.
21 Telegram, Churchill to Roosevelt, 7 December 1940, in Warren F. Kimball (ed.), *Churchill and Roosevelt, The Complete Correspondence*, vol. 1, *Alliance Emerging, October 1933–November 1942* (Princeton: Princeton University Press, 1984), 102.
22 Dallek, *Franklin D. Roosevelt: A Political Life*, 403–4.
23 Franklin Delano Roosevelt, 'The Great Arsenal of Democracy', delivered 29 December 1940. Available online: https://www.americanrhetoric.com/speeches/fdrarsenalofdemocracy.html (accessed 27 April 2022).
24 Franklin Roosevelt, 'State of the Union (Four Freedoms)', 6 January 1941, Presidential Speeches, Franklin D. Roosevelt Presidency (University of Virginia Miller Center, 2019). Available online: https://millercenter.org/the-presidency/presidential-speeches/january-6-1941-state-union-four-freedoms (accessed 27 April 2022).
25 Franklin Roosevelt, 'Third Inaugural Address', 20 January 1941, Presidential Speeches, Franklin D. Roosevelt Presidency (University of Virginia Miller Center, 2019). Available online: https://millercenter.org/the-presidency/presidential-speeches/january-20-1941-third-inaugural-address (accessed 27 April 2022).
26 Dwyer, *Irish Neutrality and the USA*, 89–90. See also 'Irish Neutrality Lauded: Meeting Here Protests Any Attempts to Jeopardize Nation', *New York Times*, 9 December 1940.

27 National Archives of Ireland (hereafter NAI), Department for Foreign Affairs (hereafter DFA) 221/147A, *Documents on Irish Foreign Policy*, vol. VI, 1939–41, Telegram from Joseph P. Walshe to William Warnock (Berlin), 2 January 1941, no. 378.
28 NAI DFA Secretary's Files P35, Telegram from Robert Brennan to Joseph Walshe concerning a meeting between Frank Aiken and President Franklin D. Roosevelt, 7 April 1941, no. 38 and NAI DFA Secretary's Files P 35, *Documents on Irish Foreign Policy* vol. VII, 1941–5, Letter from Robert Brennan to Joseph Walshe (Confidential), 10 April 1941, no. 40. See also EdV Papers, UCD, P150/2604, From Mr. Brennan on Mr. Aiken's Interview with President Roosevelt of 7th April 1941.
29 Girvin, *The Emergency*, 215.
30 Lynne Olson, *Those Angry Days: Roosevelt, Lindbergh, and America's Fight over World War II, 1939–1941* (New York: Random House, 2013), 274–7.
31 EdV Papers, UCD, P150/2635, Clear Cablegram from Washington Legation, 11 July 1941.
32 Franklin Roosevelt Presidential Library, Hyde Park, NY (hereafter FDR Library), David Gray Papers (hereafter DG Papers), box 6, David Gray to Franklin Roosevelt, 18 July 1941. See also FDR Library, Franklin Roosevelt Papers, (hereafter FDR Papers), President's Secretary's File: Ireland 1941, box 40, Minister to Ireland David Gray to Franklin Roosevelt, 28 July 1941.
33 Maurice Manning, *James Dillon, A Biography* (Dublin: Wolfhound Press Ltd, 1999), 165–6.
34 Girvin, *The Emergency*, 283–4, citing document dated 21 August 1941.
35 From 1939–43, both British and German spies infiltrated Ireland. See Max Hastings, *The Secret War: Spies, Ciphers and Guerillas, 1939–1945* (New York: HarperCollins, 2016), 329.
36 FDR Library, DG Papers, box 9, David Gray, 'Notes on Axis Activities in Ireland,' 20 July 1941. See also Smith College, Northampton, MA, Sophia Smith Collection, Helen Paull Kirkpatrick Papers (hereafter HPK Papers), CA-MS-01132, box 2, 'Notes on Axis Activities in Ireland'.
37 'Memorandum by SS Standartenfuhrer Veesenmayer, 24 August 1941, Proposal for the Ireland Operation', Doc. 234, in *Documents on German Foreign Policy, 1918–1945*, vol. 11 'The War Years, June 23–December 11, 1941' (Washington DC: Government Printing Office, 1964).
38 Interview with Helen Kirkpatrick Milbank by Anne Kasper, Women in Journalism, Oral History Project of the Washington Press Club Foundation, April 3–5, 1990, in the Oral History Collection of Columbia University and other repositories.
39 HPK Papers, box 2, 'Memorandum on Eire, To: The American Ambassador, From: Helen Kirkpatrick', 25 August 1941.
40 HPK Papers, box 2, David Gray to Helen Kirkpatrick, 2 September 1941.
41 FDR Library, DG Papers, box 4, Helen Kirkpatrick to David Gray, *c.* 28 August 1941; HPK Papers, box 2, Typescript for *Chicago Daily News* sent via cable, 28 August 1941: 'German propaganda working through news bulletins broadcasts and agents is trying to upstir [sic] anti-American feeling in Ireland and to incite extremist Irish in America against [US] Government. Evidences of this are very apparent in Ireland and according to American official sources in United States.'
42 HPK Papers, box 2, Frank Gallagher to Helen Kirkpatrick, 1 September 1941.
43 NAI DFA Secretary's Files P48A, *Documents on Irish Foreign Policy* vol. VII, 1941–5, Doc. No. 125, Letter from Joseph Walshe David Gray, 11 September 1941.

44 HPK Papers, box 2, Helen Kirkpatrick, 'People Sympathize with US but Eire Clings to Neutrality', *Chicago Daily News*, 26 December 1941; FDR Library, FDR Papers, President's Secretary's Files: Ireland, 1941, box 40, David Gray to Franklin Roosevelt, 17 December 1941.
45 HPK Papers, box 3, Kirkpatrick, 'Gen. Chaney, Air Expert, Heads Yanks in Britain', *Chicago Daily News*, 27 January 1942.
46 NAI DFA Secretary's Files P43, *Documents on Irish Foreign Policy*, vol. VII, 1941–5, Doc. No. 173, Clear telegram from the Department of External Affairs to the Irish Legations at Washington (No. 24) and the Holy See (no. 10) and to the High Commission in London (no. 11) 27 January 1942. See also EdV Papers, UCD, P150/2604, Official Statement issued in Dublin on 27 January 1942.
47 Duggan, *Herr Hempel*, 189–90.
48 Letter from David Gray to Éamon de Valera (Dublin) 'The American Note' (no. 410), 21 February 1944, Doc. No. 369 UCDA P150/2658, *Documents on Irish Foreign Policy*, vol. VII, 1941–5.
49 David McCullagh, *De Valera: Rule, 1932–1972* (Dublin: Gill Books, 2018), 241–3; Girvin, *The Emergency*, 249–50.
50 Clair Wills, *That Neutral Island: A Cultural History of Ireland during the Second World War* (London: Faber and Faber Ltd, 2007), 387.
51 McCullagh, *De Valera: Rule, 1932–1972*, 243. See also Wills, *That Neutral Island*, 388.
52 John Day Tully, *Ireland and Irish Americans, 1932–1945: The Search for Identity* (Dublin: Irish Academic Press, 2010), 153; Mark A. Stoler, 'The Second World War in US History and Memory', *Diplomatic History* 25, no. 3 (2001): 384–8.
53 Girvin, *The Emergency*, 327–8.

7

An 'irregular intellectual'

Elizabeth Wiskemann in Berne

Guy Woodward

As author of *The Rome-Berlin Axis* (1949) and *Europe of the Dictators* (1966), the historian Elizabeth Wiskemann was influential in shaping mid-twentieth-century perceptions of the Second World War. This chapter re-examines Wiskemann's own wartime career in Switzerland, however, to which she was despatched in 1940 with a 'roving commission' to gather intelligence by the secret British department of enemy propaganda Electra House (EH), subsequently known as SO1 as part of the Special Operations Executive (SOE), and which later became the Political Warfare Executive (PWE) in 1941.[1] As a self-described 'irregular intellectual' based in the British Legation in Berne, Wiskemann established contacts with a wide range of individuals who travelled between Switzerland and belligerent or occupied territories including the German Reich, Italy, France, Hungary, Yugoslavia, Romania and Bulgaria.[2] These contacts provided her with detailed information regarding living conditions, public morale and resistance activities in these places, which she relayed to London via encrypted telegram. Wiskemann described her intelligence-gathering activities in the memoir *The Europe I Saw* (1968), but gave no indication of how the information she sent back was used. Documents in the PWE papers reveal that some reports were used in the preparation of black propaganda campaigns, which sought to foment discord and resentment between civilian or military populations and their leaders. The papers also show that while in Switzerland, Wiskemann was involved in the dissemination of British propaganda publications and may have conducted espionage work on behalf of the Secret Intelligence Service (SIS/MI6). Drawing on research in these papers, this chapter attempts to clarify and extend our understanding of Wiskemann as a 'secret agent' – a term used in a recent account of her career – but also outlines the significance of neutral Switzerland to these activities.[3]

Before the Second World War

Wiskemann's pre-war career embedded her in networks which proved crucial for her wartime involvement in intelligence and political warfare. After postgraduate study at the University of Cambridge pursuing research into the French Second Empire, she divided her time between lecturing work at the university and vacation travels in Europe, reporting on the Nazis' rise to power during the 1930s for the *New Statesman*. On her arrival in Berlin in 1930 she was introduced to German intellectual circles by the *Manchester Guardian*'s Frederick Voigt, later of the Foreign Office and who worked on British propaganda to Germany in the early years of the war. Wiskemann also met a range of significant German political figures, including Chancellor Heinrich Brüning and Ernst Hanfstaengl, 'Hitler's clever choice of propagandist for foreigners'.[4] In January 1931, she attended a rally at the Berlin Sportpalast, at which the future German Chancellor Adolf Hitler's chief propagandist Joseph Goebbels spoke. Besides Voigt, it is striking how many figures associated with British wartime propaganda Wiskemann had already encountered in the interwar period. In Britain, she knew Hugh Dalton, David Garnett, Rex Leeper and R. W. Seton-Watson; in Berlin, she associated with Vernon Bartlett, Darsie Gillie, Hugh Carleton Greene, Ivone Kirkpatrick, Arthur Koestler and Cecil Sprigge. Wiskemann's 1930s career indicates the extent to which British wartime propaganda organizations drew on pre-existing academic, diplomatic and journalistic networks and also suggests that direct experience of Weimar and Nazi Germany motivated individuals to pursue wartime roles in intelligence and propaganda.

Travelling to Berlin a few days after Hitler's appointment as Chancellor on 30 January 1933, Wiskemann sensed that terrible changes were occurring in Germany. Reporting on the Federal elections a few months later, she became aware that a concentration camp had been established at Dachau.[5] Returning to London she sought meetings with political figures to discuss what was happening but made little headway. In July 1936, she was arrested and questioned by the Gestapo following a visit to Danzig and left Germany the next day. In London, she called on Leeper at the Foreign Office; he advised her to continue writing about the Nazis but not to attempt to return to Germany.[6] In early 1937, she was commissioned by the Royal Institute of International Affairs (also known as 'Chatham House') to write a study of Czech–German relations, an extended project which required her to give up her teaching post in Cambridge and spend much of the year researching the book in Czechoslovakia. On the outbreak of war in 1939, Wiskemann moved first with Chatham House to Oxford, where she worked for Arnold Toynbee's foreign research and press service. Finding this work unsatisfying, after six weeks she returned to London and set about trying to persuade the Foreign Office to send her to Switzerland, reasoning that she had trained herself as 'an observer abroad' and had helpful contacts in a country which occupied a 'key position' in Europe.[7]

Wiskemann moves to Switzerland

Perhaps in the interests of secrecy, Wiskemann's published account of her recruitment to work in enemy propaganda is vague, but she recorded that she followed several friends into Sir Campbell Stuart's department EH, which by Christmas 1939 decided to send her to Switzerland 'although only in a semi-official capacity'.[8] A contract with Oxford University Press to write a book on the country was arranged, as a means of explaining her presence to the Swiss authorities and of providing cover for her travels around the country and encounters with a wide range of contacts. In January 1940, Wiskemann travelled via Paris to Zurich, where she spent several months getting to know as many Swiss journalists and writers as possible. In May 1940, she was ordered to move to Berne, where a British Foreign Press Reading Bureau was being established at the British Legation, to scour the print media of belligerent and neutral countries for information to assist British intelligence and propaganda agencies (similar bureaux were established in Istanbul, Lisbon, Madrid and Stockholm).

The invasion of the Low Countries that same month necessitated the switch of systematic reading of the German press to Berne, and in addition to her conversational intelligence gathering, Wiskemann also began to compose summaries of German newspapers.[9] Some publications were readily available in the Swiss capital, while others had to be sourced in the countries of publication and brought over the border by agents and associates. Over the course of the war EH, SO1 and the PWE drew heavily on information gleaned from the foreign press: according to one document, SO1's French Section had become dependent on reports from Berne by August 1941.[10] The British Minister to Switzerland David Kelly was aware of Wiskemann's work for EH, and she appears regularly to have shared her reports with him, recalling that Kelly 'liked a few irregular intellectuals enrolled in war-time about the place, and gave me a remarkably free run then and later'.[11]

In her memoir Wiskemann suggested that 'My employers in London wanted above all to be informed about the *Stimmung* [atmosphere/mood] in Germany'.[12] The PWE papers show that she also relayed suggestions for British propaganda campaigns, however. Reporting in February 1941 that a Swiss contact had told her that rumours were circulating in Vienna that Hitler planned to invade England with Austrian troops, Wiskemann suggested that these fears could be played upon in propaganda 'to show exploitation and sacrifice of Austrians by Germans'.[13]

Recalled to Britain

In early 1941, the Foreign Office moved to recall Wiskemann to London. She had already become 'dissatisfied' with her position and put in requests to return.[14] Writing to Leeper she suggested that relations with other legation bureaucrats were poor and that the work had become 'demoralising', since she had no idea for whom she was working, 'what was wanted, or whether what I sent ever reached anyone'.[15] In April, she began her journey home via Vichy France, Spain and Lisbon. Bureaucratic obstacles and a shortage of transport mean that she spent nearly four weeks in the Portuguese capital, which in contrast with sober Berne was a place of 'the wildest cloak-and-dagger stories'.[16] She was initially regarded with suspicion by the British authorities there, even after telling them she worked with Campbell Stuart; only the intervention of SIS officer Rita Winsor prevented her from being treated as an 'impostor'.[17]

Wiskemann's exact involvement with SIS in Berne is unclear, but a memo suggests that Claude Dansey, SIS chief of active espionage – who had run SIS operations in Switzerland at the end of the First World War and also worked in Berne in late 1939 – was keen to see Wiskemann on her return.[18] SO1 were in turn anxious to prevent her meeting Dansey until she had reported to them: one internal note advised that Wiskemann would have to be 'very carefully instructed on her return to London' to 'prevent her from going all over the place'.[19] She expressed some apprehension about this situation in a letter to SO1's Thomas Barman, asking if she could be met in London by someone who could pass on instructions 'as to whither to proceed etc. . . . I won't know how to behave these days'.[20]

Arriving in Britain in mid-May, she was sent to SO1's country headquarters in Bedfordshire, where it is likely that she briefed propagandists on her findings in Switzerland and was trained for future activities. From there she wrote to Leeper on 23 June that she had 'dealt . . . with Germany + Italy' and was moving on to France and the Netherlands.[21] Whenever she could, Wiskemann escaped Bedfordshire to London, Cambridge or Oxford, where a hectic schedule of overlapping professional and social engagements with contacts at the Foreign Office, the BBC and SIS awaited; she also met a series of Czechoslovak, Polish and Yugoslav exiles. Her position between SIS and SO1 appears to have been delicate and subject to conflict, and both agencies made plans to send her back to Berne on their behalf. Although this tug of war was won by SO1, documents in the archive suggest that she worked in some way with SIS in Switzerland. For example, Wiskemann mentioned in a letter to the PWE's Director General R. H. Bruce Lockhart in August 1942 that she had been working well with Count Frederick Vanden Heuvel, SIS chief of station in Berne, 'who most definitely wishes me to stay here'.[22]

Returning to London, she arranged a short-term post at the Ministry of Information (MoI) with an old Chatham House associate. July and August were frustrating months, however, as her future status and prospects of returning to Switzerland on a more secure footing remained unclear. The nascent PWE appears to have been determined to retain her services: Leeper wrote on 29 August 1941 that Wiskemann would be returning to Switzerland as 'our representative in Berne' and that her salary would be paid by the PWE, although her 'exact status' was a matter for the Foreign Office.[23] In the end she returned on an MoI salary, with legation cover of Assistant Press Attaché. Despite this, the PWE's Michael Balfour (also a historian who had travelled in Germany before the war) wrote in August 1942 that '[t]he whole of her time is occupied in obtaining intelligence for PWE'.[24] To the apparent 'horror' of administrators at the legation she was given a diplomatic passport and full diplomatic status.[25] Wiskemann returned to Berne in late September, with daunting instructions 'to collect and convey home all possible non-military information about all enemy and enemy-occupied Europe, roughly the whole Continent, the *Festung Europa*'.[26]

Return to Switzerland

Wiskemann's work involved frequent travel around Switzerland, and by late 1942 she was spending two or more days a week outside the capital. Rising at 5 am, she would take a train at around 6 am to another city such as Geneva or Lugano for a 'long talk over lunch'. In September 1942, Balfour reported that Wiskemann is 'the kind of person who will do much better if left to her own devices':

> Hers is very much a 'personal' show. She moves around as widely as she can, trying to establish friendly relations with sources which seem likely to be valuable. She gets the information she does – of a political or social rather than an economic or military character – because she gains the trust of people she talks to. . . . It would be fatal to try to formalise her too much.[27]

Wiskemann observed to Balfour the following month that 'I have to pick things up in conversation mostly without betraying too much interest'.[28] Her contacts were many and various. One source, Raymond Gautier, acting director of the Geneva-based League of Nations Health Organization (predecessor of the WHO), observed that 'she knew everyone in Switzerland and had their complete confidence'.[29] Gautier was able, through Wiskemann, to pass on information from doctors of various nationalities.[30] Other sources also held posts in the international organizations based in the country, such as Carl Buckhardt of the International Red Cross and Willem Visser t'Hooft, a Dutch pastor who served as provisional general secretary of the World Council of Churches in Geneva, and had contacts among Dutch, French and German resistance groups. Unlike most legation staff, Wiskemann was allowed to meet enemy subjects; she reported that one contact at the Vichy French Embassy ('100 per cent anti-German') was a particularly useful source of information.[31] Soon after her return from London in autumn 1941, she was introduced to a German Catholic journalist based in Berne, who, 'went in and out of the German Legation as he chose', was constantly meeting arrivals from Germany and Italy and in whose presence German Legation staff spoke freely.[32] Wiskemann recalled that this unnamed figure, who regarded Hitler as a 'fiend' and wished to help the British defeat him, provided her with 'information of great value' every other week until late in the war.[33]

Frequent travellers were also useful sources: Wiskemann spoke to Swiss journalists based in Germany when they returned home to visit their editors, and businesspeople who travelled between Switzerland and neighbouring territories. Sources cited in December 1942 include an Italian monarchist, a Berlin clergyman, some 'Dutch printers escaped to Switzerland', a 'Reliable German industrialist' and an 'Austrian Baroness domiciled in Switzerland', recently returned from a visit to relations in Vienna and Graz in Austria and Maribor in occupied Slovenia, where she reported that resistance to the occupiers was strong.[34] A young Montenegrin, ostensibly studying theology in Berne, was one of several Yugoslav Communist contacts who brought Wiskemann news of Tito and the Partisans. Evidence mounted in their reports that the Partisans were doing the bulk of the fighting against the Axis while General Draža Mihailović's royalist resistance forces backed by the Allies were holding back or even collaborating with the occupiers. Against the advice of the anti-communist Director of the US Office of Strategic Services in Switzerland, Allen Dulles, Wiskemann relayed this intelligence back to London – a Pilot telegram dated 4 December 1942 notes that Mihailović was 'unreliable and inactive'.[35] She later claimed that her intervention had contributed to the Allied switch to support Tito towards the end of 1943.[36]

Wiskemann's reports

Wiskemann's reports were sent to the Foreign Office via Empax telegram or Pilot cyphers where the PWE's more secret activities were concerned. The Foreign Office passed down these communications to the PWE, which played a gatekeeper role in relaying information to the BBC's European Intelligence Unit, the Ministry of Economic Warfare and the Service departments.[37] Wiskemann reported regularly on the reception of propaganda, identifying several causes of dissatisfaction with BBC radio broadcasts. She was not shy of offering advice regarding propaganda strategy. Writing to Balfour in August, she repeatedly advises that British propaganda should aim to 'pierce the screen' and make Germans aware of atrocities committed by the Gestapo in occupied countries.[38] It is unclear how welcome such suggestions were, but when Wiskemann proffered advice gathered from a French contact who recommended scattering more 'drops of poison' – using written materials and rumours in addition to broadcasting – the PWE's Colonel Nigel Sutton responded enthusiastically, replying that further 'definition' on this would be helpful.[39]

Other reports feature striking details of life in German and occupied Europe, the granularity of which appear designed to contribute to the PWE's rumour and black propaganda campaigns. In his official history of the agency, Garnett noted that 'the kind of gossip and rumours circulating among Germans hostile to the Hitler regime' picked up by Wiskemann were 'of considerable value to our Black propaganda'.[40] Walter Adams, the PWE's coordinator of propaganda intelligence, similarly observed in May 1942 that Wiskemann's reports 'consist chiefly of gossipy items gleaned ... in conversations, etc. Information of this type proves very useful in black work, but requires extreme caution and expert regional knowledge before it is used as background intelligence or for publicity purposes'.[41] The level of detail is sometimes extreme. One telegram dated 4 February 1943 reported on conditions at an aluminium factory in Wutöschingen, just over Switzerland's border with Germany. Wiskemann reported the salaries of workers at the factories, the costs of their board and lodging, and gives details of rations provided in the factory canteens. In addition, she noted that a little butter is provided on Fridays and Saturdays, and that workers received 'Black ersatz coffee early in the morning. Beside this only beer, lemonade and cigarettes can be bought at the canteens'.[42] In previous years she reported that a friend had spoken to a French woman from Toulouse, who observed that a portrait of Marshal Pétain, the leader of Vichy France, has been removed from the wall of her workplace.[43] Another contact reported shortages of darning wool and typewriters; another, coming from Paris, 'had seen German soldiers there buying books by Thomas Mann'.[44]

John Baker White, one of the PWE agents who sifted through her reports, recalled in his post-war memoir *The Big Lie* (1955) searching for 'intimate little details upon which rumour, deception and morale-breaking are built up'.[45] Wiskemann's correspondence affords a rare glimpse into how these details were sourced in the field. Some of her reports featured gossip about senior Nazis, which appear intended for use in propaganda (often rumours or 'sibs') designed to undermine German trust in political leaders by spreading tales of their luxurious and promiscuous lifestyles, or their mental and physical frailties.[46] A Pilot telegram on 27 November 1942, for example, reported a conversation with a source in contact with a German actor recently returned from the Eastern Front, who had described 'marvellous theatrical shows there, champagne distributed from Hitler, etc.' Another had recently been entertained in the house of the Nazi Propaganda Minister, Joseph Goebbels, in Berlin and had been 'amazed by [the] luxury in which the whole of Goebbels' family lived. Frau Goebbels ordered present of nescafe [*sic*] to be thrown away because she did not relish it'.[47] The following month Wiskemann reported a conversation with a source who had told her that senior Nazis, Heinrich Himmler and Joachim von Ribbentrop, were both in poor health and frequently disappeared into nursing homes for periods of weeks. Hitler's condition, meanwhile, was said to alternate between 'outbursts of rage and long dazed periods of frightened silence. He has recently been supplied with a certain Fraulein Braun with whom his behaviour is pathologically depraved'.[48]

On at least one occasion Wiskemann relayed intelligence which turned out to be the product of the PWE's own rumour-mongering: in April 1942, she passed on a report that Germans had locked French workmen into a Renault factory at the time of an air raid by the British Royal Air Force and advised that the BBC publicize this cruelty. Colonel Sutton noted that this was in fact 'one of our own sibs which caught on with extraordinary rapidity' – or, he conceded, might have been fabricated 'by like-minded people in Paris'.[49] And just before the shutdown of the PWE's German black radio station *Wehrmachtsender Nord* [translating as 'Wehrmacht Transmitter North'] in early February 1943, it was reported that the station had 'notched a first-class come-back from Miss Wiskemann in Switzerland'. 'Come-backs' were instances where PWE rumours were detected in general circulation, indicating that once again Wiskemann had relayed information which had derived from the agency's own broadcasts.[50]

Reactions to Wiskemann's reporting

Indicating the extent to which the PWE leadership had direct access to raw intelligence, Wiskemann's reports were circulated at the highest levels of the agency. Many of the Pilot telegrams in the archive are stamped with the following names: Director General R. H. Bruce Lockhart, Deputy Director and head of the military wing Major-General Dallas Brooks, 'PWE Manager in the BBC' Ivone Kirkpatrick, head of the Political Warfare Intelligence Directorate Brigadier Eric Sachs, Director of Plans and Campaigns Peter Ritchie Calder and head of the German Section Richard Crossman. Reactions to her work were often favourable. Balfour noted in August 1942 that the PWE found her work to be of 'great value', and the high esteem in which he held her contributions is indicated by his later recommendation that she be granted an extra allowance of £400 per annum.⁵¹ A September 1942 note by a Miss Maxwell of the Italian Section observed that 'Miss Wiskemann's contributions are among the more useful pieces of information we receive from secret sources and in view of the dearth of reliable intelligence about Italy, her work may be considered valuable to the Section'.⁵² Sachs also appreciated her reports, writing towards the end of 1944 that 'Berne has become an increasingly important centre for intelligence and has continued to produce valuable material. Liaison has been assisted by the re-opening of communications and the visit of hard-pressed Miss Wiskemann'.⁵³

Others were more sceptical, however. An anonymously written PWE note from January 1943 casts doubt on intelligence Wiskemann passed on from subversive groups within Germany, observing that these reports 'have referred exclusively to "decent German" groups at a high level, who do not like atrocities and the extremes of Nazi doctrine, and who have good connections in [German] F.O., Church and Army', and suggesting that the communications had been 'allowed if not inspired by the German authorities'.⁵⁴ An August 1944 memo by intelligence official Clifton Child dismissed reports from Wiskemann on atrocities committed by Germans in the occupied territories as 'of no earthly use to us', and requested that instead of 'generalisations about morale' the PWE required specific information on topics including the breakdown of police authority and the inequality of hardships suffered by the German people and their leaders.⁵⁵ Finally, the PWE's black propaganda supremo Sefton Delmer declared himself unimpressed following a meeting with Wiskemann in November 1944, describing her as 'thoroughly uncollaborative' and 'much too Scarlet Pimpernel-minded for the humdrum needs of mere Black propaganda', suggesting that he found her overly adventurous and conspiratorial.⁵⁶ He subsequently requested the appointment of a second PWE representative in Berne, but this was turned down by Bruce Lockhart.⁵⁷

Eccentric tasks

It is possible that Wiskemann's perceived Pimpernel mindset was encouraged by some of the more demanding and eccentric tasks she was assigned, some of which verged on espionage. Over the course of 1942, for example, the PWE's Balkan Section made a series of curious requests. In March, Wiskemann was asked to get in touch with a Croat Rowing Club in Switzerland. In June, the same section requested details of twenty-one Slovene resistance fighters being tried before a special tribunal in Rome, emphasizing that obtaining the names of some of these figures was 'extremely important for our ... black work'.⁵⁸ In July, she was asked to interview a group of Serb children recently arrived via Italy in Ticino/Tessin in the south of Switzerland.⁵⁹ Wiskemann discussed their arrival with a Yugoslav diplomat in Berne and discovered that the children were aged between five and ten, had been sent with the agreement of the Germans by the Serbian puppet regime of Milan Nedić and accordingly were 'probably the least interesting small Serbs one could find'. Since the children were under strict Axis surveillance, Wiskemann arranged that 'certain Yugoslav wives of Swiss people who naturally visit these children . . . should try to find out for me what they say about their life at home'.⁶⁰

Aside from intelligence gathering, there is evidence to suggest that Wiskemann was also charged with the dissemination of propaganda materials. A letter to Adams towards the end of May 1942 appears to attest to her success in this field; having just received a bag of the Free French cultural and political review *La France Libre* [translating as 'Free France'] and other pamphlets, she reported that she knows of 'at least 4 lots of people who are able to get any number of these things into France and are always begging me to produce more'.⁶¹ An October 1942 memo noted that she had been requesting miniature propaganda for many months for smuggling into France and had developed 'excellent channels' for doing so.⁶² Writing to London the same month, Wiskemann requested a regular supply of *La France Libre* and the PWE digest *La Revue de la Presse Libre* ['The Free Press Review']. The French Section's H. A. Paniguian added: 'Not only is she ideally placed to reach the most influential persons connected with Vichy France in Switzerland, not only has she developed suitable channels to get material into Unoccupied France, but we know that whenever she has received material, she has been able to despatch it to Eastern and Central Europe as well.'⁶³

Challenges and problems

Sending material to Wiskemann, particularly on the Lisbon–Berne leg of the journey, was difficult – in part due to Switzerland's complete encirclement by Axis forces following the Nazi occupation of Vichy France in November 1942. Space was also tight in the British diplomatic bag, and PWE material appears to have taken second place to Foreign Office and MoI papers which were seen as more important or respectable. Wiskemann was still receiving copies of *La Revue de la Presse Libre* and *La France Libre* the following April, when it appears material was also being sent for local reproduction as well as distribution.

It appears that the greatest impediments to Wiskemann's work were posed not by hostile enemy actors but by figures within the walls of the Berne Legation. Although she got on well with Kelly and with Arthur 'Boofy' Gore (Lord Arran), Assistant Press Attaché at the legation until his transfer to Lisbon in early 1941, relations with other members of the legation were less than harmonious. It is possible that Wiskemann had a combustible or rebarbative personality – she was reportedly 'on vile terms' with an SOE representative in Berne – but both her memoir and the PWE papers suggest that her gender presented the main problem.⁶⁴ The grinding casual sexism experienced by Wiskemann during her wartime career is indicated by her recollection of being vetted by a senior British security official who told her that she was 'not nearly such a fool as he had expected a woman would be'.⁶⁵ At the legation in Berne, she felt that for the first time since Cambridge she was 'up against serious resentment of an independent female'.⁶⁶ Writing to Bruce Lockhart in August 1942, she complained of a 'fresh outburst of misogyny' at the legation and asked him to 'have a word' with Minister of Information Brendan Bracken.⁶⁷ Although Wiskemann's gender very likely assisted her in some contexts to gather information without raising suspicions, it appears to have prevented her from being given a better-defined operational role in disseminating black propaganda. In March 1942, the PWE discussed sending an official representative to Switzerland, outside the auspices of the MoI, who would disseminate rumours through Swiss newspapers or by word of mouth 'in conversation with Swiss business men' and would undertake the production and dissemination of 'subversive literature'. The memo further suggested that this putative agent – significantly imagined using male pronouns – could move in less-elevated 'working-class' social circles to Wiskemann.[68] The appointment was never made, however. Wiskemann appears to have posed challenges to two intersecting fields – diplomacy and intelligence – which proved notoriously hostile to women until the later decades of the twentieth century.

The other main problem Wiskemann faced was that of overwork. She recalled in her memoir that at the time of her reappointment it had been 'vaguely presumed that I could find assistants in Switzerland'.[69] Before returning to Switzerland, she wrote to Leeper in August 1941 that she worried about how to do everything that Woburn had asked for since she had been given enough work for 'a team of 10 of me'; the following month she suggested she had been assigned duties suitable for twenty.[70] These problems appear to have continued for the duration of Wiskemann's posting, and the files feature repeated requests for assistance. In September 1944, she reported that she had been 'overworking for three years, practically without leave'.[71] Despite these pressures, towards the end of the war she appears to have harboured some hopes of continuing in the field: just prior to VE Day, she wrote to London noting that the US Office of War Information representatives in Berne were 'full of plans for carrying on here' and asked whether there were any similar plans for the British to maintain an operation in Switzerland.[72] There were not, and Wiskemann left Switzerland to return to London on 26 June 1945.[73]

Conclusion

Garnett's confident assertion that Wiskemann was 'unaware of the extent and nature of PWE Black propaganda and of the way in which much of her material was used' suggests that the gendered nature of covert wartime service has been recapitulated in its historiography: given her numerous contacts in various branches and at all levels of the PWE, it is difficult to believe that she was completely in the dark about these activities, and as we have seen, references to rumours specifically feature repeatedly in her reports to London.[74] If Wiskemann's wartime career points to the chauvinism in the fields of intelligence and diplomacy at this time, it also presents an intriguing picture of the type and extent of work carried out by PWE field officers in neutral countries and shows how the gossip on which black propaganda campaigns – and specifically rumours or 'sibs' – depended was sourced. Finally, her activities highlight the value of neutral Switzerland as a staging post in the wartime exchange of information and disinformation.

Notes

1. The UK National Archives, Kew (hereafter TNA), Foreign Office files (hereafter FO) 898/256, David V. Kelly to H.L. d'A. Hopkinson, 16 April 1941. The files of the Political Warfare Executive are held at the UK National Archives in the FO 898 series; most of the files referred to in this chapter have been digitized by Gale for the "Archives Unbound" database. Available online: https://www.gale.com/intl/primary-sources/archives-unbound (accessed 27 April 2022). For more on the transitions from EH to SO1 to the PWE, see David Garnett, *The Secret History of PWE: The Political Warfare Executive 1939–1945* (London: St Ermin's Press, 2002), 1–73.
2. Elizabeth Wiskemann, *The Europe I Saw* (New York: St. Martin's Press, 1968), 141.
3. Geoffrey Field, 'Elizabeth Wiskemann, Scholar-Journalist, and the Study of International Relations', in *Women's International Thought: A New History*, ed. Patricia Owens and Katharina Rietzler (Cambridge: Cambridge University Press, 2021), 206.
4. Wiskemann, *Europe*, 18.
5. Ibid., 36.
6. Ibid., 59.
7. Ibid., 139.
8. Ibid.
9. TNA, FO 898/256, Kelly to Hopkinson, 16 April 1941.
10. TNA, FO 898/256, Anon to Stevens, 11 August 1941.
11. TNA, FO 898/256, Kelly to Hopkinson, 16 April 1941; Wiskemann, *Europe*, 141.
12. Wiskemann, *Europe*, 147.
13. TNA, FO 898/256, telegram from Elizabeth Wiskemann, 12 February 1941.
14. Wiskemann, *Europe*, 153.
15. TNA, FO 898/256, Wiskemann to Rex Leeper, 19 August 1941.
16. Wiskemann, *Europe*, 155.
17. TNA, FO 898/256, telegram from Sir R. Campbell to Foreign Office, 23 April 1941; TNA, FO 898/256, Wiskemann to Thomas Barman, 25 April 1941; Nigel West notes that Winsor was 'a key figure in the local SIS station and formerly a member of the pre-war SIS station in Zurich', see Nigel West, *Historical Dictionary of British Intelligence* (Lanham: Rowman & Littlefield, 2014), 419.
18. TNA, FO 898/256, memo by H.V., 25 April 1941.
19. TNA, FO 898/256, Anon to Walter Adams, n.d.
20. TNA, FO 898/256, Wiskemann to Barman, 25 April 1941.
21. TNA, FO 898/256, Wiskemann to Leeper, 23 June 1941.
22. TNA, FO 898/256, Wiskemann to R. H. Bruce Lockhart, 4 August 1941; Stephen Dorril, *MI6: Inside the Covert World of Her Majesty's Secret Intelligence Service* (New York: Touchstone, 2000), 140.
23. TNA, FO 898/256, Leeper to Walter Stewart Roberts, 29 August 1941.
24. TNA, FO 898/256, Michael Balfour to P. W. S. Y. Scarlett, 13 August 1941.
25. TNA, FO 898/256, Wiskemann to Nigel Sutton, 21 October 1941.
26. Wiskemann, *Europe*, 157.
27. TNA, FO 898/256, Balfour to Gage, 12 September 1942.
28. TNA, FO 898/256, Wiskemann to Balfour, 28 October 1942.
29. TNA, FO 371/34873, Foreign Office minute, 'Switzerland: Position of Miss Wiskemann', 11 January 1943.
30. Wiskemann, *Europe*, 161.

31 TNA, FO 898/256, Wiskemann to Sutton, 26 October 1941.
32 Wiskemann, *Europe*, 159.
33 Ibid.
34 TNA, FO 898/256, Berne to Foreign Office, 1 December 1942, 3 December 1942, 5 December 1942 and 9 December 1942.
35 TNA, FO 898/256, Berne to Foreign Office, 4 December 1942.
36 Wiskemann, *Europe*, 171.
37 TNA, FO 898/256, Anon to Hubert Howard, 16 September 1942.
38 TNA, FO 898/256, Wiskemann to Balfour, 26 August 1942.
39 TNA, FO 898/256, Wiskemann to Sutton, 21 October 1941; Sutton to Wiskemann, 4 November 1941.
40 Garnett, *PWE*, 142.
41 TNA, FO 898/256, Adams to Ivone Kirkpatrick, 11 May 1942.
42 TNA, FO 371/34382, telegram from Berne to Foreign Office, 4 February 1943.
43 TNA, FO 898/256, note by Wiskemann, 8 August 1942.
44 TNA, FO 898/256, note by Wiskemann, 29 October 1941.
45 John Baker White, *The Big Lie* (London: Evans Brothers, 1955), 105. Correspondence from November 1942 indicates that Baker White was also involved in sending propaganda material to Wiskemann for distribution. See TNA, FO 898/256, memo from Baker White to G.S.O. (Country), 2 November 1942.
46 The word derives from the Latin *sibillare*, meaning to hiss or whisper. See Sefton Delmer, *Black Boomerang: An Autobiography: Volume Two* (London: Secker & Warburg, 1962), 66.
47 TNA, FO 898/256, Berne to Foreign Office, 27 November 1942.
48 TNA, FO 898/256, Berne to Foreign Office, 19 December 1942.
49 TNA, FO 898/256, Sutton to Adams, 25 April 1942.
50 TNA, FO 898/108, 'Notes on German Black', n.d.
51 TNA, FO 898/256, Balfour to Scarlett, 13 August 1942; TNA, FO 898/256, Balfour to J. Arrow, 21 October 1942.
52 TNA, FO 898/256, Miss Maxwell to Balfour, 15 September 1942.
53 TNA, FO 898/35, 'P.W.I. Directorate: Report for 1944', 20 January 1944.
54 TNA, FO 898/108, 'Reply to Points Raised in David Bowes Lyon's Letter of 21st January', n.d.
55 TNA, FO 898/257, Clifton Child to Lt. Col. Kerr, 12 August 1944.
56 TNA, FO 898/257, Delmer to Kerr, 11 December 1944. A handwritten note by Kerr casts doubt on the severity of his judgement, however, describing it as a 'slice of vitriol'. See TNA, FO 898/257, note signed by Kerr, 16 December 1944.
57 TNA, FO 898/61, minutes of PWE (Enemy & Satellite) 'Black' meeting, 16 November 1944.
58 TNA, FO 898/256, Adams to Scarlett, 25 June 1942.
59 TNA, FO 898/256, MoI to Berne, 11 July 1942.
60 TNA, FO 898/256, 'Extract from Letter of August 11th, 1942, from Miss Wiskemann to Mr. Roberts'.
61 TNA, FO 898/256, Wiskemann to Adams, 29 May 1942.
62 TNA, FO 898/256, David Alexander to H. A. Paniguian, 21 October 1942.
63 TNA, FO 898/256, Paniguian to Scarlett, 22 October 1942.
64 TNA, FO 898/256, Balfour to Scarlett, 13 August 1942.
65 Wiskemann, *Europe*, 140.
66 Ibid., 141–2.

67 TNA, FO 898/256, Wiskemann to R. H. Bruce Lockhart, 4 August 1941.
68 TNA, FO 898/256, 'Memorandum on Work to be Performed for P.W.E. in Switzerland', n.d.
69 Wiskemann, *Europe*, 157.
70 TNA, FO 898/256, Wiskemann to Leeper, 19 August 1941; Wiskemann to Leeper, [obscured] September 1941.
71 TNA, FO 898/257, Wiskemann to 'the General Secretary P.W.E.', 21 September 1944.
72 TNA, FO 898/257, Wiskemann to Kerr, 5 May 1945.
73 Wiskemann, *Europe*, 203.
74 Garnett, *PWE*, 142.

8

Propaganda and Vichy France's 'neutrality'

The impossible challenge

Richard Carswell

In May 1940, German armed forces invaded the Benelux countries[1] and France, resulting in the capitulation of the Netherlands and Belgium, the German annexation of Luxembourg, the expulsion of the British Expeditionary Force from the continent and the conclusion of armistices between France, on the one hand, and Germany and Italy, on the other. The armistices came into force on 25 June, six and a half weeks after the start of the German military offensive.

In order to dissuade the French government under Marshal Philippe Pétain from moving abroad and continuing the war, Hitler allowed France to retain its navy and its empire. Nevertheless, the other terms of the armistice were onerous and severely constrained France's room for manoeuvre, politically, economically and militarily. Three-fifths of metropolitan France, including the whole of the Atlantic seaboard and Channel coast, were to be occupied by German forces. The unoccupied zone was confined to the poorer south and east of the country – including the small spa town of Vichy, where the French government moved in July 1940. The artificially inflated costs of the German occupation were to be borne by the French state, a huge burden on its economy. France's official representatives were obliged to cooperate with the occupying authorities in the administration of the occupied zone. Nearly two million French prisoners of war (PoWs) were to be kept in captivity pending the conclusion of a peace treaty, in effect hostages. France's army was reduced to 100,000 men, only enough to maintain law and order. Its navy and air force were to be disarmed under Axis supervision.[2]

In addition to the simple division of the country into occupied and unoccupied zones – separated by a rigidly regulated demarcation line, a sort of internal frontier – the Germans also hived off other areas for different administrative treatment and potential annexation. The departments of the Nord and Pas de Calais came under the direct authority of the German military commander in Brussels. Ignoring the formal terms of the armistice, the Germans annexed Alsace-Lorraine and expelled those sections of the local population considered undesirable. In short, metropolitan France became a 'jigsaw puzzle' which was extremely difficult for the Vichy government to control.³ Article 3 of the armistice agreement gave the Reich 'all the rights of the occupying power'. Moreover, it specified that 'the French government will immediately invite all the French authorities and administrative services of the occupied territory to comply with the regulations of the German authorities and collaborate with them in a correct manner'.⁴ Unlike other countries occupied by Germany, theoretically the French government's writ ran over the whole of France, but, in practice, the country's territorial sovereignty was subverted.⁵ Under Article 10 of the armistice agreement, the French government undertook 'to commit in future no hostile act against the German Reich with any part of the armed forces left to it or in any other way'. The article also prohibited French arms and forces being transferred to Britain or abroad. All French citizens were forbidden to fight for any state at war against Germany.⁶

This chapter will explore how the Vichy government tried to assert itself as a neutral power through its policies and propaganda, but that ultimately it was unable to resolve this impossible challenge due to German pressure and occupation and ultimately by the actions of the Allies in Syria, North Africa and on the beaches of Normandy.

Vichy 'out of the war'

Marshal Pétain's government was officially recognized by Germany and internationally. At various stages in its brief history, Vichy France had formal diplomatic relations with some thirty-four countries, including Canada, the Vatican, the Soviet Union and the United States, but not Britain. These countries' embassies followed the government to Vichy. Abroad, where Vichy was recognized diplomatically, France's embassies continued to operate more or less as before.⁷

Britain, by contrast, recognized Charles de Gaulle's 'Free French', in exile in London. De Gaulle appealed on British Broadcasting Corporation (BBC) radio to French servicemen and women in Britain and elsewhere to join him in pursuing the war. De Gaulle argued that the fall of metropolitan France was but one battle in a world war which the Allies would ultimately win. For him and his very small band of followers, the armistice was not only a shameful act, it was a fundamental mistake.⁸

However, officially Pétain's France had now withdrawn from the war. Vichy classed itself as neutral and soon became an authoritarian country. In July 1940 – amid the chaos of military defeat, millions displaced and widespread administrative breakdown – France's national assembly delegated plenary constitutional powers to Marshal Pétain. The assembly was then mothballed, and the Third Republic ceased to exist. The old political parties were soon banned. Pétain was the Hero of Verdun in the First World War and the man who now in the country's hour of need had made 'a gift to France of his person to mitigate her misfortune'.⁹ Who better to embody and revive the country than Marshal Pétain? In the words of the slogan on a poster featuring a portrait of the marshal: 'Are you more French than him?'¹⁰

Pétain declared himself head of the new French state. The ideology of the new regime was based on traditional social hierarchies, a wise leader, conservative values and a powerful state. The motto of the defunct republic *Liberté, Égalité, Fraternité* [Liberty, Equality, Fraternity] was replaced by *Travail, Famille, Patrie* [Work, Family,

Homeland]. France had erred and now had to rebuild morally and materially. Such was the aim of Vichy's so-called National Revolution.¹¹ It was an ideological project, antidemocratic in character and therefore antithetical in principle to the liberal democracy of the Allies.

The National Revolution would depend on France staying out of the war. Vichy's strategic thinking was dominated by two grand assumptions. First, a resumption of French participation in the war would create dangerous social upheaval in France. Second, the war was a European war, not a global one; it would end soon. Britain would sue for peace, while Germany would determine the future of the continent. For Pétain and Vichy, neutrality was the means by which to safeguard France's sovereignty and preserve its new internal political organization. France had to avoid war and find its proper place in Hitler's New Order. Vichy believed that, come the negotiation of a final peace treaty with Germany, it had two valuable bargaining chips: France's empire and its navy. Many in Vichy's elite believed that, despite what they claimed was the decadence of the Third Republic as the cause of the military defeat, France was still a great nation, albeit in need of repair.¹²

Neutrality and propaganda

Like all authoritarian governments and dictatorships, Vichy controlled the media. It inherited a governmental information service, which it upgraded and expanded with the aim of influencing public opinion.¹³ It wielded the tools of persuasion, censorship, sanction and propaganda. News agencies, press, radio and cinema were subjected to detailed control by the regime. They were expected to conform to 'guidance' on how to present the news and which stories to run and which to omit. Thus, for example, newspapers were ordered to lay out news items on their pages according to a specified format. The press was also required to insert articles prepared by the government. The result was a dull uniformity across the whole of the press, although it was possible to read between the lines and detect differences of nuance between those newspapers fully behind the regime and those which were sceptical.¹⁴

Propaganda was crafted to mobilize support for the regime, in particular, to glorify Pétain, to proselytize the National Revolution, to stress the beneficial results of collaboration with Germany and to defend the regime's legitimacy against those who, like de Gaulle's Free French, contested it.¹⁵ Its conservative values were exemplified by the accent on family values and youth as the future of the country. A poster of Pétain depicts him seated with two young girls and has the strapline 'the Marshal protects the family'.¹⁶ Equally significantly, according to the regime, France's national community had to be defended against the country's internal and external enemies: Jews, freemasons, communists and the Anglo-Americans.¹⁷

As Dominique Rossignol outlines, Vichy's propaganda – as distinct from the German-controlled propaganda emanating from the occupied zone – was coordinated officially by Vichy's Ministry of Information, headed for the majority of the period by Paul Marion – although a number of other leading figures of the Vichy regime, such as Bernard Ménétrel, Paul Creyssel, Pierre Laval and Philippe Henriot, also had

Figure 8.1 '*N'oubliez pas Oran!*' [Don't forget Oran!], Vichy French poster, *c*. 1940. Courtesy Getty Images.

significant influence and roles to play.[18] Vichy's propaganda maintained that France's neutrality and independence were intertwined. 'La France seule' ['France alone'] had to concentrate on itself. It had no need of foreign entanglements, as they had brought disaster. France had to rebuild the country shattered by a war criminally embarked upon by the warmongers of the Third Republic, duped by the former British Prime Minister Neville Chamberlain and the moneyed interests of the City of London. After all, it was Britain and France which had declared war on Germany. In the words of an instruction issued by Vichy's censorship authorities in December 1940: 'For the time being, France is passing through a period of withdrawal. All that she can do is observe the unfolding of world events, while at the same time pressing ahead with her material and moral reconstruction.'[19]

Vichy's propaganda initially ignored the outside world.[20] In its cinema newsreels, it was as if the rest of the world scarcely existed. France was depicted as a land of serenity, almost alone on the planet. Occasionally there were reports about neighbouring Spain and Switzerland, both, of course, neutral countries themselves. When momentous events elsewhere were impossible to disregard, the tone of Vichy's news reports was detached.[21] But, whether it liked it or not, Vichy was caught in the middle of the continuing war between Britain and Germany.[22] Britain imposed an economic blockade on France and its empire, in order to prevent goods passing to Germany. British fears that the French naval fleet would come under German control led to the seizure of French ships in British ports, the neutralizing of the French squadron at Alexandria (Egypt) and, most spectacularly of all, the Royal Navy shelling ships of the French fleet at anchorage at Mers el-Kébir near Oran (Algeria), in July 1940, killing nearly 1,300 French sailors. Vichy broke off the diplomatic relations that France had had with Britain and bombed Gibraltar several times, although without causing any casualties.[23] Vichy's propaganda would make much of the British attack at Mers el-Kébir (see Figure 8.1).

The fact was that Vichy's claim to be a great power was illusory. Vichy could neither escape the war nor defend metropolitan France and its empire.[24] All three armed forces were weakened by the terms of the armistice. At any moment, Germany could revoke the agreement if it deemed France was not in compliance. In short, France had surrendered its ability to follow an independent foreign policy.

The French Empire

As part of its assertion that France was still a great power, Vichy's propaganda made much of France's imperial pre-eminence.[25] And, indeed, together with its protectorates and mandates, France's empire was the second largest in the world at the time, stretching from islands in the Caribbean and North Atlantic, to North Africa, large parts of West and Equatorial Africa, trading posts in India, the whole of Indo-China and islands in the Pacific. Typical Vichy propaganda slogans included 'The empire: secret of the nation's survival' and 'The empire: guarantee of France's future'.[26]

The message was intended to remind the French people of the country's civilizing mission and of the empire's vastness and rich resources which contributed to France's greatness. Propaganda was directed particularly to the cream of the nation's youth, to divert their attention from the difficulties at home and to stimulate their potential interest in a career in the colonies.[27]

Figure 8.2 'Dakar-Mers El-Kébir', Vichy French poster, October 1940. Courtesy Getty Images.

But the French Empire was prey to predators, the Free French and others, including Spain in North Africa and Japan in Indo-China.[28] And despite the armistices, Germany and Italy, too, had their designs on France's imperial possessions.[29] Vichy was constrained to make concessions to Japan and was forced to accept American limitations on its fleet and colonies in the western Atlantic and Caribbean. Yet, Vichy's orders to its imperial governors and military commanders were to resist *all* attempts by *all* outsiders to encroach on France's overseas territories. This posture was partly a consequence of its suspicions that the Allies wanted to confiscate France's possessions. Moreover, as Peter Jackson and Simon Kitson remark, 'in order to fulfil France's armistice obligations, Vichy officials had no choice but to resist any Allied attack on its possessions in Africa and the Mediterranean'.[30]

The French Empire was soon under attack. Although they had a foothold in Britain, it was vital for the Free French to secure a French territorial base if they were to claim any form of political legitimacy.[31] Assisted by the British, the Free French secured their first territorial base by capturing the colonies of French Equatorial Africa and the French mandate of Cameroun in August 1940. The following month the British and the Free French attempted to land at Dakar in modern-day Senegal, to occupy French West Africa. They failed in the face of armed resistance by the local forces loyal to Vichy.[32] In 1941, British and Free French forces overran the French mandate of Syria. In 1942, British forces landed in the French colony of Madagascar. And later that year they and the Americans landed in French North Africa. In short, Vichy's neutrality was nullified by the Allies. Their policies and actions served to aggravate Vichy's underlying Anglophobia, which was reflected in its propaganda. A poster (see Figure 8.2) entitled 'Dakar-Mers El-Kébir' portrays a grotesque, smirking Churchill contemplating the smouldering ruins of French naval vessels and the crosses on the graves of the dead French servicemen.[33]

Collaboration

That Vichy's neutrality was ambiguous is also evident from its policy of collaboration with Germany. Vichy was sure that Germany would win the war and shape the European peace that followed. The Reich would therefore decide France's place in the new continental order. In the minds of many of Vichy's leaders – but not all – collaboration would secure a position for France in a German-dominated Europe that was commensurate with France's status as an imperial power. It was also vital for Vichy that the final peace treaty should remove the very heavy burden of the armistice terms weighing down on the country, its economy and its people. For the Germans, however, collaboration was seen in quite a different light. Collaboration meant keeping France on a leash and gaining access to French economic resources, in order to boost Germany's war economy. It also meant putting pressure on Vichy to give Germany military logistical support in the French Empire.[34]

Vichy's policy of collaboration became public knowledge as a result of the widely reported meeting between Pétain and Hitler at Montoire in central-northern France on 24 October 1940 (see Figure 8.3).[35] The regime was soon aware that French public opinion was taken aback by the meeting and by the notion of collaborating with the

Figure 8.3 Pétain and Hitler shaking hands at Montoire, 24 October 1940. Courtesy Getty Images.

erstwhile enemy.[36] Public opinion was assessed monthly by Vichy's prefects in both the occupied and unoccupied zones. Their assessments were based on information gleaned by the security services, the police and other official bodies and by means of listening to gossip, phone-tapping and intercepting postal correspondence.[37] Pétain justified his decision to meet Hitler in a radio broadcast on 30 October. He had agreed to the principle of collaboration, he declared, in order to preserve French unity and the empire and to lessen the burdens of the armistice. He alone took responsibility for the decision and he would be judged by history.[38] In the event, the Montoire meeting turned out to be essentially symbolic, since little concrete by way of practical collaboration ensued.[39] Nevertheless, Vichy tried to make capital out of it by appearing to put France and Germany on an equal footing. One poster depicted Pétain and Hitler shaking hands on a deserted battlefield, with the inscription summarizing the theme of the Marshal's radio broadcast: 'It is with honour that today I embark on the process of collaboration. Marshal Pétain.'[40]

Vichy's search for collaboration was based on pragmatic considerations of France's economic needs and the future of French PoWs in German camps. But it was also the product of a generalized Anglophobia and atavistic hatred and fear of British imperialism. Two of Vichy's leading figures – both vice-presidents under Pétain at various times – Pierre Laval and Admiral François Darlan were Anglophobes. But as it became clear in 1940–1 that Britain would not make peace with Germany and that the war was not coming to an end, French public opinion turned largely in favour of the Allied cause.[41] This change acted as a brake on Vichy's policymakers.

At various stages during the war, the Germans tried to persuade Vichy to declare war on Britain and, at one point, even on America. That such a fateful step was not taken was due as much to Hitler's changing priorities and deep-seated mistrust of France, as it was to internal divisions among Vichy's leaders and the regime's ministerial instability and incoherence. The British and Americans tried to persuade Vichy to abrogate the armistice and resume the fight against Germany. Pétain refused both sides, partly due to the inertia of old age. More important was his belief that rejoining war would bring social disorder and benefit France's internal enemies, the freemasons, Jews and communists.[42]

How did Vichy's policy of collaboration compromise France's neutrality? In essence, economic collaboration strengthened the German economy and thus prolonged the war. Military collaboration provided Germany with the logistical support which it would not otherwise have had. A good example of the latter were the airfields in Syria offered to German aircraft in May 1941, as part of an operation to assist the anti-British rebellion in Iraq, although the rebellion was quickly put down by the British.[43] At first, Vichy viewed the German attack on the Soviet Union in June 1941 with the same detached eye as it viewed the outside world. Radio Vichy announced the invasion as an event 'of great importance' whose outcome was 'unpredictable'.[44] Its reports on the opening campaigns were dispassionate, as if describing something in the historic past. It was a characteristic evasion of reality. But, under German pressure, Vichy broke off diplomatic relations with the Soviet Union. And, in time, Vichy became more open in its support for the campaign against the Soviet Union and it provided Germany with moral and practical support. On 22 June 1942, Laval went so far as to declare on radio that 'I desire a German victory because, without it, bolshevism would take hold everywhere'.[45]

During 1942, it became clear that the German war in the east against the Soviet Union would last longer than originally anticipated. Germany would require more manpower and resources if it was to seal its victory. One consequence was that it intensified its exploitation of the economies under its domination, the richest of which was France. The country became Germany's milch cow. This was the inevitable logic of Vichy's policy of state collaboration with Germany. The baleful result was the growing material hardship suffered by the French people. The Germans pillaged the economy and put pressure on Vichy to supply French labour to replace the German workers drafted into the armed forces to fight on the Eastern Front. Under the scheme known as La Relève [The Relief], Vichy offered to send three skilled workers to Germany in return for every one French PoW repatriated to France. Because the Germans soon demanded more, Vichy also established a compulsory work scheme, the Service du Travail Obligatoire [Compulsory Labour Service].[46]

Propaganda and its contradictions

By 1941–2, it was impossible for Vichy's propaganda to ignore the full reality of the international situation. France alone, the impartial observer of world events, became France the victim. Vichy claimed that the British were punishing innocent victims by making the French people go hungry. Why French men, women and children

Figure 8.4 '*L'Europe en marche contre le bolshevisme*' [Europe on the march against Bolshevism], Vichy French poster, c. 1942. Courtesy Getty Images.

were short of food – because the Germans were requisitioning French agricultural produce – was left unsaid. In the minds of Vichy's policymakers, the British economic blockade, the Allied encroachments on the French Empire and the menace of Soviet communism became conflated. When in March 1942 the Royal Air Force bombed Boulogne-Billancourt near Paris, targeting the Renault factory producing tanks for the German Army, Vichy's censorship authorities ordered the press to use the following headline: 'The English and the Communists unite to assassinate France'.[47]

From Vichy's point of view, worse was to come. On 8 November 1942, the Americans and British landed in French North Africa (under the codename 'Operation Torch'). After a brief bout of fighting, French North Africa switched sides and joined the Allies. In retaliation, the Germans occupied the rest of metropolitan France within days (i.e. the area nominally under the control of the Vichy regime and previously unoccupied by Germany). Vichy may have been a sovereign nation on paper. Now it became nothing more than a puppet regime manipulated by the Germans. More and more countries closed their embassies in Vichy.[48]

With metropolitan France under total occupation, Vichy's propaganda was subjected to German control, to the extent that it was barely possible to differentiate between Vichy and Nazi propaganda. By now, Germany and Vichy needed each other even more: Germany needed France's economic resources. Vichy needed German troops on French soil to guarantee its survival as a regime. From London, the Free French and the BBC urged the French people to avoid contributing to the German war economy by working in Germany or for the Germans in France.[49] Vichy's propagandists, on the other hand, highlighted the benefits of working in Germany and the service to France. In a poster showing a hand clasping a key, the message was clear: 'You have the key to the camps. French workers: you free prisoners by working in Germany.'[50] Vichy also put up posters in praise of the German soldiers on the Eastern Front: 'They give their blood. Give your work to save Europe from Bolshevism.'[51] The fight against communism was not just Germany's battle. It was now a united European crusade, France included (see Figure 8.4).

Liberation or civil war?

In the east, German armed forces were now being pushed back, following the Battle of Stalingrad in February 1943. Yet the intensity of Vichy's antipathy to communism and liberal democracy goes some way to explain why the regime continued to favour collaboration, even as a Germany victory in the east became more and more elusive. Moreover, in the West, it would not be long before France faced invasion by the Allies. But, according to Vichy's propaganda, invasion would not bring liberation. It would foster Bolshevism, the great enemy.[52] While attacking Anglo-American liberal democracy would not be credible, it could assert that Bolshevism would lead to civil war, and civil war was being stoked by France's internal resistance – deemed terrorists by Vichy and the Germans – and by the Allies' bombing of the country.

The ablest and most notorious exponent of Vichy's propaganda was the new Minister of Information, Philippe Henriot, appointed early in 1944.[53] Described by the

French Resistance as the 'merchant of terror', Henriot used his talks on the radio twice a day to describe in blood-curdling detail the effects of the Allied bombing of France – bombing which intensified as D-Day approached in June 1944. At first, Henriot dismissed the likelihood of an Allied invasion as hot air, bluff on the part of Vichy's enemies. When reality could no longer be ignored, he claimed the invasion would bring not liberation but death and destruction to an innocent – and neutral – people.[54]

Most French radio listeners did not believe Henriot, however entertaining some found his adept use of language. The documentary evidence tells us that Vichy's message fell on deaf ears for the most part. In fact, from the autumn of 1940 onwards and until France's liberation in 1944, French public opinion was largely pro-British and anti-German. Out of hatred of the Germans, even some anti-Vichy Anglophobes were pro-British. As the journalist of the catholic newspaper *La Croix*, Pierre Limagne, quipped in his notebook, 'the Anglophiles are the people who hope for the victory of "our friends the English"; the Anglophobes are the people who hope for the victory of "those English swine".'[55]

Conclusion

Ultimately, Vichy's propaganda failed to convince. The initial representation of France as an island of tranquillity in a world at war belied the fact that France was caught in the crossfire between opposing belligerents. It glossed over the traumatic upheaval of the German invasion and occupation. It portrayed Britain as the perfidious Albion[56] of old, intent vulture-like on snatching pieces of the French Empire. As the war lengthened, Vichy went on to allege that Britain and its puppet de Gaulle were in the hands of international capitalism, Jewry, freemasonry and communism.[57] It was an unlikely combination. And increasingly in step with Nazi propaganda, Vichy claimed this alliance was bent on harming France and the French people. Vichy's propaganda was ineffective externally as well. In neutral Sweden, for example, the press quickly put Vichy France into the German camp. The Swedes simply did not believe that Vichy France was a neutral country.[58]

For propaganda to be effective, it has to have an element of credibility. Vichy's propaganda was far from credible. Vichy's neutrality was at best ambiguous, at worst fiction. It is true that Vichy's room for manoeuvre was limited, given the heavy burdens of the armistice, the German occupation and the British blockade. As Jackson and Kitson have commented, 'the regime found itself waging undeclared war against the external threats posed by Britain, the British-sponsored Gaullist movement and later the United States, as well as the growing internal threat from the French resistance'.[59] It was inhibited from pursuing a more aggressive policy towards Britain, partly by French public opinion and partly by the fear of greater retaliation. However, instead of maintaining a strict neutrality, Vichy chose to collaborate with Germany and by doing so, it entered a downward spiral of making more and more concessions without receiving commensurate benefits in return. As two distinguished French historians have written, waiting for German concessions was like waiting for Godot, in a reference to the post-war play by Samuel Beckett, in which the main characters await a protagonist who never arrives.⁶⁰ Moreover, even if Vichy had wanted to join forces formally with Germany, Hitler never saw France as an ally, nor even as a satellite. Vichy's purported neutrality was even a conceit in the deluded minds of some of Pétain's supporters. As one told the resister Daniel Cordier, once the Soviets and Germans had torn themselves apart, France's neutrality, guaranteed by Pétain, would give the French 'the opportunity to be the arbiters of the peace'.⁶¹

Could Vichy have maintained a strict neutrality, if it had wanted to? Not according to one contemporary witness, Professor Denis Brogan of Cambridge University. In a research note written for the Foreign Office, he argued:

> If France were neutral like Portugal she could insist on the evacuation of her territory by the Germans. It is in Brest that the *Gneisenau* and *Scharnhorst* lie licking their wounds. Have they been forced to put to sea after the maximum delays of international law? Have the German aerodromes in northern France been demilitarised? Of course not, and we know that France cannot help this use of her soil, of her ports; it is a consequence of her disasters. But France which has to suffer these indignities, France from whose shores Germany conducts her war, cannot be neutral. For if the government of Vichy, of the so-called Free Zone disdains all responsibility for what goes on in the occupied zone, it reveals what we all know, its own impotence. There is not one France; there are two or more. None of these Frances is really neutral; some are more openly assimilated to the Nazi system than others. But that is all.
>
> . . . Real neutrality for France is impossible. The Germans will not permit it; they do not permit it. What they permit is the exploitation of legal fictions, of the discipline of the French forces, of the loyalty of the French colonists to aid them in their war. The moment that they have squeezed this orange of legal neutrality dry, they will turn on their accomplices. Can we wonder that the English, fighting for their own and for French and European deliverance from the Nazi gangsters, refuse to take their lawyers' tricks seriously? Darlan for his German client is exhausting all the resources of chicane [sic], but they do not and will not serve him. The French people sees the truth.⁶²

In short, Vichy's propaganda was bound to fail. The assertion that France was neutral could not be sustained. The assertion was a pretence, and the pretence was a challenge that was impossible to meet.

Notes

1. 'Benelux' is the portmanteau term for Belgium, the Netherlands and Luxembourg.
2. Julian Jackson, *The Fall of France: The Nazi Invasion of 1940* (Oxford: Oxford University Press, 2004); Jean-Pierre Azéma, *1940 L'Année noire* (Paris: Fayard, 2010). For a succinct overview of France in the Second World War, see Chris Millington, *France in the Second World War: Collaboration, Resistance, Holocaust, Empire* (London: Bloomsbury, 2020).

3 Alya Aglan, *La France à l'envers: la guerre de Vichy (1940–1945)* (Paris: Gallimard, 2020), 148–55.
4 Jean-Baptiste Duroselle, *Politique étrangère de la France: L'abîme 1939–1944* (Paris: Imprimerie nationale, 1986), 265–6.
5 Occupied Denmark also retained its own government. Formally speaking, the country was not occupied but under German 'protection'.
6 Duroselle, *Politique étrangère de la France*, 245–56.
7 On Vichy's unusual diplomatic status in Britain, see Nicholas Atkin, *The Forgotten French: Exiles in the British Isles 1940–1944* (Manchester: Manchester University Press, 2003).
8 For an up-to-date and comprehensive biography of de Gaulle, see Julian Jackson, *A Certain Idea of France: The Life of Charles de Gaulle* (London: Penguin, 2018).
9 Bénédicte Vergez-Chaignon, *Pétain* (Paris: Perrin, 2018), 416–17. For a short biography of Pétain in English, see Nicholas Atkin, *Pétain* (London: Longman, 1998). Translation from the French here and in later quotations by the author.
10 Stéphane Ducreux and Jean-Luc Messager, *La France et les Français dans la Seconde Guerre Mondiale* (Paris: Éditions LBM, 2014), 35.
11 For a rich analysis of Vichy's ideology, see Debbie Lackerstein, *National Regeneration in Vichy France: Ideas and Policies 1930–1944* (London: Routledge, 2012).
12 For two concise introductions to Vichy's external relations, see Robert Frank, 'Vichy et le monde, le monde et Vichy: perceptions géopolitiques et idéologiques', in *Le Régime de Vichy et les Français*, ed. Jean-Pierre Azéma and François Bédarida (Paris: Fayard, 1992), 99–121; Peter Jackson and Simon Kitson, 'The Paradoxes of Vichy Foreign Policy 1940–1942', in Jonathan *Hitler and His Allies in World War II*, ed. R. Adelman (London: Routledge, 2007), 79–115. On the notion of decadence as the cause of France's military defeat in 1940, see Richard Carswell, *The Fall of France in the Second World War: History and Memory* (London: Palgrave, 2019).
13 For a detailed account of the structural and administrative changes to the government's information service, see Philippe Amaury, *Les Deux Premières Expériences d'un Ministère de l'Information en France* (Paris: Librairie Générale de Droit et de Jurisprudence, 1969). For a brief introduction to the information service's leading personalities, see Claude Lévy and Dominique Veillon, 'Propagande et modelage d'esprits', in *Le Régime de Vichy et les Français*, ed. Jean-Pierre Azéma and François Bédarida (Paris: Fayard, 1992), 184–202.
14 Claude Lévy, 'La propagande', in *La France des années noires, vol. 2: de l'Occupation à la Libération*, ed. Jean-Pierre Azéma and François Bédarida (Paris: Seuil, 1993), 47–64.
15 Jean-Pierre Azéma and Olivier Wieviorka, *Vichy 1940–1944* (Paris: Perrin, 2004), 142–4.
16 David Welch, *World War II Propaganda: Analysing the Art of Persuasion during Wartime* (Santa Barbara: ABC-CLIO, 2017), 151–4.
17 Dominique Rossignol, *Histoire de la Propagande en France de 1940 à 1944: l'utopie Pétain* (Paris: Presses Universitaires de France, 1991), *passim*.
18 Ibid., 9–11.
19 Archives Nationales, Paris, F 41-107, Instructions pour les censeurs, Vichy, 26 December 1940, quoted in Aglan, *La France à l'envers*, 57.
20 Julian Jackson, *France: The Dark Years 1940–1944* (Oxford: Oxford University Press, 2001), 252–6.
21 Ibid., 255.

22 For general accounts of relations between Britain and Vichy, see R. T. Thomas, *Britain and Vichy: The Dilemma of Anglo-French Relations 1940–1942* (London: Macmillan, 1979); Warren Tute, *The Reluctant Enemies: The Story of the Last War between Britain and France 1940–1942* (London: Collins, 1990); Colin Smith, *England's Last War against France: Fighting Vichy 1940–1942* (London: Weidenfeld & Nicolson, 2009). For a wider view, see Peter Mangold, *Britain and the Defeated French: From Occupation to Liberation 1940–1944* (London: I.B. Tauris, 2011).
23 Hervé Coutau-Bégarie and Claude Huan, *Mers-el-Kébir 1940: la rupture franco-britannique* (Paris: Economica, 1994).
24 Martin Thomas, *The French Empire at War 1940–1945* (Manchester: Manchester University Press, 1998).
25 Charles-Robert Ageron, 'Vichy, les Français et l'Empire', in *Le Régime de Vichy et les Français*, ed. Jean-Pierre Azéma and François Bédarida Bédarida (Paris: Fayard, 1992), 122–34.
26 Ibid., 128.
27 Amaury, *Les Deux Premières Expériences*, 371.
28 On Spain and Morocco, see Ángel Viñas, *Sobornos: de cómo Churchill y March compraron a los generales de Franco* (Barcelona: Planeta, 2016), 166–87 and María Antonia Paz Rebollo, 'La propaganda francesa en España 1940–1944', *Mélanges de la Casa de Velázquez* XXXI, no. 3 (1995): 226; on Japan and Indochina, see Eric T. Jennings, *Vichy in the Tropics: Pétain's National Revolution in Madagascar, Guadeloupe and Indochina 1940–1944* (Stanford: Stanford University Press, 2002).
29 Chantal Metzger, *L'Empire colonial français dans la stratégie du Troisième Reich (1936–1945)* (Paris: Lang, 2002).
30 Jackson and Kitson, 'The Paradoxes of Vichy Foreign Policy', in *Hitler and His Allies*, ed. Jonathan Adelman (London: Routledge, 2020), 102.
31 Jean-Louis Crémieux-Brilhac, *La France Libre: de l'appel du 18 juin à la libération* (Paris: Gallimard, 1996); Eric T. Jennings, *Free French Africa in World War II: The African Resistance* (Cambridge: Cambridge University Press, 2015).
32 Hervé Coutau-Bégarie and Claude Huan, *Dakar: la bataille fratricide* (Paris: Economica, 2004).
33 Jacques Marseille and Régis Bénichi, *Les 100 dates de la France en guerre 1939–1945* (Paris: Perrin, 2004), 61.
34 François Broche and Jean-François Muracciole, *Histoire de la Collaboration 1940–1945* (Paris: Tallandier, 2017), 181–3.
35 Michèle Cointet, *Nouvelle histoire de Vichy* (Paris: Fayard, 2011), 368–71; Broche and Muracciole, *Histoire de la Collaboration*, 98–103.
36 Pierre Laborie, *L'opinion française sous Vichy: les Français et la crise d'identité nationale 1936–1944* (Paris: Éditions du Seuil, 2001), 245–7.
37 Philippe Burrin, *Living with Defeat: France under the German Occupation 1940–1944* (London: Arnold, 1996), 177–8.
38 Vergez-Chaignon, *Pétain*, 617–22.
39 Jean-Paul Cointet, *Hitler et la France* (Paris: Perrin, 2017), 248–55.
40 Rossignol, *Histoire de la Propagande en France*, 199.
41 Burrin, *Living with Defeat*, 178.
42 Cointet, *Nouvelle histoire de Vichy*, 573–86.
43 Jean-Paul Cointet, *Histoire de Vichy* (Paris: Perrin, 2003), 193–200.
44 Jackson, *France: The Dark Years*, 256.
45 Fred Kupferman, *Laval* (Paris: Tallandier, 2006), 388–91.

46 Cointet, *Histoire de Vichy*, 244–50.
47 Lévy, 'La propagande', 63.
48 Jean-François Muracciole, *La France pendant la Seconde Guerre mondiale: De la défaite à la Libération* (Paris: Le livre de poche, 2002), 444.
49 Aurélie Luneau, *Radio Londres: les voix de la liberté (1940–1944)* (Paris: Perrin, 2010), 236–46.
50 H. Roderick Kedward, 'STO et Maquis', in *La France des années noires vol. 2*, ed. Jean Pierre Azéma and François Bédarida (Paris: Seuil, 2000), 272.
51 Thomas Fontaine and Denis Peschanski, *La collaboration: Vichy, Paris, Berlin 1940–1945* (Paris: Tallandier, 2018), 221.
52 Laborie, *L'opinion française sous Vichy*, 293.
53 Kay Chadwick, 'Radio Propaganda and Public Opinion under Endgame Vichy: The Impact of Philippe Henriot', *French History* 25, no. 2 (2011): 232–52.
54 Christian Delporte, *Philippe Henriot: la résistible ascension d'un provocateur* (Paris: Flammarion, 2018), 291–6.
55 Pierre Limagne, *Éphémérides de quatre années tragiques 1940–1944* (Lavilledieu: Éditions du candide, 1987), 47.
56 The phrase 'perfidious Albion' has been used to describe British foreign policy since at least the seventeenth century, denoting self-interest, and often in relation to Anglo-French relations but also more broadly, including in the propaganda of Nazi Germany. See H. D. Schmidt, 'The Idea and Slogan of "Perfidious Albion"', *Journal of the History of Ideas* 14, no. 4 (1953): 604–16.
57 Tim Brooks, *British Propaganda to France 1940–1944: Machinery, Method and Message* (Edinburgh: Edinburgh University Press, 2007), 116.
58 Frank, 'Vichy et le monde, le monde et Vichy', 117.
59 Jackson and Kitson, 'The Paradoxes of Vichy Policy', 102.
60 Azéma and Wieviorka, *Vichy 1940–1944*, 53–5.
61 Daniel Cordier, *Alias Caracalla* (Paris: Gallimard, 2009), 550.
62 Imperial War Museum, London (IWM), 92/25/1, Brogan, *The Fiction of French Neutrality*, Research Unit (Overseas), Report No. 6, undated but probably 1941.

9

Turkey's struggle for neutrality and the surveillance of Nazi propaganda

Yasemin Türkkan Tunalı* and Yasemin Doğaner

The Lausanne Peace Treaty – an agreement that recognized the sovereignty and integrity of modern Turkey in 1923 – ushered in a new era for rational, realistic and most importantly, peaceful Turkish foreign policy. With its transition from an empire to a nation state after the period of *Millî Mücadele* ['the National Struggle'],[1] Turkey needed an environment of peace and stability for the political, economic and social revolutions to settle. The principle of maintaining the status quo and peaceful international relations served as a basis for the position adopted by Turkey in the Second World War. However, this 'state policy' was determined by a very narrow cadre holding the decision-making authority.[2] After the death of Mustafa Kemal Atatürk, the founding father and first president of the Republic of Turkey, in November 1938, his closest associate, İsmet İnönü, was elected president and also became chairman of the Cumhuriyet Halk Partisi (CHP) [the Republican People's Party]. To fill the potential power vacuum that could have arisen in the absence of a charismatic leader, İnönü took the necessary steps to establish his authority both within the party and at the state level. Thus, in this period of one-party rule – in which deputy candidates were determined by CHP – the Grand National Assembly of Turkey, the party group and the Council of Ministers all became extensions of İnönü's political administration. In addition, the press was prevented from interfering with politics and controlled through the amendments to the Press Law of 1931 and the enactment of the Press Union Law in 1938.[3] Likewise, the absence of non-governmental organizations and the low participation of the masses in politics[4] helped the concentration of the decision-making at the state's highest level. Consequently, by 1939, President İnönü himself emerged as the authoritarian leader, who was the master of both the domestic and foreign policy of Turkey. With the outbreak of the Second World War, his foreign policy was directed towards maintaining a neutrality that would distance Turkey from any armed conflict – a policy that was also shared by the Turkish political elite. The inadequacy of the military, the lack of armaments production and the inability of the country's economy to withstand a new conflict were realities that no one could ignore.

In addition to the points above, a new factor presented a further challenge to the Turkish administration: the emergence of war propaganda. In fact, with the Nazi

Party coming to power, Germany had begun to make inroads into Turkish education, industry and economy to influence Turkish public opinion and foreign policy even before the Second World War. The participation of the Allied powers in this trend with the onset of the armed conflict turned Turkey into a propaganda battleground of the warring states. The Turkish administration cautiously monitored these propaganda activities with its intelligence network and developed control mechanisms to try to limit their effects as much as possible. This chapter will explore Turkey's struggle for neutrality within this context as well as the Nazi propaganda organization in Turkey, its methods and aims reflected in Turkish intelligence reports, and present the measures taken by the Turkish authorities during the Second World War.

The construction and maintenance of Turkish neutrality

Italy's expansionist movements in the Eastern Mediterranean[5] and militarization of the Dodecanese Islands, just off the Turkish coast, prompted Turkey to take a number of initiatives. These included signing of the Montreux Convention[6] in 1936, which ensured Turkey's full sovereignty over the Straits of the Dardanelles and the Bosphorus that joined the Mediterranean and Black Seas, and also the Non-aggression pacts with its Balkan and Eastern neighbours through the Balkan Entente[7] in 1934 and the Saadabad Pact[8] in 1937. Moreover, the Italian invasion of Albania in April 1939 brought together Turkey and Britain, and on 12 May 1939, the two states signed a Joint Declaration which established cooperation in case of an armed conflict in the Mediterranean. On 23 June 1939, Turkey signed a new agreement with France, which expanded the military alliance with the Allies against the Axis, with an expectation that the Soviets would soon join to complete the circle.[9]

However, the signing of the German–Soviet Non-aggression Pact on 23 August 1939 left Turkey no choice but to conclude its alliance with the Western states without the Soviets. Unacceptable demands made by the Soviets on Turkey regarding the Turkish Straits and its eastern borders also catalysed this decision.[10] The Treaty of Mutual Assistance signed on 19 October 1939 between Britain, France and Turkey guaranteed mutual collaboration and assistance in case of an aggression leading to a Mediterranean war. However, Protocol No. 2 of the Treaty declared that the obligations undertaken by Turkey could not compel or draw the country into an armed conflict with the Soviets (known as 'the Soviet reservation').[11] It could be argued that due to the military obligations imposed by the Treaty, Turkey was no longer a neutral state and openly joined on the side of the Allied powers.[12]

However, with the changing nature of the war, Turkey pursued a 'policy of balance' between those three powers and developed new manoeuvres to stay out of the conflict. First, the German advance on France in May 1940 and the consequent participation of Italy on the side of the Axis forced the Turkish government to refuse the British request of Turkey's entry into the war because of 'the Soviet reservation'. Turkey once again responded negatively to the same request after Italy attacked Greece in October 1940. In this period, Turkish authorities tried to persuade both sides of the war of the benefits of Turkey's neutrality.[13] Obviously, the main factor that motivated this 'policy of balance' was the rapid defeat of France by Germany and the consequential French withdrawal from the war. In the meantime, Germany – which stopped German–Turkish trade completely in August 1939, in response to the joint Turkish–British–French declarations[14] – decided it was in its interests to refrain from pushing Turkey further towards the Allies. The revival of Turkish–German military–commercial relations from 1941 onwards, which enabled the export of Turkish chrome at a high price in exchange for the provision of German weapons,[15] provided Turkey with leverage against the pressures of the Allied powers. The Treaty of Friendship signed with Germany on 18 June 1941 established guarantees of mutual respect for territorial integrity and provided Turkey a further gain. This was that Germany, which had previously tried to separate Turkey from the Western alliance, had to confirm during the negotiations of the treaty that it recognized Ankara's adherence to its existing alliance obligations.[16] From this time onwards, Turkey entered an 'active neutrality' period in which it continued its relationship with both sides of the war but without jeopardizing its neutral position outside the war.

Germany's attack on Russia on 22 June 1941 gave the Turkish authorities a sigh of relief as it meant neither of those two powers was likely to pose a direct threat to Turkish territory for a while.[17] However, Ankara's suspicion as to whether Britain would be ready to sacrifice Turkey to attract the Soviets to its side[18] was reinforced by the joint Anglo-Soviet invasion of Iran, convincing Turkey to maintain its neutrality more than ever before. German efforts to persuade Turkey to join its fight against the Soviets at that time made no impact on Ankara.

Since the war started turning in the Allies' favour in 1943, Turkey's game of balance faced new challenges. While Germany aimed to guarantee Turkish neutrality to keep its southern borders secure, the Allies increased their pressure for Turkey's participation in the war with the desire to use its air and ground bases in their fight against Germany. Such demands were not only considered in the conferences that took place in Casablanca, Adana, Moscow and Tehran, but also in the meeting between US President Franklin D. Roosevelt, British Prime Minister Winston Churchill and President İnönü in Cairo on 4–6 December 1943.[19]

Although at the Cairo Conference İnönü agreed in principle that Turkey would join the war, he did not commit to doing anything specific, particularly while the country was not ready for war. In the meantime, with the objective of reducing the pressure from the Allies, Turkey tried to fulfil all the requests made as long as they did not involve the risk of open hostilities. In April, Turkey stopped its chrome exports to Germany; in June, the Turkish Foreign Minister Numan Menemencioğlu – considered by the Allies to be pro-German – resigned and Turkey broke off relations with Germany on 2 August 1944.[20] Likewise, the arrest of the leading names of *Turan* [pan-Turkist] ideology[21] and the permission given to the Allied ships carrying war equipment through the Turkish Straits in November 1944 were measures taken to calm the Soviet Union's accusations and threatening policies.

These developments actually show that as of 1944, Turkey had come out of 'active neutrality' and adopted 'neutrality in favour of the Allies' designated to stay close to the Western powers, but not to enter the war until the last moment. However, this moment came on 23 February 1945, when Turkey officially – and at the same time symbolically – declared war on the Axis powers just a few weeks before the conclusion of the conflict. Four days later, on 27 February, Turkey signed the Declaration of the United Nations, becoming a founding member of the organization and integrating into the international system established by the victorious powers.[22]

It can be argued that Turkey's neutrality struggled mostly against the pressures of the Allied powers in wartime. However, until the Soviet demands at the end of 1939, Turkey believed that Germany and Italy – due to their expansionist policies and the latter's geographical proximity – posed a greater threat to its territorial integrity. For this reason, the Turkish government attached importance to the monitoring of the German propaganda and intelligence organization, which started its activities in Turkey some time before the war. The general attitude of the Turkish administration towards the propaganda organizations of the warring states was to ensure that their activities and impacts on the Turkish public opinion remained within such limits that would not endanger the Turkish neutrality.

German propaganda in Turkey

The Turkish authorities' policy to balance the Allied and Axis powers at the level of interstate relations also required them to keep a close eye on their propaganda and intelligence activities in Turkey. Britain and Germany took the lead in the propaganda struggle which started immediately after the outbreak of the war.[23] In fact, Germany's efforts to have an impact on Turkey went back much earlier. The memorandum titled *Policy of zones of influence – Cultural policy* prepared by Dr Kurt Köhler, Professor Oluf Krukmann and Dr Wilhelm Eliers in 1935 emphasized that the east and southeast of Europe, the Middle East and Egypt constituted a suitable zone for German *Lebensraum* [Nazi concept of further 'living space']. Therefore, a state-backed cultural propaganda campaign in Anatolia – considered as a geopolitical gateway to this area – was crucial for Germany to expand to the Middle East. The conduct and means of propaganda suggested in the report were as follows:

1. The attraction of Turkish students to education in Germany;
2. The penetration to the Turkish education system through the employment of German scientists;
3. The creation of sympathy for Germany among Turkish students (both Turkish graduate–doctorate students studying in Germany and those taking lessons from German academics in Turkish universities and high schools); and
4. The use of publications and the press.[24]

During the years of the Second World War, all these suggestions were put into practice by the German Ministries of Propaganda and Foreign Affairs and also by the Nazi Party's Auslands-Organization [Foreign Countries Organization].[25] The German Embassy in Ankara and the consulates in Istanbul and Izmir became the headquarters of the German propaganda campaign in Turkey. The leading figures were Franz

Frederik Schmidt-Dumont – the Press Attaché of the Embassy – and Walter Brell – the president of the Deutsche Nachrichtenbüro (DNB) [the German News Agency] in Turkey. The activities were also complemented by the efforts of the Teutonia Club, the German Church, the office of the newspaper *Türkische Post* – founded by the German Embassy in 1926 – and the German bars and pubs that had opened in Istanbul. Almost every German living in Turkey was operating as a member of the Auslands-Organization. Their duties were to instil Nazi sympathy among both Turkish citizens and foreigners, to facilitate and provide German publications to those sympathizing with Nazism, to give financial support to pro-German and anti-Semitic publications, and of course, to obtain intelligence from locals at every opportunity and through organized events like balls, parties or meetings.[26]

Milli Emniyet Hizmetleri Riyaseti (MEH) [the Presidency of National Security Services], affiliated to the Prime Ministry, was in charge of the surveillance of all foreign intelligence activities in Turkey. Its large staff consisted of soldiers of the Ministry of National Defence, personnel from the Ministries of Interior and Foreign Affairs, the Turkish General Directorate of Security and also civilians.[27] As the central institution of Turkish intelligence, the MEH not only turned a blind eye to both Axis and Allied agents spying on each other but also took advantage of this rivalry to further Turkish interests. Thus, MEH's information pool on the German propaganda activities was also fed by the British agents alongside the undercover Turkish security personnel and civilian agents that it infiltrated into German organizations.

According to Turkish intelligence reports between 1939 and 1945, the Nazi propaganda activities in Turkey were carried out by five groups, especially after the headquarters were moved from Vienna to Istanbul. The first group kept in touch with the German Nazis in Turkey. The second group worked to instil national socialism and create an atmosphere against Britain – and the 1939 Turkish–British–French agreement – in Turkish public opinion. The third group, operating through the Teutonia Club, tried to win over the Austrians living in Turkey, who were generally resentful towards Germany after its annexation of Austria. The fourth group, which led the Nazi Youth Organization, aimed to create national socialist sentiments among Turkish youth in economic, political and cultural terms. The last group was also in charge of tracking the press and making propaganda through newspapers, magazines and brochures.[28]

The Turkish intelligence reports also reveal that the channels of the Nazi propaganda in Turkey were activated in accordance with the *Policy of zones of influence – Cultural policy* memorandum of 1935: social gatherings, educational institutions, publications and the press. The target audience of some of these social meetings were the German community residing in Turkey, and some were directed to Turks who sympathized with the Nazis. The first interesting meeting reported was held on 20 April 1939, at the Teutonia Club in Istanbul's Beyoğlu district, on the occasion of Hitler's fiftieth birthday. According to the report, the German community and the members of the Italian Embassy attended the meeting, in which they sung the Nazi Anthem and gave speeches praising Hitler emphasizing how he had increased the prestige and influence of Germany. The ceremony ended with a parade and the singing of the German national anthem.[29] The annual celebrations of Hitler's birthday[30] and the Workers' Day[31] aimed to strengthen the ties of Germans – and also Italians invited to those events – living in Turkey with their homelands. Conferences on the economic and military power of Germany were organized at the diplomatic centres in Ankara, Istanbul and Izmir, and they aimed to keep the Nazi sentiments alive among the German audience. Some of the conferences were hosted by the German Ambassador Franz von Papen,[32] Kresten Meves – the head of the Nazi organization in Turkey,[33] Victor Frederick – the bureau chief in Ankara, Alfons Volpel – an officer in the German Ministry of Interior,[34] Bavarian Volpen[35] – a member of the Nazi Party, and Dr Eduard Schafer – the *Türkische Post*'s executive editor between 1937 and 1944.[36]

In such gatherings, the German colony was given instructions to stop shopping from the Jewish-owned businesses, to provide jobs to Germans who would come to Turkey and to employ so-called pure Germans and to dismiss the Jews working in the German-owned factories.[37] According to the intelligence reports, other anti-Semitic measures of the Nazi organization in Turkey were the doubling of the tuition fees of German schools, expelling Jewish students who could not afford the fees and placing those who could afford the fees in isolated classes with the aim of driving them away.[38] The correspondence sent by the Turkish Ministry of Foreign Affairs to the Interior on 28 January 1936 demonstrates that the German Embassy organized similar meetings long before the war, and Turkey's sensitivity to propaganda dated back to then: 'such meetings held at the Embassy were not permissible, however, it was impossible to intervene with them, either'.[39]

The ceremonies – targeting the Turkish public and especially to the Nazi sympathizers among the Turks – emphasized the historical Turkish–German friendship. See, for instance, the German Consulate's memorial ceremony in Istanbul on 15 May 1942 – held in honour of the soldiers who died in the First World War and in particular for Field Marshal Colmar Freiherr von der Goltz (known as 'Goltz Pasha'), who was the Commander of the Ottoman's 6th Army in Iraq; the celebration of the seventy-fifth anniversary of the German High School in Istanbul on 16 June 1943 and the German Evangelical Church's annual rites.[40] According to Turkish official correspondence, the German community came together on traditional and religious occasions and expressed its good wishes and devotion to Turkey, in the context of Nazi propaganda.[41]

During the war years, Turkish intelligence closely monitored any German suspected of being a member of the Nazi propaganda organization in the country. In the big cities of Istanbul, Izmir and Ankara, many were identified as propagandists or collaborators who allocated their workplaces for meetings of the organization.[42] On the other hand, German scientists and technicians working in Turkish public institutions, such as Dr Friedrich Falke[43] – the rector of the Higher Agricultural Institute; Dr Walter Ruben – professor at the Faculty of Language, History, and Geography; Dr Alber Stummvoll[44] – director of the Higher Agricultural Institute Library and German teacher of the Istanbul Military Academy; Walther Hetzer[45] – German teacher in Istanbul German High School; Herr Lohman[46] – expert at the İvriz Hydroelectric Power Plant in Konya; and Dr Herman Foeyer[47] – expert at the Turkish Mining Research Institute in Ankara, were among the list of people whom Turkish agents monitored.[48]

The educational institutions were conducive environments for German propaganda. It should be remembered that Turkey had been inviting and assigning foreign scientists since the presidency of Atatürk, with the objective of supporting the reforms in the fields of education, agriculture, urbanization and industry.[49] However, with the outbreak of the war, the German administration ensured that the process resulted in assigning people who would serve for the Nazi propaganda. Furthermore, it even sought to target German and Austrian academics of Jewish origin – who had taken refuge and employed in Turkish universities – with the aim of instilling anti-Semitism among the Turks.[50] Turkish intelligence drew attention to the rise of sympathy towards the Nazi point of view among the Turkish associate professors as a consequence of the propagandist suggestion that Jewish professors occupied the roles to which Turkish scientists were entitled.[51] Other reports informed that Turkish university students were frequently visiting the German Library in Istanbul and giving the Nazi salute to the Germans working there, demonstrating the rise of Nazi sentiments among the educated youth. Intelligence reports confirmed that Nazism had also gained ground among Turkish students (and officers) who had higher education or training in Germany recently.[52] Accordingly, and as a condition of obtaining a diploma, these students were made to take exams on Nazi methods and ideology in Germany. Some of them even returned officially affiliated to the Nazi organization.

In addition to these, reports by the Istanbul Police Department also confirmed the presence of Axis propagandist activities in the pre-university education institutions in Turkey. For example, Italian nationals who were students of the Italian State High School in Istanbul were forced to join the fascist organization, given badges with 'Rome-Berlin' inscribed on them, together with the swastika and busts of Adolf Hitler and Benito Mussolini, and they were also sent to summer camps in Italy where they were trained as propagandists. The Department acknowledged that it was taking measures to prevent such activities spreading to other schools.[53]

German propaganda in Turkey was carried out in every form of printed material: books, magazines and brochures. Those publications were first exhibited in the embassy and consulates and later were provided free of charge to bookstores in Ankara and Istanbul to be sold at very low prices.[54] Even pocket calendars printed in Germany with Hitler's picture and propagandist images were distributed by the consulate staff to newsagents.[55] Such images were also concealed in open spaces to appeal to the public's subconscious. For example, the swastika featured in the illuminated billboard of a German car tyre shop[56] and the German pavilion at the Izmir Fair featured a large swastika alongside the Turkish flag, as well as images of various German achievements.[57]

However, the most effective method of German propaganda was the penetration of the Turkish press. The invitation of a group of Turkish journalists to Germany by Herr Knothe – the Turkey officer of the German Ministry of Propaganda – and Hitler's receiving them in 1935[58] marked the beginning of these activities. In the early years of the Second World War, Turkish newspapers and Anadolu Ajansı [the Anatolian Agency – the Turkish press agency] followed the developments in the war mainly from the Allied news agencies of Havas and Reuters. To change this situation, German news agencies DNB, Transcontinent Press, Transocean, Nachrichten Press Dienst and Europa Press, all officially or semiofficially affiliated with the Nazi administration, started to provide free news to national and local newspapers in Turkey. Some local newspapers such as *Istanbul*, *Beyoğlu* and *Journal d'Orient* ['Oriental Diary'] were offered bribes by the German Ministry of Propaganda.[59] German-controlled newspapers such as *Frankfurter Zeitung* ['Frankfurter Newspaper'] and *Türkische Post* were distributed in Turkey, as well as the *Völkischer Beobachter* ['National Observer'] and *Deutsche Allgemeine* ['German General'], which were printed in both Turkish and German, and imported and distributed by the German bookstores.[60] All of them, alongside their efforts to increase German influence in the Turkish press, were working as intelligence centres due to their domestic and international networks.

It should be noted that while MEH monitored the German propagandist activities towards the Turkish newspapers, Selim Sarper's Matbuat Umum Müdürlüğü [General Directorate of the Press] situated within the Turkish Prime Ministry developed a more effective control mechanism over the press. For instance, the newspapers *Cumhuriyet* ['Republic'], *Son Telgraf* ['Last Telegram'], *Son Posta* ['Last Post'], the magazine *Azerbaycan Yurt Bilgisi* ['Azerbaijan Country Information'] and a number of books written by Turkish authors or published in Turkey were detected to be reconciling Nazism with pan-Turkist ideology.[61] *Akbaba* ['Vulture'] magazine, discovered to receive financial support secretly from Deutsche Bank and Bayer Company, was investigated.[62] The owners of *Açık Göz* ['Open Eye'], a local newspaper in Istanbul conducting open German propaganda, were arrested on the grounds of operating against the national interests.[63] Ahmet Muzaffer Toydemir, the managing editor of *Türkische Post* between 1926 and 1943, was fined in January 1940 for printing anti-Turkish propaganda brochure.[64] *Türkische Post* was temporarily suspended for thirty-four days by a decree by the Council of Ministers, first in March 1940 due to its publications against the foreign policy of the state, and then again in February 1944 for six weeks because of a political cartoon.[65] However, by contrast when the *Berliner Ilustrirte Zeitung* ['Berlin Illustrated Newspaper'] promoted the extent of German military power in a supplement of *Signal* magazine on 15 June 1940 and caused a great reaction within the Turkish press, no sanction was imposed by the Press Directorate because it did not contain anything directly against Turkey.[66]

Depending on the changing course of the war, although the Turkish authorities sometimes allowed publications in favour of one of the warring parties to dominate, they also followed the policy of balance in the press. Warnings, fines, short-term closure and licence withdrawal penalties were not only imposed on the newspapers and magazines which made German propaganda but also on those with anti-fascist and communist contents. Between 1938 and 1949, the number of decrees issued by the Council of Ministers suspending the publication or prohibiting the import of newspapers, magazines and books was 177. Seventy-nine of those cited disturbance of public opinion, communist propaganda and content against the foreign policy of the state as grounds.[67] To counterbalance the trips of the Turkish press delegation to Germany upon invitation in 1939 and 1942, the government took care to also respond positively to the joint invitations of Britain and France in 1940, as well as Britain and the United States in 1942.[68]

Conclusion

The study of intelligence reports and official correspondence of Turkish administrative units demonstrates that German propaganda organization's objective in Turkey, rather than including Turkey in the war along the Axis, was to create sympathy for Germany and Nazism, to instil anti-Semitism and anti-British sentiment, and establish in Turkish public opinion the perception of Germany's invincible military, economic and technological power.

Although this goal was achieved to a certain extent, especially among educated people who were the primary target audience, it can be argued that it had been unsuccessful across the entire Turkish public opinion. This fact was even acknowledged by the Counter-espionage Office of the Commander-in-Chief of the German Western Armies in March 1940,[69] which held Brell and Dr Schmidt-Dumont responsible for the failure. Ambassador Von Papen, on the other hand, attributed that to the delay in his assignment to Ankara.[70] The primary reason for German propaganda's limited impact on the masses can be attributed to the language barrier. Yet, even in the mass media where that obstacle was overcome to an extent and the propaganda was most active, the government had both direct and indirect control, through either the press laws and the Directorate of Press or through leading newspaper owners also being CHP deputies. The Turkish administration's determination of not being involved in the war in which it had no interest had been the basis of its surveillance and control mechanisms. This policy, supported by the reality of Turkey's military and economic inadequacy, remained unhindered under President İnönü's authority and succeeded in resisting the pressures of the warring powers during the Second World War. The propaganda of German economic and technological power in Turkey would, however, give its belated fruits in the post-war era, especially by the mid-1950s, with the increase in economic relations of the two countries.

Notes

* Yasemin Türkkan Tunalı is the corresponding author for this chapter.
1. 'The National Struggle' is the phrase recognized in Turkey for the period dating May 1919–July 1923 encompassing the military resistance against the Allied occupation and also the political activities of the Turkish national revolutionaries against the Ottoman government.
2. Selim Deringil, *Denge Oyunu* (Istanbul: Tarih Vakfı Yurt Yayınları, 2009), 38–57.
3. H. Emre Bağce, 'Milli Şef Döneminde İktidar-Basın İlişkisi', in *Medya ve Siyaset 2: 1923–1946 Tek Partili Dönem*, ed. Tolga Yazıcı (Kocaeli: Volga Yayıncılık, 2016), 98.
4. Seyfettin Aslan, 'Türkiye'de Sivil Toplum', *Electronic Journal of Social Sciences* 9, no. 31 (2010): 267–8.
5. Yücel Güçlü, 'Fascist Italy's "Mare Nostrum" Policy and Turkey', *Belleten* 63 (1999): 813–18.
6. 'Convention Regarding the Regime of the Straits, with Annexes and Protocol. Signed at Montreux, July 20th, 1936', *League of Nations Treaty Series (1936–1937)*, 173, no. 4015: 213–41.

7 'Pact of Balkan Entente, and Protocol-Annex. Signed at Athens, February 9th, 1934', *League of Nations Treaty Series (1934)*. 153, no. 3514: 154–9.
8 İsmail Soysal, *Tarihçeleri ve Açıklamaları ile Birlikte Türkiye'nin Siyasal Antlaşmaları (1920-1945)* (Ankara: TTK, 2000), 592–5.
9 Cemil Koçak, *Türkiye'de Milli Şef Dönemi (1938-1945)* (Istanbul: İletişim Yayınları, 2017), 243–55.
10 Negotiations on a Turkish–Soviet alliance between 26 September and 17 October 1939 had failed due to the same demands. Kamuran Gürün, *Dış İlişkiler ve Türk Politikası (1939'dan Günümüze Kadar)* (Ankara: SBF Yayınları, 1983), 63–72; Koçak, *Türkiye'de*, 257–70.
11 İsmail Soysal, '1939 Türk-İngiliz-Fransız İttifakı', *Belleten* XLVI, no. 182 (1982): 367–414; Figen Atabey, 'İkinci Dünya Harbi Öncesi Türk-İngiliz-Fransız Ortak Deklarasyonu', *The Journal of International Social Research* 7, no. 31 (2014): 296–304.
12 Even Turkish Foreign Minister Saraçoğlu in one of his public speeches in February 1940 defined Turkey's position as not impartial/neutral (*bitaraf*), but just out of war (*harb hârici*). See Koçak, *Türkiye'de*, 301.
13 Mustafa Yılmaz, 'İnönü Dönemi Türk Dış Politikası', *Selçuk Üniversitesi Atatürk İlkeleri ve İnkılâp Tarihi Araştırma ve Uygulama Merkezi Dergisi*, no. 8 (1999): 19.
14 Koçak, *Türkiye'de*, 440.
15 Nuri Karakaş, 'İkinci Dünya Savaşı Yıllarında Türkiye'nin Krom Satışı ve Müttefik Politikaları', *Tarih İncelemeleri Dergisi* XXV, no. 2 (2010): 447–82.
16 Koçak, *Türkiye'de*, 591; Deringil, *Denge*, 144–5.
17 President İnönü had a fit of laughter when he was woken up and informed that the German–Russian war had begun. Metin Toker, *Tek Partiden Çok Partiye 1944-1950* (Ankara: Bilgi Yayınevi, 1990), 21. Turkey officially announced its neutrality in the German–Soviet war on the same day. See Türkiye Cumhuriyeti Cumhurbaşkanlığı Devlet Arşivleri Başkanlığı, Cumhuriyet Arşivi (hereafter BCA), 30.18.1.02/95-54-1. Note: The BCA files used in this chapter are not classified and therefore do not have official titles for the documents.
18 Deringil, *Denge*, 151.
19 Tuğrul Otaç, 'İkinci Dünya Savaşı'nda Müttefik Konferansları ve Türkiye İçin Önemi', *Journal of General Turkish History Research* 1, no. 1 (2019): 97–126.
20 Sina Akşin, 'Turkey's Declaration of War on Germany at the End of World War II', *The Turkish Yearbook of International Relations* 33 (2002): 289.
21 Alpaslan Öztürkci, 'Cumhurbaşkanı İnönü'nün TBMM'yi Açış Konuşmaları Bağlamında Türk Dış Politikası ve Türkçü-Turancı Akımlar (1939-1944)', *Van Yüzüncü Yıl Üniversitesi Sosyal Bilimler Enstitüsü Dergisi* 49 (2020): 123–5.
22 *TBMM Tutanak Dergisi*, vol. 15 (Ankara: TBMM Basımevi, 1945), 126–35.
23 For the British propaganda organization and activities, see Edward Corse, '"To accustom Turkish minds to a state of belligerency": The Delicate Balance of British Propaganda in Turkey during the Second World War', *Journal of Balkan and Near Eastern Studies* 23, no. 6 (2021): 896–913.
24 Süleyman Seydi, *1939-1945 Zor Yıllar! 2.Dünya Savaşı'nda Türkiye'de İngiliz-Alman Propaganda ve İstihbarat Savaşı* (Ankara: Asil Yayın, 2006), 19.
25 Johannes Glasneck, *Türkiye'de Faşist Alman Propagandası*. Translated by Arif Gelen (Ankara: Onur Yayınları, n.d.), 177.
26 Seydi, *Zor Yıllar*, 28–30.
27 Erdal İlter, *Millî İstihbarat Teşkilatı Tarihçesi* (Ankara: MİT Basımevi, 2002), 17.

28 BCA, 34.171. 01, 129,130; BCA, 33.170.01, 66–9; Yasemin Doğaner, 'İkinci Dünya Savaşı Yıllarında Türkiye'de Nazi Propagandası (Emniyet Genel Müdürlüğü Raporlarına Göre)', *Türkiyat Araştırmaları*, 17, no. 17 (Güz 2012): 66.
29 BCA, 33.170.01, 155–6. A similar ceremony was organized by the Italian Consulate for the eighteenth anniversary of Mussolini's coming to power. The consul was reported to have praised the neutrality of Turkey in his speech. BCA, 34.175.01, 3–4.
30 BCA, 34.171.01, 10; BCA, 34.171. 01, 18.
31 BCA, 34. 171.01, 154; BCA, 34.173.01, 16–18.
32 BCA, 33.170.01, 5.
33 BCA, 33.170.01, 155, 156.
34 BCA, 34.175.06, 2.
35 BCA, 33.170.01, 4.C.11, 24.04.1939.
36 BCA, 34.170.01, 154.
37 BCA, 33.170.01, 36–7; BCA, 33.170.01, 214.
38 BCA, 33.170.01, 74–8.
39 BCA, 33.169. 01, 2-A-9.
40 BCA, 34.171.01, 24; BCA, 34.171.01, 9.B.12, 21.06.1943; BCA, 34.171.01, 4–7.
41 BCA, 34.171.01, 4–7.
42 BCA, 34.172.01, 15–18; BCA, 34.172.01, 39–54; BCA, 34.172.02; BCA, 34.175.04, 3; BCA, 33.170.01, 40,41; BCA, 33.170.01, 138, 139; BCA, 33.169.01, B12-B14, C1–C3.
43 BCA, 33.170.01, 49.
44 BCA, 34. 173.01, 70, 71.
45 BCA, 33.169.01, 2-A-13.
46 BCA, 34.171.01, 176.
47 BCA, 33.170.01. 50.
48 Measures taken by the Turkish authorities against the people deemed subversive were the termination of employment of those working in official institutions or not extending their residence or working permits. BCA, 34. 173.01, 36, 37; BCA, 34.173. 01, 1/C5-1/C6; BCA, 34.172.02; BCA, 33.169.01, 2-A-6, 2-A-7.
49 Sezen Kılıç, *Türk-Alman İlişkileri ve Türkiye'deki Alman Okulları (1852'den 1945'e kadar)* (Ankara: Atatürk Araştırma Merkezi, 2005), 159; Alev Gözcü, 'Atatürk Döneminde Türkiye'de Tarımın Gelişiminde Alman Etkisi', *Journal of Modern Turkish History Studies*, 18, no. 36 (2018): 107–37.
50 Fahri Türk-Servet Çınar, 'Türkiye ile Almanya Arasındaki Bilimsel İlişkiler: Türk-Alman Üniversiteleri', *Gazi Akademik Bakış* 7, no. 13 (2013): 50; Sevtap Kadıoğlu, 'Ankara Yüksek Ziraat Enstitüsü'nde Mülteci Bilim Adamları', *Osmanlı Bilimi Araştırmaları* IX, no. 1–2 (2007–2008): 183–97; Ali Özden, 'Ord. Prof. Dr. Erich Frank', *Güncel Gastroenteroloji* 14, no. 4 (2010): 163.
51 BCA, 33.170.01, 24.
52 BCA, 33.170.01, 55, 63.
53 BCA, 33.166.02, 1–3.
54 BCA, 34.174.02, 9–12; BCA, 34. 174.05, 21.D.3-21.D.6; BCA, 34.175.01; BCA, 34.175.03, 10-13; BCA, 33.170.01, 5.D.5-5.D.10.
55 BCA, 34.175.03, 13; BCA, 34.175.04, 10.
56 BCA, 34.171.01, 8-D-2; BCA, 34.173.01, 87.
57 M. Sinan Niyazioğlu, *İroni ve Gerilim: İkinci Dünya Savaşı Yıllarında İstanbul'da ve Ankara'da Savaş Algısı* (Ankara: Koç University Vekam, 2016), 182–93.
58 Asım Us, *Hatıra Notları* (Istanbul: Kitabevi, 2012), 89.
59 Seydi, *Zor Yıllar*, 26.

60 Ibid., 58.
61 BCA, 33.170.01, 24, 25.
62 BCA, 34.175.04, 3.
63 Seydi, *Zor Yıllar*, 33–6.
64 Resul Alkan, 'Die "Türkische Post": Türkiye'de Bir Nazi-Propaganda Gazetesi ve Matbuat Umum Müdürlüğü', *SUSBED* 42, no. 1 (2019): 205.
65 BCA, 30.18.1.02, 90-29-2; BCA, 30.18.1.02, 104-14-3.
66 BCA, 34.175.01, 3–15. Also see Chapter 14 of this volume for a more general analysis of the German magazine *Signal*.
67 Mustafa Yılmaz-Yasemin Doğaner, *Cumhuriyet Döneminde Sansür (1923–1937)* (Ankara: Siyasal Kitabevi, 2007), 18.
68 Us, *Hatıra*, 383, 469–82; Gül Karagöz Kızılca, '1942 Yılında Mihver ve Müttefik Devletlerce Düzenlenen Türk Basın Gezileri', *Kebikeç* 14 (2002): 5–27.
69 Seydi, *Zor Yıllar*, 34.
70 BCA, 33.170.1, 5.

10

Beyond neutrality

Italian cultural propaganda in Portugal

Simone Muraca

In June 1940, as France was falling in the face of the German war machine, and Italy had decided to become a belligerent alongside Germany, the Portuguese single-party União Nacional [National Union] published an internal note stating that Portugal was overwhelmed by the propaganda of the belligerent states. The right-wing conservative and authoritarian dictatorship was led by the former Coimbra University professor António Oliveira Salazar, who had been in power since 1932, but Minister of Finance since 1928. Salazar had kept the small country at the western edge of Europe outside the war, despite the historical ties with their British ally on one hand (through the old Anglo-Portuguese alliance of the fourteenth century[1]), and the political sympathies and regime similarities with Italian fascism on the other. For such small states, as Leos Müller wrote, 'the best way to survive the storm was to rely on one's neutrality and to accommodate the belligerents'.[2] Portuguese neutrality could happen only in synergy with Spain, within a broader framework of Iberian neutrality. Francisco Franco's victory in the Spanish Civil War (in 1939) had reshaped the relations between the two countries. Both ruled by right-wing authoritarian dictators, the new phase in relations was formally sealed with a treaty of friendship and non-aggression signed in March 1939 (the 'Iberian Pact'), in which it was agreed not to help an aggressor of the other party.[3]

But in June 1940 the situation in Lisbon was unbearable for Salazar's government. According to the party report, 'from a nationalistic point of view' the propaganda saturation was 'completely harmful' for the country. It was stated that 'Portuguese public opinion [was] intoxicated, and it became impossible for our people to distinguish fantasy from reality'.[4] Nazi Germany, Britain, France and Italy all contended the stage of Portuguese public opinion.

By the spring of 1940, Lisbon had rapidly experienced the effect of the escalation of both Axis and Allied propaganda narratives about the ongoing war, while the city was on its way to becoming an international centre of espionage and intelligence deception.[5] From the beginning of the war, Salazar's government tried to prevent such activities through implementing controls over the media (especially the press and radio), which were strong in theory, but the results were often limited. Especially in the early phases of the war, German propaganda was often tolerated by Portuguese censors and the press popularized the military successes obtained by Hitler.[6] Thus, as the historian Neil Lochery wrote, 'the greater the success, the more reluctant the Portuguese were becoming to mention the old alliance with Britain for fear of antagonizing the Germans'.[7]

As the war evolved, the volumes of propaganda increased accordingly, in a harsher competition to obtain the attention of Portuguese public opinion. After the campaign against France and the Italian declaration of war on 10 June 1940, the situation in Lisbon escalated in a way that the Portuguese government felt it could not postpone an intervention any further. Progressively, during the second half of 1940, Salazar's government forbade foreign associations and institutions to explicitly undertake political propaganda and or act with hostility towards the representatives of other powers.[8] As a result, the Portuguese preventive sanctions led Britain, Nazi Germany and Italy to adopt different tactics, moving away from political propaganda to cultural propaganda. Historians have argued that the use of national culture as a diplomatic instrument to gain international legitimation, foreign consensus and the power of persuasion and influence emerged at the end of the nineteenth century, but extensively became part of major powers' foreign affairs policies only from the interwar period.[9] According to Jo Fox, propaganda during the Second World War operated with the potential to mobilize mass opinion and structure social relationships, attitudes and behaviour, but at the same time 'it also operates through a series of intricate and flexible interactions between the propagandist and the recipient', in the sense that 'public opinion and propaganda mutually limit and influence each other' in a reciprocal transaction.[10] In the case of neutral Portugal, in the Second World War period, propaganda and cultural diplomacy became indissolubly interconnected – simultaneously limited and influenced by the Portuguese audience. All the major powers had institutions in Lisbon designed for conveying such cultural propaganda. By the late 1930s, all the major powers had established institutes of culture in Lisbon: the Institute Français, the German Institute of Culture and the British Institute were founded.[11] In the case of Fascist Italy, it was the Istituto Italiano di Cultura [Italian Institute of Culture], located in Rua do Salitre, in Lisbon's residential neighbourhood of Rato.[12]

The chapter aims to analyse the role of the Italian Institute of Culture in Lisbon during the Second World War. By providing the main features of Italian cultural propaganda carried out by the institute, and by studying the work of the two directors who managed the institute in wartime, this chapter will cover both the period when Italy was part of Nazi–Fascist alliance and the years that followed the fall of the Italian Fascist dictator, Benito Mussolini, in 1943.

The Italian Institute of Culture before Italy joins the war

The Italian Institute of Culture in Lisbon, originally called Regio Instituto Luso-Italiano [translating as Royal Portuguese-Italian Institute], was first established in 1928. However, it was only after the Abyssinian[13] war in 1935–6 that the Italian Minister of Foreign Affairs allocated steady funds to the institute as well as human resources which aimed to extend the influence over the country. Teachers, language professors, university lecturers and functionaries were sent over to Lisbon, and soon the Italian Institute of Culture became a central node of a network of agents, both institutional and informal, aiming to spread 'the Fascist message' within Portuguese right-wing cultural, political and bureaucratic elites.[14]

The first director appointed to achieve this task was among the most experienced cultural agents at the service of Italian foreign affairs: the journalist and writer Aldo Bizzarri. Born in 1907 and enlisted in Fascist National Party since 1925, Bizzarri was a professor with literary ambitions. In the late 1920s, he founded a modernist and Futurism-inspired magazine called *I Lupi* ['The Wolves'] and, after some years employed in senior positions at the Fascist Confederation of Professionals and Artists [Confederazione fascista dei professionisti e degli artisti], he moved out of Italy to undertake a diplomatic career. For a while he was an agent of cultural activities in Chile and Argentina in South America, and then, from 1935, he was transferred to France and later appointed as director of the revitalized Italian Institute of Culture in Lisbon.[15]

Arriving in the Portuguese capital shortly after Mussolini's proclamation of the Italian Empire, Bizzarri organized the activities performed by the institute with conferences, exhibitions, cultural courses, books donations to public libraries and a twice-a-year cultural review named *Estudos Italianos em Portugal* ['Italian Studies in Portugal'].

By 1939, as instructed by official guidelines, the institute was the channel aimed to deliver in Portugal: 'literary and artistic themes intended to illustrate our heritage of culture, science and beauty ... themes relating to present-day Italy, the achievements of Fascism, and the legislative provisions of the Fascist regime: everything, in brief, that represents the great social and universal construction that we owe to the spirit of Mussolini'.[16] Conferences and lessons included notions of geography, history, literature and fine arts, but also information about 'the new Italian lifestyle' which had emerged after Mussolini's rise to power through the 1922 Fascist Revolution. What Edward Corse wrote about the British Council's propaganda work during the Second World War perfectly applies also in the case of Italian cultural strategy in Portugal. Corse wrote:

> The British Council's propaganda work was not focused on the war situation, and at times blithely ignored that there was a war on at all. Instead, it took a long-term, positive image of the British way of life and presented it in a way that was attractive to its audience and not in a way that appeared to impose a way of life or a way of thinking onto its audience.[17]

To this extent, similarly to what the British were doing, a central role was taken by the lessons, exhibitions or conferences in which the achievements of the regime in social affairs were described, namely the construction of new infrastructures or buildings, or the resolution of social conflicts due to the 'third way' corporatist system. Indeed, the topic was of particular strategic importance in Portugal. From 1933 onwards, Portugal had promulgated a corporatist constitution and some reforms directly inspired by Italian Fascist laws, such as the School Charter and the Labour Charter. For this reason, Italian cultural propaganda's main narratives delivered by the Institute of Culture tended, in this phase, were to stress the similarities between the two regimes, underlining the corporatist affiliation as a consequence of the common Latin roots (also known as Latinity):[18] a same foundation restored by the modernity of the two regimes, capable of dismissing and outclassing the early twentieth-century liberal democracy and its legacy of crisis.[19]

At the beginning of the Second World War, after three years since Bizzarri's arrival, the institute thus held an important spot in Lisbon's cultural horizon. Italy and Portugal shared anti-communist and anti-liberal-democratic values, and along with the cultural exchange, it created a synergy that helped the institute to gain a strategic position for Fascist cultural diplomacy. Apart from the activities themselves, it seems that Bizzarri was particularly able to create an intellectual network around the institute – a network which guaranteed a constant number of participants at institute's events. These included a select audience of Portuguese officials and high-profile personalities of politics, administration, education and culture, such as writers, journalists, professors and academics.[20]

Italy joins the war and the effect on the institute

This favourable and stable situation did not last any longer. With the outbreak of the Second World War, Italian cultural propaganda in Portugal suffered the consequences of structural changes determined by both the international context and fascist propaganda policies.

During the 1930s, the ministries responsible for domestic propaganda within Italy were reorganized by Galeazzo Ciano, the son-in-law of Mussolini, but his new master plan did not include any adjustment for the war propaganda which was promoted abroad. In the first place, the regime never clearly defined which institutional body had to oversee the activities of propaganda abroad. As a result, the Ministry of Foreign Affairs [Ministero degli Affari Esteri], the Ministry of Popular Culture [Ministero della Cultura Popolare] and the Fascist National Party, through the presence of 'Italian Fascism Abroad' [Fasci Italiani all'estero], became competitors with no centralized orders and targets. The effectiveness of the action was thus reduced by the multiple presence of different subjects and this multiplicity determined a dissipation of the economic resources allocated by the regime to expand fascism influence abroad. According to the Director-General of propaganda at the Ministry of Popular Culture, Ottaviano Koch, the funds were too meagre to fulfil the 'imperious needs of a great country'. The means were 'too limited, if we think of the various millions spent by the other States for propaganda activities and cultural and political penetration in foreign countries'.[21] Moreover, while after 1940 Koch reportedly suggested increasing the budget for propaganda work – seeing the need for 'a great intensification of propaganda inside and outside our borders' due to the war – Mussolini limited the budget allowed and never fully agreed on the strategic importance of cultural diplomacy as a diplomatic tool.[22] In this respect, as shown by the historian Francesca Cavarocchi, the history of fascist propaganda abroad, in particular after 1940, was marked by a constant lack of financial resources and failed attempts towards a more efficient coordination of energies and expertise of the many actors involved until the very end of the regime.[23]

Only in late 1942 was the internal dispute between governmental bodies resolved. A ministerial circular of instructions signed by Mussolini himself ordered that every official initiative of propaganda concerning foreign targets (which could be either institutions or people) had to have prior authorization by the Ministry of Foreign Affairs.[24]

Shortly after the beginning of the war, the Fascist regime focused its cultural influence efforts towards the Axis, Allied or occupied countries, particularly in Eastern Europe and the Balkans. Here, the Nazi–Fascist 'New Order' for European culture was an ongoing process of consolidation, however contradictory, as shown by Stefano Santoro's research on fascist cultural diplomacy in Eastern Europe.[25] Such a focus on the Eastern Front loosened the Italian aspirations of cultural and political influence over Salazar's regime. In this regard, the peripheral offices of Lisbon, at the opposite geographical extreme in Europe, lost all its importance in Mussolini's eyes, and despite the success of fascist cultural diplomacy of the late 1930s, the activities of the Italian Institute of Culture were gradually reduced.

On 23 September 1940, Attilio de Cicco, the deputy chair of the cultural office at the Italian Ministry of Foreign Affairs, wrote to the Honorary President of the Italian Institute of Culture in Portugal, Luigi Federzoni – a first-class member of fascist political elite. The official informed Federzoni that Bizzarri was being immediately transferred to Budapest, Hungary. His 'admirable skills' of intellectual networking and cultural management were considered wasted in the peripheral and neutral Lisbon, and according to the new cultural and propagandistic policy embraced by the fascist regime during the 1940s, his work was instead needed in Eastern Europe.[26]

The appointment of Gino Saviotti

The selection process of his successor testifies to the new Italian lack of interest towards neutral Portugal. The Ministry of Foreign Affairs refused to appoint any important resource at their disposal, and the range of names quickly reduced to one: Gino Saviotti, a professor at the institute's branch of Porto (Oporto). 'He seems particularly fit for education and sensitive to assume the task in this delicate moment', wrote Attilio de Cicco in the aforementioned communication to Federzoni.[27]

Before his employment in Porto, Saviotti was a professor of literature and a writer with some novels of moderate success in both public and of critique published in the 1920s. He began his cultural diplomacy career quite late in his life. Bizzarri's first service was at the age of twenty-nine, while Saviotti first entered diplomacy in his late forties. Most importantly, he was surprised by his promotion and, at the moment of the inauguration of 1940–1 academic year (which was also the first year that Italy was a belligerent country), Saviotti had no important contacts in Lisbon, nor did he belong to any networks, either intellectual or political. He was basically an unknown Italian cultural officer, and he was far away from the 'perfect Fascist'. While he was regularly involved in Fascist Party activities, his record at the Ministry of Foreign Affairs archives shows that he had been the subject of an inquiry for suspected anti-fascist activities in 1925.[28]

If we consider that the previous success of the institute was largely built on the former director Bizzarri's ability of networking in public relations, his departure resulted in a drastic reduction in the institute's chances to play a role of influence within Lisbon's cultural and political environment. The appointment of an unknown professor coming from Portugal's second city, with no significant connection in the political or cultural world of the Portuguese capital, did not help at all.

Furthermore, Saviotti had to deal with another cause of deterioration of interest in, and enthusiasm from, the Portuguese audience in Italian cultural propaganda. After the Italian attack on France in June 1940, the Portuguese elites changed their sentiments towards the Italians. There was never a dramatic cut in relationships, official nor informal, but after 1940 the institute never experienced again, in quantity and quality, the publicity and the successes of the previous period. More generally, the traditional diplomatic relations were also affected by the war. After the Spanish Civil War – a stage in which both Portugal and Italy fought side by side against communism – the Italian declaration of war against the Allies produced a stagnation and a regression of the Luso-Italian friendship.[29]

Indeed, shortly after the Italian declaration of war, the situation in Lisbon was quite difficult to handle by Italian authorities in the country. Shortly after the public announcement, Salazar received the Italian Minister in Lisbon, Renato Bova Scoppa, in his office at São Bento Palace. At this meeting, Salazar mentioned to the Italian diplomat his admiration for the aggressive Fascist foreign policy, but he also expressed disappointment. Salazar trusted Mussolini to keep the peace on the continent and leave the Mediterranean area outside the conflict.[30] The Portuguese leader's main concern at this early stage of the war was a potential Spanish involvement alongside the Axis powers. In this sense, a new battlefront in the Mediterranean might involve the Spanish dictator, General Francisco Franco, becoming entangled in the war, leading to the collapse of the Iberian Pact which guaranteed Iberian neutrality. Salazar was worried by the implications for Portuguese foreign policy. Moreover, he was particularly concerned by the strengthening of the Rome–Berlin Axis. Salazar had been an admirer of Mussolini from the beginning of the Fascist Revolution, to the point that he had kept for many years a signed portrait of Mussolini on his office table, but at the same time he was afraid of Italian reliance on Nazi Germany. After the Nazi's rise to power, Salazar looked at Germany with caution. He expressed more than once his aversion towards Hitler's imperialistic aspirations. A 'Germanized Europe', he stated in 1940, was against European tradition. The continent would have been ripped from its true cultural roots in favour of 'a neo-paganism of mystic and racist origin that is contrary to our Roman and Catholic traditions'.[31] In January 1941, Bova Scoppa wrote that the thought of a domino effect of the Latin nations (France, Spain, Belgium, Romania) falling under German influence caused Salazar ('a true Latin man') 'intimate suffering'.[32] Thereby, in Salazar's view, the alliance between Hitler and Mussolini would jeopardize Latinity and it is not by chance that, after the summer of 1940, Italy experienced a backlash in diplomatic relations with Portugal. Symbolically, it was the very news of the Italian declaration of war that induced Salazar to remove the portrait of the Italian leader from his desk.[33]

The difficult situation the institute had to face from September 1940 onwards is well described in a letter of one of its employees, Lorenzo di Poppa, to a bureaucrat of the Italian Ministry of Foreign Affairs:

> This year is particularly difficult for us: I cannot say if it is for political reasons or because of our passiveness in propaganda action. The Germans are doing well. They distribute an enormous quantity of books and journals about the war; we don't have anything to deliver. Not a single printed paper for interested people and newspapers. Now, an efficient propaganda, especially during these hard times, cannot be held only through cultural activities. We need new things, up to date, if we don't want to disappear from the public arena.[34]

But the 'new things' di Poppa wanted were not in sight. Thus, Saviotti decided to pursue a policy of working towards diffusing the Italian language all over Portugal, as a future channel for penetration once the situation was more favourable to Italy. The targets were in first place students from secondary schools and universities, but also young Portuguese who were still fascinated by 'the language of Fascist culture'. If overt propaganda was forbidden, then education – 'a sacred factory of souls', as Salazar considered it – was the 'silent vehicle' to keep transmitting fascist achievements and ideas.[35] Therefore, Italian classes were inaugurated all over the country, from the universities of the main cities to the high schools of inland towns. Despite the political divergences, Italian cultural diplomacy still managed to hold its status. In Lisbon, the attractiveness of the language classes is demonstrated by the fact that Italian remained a mandatory language subject in two important Lyceums, the Pedro Nunes and the Gil Vicente, and by 1941 it was taught in all capital's Lyceums, art schools and trade secondary schools.[36] At higher education level, the Italian lecturer Giuseppe Carlo Rossi held more than a dozen courses in five different universities (Instituto Superior de Ciências Económicas e Financeiras [the 'Higher Institute of Economic and Financial Sciences'], the Instituto Superior Técnico [the 'Higher Technical Institute'], the Faculty of Science, the Faculty of Veterinary Medicine and the Faculty of Letters in 1942–3).[37] It seems that the language classes diluted their political content year after year. References to fascism and its culture were slowly replaced by cultural-only content devoid of their political connotations. Safe and uncontroversial content such as Dante Alighieri's Comedy lectures and fine Renaissance art and architecture regained the centre stage.[38]

'Those lectures on language and Italian civilization, ancient and modern culture, are aimed to clarify the spiritual values and our intimate force', Saviotti wrote in one of his official reports of 1940.[39] Nonetheless, some of the professors in the peripheral branches still acted according to the fascist instructions of propaganda. The cultural delegate in Setùbal, Luigi Felici, stated that his cultural work let the Portuguese youth understand 'the essence of various cultural problems of the two nations' and allow them to think about how fascism enlightened 'the millenary Roman civilization that lies at the very origins of both our cultures'.[40]

The deputy director of the institute's branch of Porto expressed a similar opinion. The syllabus of the language and culture course for Lyceums he edited disseminated its propagandistic purpose through a political-oriented teaching of the most notable Italian literary authors. The syllabus was entitled, a selection 'from Dante to the present day', which also included several of Mussolini's works. 'In this way', Porto's branch deputy wrote in a report, 'I'll have the chance to overcome the political caution of today'.[41] According to a working report of early 1943 from Porto, the final aim of the cultural strategy conducted there was to 'let the sympathy, the interest, and the comprehension for the great historical and racial qualities of our people rise in the student body'. They would become a sort of future 'fifth column' of Italian propaganda, with close ties to the Institute of Culture through both its activities and its intellectual network. A long period of cultural and political loyalty, empowered by scholarships funded by the Ministry of Foreign Affairs for living and studying in Italy or funded short-term visits to Rome and the key places of Fascist revolution.[42]

Regardless of this difference in approach between Lisbon and Porto, the military defeats suffered by Axis armies during the course of 1942 changed the context once again. The lack of control exercised by the Ministry of Foreign Affairs allowed Saviotti to ease political references in his work, until the point of ceasing them entirely. By the end of the 1942–3 academic year, in June 1943, Italian diplomatic representatives in Porto submitted to the Italian Minister in Lisbon an official request for an inquiry into Saviotti's anti-fascist management of the institute. They were too late, though, to make a difference. Only a few weeks later the last meeting of the Fascist Grand Council voted against Mussolini. After twenty years of dictatorship, the Italian Duce was overthrown by his senior officials, in the same weeks Allied forces reached Italian shores.[43]

The effect of the Italian change of sides in the Second World War

A new phase for Italian propaganda in neutral Portugal began in the summer of 1943. After the Fascist regime collapsed, the Nazis invaded Italy from the north and the Allies liberated the country from the south. In September 1943, a new Italian government led by Marshall Pietro Badoglio signed an armistice and the next month the liberated Italy declared war against Nazi Germany and Mussolini's new puppet state – the Italian Social Republic [the Repubblica Sociale Italiana, RSI] – established in northern Italy.[44] So far, historiography has not paid enough attention to the projection abroad of the Italian internal conflict and effective civil war. How, for example, did the political subversion affect the relationships among the Italian communities of emigrants and between the communities and their diplomatic representatives?

In Portugal, the disintegration of the Fascist regime caused a suspension of the whole of Italian activities. The Italian Legation, upon which the institute was subordinate, took the side of the new government and waited for clear instructions from the post-Fascist authorities. For this reason, Saviotti postponed the organization of the 1943–4 academic year until he had the approval of the Allies to continue.[45] Meanwhile, almost all the employees and professors of the institute were dismissed and returned to Italy.

At first, it comes clear from the records in the archives that British and American diplomats in Lisbon discussed intensely whether the institute had to cease its activities or not. The reason was simple. The Italian Institute of Culture was created according to a 1926 Fascist Law written by the Fascist Minister and known philosopher Giovanni Gentile. It was an institution designed for fascist propaganda, and in Lisbon it was universally recognized as such. Therefore, in the last months of 1943, from the Allied point of view, there were no reasons to keep the offices of Italian cultural propaganda running any further.

However, the talks led in the opposite decision. The Allied representatives in Lisbon decided to keep the institute open and, in fact, managed by the very same director as before, Gino Saviotti. On his side, it was appreciated that he had had detachment from fascist propaganda for a number of years. The project behind the institute was to use it as an anti-fascist propaganda centre for the Italian community in Portugal. Indeed, after the armistice and the foundation of the RSI in northern Italy, a group of Portugal-based fascists established an RSI Committee funded by Nazi Germany authority in Lisbon. Among the founders of the committee there were all the top intelligence officials of Italian services in Portugal: some former agents of propaganda, two former professors of the Institute of Culture and some of the most prominent Italian businessmen in Portugal.[46]

Shortly after the organization, the fascist group of dissidents, led by the former Italian military attaché in Lisbon, Vittorio Terragni, began a significant effort in pushing RSI propaganda. It was addressed to the other compatriots who were confused from the shortage of information about their motherland. They were targeted with airmail pamphlets against Badoglio, and the new Allied-backed Italian government, who was depicted as a cruel and lawless illegitimate ruler.[47] The institute was given the task to counter-attack these actions.

In the following months of 1944, the institute and the Fascist Committee were the contenders of a war of propaganda fought within the Italian community in Portugal. Each side produces a weekly bulletin sent to hundreds of people all over Portugal, both Italians and Portuguese, who had been members of the institute's network in the 1936–43 period. The two bulletins presented similar features. The main difference was visual. The bulletin issued by the fascist side of the community had the former logo of the Lisbon's Casa del Fascio (the local Fascist headquarters) and the motto 'Believe, Obey, Fight' [*Credere, Obbedire, Combattere*], whereas the bulletin issued by the Institute of Culture had a blue headline '*Bollettino della Legazione Italiana*' [Bulletin of the Italian Legation] with Italian Legation's symbols on it.[48]

Both bulletins were three to six pages long and they mostly focused on war events in Italy, with long accounts of the military operations taken from the official military dispatches of the two sides. They both used apocalyptic rhetoric describing the enemy's occupation. Almost every issue of the Nazi–Fascist paper gave a long account of starving people in the Anglo-American-controlled south of Italy. By contrast, the bulletins written by the Italian Institute remained on the same theme but with the complete opposite view: northern Italy was described as a German province, with mass executions of partisans and mass conscriptions of teenagers sent to die on the Front, without any chance of survivors.[49]

Conclusion

In conclusion, the foundation of the Italian Institute of Culture in Lisbon represented an important tool for Italian diplomacy and fascist political and cultural relations with Salazarist Portugal. Nevertheless, after the outbreak of the Second World War, the neutral positioning of Portugal, the Italian focus on Eastern Europe and a reduction of the expendable budget for propaganda due to the economy being dedicated to the war caused strong limitations in the spectrum of the activity conducted by the institute and its directors.

The collapse of Mussolini in July 1943 represents another rupture point. A reproduced propaganda conflict between the supporters of the two sides in the Italian civil war lasted almost until the end of the Second World War itself. In the autumn of 1944, some fascist bulletins were prohibited by Portuguese Police, and afterwards the publications started to lose the ability to be printed on a regular basis, failing to keep their readership and general appeal. The last bulletin from fascist side appeared in early 1945. Five months before the war ended, nearly all of the members of the Fascist Committee in Portugal had left the country, moved back to northern Italy for the last defence of fascism in Italy or resigned and retired into a low-profile private life.[50]

On the other side, Saviotti and the Institute of Culture carried on as a convening centre for the Italian community of Portugal. After the collapse of the Fascist Committee, the institute was finally able to reopen its language courses. After two years of inactivity, in 1945, the first eighty-three Portuguese students were enrolled. Saviotti, without any public funds and with a budget limited to the enrolment fees, was the only teacher. It was the new start for the post-fascist Italian cultural diplomacy institution. Saviotti directed the institute until 1950 and spent most of his life in Lisbon, a long-standing reference for both the Italian community and Portuguese cultural environments.[51]

Notes

1 Joaquim da Costa Leite, 'Neutrality by Agreement: Portugal and the British Alliance in World War II', *American University International Law Review* 14-1 (1998): 185–99. See also Chapter 4 of this volume with regard to the Anglo-Portuguese alliance and Portugal's position in the First World War.
2 Leos Müller, *Neutrality in World History* (London: Routledge, 2019), 144.
3 Maria Inácia Rezola, 'The Franco–Salazar Meetings: Foreign Policy and Iberian Relations during the Dictatorships (1942–1963)', *e-Journal of Portuguese History* 6, no. 2 (2008): 58–68.
4 António Josè Telo, *Propaganda e Guerra Secreta Em Portugal. 1939-1945* (Lisboa: Perspectivas e realidades, 1990), 14. Translation from the Portuguese (and Italian) here and in later quotations is by the author.

5 Neil Lochery, *War in the Shadows of the City of Light, 1939–1945* (New York: Public Affairs, 2011).
6 Claudia Ninhos, *Portugal e os Nazis* (Lisboa: Esfera do Livros, 2017).
7 Lochery, *War in the Shadows of the City of Light*, 29.
8 Archivio Storico-diplomatico Minstero degli Affari Esteri (hereafter ASMAE), Rome, Italy: Series: Affari Politici (hereafter AP) Portogallo, box (b.) 9, folder (f.) 'Conflitto europeo. Neutralità'.
9 Among the many titles in international historiography, see Ruth E. McMurry and Muna Lee, *The Cultural Approach: Another Way to International Relations* (Chapel Hill: University of North Carolina Press, 1947); Jessica Gienow-Hecht and Mark Donfried (eds), *Searching for cultural diplomacy* (New York: Berghahn Books, 2010).
10 Jo Fox, 'The Propaganda War', in *The Cambridge History of the Second World War*, ed. Richard J. B. Bosworth and Joseph A. Maiolo (Cambridge: Cambridge University Press, 2015), 91.
11 On Institute Français, see 'O Instituto'. Available online: https://www.ifp-lisboa.com/o-instituto (accessed 15 March 2022); on British Institute, see Edward Corse, *A Battle for Neutral Europe. British Cultural Propaganda during the Second World War* (London: Bloomsbury, 2013), 27, and 'A nossa história'. Available online: https://www.britishcouncil.pt/sobre/historia (accessed 15 March 2022). On German Institute, see Ninhos, *Portugal e os Nazis*.
12 In 1942, the British Institute, which had opened on the Bairro Alto hill of Lisbon, was transferred close to the Italian Institute in Rato.
13 Abyssinia is now known as Ethiopia.
14 Mario Ivani, *Esportare il fascismo. Collaborazione di polizia e diplomazia culturale tra Italia Fascista e Portogallo di Salazar (1928–1945)* (Bologna: CLUEB, 2008), 157–81.
15 ASMAE, Direzione Generale Italiani all'Estero (DGIE), Archivio Scuole (AS) 1920–1950. Fascicoli personali, box 70, folder Aldo Bizzarri. Also see Robert S. C. Gordon, 'An Intellectual at Mauthausen: Aldo Bizzarri between Essay, Fiction (and cinema)', *Laboratoire italien* 24 (2020). DOI:10.4000/laboratoireitalien.4521.
16 'Istituti di Cultura – Cattedre e Lettorati Universitari – Istituto Interuniversitario Italiano' (Direzione Generale Italiani all'Estero, 12/1/1937, no. 1), in *Raccolta delle circolari e delle istruzioni ministeriali*, ed. Angelo Toscani (Rome: Ministero degli Affari Esteri, 1938).
17 Corse, *A Battle for Neutral Europe*, 185.
18 See also Chapter 2, which considers Latinity in the context of Argentina in the First World War.
19 Rita Almeida de Carvalho and Annarita Gori, *Los intelectuales Portugueses y el mito de la Latinidad (1915–1940)*, in *Fascismo y modernismo. Política y culturaen la Europa de entreguerras (1918–1945)*, ed. Francisco Cobo Romero et al. (Granada: Comares, 2016), 223–39.
20 Annarita Gori and Rita Almeida de Carvalho, 'Italian Fascism and the Portuguese Estado Novo: International Claims and National Resistance', *Intellectual History Review* 30 (2019): 295–319.
21 Archivio Centrale dello Stato (ACS), Rome, Italy: MinCulPop, Gabinetto, box 95, folder entitled: 'Gabinetto. Relazioni sull'attività della Dir. Gen. della propaganda'. Document entitled 'Relazione sull'Attività Tecnico-Amministrativa svolta dalla Direzione Generale per i Servizi della Propaganda durante l'Esercizio Finanziario 1940-41', 14 February 1941.
22 Ibid.

23 Francesca Cavarocchi, *Avanguardie dello spirito. Il fascismo e la propaganda culturale all'estero* (Rome: Carocci, 2010), 165.
24 Circolare n. 7 del 14 February 1942, in *Raccolta delle circolari e delle istruzioni ministeriali*, ed. Angelo Toscani (Rome: Tipografia del Ministero degli Esteri, 1934).
25 Stefano Santoro, *L'Italia e l'Europa orientale. Diplomazia culturale e propaganda 1918-1943* (Milan: Franco Angeli, 2005), 322. See also Benjamin Martin, *The Nazi-Fascist New Order for European Culture* (Cambridge, MA: Harvard University Press, 2016).
26 ASMAE, DGIE AS 1920-50. Fascicoli personali, box 70, folder Aldo Bizzarri: Nota di De Cicco, 23 September 1940.
27 ASMAE, DGIE AS 1920-50. Fascicoli personali, box 70, folder Aldo Bizzarri: Nota di De Cicco, 23 September 1940.
28 ASMAE, DGIE AS 1920-50. Fascicoli personali, box 484, folder Gino Saviotti.
29 Vera de Matos, *Portugal e Itália: relações diplomáticas (1943-1974)* (Coimbra: Imprensa da Universidade de Coimbra, 2010), 24-5.
30 The Minister in Lisbon Bova Scoppa to the Minister of Foreign Affairs Galeazzo Ciano, Document number 10, 12 June 1940, Documenti diplomatici italiani (DDI), *Nona serie*, vol. V (Rome: Istituto Poligrafico dello Stato, 1965), 7-9.
31 Richard A. H. Robinson, *Contemporary Portugal: A History* (London: George Allen & Unwin, 1979), 87.
32 The Minister in Lisbon, Bova Scoppa, to the Minister of Foreign Affairs, Galeazzo Ciano, Document number 495, 25 January 1941, DDI, *Nona serie - Vol. VI* (Rome: Istituto Poligrafico dello Stato, 1986), 500-1.
33 Tom Gallagher, *Salazar. The Dictator Who Refused to Die* (London: Hurst & Company, 2020), 84.
34 ASMAE, DGIE AS 1936-1945, box 77, folder Istituto di cultura portogallo. Sezione di Oporto-Coimbra, 1939-1940: Letter from Di Poppa to Ferrari, 22 November 1940.
35 António O. Salazar, *Discursos (1928-34)* (Coimbra: Coimbra editora, 1939), 302.
36 ASMAE, DGIE AS 1936-45, box 107, folder Lisbona 1941: Report by Giacinto Manuppella, 16 January 1943.
37 ASMAE, DGIE AS 1936-45, box 107, folder Lisbona 1941: Report by Giuseppe Carlo Rossi, 15 January 1943.
38 ASMAE, DGIE AS 1936-45, box 77, folder Istituto di cultura italiana Portogallo- Sede Centrale Lisbona, final reports.
39 ASMAE, DGIE AS 1936-45, box 77, folder Istituto di cultura italiana Portogallo-Sede Centrale Lisbona. Relazioni periodiche 1939-40: Report by Gino Saviotti, 30 November 1940.
40 ASMAE, DGIE AS 1936-45, box 107, folder Lisbona 1941: Report by Luigi Felici, 19 January 1943.
41 ASMAE, DGIE AS 1936-45, box. 77, folder Istituto di cultura italiana Portogallo. Sede centrale Lisbona. Relazioni periodiche 1939-40: Report by Lorenzo Di Poppa, 12 December 1940.
42 ASMAE, DGIE AS 1936-45, b.107, f. Lisbona 1941: Report by Leo Pessina, 15 January 1943.
43 See Emilio Gentile, *25 luglio 1943* (Rome-Bari: Laterza, 2018).
44 H. James Burgwyn, *Mussolini and the Salò Republic, 1943-1945. The Failure of a Puppet Regime* (London: Palgrave Macmillan, 2018).
45 Lorenzo Medici, *Dalla propaganda alla cooperazione. La diplomazia culturale italiana nel secondo dopoguerra* (Padua: Cedam, 2009), 73-101.

46 Marino Viganò, *Il Ministero degli Affari Esteri e le relazioni internazionali della Repubblica Sociale Italiana (1943–1945)* (Milan: Jaca Book, 1991), 341–56.
47 ASMAE, Fondo RSI, box 37 Portogallo, folder Affari Politici: Political situation of RSI Committee in Portugal, 10 March 1944.
48 Copies of the bulletins are conserved in ASMAE, AP 1931–1945 Portogallo, box 17, folder Stampa.
49 ASMAE, AP 1931–1945, Portogallo, box 17, folder Stampa: Italian Legation's activities and propaganda counterattack, 3 December 1943.
50 ASMAE, DGIE AS 1936–45, box 171, folder 'Istituto Italiano di Cultura. Portogallo. Relazioni iniziali e finali: Costituzione e attività dell'istituto dal settembre 1943'.
51 Laura Melania Rocchi, 'Presenza culturale Italiana in Portogallo nei primi decenni del XX secolo', *Imprensa da Universidade de Coimbra*, no. 2 (2007): 374. Available online: https://digitalis-dsp.uc.pt/bitstream/10316.2/42652/6/Presenza_culturale_italiana_in_Portogallo.pdf (accessed 6 March 2022); Deborah Holmes, 'Gino Saviotti (1891–1980)', in *The Oxford Companion to Italian Literature*, ed. Peter Hainsworth and David Robey (Oxford: Oxford University Press, 2002), 228.

11

British propaganda and contingency planning for Spain

Marta García Cabrera

Spain's strategic location and the ambiguous position adopted by the regime of Francisco Franco favoured the country in becoming an active participant in the Second World War in some form. Wartime Spain's alignment with the Axis – characterized by a shared ideology that consisted of conservative, authoritarian, anti-democratic and anti-communist ideas – had its roots in the debt incurred during the Spanish Civil War. However, when the European war broke out in 1939, Franco assumed an official position of strict neutrality. Nevertheless, this was a neutrality which concealed an evident inclination towards the Axis – a position particularly manifested through constant collaboration with Germany in political, economic, logistical, propagandistic and military spheres. Furthermore, and despite Spanish neutrality, the country did not rule out the negotiation of and preparation for its participation in the war alongside Germany. Especially between 1941 and 1943, Spain took a particularly dangerous position, which raised the alarm among the Allies.

The ways in which Spain could be involved in the war, and consequently impact the Allies, were numerous. Spain could, for example, strengthen its cooperation with the Axis, and the Spanish population could succumb to the German influence. Spain could voluntarily participate in the conflict in response to Franco's colonial aspirations and Spain's belief in a short war. Spain could also give up its neutrality by favouring a German attack on Gibraltar or even lose its neutrality involuntarily by succumbing to the military advance of the Third Reich. It was also conceivable that Germany might occupy the Balearic Islands or invade the Canary Islands; the latter were seen by Britain as a strategic alternative to the loss of Gibraltar – its most important naval base in the Mediterranean region. Any of these scenarios would immediately tilt the balance of the war, considerably aggravating the Allied front in the Atlantic and Mediterranean. Spain was therefore seen as a dangerous neutral country: a strategic territory that needed to be controlled and persuaded throughout the war. Britain resorted to a number of different options to maintain Franco's strict neutrality and avoid Spanish cooperation with Nazi Germany – such as diplomacy, bribery and economic pressure.[1] However, Britain also prioritized the activation of a propaganda campaign of significant proportions.[2] Its initial attempts were characterized by a lack of coordination and ineffectiveness, but the efforts progressively evolved from what was needed to help Britain survive to focusing more on what was required to defeat Germany. The British effort was therefore a combination of diplomacy and propaganda which, although not dispensing with clandestine and subversive movements, always preferred cordial relations and understanding with the established regime.

However, Spain was also within scope of the planning by the Political Warfare Executive (PWE), a clandestine body that organized campaigns of operational propaganda – aimed at complementing military campaigns – in countries usually already occupied by or aligned with Nazi Germany.[3] Spain's growing inclination towards the Third Reich and the German advance in Europe alarmed the Allies, who feared Franco's belligerent participation or a Nazi invasion of Spanish territory, especially between 1941 and 1942. If the war reached the Iberian Peninsula, the diplomatic propaganda that had been distributed until then would not suffice. Therefore, the PWE designed several contingency plans which, at least in theory, prepared Allied propaganda for a scenario of greater belligerence.[4] Although the PWE's contingency plans conceived Spain as a territory involved in the war, a large proportion of the proposed campaigns continued to include neutrality and freedom as prominent symbols within the messaging. The Allied victories of 1942 and 1943 resulted in a slow return of Spain to its official neutrality.[5] From this time on, British propaganda no longer focused on the potential for enemy invasion, and instead redirected its efforts towards guaranteeing Spain's neutrality for the remainder of the war.

This chapter analyses the propaganda campaigns launched by Great Britain in Spain during the Second World War. Propaganda activities will be examined in three distinct phases: firstly, during the Franco regime's initial phase of neutrality (1939–40); secondly, during Spain's phase of non-belligerence, as distinct from neutrality (1940–2); and finally, during the period in which the Franco regime adopted another position of neutrality (1943–5). This chapter also analyses the instruments and content of British propaganda in a variety of forms to maintain Spain's neutrality when Franco was increasingly tempted to become involved in the war itself. However, this study also devotes special attention to the British design of 'operational propaganda' which, between 1941 and 1942, prepared Spain for various scenarios of war. This chapter will emphasize Spain's prominence on the international stage, the changeable nature of its neutrality and the continual realignment of British propaganda to these changing circumstances. Furthermore, this case study highlights the multiplicity of propaganda campaigns aligned to several alternative projected scenarios, and the potential for operational propaganda, understood as a complement to military operations which, in Spain, continued to be directed towards the shoring up of its neutrality.

British propaganda and Spain's fluctuating neutrality (1939–45)

Spain has always played a prominent role on the international stage and its strategic position was once again enhanced between 1939 and 1945. Its territory was in the middle of important trade routes, at the crossroads of strategic communication routes and the intersection of three continents. The Spanish coasts were an ideal refuge for the Axis ships and the country's territory also offered direct access to Gibraltar. 'The Rock', as Gibraltar is known, was Great Britain's main naval base in the Mediterranean region and its fall, or at least rendering it useless for military activity, was consequently a vital strategic military objective for Germany. Understanding this led to British military planners drawing up contingency plans for military action in the Canary Islands, considering the archipelago to be an excellent alternative naval base in the Atlantic.

Exhausted by the effects of its own Civil War and unable to mobilize a new war effort, Franco declared Spain's neutrality when war broke out in September 1939. However, and despite this status of official neutrality, the Spanish government prepared for its participation in the war and was not shy in demonstrating its ideological preferences, especially in two distinct phases. The first of these was after the fall of France in June 1940 when Spain adopted a position of 'non-belligerence', rather than strict neutrality, which favoured the Axis powers. Between August 1940 and February 1941, Europe witnessed a critical moment of negotiations between Spain and Germany, which, although it did not finally culminate in the formal military participation of Spain, it did reinforce its involvement in the war. This phase of temptation towards belligerency by Franco was later intensified – between June 1941 and June 1942 – with the German advance on the Soviet Union and the revival of Spanish anti-communism, which justified renewed Spanish interest in the war,[6] manifested, for example, through the dispatch of the Blue Division to the Eastern Front.[7] Economic and diplomatic pressures exerted by the United Nations (as the United States, Great Britain and other Allied nations fighting the Axis were described at the time) resulted in Spain slowly returning to its official status of neutrality after the Allied victories of 1942. However, the actual change in Spain's foreign policy only took place at the end of 1943, when the new military achievements of the Allies finally tempered the blatant Germanophilia of the Spanish government.[8]

For the Francoists, both France and Great Britain were the sacred enemies of the Spanish nation – a perception that was reinforced not only by the memory of the Napoleonic invasion and the popular resentment over Gibraltar but also by the Allies' position in the Civil War. The Francoists shared nothing with the democracy, monarchy and the Anglicanism that generally defined British politics and culture. And to top it all, Britain allied with the Soviet Union from the summer of 1941, which endowed Franco's anti-Allied cause with an anti-communist crusade component. The Spanish regime led its own national struggle against democracies and communism that hindered Franco's sympathies with the Allies and favoured Spain's alignment with the Axis. Even though Spain did not finally participate in the war, the Franco government offered constant collaboration with Nazi Germany, which included the trade in war materials, the use of the Spanish merchant navy and the supply of German submarines in national ports. The Spanish government offered support to the espionage, intelligence and subversion activities deployed by the Reich, also contributing to the development of its propaganda campaign while hindering the one promoted by the democracies.[9] The ambiguous position adopted by the Franco government activated the alarm of the

Allied powers, who feared that the Spanish territory would become a new war front – directly or indirectly, voluntarily or involuntarily.

Therefore, Great Britain attempted to control Franco's neutrality through different campaigns: diplomatic, economic, clandestine, strategic and, most importantly for this study, propagandistic. Spanish territory was the scene of a propaganda battle of significant proportions that involved the very powers that were killing each other on the front lines. Hitler's Germany kept Spain in a prominent position in its planning, by mounting a persuasive campaign that had the connivance and support of the Franco regime. Nazi propaganda was channelled from Hans Lazar's Press Office within the German Embassy in Madrid.[10] Along with Ambassador Eberhard von Stohrer, Lazar tried to exploit Franco's Germanophilia to the greatest extent by emphasizing totalitarian solidarity and undermining Allied propaganda campaigns – such objectives were set out in the German *Grosse Plan* [translating as 'Great Plan']. France and Britain rolled out their persuasive efforts in a measured way, fighting against the obstacles imposed by the Spanish regime, and, given Germany's advantageous position, just trying to ensure survival of Allied messaging. Although France mobilized its activities in an uncoordinated and ineffective manner, the French initiative led the Allied campaign at the beginning of the war and, indeed, its early moves triggered increased interest from the British agencies.

After the fall of France, Britain took the lead in seeking to control Spanish public opinion for the remainder of the conflict. Although the British initially mounted a weak, defensive and uncontrolled campaign, their activities progressively evolved. Its activities were conducted mainly through diplomatic and clandestine channels, which were also mobilized by British residents and Spanish citizens. Britain's campaign sought to maintain Spain's neutrality, weaken the Axis image and guarantee post-war economic and commercial interests. Britain's propaganda mission was leveraged by the British Ministry of Information (MoI) through a diverse network of specialized sections – such as the Foreign Publicity Department, the Overseas Planning Committee, the Roman Catholic affairs section and multiple geographic subdivisions – that included Spain as a priority. The section responsible for propaganda in the Iberian zone was initially controlled and directed from London by William (Billy) McCann. Michael Stewart and Denys Cowan were in charge of the Spanish area, while the Lord Chancellor was responsible for propaganda policy in Portuguese territory.[11] Their stances were also overseen by the War Office and the Foreign Office, which, alongside the embassy and the consulates established in Spain, helped to coordinate the propaganda campaign in the neutral territory.[12]

In Madrid, the office was initially supervised by Thomas Pears, who, although he gave an initial boost to the persuasive activity in the country, launched a campaign that was limited in effect.[13] It was Franco's rapprochement towards Nazi Germany – from the summer of 1940 – that catalysed the actions of Great Britain, which then reinforced its diplomatic, strategic and propaganda activities in Spain. The mission began with the arrival of a new Ambassador, the influential former Foreign Secretary, Sir Samuel Hoare. He came to Madrid with the brief to keep Spain out of the international conflict by maintaining an amicable understanding with Franco without dispensing, however, with instruments of pressure and persuasion. Nonetheless, the main boost to British propaganda in the country came from a new press attaché, Thomas Ferrier Burns (1906–95), who left his post at the MoI's Roman Catholic affairs section to coordinate propaganda activity in Spain.[14] In Barcelona, the British established a second semi-diplomatic press section run by Paul Dorchy, a talented British citizen, polyglot, with great social skills and experienced in advertising and propaganda.[15] In the rest of the country, propaganda was channelled through the consular authorities, which spread the propaganda messages to all the territories alongside the British community and Anglophile Spaniards who wished to play their part.[16] Despite the ambassador's refusal to use subversive and clandestine tactics, the Special Operations Executive (SOE) representative in Gibraltar – Hugh Quennell – also promoted some propaganda campaigns in the country.[17]

Despite Spanish interference, Great Britain channelled its propaganda through multiple channels and instruments. The press was the most censored channel, and it was therefore difficult to influence. Therefore, the British directed their efforts towards exploiting printed material in the form of leaflets, pamphlets, flyers, magazines and newsletters. The BBC Spanish Service from London became the most combative and influential medium, while film was intended for diplomatic or private events. However, the British also took advantage of the potential of spoken and social propaganda while giving special attention to religious campaigns. Moreover, the SOE was responsible for transmitting manipulated rumours that sought to weaken the enemy from within. Great Britain emphasized its role as a nation that protected freedoms, in a struggle between good and evil that would be won by Allied power and unity. The propaganda themes highlighted the Allies' military, socio-economic and political strength while attacking the weakest points of the enemy powers: their ruthless actions, exploitation of neutral countries and tendency to lie.[18]

The toying with belligerency by the Spanish regime, and the constant threat of German expansion between 1941 and 1942, intensified Great Britain's propaganda campaigns in Spain. Its channels, messages, instruments and agents were multiplied in an effort to maintain the country's neutrality. However, the British also resorted to designing operational propaganda that would be deployed to complement their potential military interventions in the country if these ever materialized. They prepared the propaganda activities for a scenario where Spain joined the war in some form.

British strategy in Spain and planning operational propaganda (1941–3)

War propaganda is an instrument of recruitment and persuasion deployed when a country is involved in a conflict. However, not all war propaganda campaigns are directly related to military and strategic action in a narrow sense. As we have seen, a large proportion of the persuasive campaigns launched in Spain during the Second World War pursued well-defined political, socio-economic, ideological or cultural objectives: the maintenance of neutrality, the alignment of support, the reduction of enemy influence, the search for economic advantages and the preparation for the post-war period, among many others. Only one part of war propaganda – operational propaganda[19] – is actually designed to support direct military activities. It uses persuasive campaigns that prepare the ideological and sociocultural ground for the deployment of military operations (invasion, advance, occupation or counterattack). This form of propaganda is usually aimed towards active areas of conflict, for example, war fronts, occupied areas or enemy territories. However, operational propaganda campaigns can also be designed for neutral countries, which are understood as strategic locations that, although not part of the war, may become a part of it either forcibly or voluntarily. Operational propaganda was part of the government machinery of the belligerent powers. For instance, the Psychological Warfare Division and the PWE were responsible for controlling Allied operational propaganda, especially from the summer of 1941 onwards.[20]

Although Spain never left its position of neutrality, the Franco regime adopted a position of non-belligerence, which, in practice, meant a clear swaying towards the Axis powers. For the Allies, the main risk of Spain's position between 1941 and 1942 was its possible involvement in the war or the German occupation of its territory. If this new war front became a reality, it could completely tilt the balance of power, diminish British control in the Atlantic basin and the western Mediterranean, aggravate maritime communications with French ports in North Africa and, at the same time, make any offensive in the area more difficult. To prevent Spanish belligerence, the United Nations used instruments of diplomatic and economic pressure, intelligence activities and subtle propaganda campaigns. However, the threat of Spain no longer being neutral was becoming increasingly concerning for Britain. This situation favoured Britain including Spain in the planning of the armed forces, intelligence agencies and subversive propaganda departments. Spain was a target of Allied military planning, which, in a context of aiming to forestall a German advance and avoiding the potential for Spain to join the war, also considered interventions in either the mainland or in the Canary Islands.[21] The planning of military manoeuvres also required thorough strategic and propaganda preparation. While the intelligence services of the armed forces gathered strategic information to facilitate any military intervention, the agencies in charge of operational propaganda designed persuasive campaigns that, at least in theory, sought to clear the ground for military campaigns through creating a propitious attitude and opinion among Spanish citizens.[22]

Between 1941 and 1943, the PWE drew up operational plans for Spain. Besides providing examples of subversive propaganda material, these plans included a description of core themes and persuasive instruments that could be used in case a war situation was declared. Its operations aimed to persuade the Spanish population to reject their country's belligerence by withstanding any external invasion and accepting the assistance of the United Nations – mainly the United States and Britain. Even though its plans were designed in the abstract, ahead of events and viewing Spain as a territory at war, the PWE's campaigns still considered neutrality as the main symbolic reference in propaganda slogans. These messages portrayed national resistance as an act of patriotism and Allied intervention as a liberalizing movement, all aimed at defending the freedom and inviolability of Spain – both that of its soil and its neutrality.

Between May 1941 and December 1942, the PWE drew up its most important contingency plan under the title *Plan for political warfare in the contingency that Spain or the Balearics are invaded by the Axis*.[23] The plan, which was overseen by the Joint Intelligence Division and also involved the US State Department and the US Office of War Information, prepared Allied propaganda activities in Spain in the event of military intervention in the country. To this end, two potential scenarios were considered. On the one hand, the possibility that the Germans would force Franco to declare war against the United Nations in order to use his territory for military operations, or that Franco himself would allow German troops to pass through without a declaration of war. And on the other hand, the possibility that the Germans would invade Spain and face the resistance of the Spanish Army. In any of these potential scenarios, propaganda was to be radicalized and disseminated subversively through radio broadcasts and the dropping of leaflets – especially in areas such as Madrid, Barcelona, Bilbao, Seville and the islands. To maintain Spanish unity against the enemy, propaganda themes would deliberately not evoke episodes from the Spanish Civil War or include class or ideological matters. Despite the fact that 'Latinity' was a prominent component of Franco's propaganda campaigns – as an evocation of Spain's imperial and glorious past – it was also part of the British operational theme that tried to reinforce the unity and strength of the Spanish resistance struggle.

The main objective of the PWE was to frustrate the Axis by encouraging the army, or part of the army, to resist the invasion. In addition, Spanish citizens were to be encouraged to fight for the freedom and neutrality of their country with the assurance of material support from the United Nations. Propaganda was to prepare the nation to make the invader's path 'as difficult and dangerous as possible', appealing to the people's historical memory of sabotaging previous foreign forces and associating the German invasion with a betrayal represented by the Falange – the political party of the Franco regime. The slogans and themes were clear and straightforward:

> Spain has never allowed an invader on her soil without fighting. Those in the Army on the mainland and islands should rally behind the resisting military leaders. The Army in Morocco can help the liberation of Spain by joining with the United Nations Forces in North Africa. The British Government is making immediate arrangements to supply all Spaniards who are resisting with food and arms. . . . This invasion is the culmination of conspiracy on the part of the Falange, who for the purpose of maintaining themselves in power against the will of the remainder of Spain, are betraying their country into vassalage. . . . There are thousands of Germans in Spain, all spies and agents of the Gestapo. Take action to eliminate them now before it is too late.[24]

The plan included a draft of a militant pamphlet that clearly set out all the necessary thematic guidelines in the event of military mobilization in Spain:

> Spaniards: The German attack on Spain has begun. The Nazi tyrant, in a last desperate throw, has violated Spanish soil. For the first time in more than a century, a foreign army is marching against Spain. As the tramp of the invader

resounds on your frontier, the peoples of the world have turned their eyes on you. They know that never in Spanish History have the Spanish people tolerated such a violation and they know that in 1942 all true Spaniards are ready to fight once again for the integrity of their soil.

Spaniards: The time has come for all to unite against the aggressor, to rally round those who have already taken up arms to repel him. In the Pyrenees your fellow-countrymen have set you the example: soldiers and civilians, young and old, they are fighting shoulder to shoulder. Their banner: the sacred name of Spain. Their battle-cry: the age-old sanctity of Spanish soil.

Spaniards: Unite against aggression! Fight against aggression! The South American peoples pledged to the cause of the United Nations look to you to defend the honour and integrity of their motherland, Spain, cradle of the true Hispanidad. The pressed peoples of Europe know that your resistance will bring nearer the Victory which will free them from the Nazi chains which bind them.

Already the tide of war has turned, and behind you, you have the military strength and the vast resources of the United Nations, who will fight on with you till Spain can take her place at the Victory Conference as an independent power, free from foreign interference and free to decide her own destiny.

Spaniards: Long live Spain.[25]

The messages were to remind the Spanish people of their historic and heroic fighting spirit. Moreover, propaganda campaigns would provide citizens with new reasons to fight, spreading evidence – both real and false – of the Falange conspiracy, Germany's expansionist desires in the Mediterranean, Nazi exploitation of neutral nations or the atrocities carried out by the Axis armies. Simultaneously, propaganda was to serve as a training tool, instructing citizens in the art of guerrilla warfare and sabotage. Finally, propaganda channels were to be used as an instrument of attack against the invader in order to weaken, discourage and frighten the enemy through exaggerations and manipulations.[26]

In December 1942, the PWE drew up a second plan in which propaganda would support more offensive military operations.[27] This plan dispensed with the idea that Spain would join the war because of its own actions or actions by the Axis, and instead envisaged a scenario where the United Nations initiated an intervention in the country. The military actions were again publicized as anticipatory moves against the collaborationist action of the Falange and Germany's expansionism:

The forces of the United Nations have entered Spain in order to forestall an Axis invasion of your country. An Axis invasion has been plotted in concert with Falangist traitors who, for their own ends, have been conspiring to bring about the enslavement of your country to the Axis, which would mean, as it has done in every other country Axis troops have entered, famine and harsher exploitation that you have already known. . . . We bring your arms, food, medical supplies, and clothing. We bring you the massive armed forces of the United Nations to aid you in your task. Immediately the German threat has been removed finally and forever, our forces will leave Spain – a free, neutral, and strong Spain. It is our desire to see Spain ruled by Spaniards independent of foreign influence, by Spaniards chosen by the people of Spain.[28]

However, the Allied victories of 1943 and the halting of German expansion reduced the Spanish threat. Therefore, these contingency plans were shelved. Soft and diplomatic propaganda followed its ordinary course in the process of steady expansion that was also favoured by Spain's slow return to its official neutrality and the consequent weakening of the German *Grosse Plan*. Although Spanish interference, such as censorship, was maintained against British propaganda until the end of the conflict, the efforts became easier as it became clearer the Nazi Germany would be defeated. Britain was increasingly able to project a positive image of Great Britain that sought to promote British leadership and Anglo-Spanish understanding in the post-war period ahead.

Conclusion

Great Britain's propaganda mission in the Second World War Spain adds a new dimension to the analysis of propaganda and neutrality. This study highlights the complexity, variability and changeability of Spanish neutrality between 1939 and 1945, which explains the multiple changes experienced by British propaganda activity throughout the war. Propaganda was devised as an instrument of British foreign policy, and it was a weapon that fluctuated in the heat of international events. Britain adjusted its propaganda efforts to the different modalities of Franco's neutrality, both actual and potential: from strict neutrality and non-belligerence to considering the possible active belligerence of the country. Additionally, the British launched a varied and comprehensive network of propaganda types: from soft, cultural and diplomatic propaganda to operational campaigns. Official propaganda emanated from the British Ministry of Information, which channelled its stances through diplomatic press offices located primarily in Madrid and Barcelona. They tried to disseminate subtle and passive messages through multiple channels, from the printing of persuasive material and broadcasting to the holding of film events, spreading rumours and distributing propaganda copies.

Spanish neutrality became both the target and the subject of Britain's propaganda messages. The persuasive contents tried to steer Spanish public opinion towards maintaining its neutrality and rejecting the German enemy. Although Spain never left its position of neutrality, the Franco regime became a constant threat to the Allied powers, especially between 1941 and 1942. The country was not a party to the war but could become one – forcibly or voluntarily – which favoured the planning of potential military responses and the anticipation of propaganda campaigns to pave the way for interventions. The British tried to stay ahead of the events and, through bodies such as the PWE, they designed propaganda plans that considered multiple possible war scenarios: the participation of the Franco regime in the war, the German strategic invasion of the country or the military intervention of the United Nations.

Its campaigns sought to create support for any Allied intervention by encouraging Spain's rejection – both civilian and military – of its country's belligerence and the German occupation of its territories. However, even when belligerency would have meant the end of Spanish neutrality, neutrality itself *did* continue to play a prominent role in the Allied propaganda campaign. Its slogans evidenced the power of neutrality and freedom as propaganda elements in themselves. They portrayed Spain as an occupied territory whose neutrality had been violated or betrayed, both by the political body of the Franco regime and by Germany, as a country that had lost its freedom through the imposition of totalitarian force. Consequently, Spanish neutrality would become a mythicized symbol which, as in Belgium, would be used to build upon the reaction of the Spanish population and justify the armed intervention of the United Nations.

The Allied victories on the international front and the progressive shift of the Franco regime towards a more neutral position between 1943 and 1945 reduced Spain's active threat. Contingency plans for operational propaganda in the country were never executed, and their contents were shelved. As for the British, they adjusted their assumptions and returned to more conventional means of diplomatic and cultural channels. Their campaigns sought to maintain a reciprocal benevolence between Great Britain and Spain in the post-war period ahead, using propaganda slogans promising the survival of the Franco regime against the backdrop of a new struggle scenario: the war against the Soviet enemy in the forthcoming Cold War.

Notes

1 Denis Smyth, *Diplomacy and Strategy of Survival: British Policy and Franco's Spain, 1940-41* (Cambridge: Cambridge University Press, 1986); Richard Wigg, *Churchill and Spain: The Survival of the Franco Regime, 1940-1945* (London: Routledge, 2015); Ángel Viñas, *Sobornos. De cómo Churchill y March compraron a los generales de Franco* (Barcelona: Crítica, 2016).
2 Marta García Cabrera, 'Filias y fobias en acción: propaganda británica en España durante la Primera y la Segunda Guerra Mundial', Doctoral thesis (University of Las Palmas de Gran Canaria, 2021) and *Bajo las zarpas del león: La persuasión británica en España durante las guerras mundiales* (Madrid: Marcial Pons, 2022). Also see Pedro Correa Martín-Arroyo, 'Propaganda Wars in Wartime Spain: Sir Samuel Hoare, the British Embassy, and the British Propaganda Campaign for "Neutral" Spain', Dissertation (Leiden University, 2014) and Christopher Bannister, 'Diverging Neutrality in Iberia: The British Ministry of Information in Spain and Portugal During the Second World War', in *Allied Communication to the Public during the Second World War*, ed. Simon Elliot and Marc Wiggam (London: Bloomsbury, 2020).
3 David Garnett, *The Secret History of PWE: The Political Warfare Executive, 1939–1945* (London: St Ermin's Press, 2002) and David Welch, *Propaganda: Power and Persuasion* (London: British Library, 2013), 95.
4 The UK National Archives (hereafter TNA), Foreign Office files (hereafter FO) 371/34764, Drafts of Propaganda plan for Spain, 6 April 1943, and FO 371/26953, OPC: Propaganda plan for Spain, December 1941.

5 Javier Tusell, *Franco, España y la Segunda Guerra Mundial. Entre el Eje y la neutralidad* (Madrid: Temas de hoy, 1995), 205–86; 419; Wayne H. Bowen, *Spain during World War II* (Missouri: University of Missouri Press, 2006), 52–60; Stanley Payne, *Franco and Hitler: Spain, Germany, and World War II* (New Haven: Yale University Press, 2008), 236–52.
6 Wigg, *Churchill and Spain*, 12–13; David Wingeate Pike, *Franco and the Axis stigma* (London: Springer, 2008), 50; Tusell Gómez, *Franco, España y la II Guerra Mundial: entre el Eje y la neutralidad* (Madrid: Temas de hoy, 1995), 102; Stanley Payne and Delia Contreras, *España y la Segunda Guerra Mundial* (Madrid: Editorial Complutense, 1996), 55–64.
7 Denis Smyth, 'The Dispatch of the Spanish Blue Division to the Russian Front: Reasons and Repercussions', *European History Quarterly* 24, no. 4 (1994): 537–53.
8 Gómez, *Franco, España y la II Guerra Mundial*, 205–10; 286 and 419; and Payne, *Franco and Hitler*, 236–52.
9 Manuel Ros Agudo, *Franco y Hitler 1940: de la gran tentación al gran engaño* (Madrid: Arco, 2009), 23–34 and David Messenger, 'Against the Grain: Special Operations Executive in Spain, 1941–45', *Intelligence and National Security* 20, no. 1 (2006): 174.
10 Ingrid Schulze Schneider, 'La propaganda alemana en España: 1942–1944', *Espacio Tiempo y Forma. Serie V, Historia Contemporánea*, no. 7 (1994): 370–5. https://revistas.uned.es/index.php/ETFV/article/view/2988 and Mercedes Peñalba-Sotorrío, 'Beyond the War: Nazi Propaganda Aims in Spain during the Second World War', *Journal of Contemporary History* 54, no. 4 (2019): 902–26.
11 TNA, FO 371/26951, McCann to FO, 1 August 1941 and FO 371/34766, McCann letter, 2 November 1943.
12 García Cabrera, 'Filias y fobias en acción', 258–65 and Robert Cole, *Britain and the War of Words in Neutral Europe, 1939–1945: The Art of the Possible* (New York: Macmillan, 1990), 98.
13 TNA, FO 371/23170, Thomas Pears' report, 16 November 1939.
14 TNA, FO 930/187, Telegram to Hoare, 19 October 1940. Also see García Cabrera, 'Filias y fobias en acción', 265–79 and Jimmy Burns, *Papa Spy: Love, Faith, and Betrayal in Wartime Spain* (Madrid: Debate, 2010), 53–120.
15 TNA, FO 930/179, Press attaché's visit to Catalonia, 20 February 1940.
16 García Cabrera, 'Filias y fobias en acción', 252–8 and 266.
17 TNA, FO 371/26952, SOE activities in Gibraltar and southern Spain, September 1941.
18 TNA, FO 930/20, Report: propaganda plan in Spain (1941–3), May 1943. Also see García Cabrera, 'Filias y fobias en acción', 294–356.
19 The concept of operational propaganda does not yet occupy a prominent place in historiography. However, parts of its components are present in specialized research or case studies. See, for example, Baruch A. Hazan, *Soviet Propaganda* (London: Routledge, 1976), 29.
20 Tim Brooks, *British Propaganda to France, 1940–1944* (Edinburgh: Edinburgh University Press, 2007), 34; Stanley Newcourt-Nowodworski, *Black Propaganda in the Second World War* (London: The History Press, 1996); Charles Greig Cruickshank, *The Fourth Arm: Psychological Warfare 1938–1945* (London: HarperCollins, 1977), 52–4.
21 Viñas, *Sobornos. De cómo Churchill y March*, 78–84 and 400–11. Also see Juan José Díaz Benítez, 'Los proyectos británicos para ocupar las Islas Atlánticas (1940–1943)', *Hispania Nova. Revista de Historia Contemporánea* 11 (2013): 3–10.

22 See, for example, Marta García Cabrera, 'British Geographic Intelligence during the Second World War: A Case Study of the Canary Islands', *Intelligence and National Security* 37 (2022): 1–19.
23 TNA, FO 898/248, Spain: Plan of political warfare, 4 December 1942. Also see Cole, *Britain and the War of Words*, 98.
24 TNA, FO 898/248, Spain: Plan of political warfare, 4 December 1942.
25 Ibid. Quotation from Government-produced material. Crown Copyright under the Open Government Licence.
26 TNA, FO 898/249, Preparatory action section of the Contingency Plan, 11 November 1942.
27 TNA, FO 898/249, Propaganda policy in case of contingencies, 13 December 1942.
28 Ibid.

12

Censorship and private shows
Mapping British film propaganda in Sweden

Emil Stjernholm

On 31 October 1942, the British Colony Committee in Stockholm invited friends of the Allied cause to a private showing of the film *One of Our Aircraft Is Missing* (Michael Powell and Emeric Pressburger, 1942) at the newly opened Park Cinema on Östermalm in the centre of the city. Produced under the auspices of Britain's Ministry of Information (MoI), the film's narrative revolves around a crew involved in fighting over the Netherlands who, following a German aerial attack, receive help from the Dutch resistance movement to flee back to England and to avoid capture. As military historian Simon MacKenzie notes, *One of Our Aircraft Is Missing* was part of a broader effort to promote a positive view of the Royal Air Force's bombing campaign over Europe.[1] The private screening at the Park Cinema took place several months before the distributor submitted the film to the National Board of Film Censors [Statens biografbyrå]. During the Second World War, the Swedish censorship board cooperated closely with the Sweden's Ministry of Foreign Affairs [Utrikesdepartementet] and the Government Board of Information [Statens informationsstyrelse] in assessing the potential harm that imported films might do to neutral Sweden's relations with other nations, in which case the films would be banned or partially censored. In fact, *One of Our Aircraft Is Missing* was banned on 19 March 1943, with the censor remarking that 'the film would be considered offensive to Germany and therefore it should not be approved for screening in public'.[2] Following intense discussions with the censorship board, and most importantly the editing out of 'anti-German dialogue', the film was approved for public screening in September 1943. However, long before this, Swedish counter-surveillance records show that the movie had circulated widely in Sweden, having been screened by organizations and communities such as the British Colony Committee in Stockholm, Norwegian expats in Uppsala and at the Anglo-Swedish Society in Gothenburg.[3]

While much previous research has focused on the propaganda war in Swedish cinemas, including both newsreels and feature films, little attention has been devoted to the clandestine film screenings that were organized by member clubs, friendship societies and other associations throughout the course of the Second World War.[4]

During the war, both Nazi Germany and the Allies invested heavily in propaganda in neutral Sweden. The battle for hearts and minds involved widespread dissemination of propaganda, but Stockholm also became a veritable hot spot for espionage, as well as intelligence gathering on enemies' propaganda efforts. Using previously neglected material from the Swedish Civilian Security Service's counter-espionage, as well as material from the British Foreign Office and MoI, this chapter studies the media production of the British Legation in Stockholm and tracks the circulation of British film propaganda in Sweden during the Second World War. As Jussi Parikka notes, an analysis inspired by media archaeology shifts attention from dominant representations to 'alternative histories, forgotten paths, and sidekicks of media history'.[5] Drawing on Parikka, this chapter places the centre of attention on moments of construction, innovation, failure and breakdown in the building of a film propaganda infrastructure. This raises the following central research questions: How did the British Legation circulate British film propaganda in Sweden? And what happened when these infrastructures were challenged and resisted by Swedish authorities?

Mapping British film propaganda

Two months after the outbreak of the Second World War, the Press Office at the British Legation in Stockholm was engaged in a wide variety of propaganda activities in Sweden. Working out of a British Legation building on Strandvägen 82 in the diplomatic quarter of Stockholm, the unit's two official functions were to organize the supply of information *for* the MoI and the legation – and to supply information *from* the UK for dissemination in Sweden.[6] This propaganda and information unit was headed by Peter Tennant, who arrived in Stockholm during spring 1939 and whose official title was that of press attaché, although his covert role was that of a Special Operations Executive intelligence officer.[7] Already before the outbreak of the war, a representative for the British Legation in Stockholm wrote to British Foreign Secretary Lord Halifax to argue for the urgency of intensified publicity measures in Sweden: 'Sweden is, of the Scandinavian countries, the one which is likely to play the most important role in wartime, and, although she is determined to maintain her neutrality at all costs, the nature of that role is likely to depend very largely on the extent of the sympathy felt in Sweden for British policy.'[8]

Early on, the British realized that the Germans had placed much greater emphasis on propaganda and the influencing of Swedish public opinion than they had.[9] Germany's ambitious propaganda initiatives included the illustrated journal *Signal*,[10] the radio network *Radio Königsberg* and the newsreel *Ufa-journalen*, as well as various initiatives to strengthen the institutional bonds, networks and entanglements between Germany and Sweden.[11] Rather than forming a separate information bureau, the British propaganda activities took place under the auspices of the Press Office's activities, a practice similarly adopted by the German Legation and later also the American Legation.[12] During the early days of the war, a memorandum sent to the MoI highlights that the British Legation's Press Office was engaged in several types of media production and circulation.[13] A key activity was to translate, type, stencil and distribute print material to the Swedish press, as well as valued institutions and individuals. Besides this, photographs were supplied to journalists and for display in shop windows, the wireless reception of radio was monitored and reports were sent back to the BBC, while the British Council supplied libraries with British classics, organized reading circles, planned art exhibitions and set up visits of cultural figures such as T. S. Eliot, among other things.[14] In 1940, the important British propaganda outlet *Nyheter från Storbritannien* [translating as 'News from Great Britain'], a Swedish-language news bulletin, was established by Tennant and the Press Office.[15] In terms of film, the memorandum notes, '[m]uch work has been done to improve our relations with the film industry in Sweden and steps have been taken to assure greater publicity to British feature films, shorts and newsreels'.[16] However, the establishment of a British propaganda unit, John Gilmour asserts, was chaotic and belated, and 'what the British underestimated was the extent of Swedish media regulation which constrained the British propaganda effort'.[17]

British film propaganda in Sweden has been largely neglected in previous scholarship. John Gilmour's book *Sweden, the Swastika and Stalin* (2010) provides a survey of the political challenges facing Sweden during the Second World War, but only one chapter is dedicated to the topic of propaganda, with film propaganda only mentioned in passing.[18] Meanwhile, the regulation of film propaganda in Sweden during the war has been the subject of previous research, for example in Arne Svensson's Swedish-language monograph on politically motivated censorship. Notably, neither Gilmour nor Svensson deal in depth with the private film screenings that the belligerent legations organized in neutral Sweden throughout the war. This chapter thus aims to fill this knowledge gap.

A transnational and transmedial perspective

Theoretically, this chapter takes inspiration from media archaeology and the field of cultural-historical media research. A key aim within cultural-historical media research, an interdisciplinary branch of study which has gained momentum over the past decade, has been to broaden existing definitions of the media concept. Lisa Gitelman, for instance, has noted that 'media are unique and complicated historical subjects. Their histories must be social and cultural, not the stories of how one technology leads to another, or of isolated geniuses working their magic on the world'.[19] Drawing on this principle, scholars working with a cultural-historical perspective on media history tend to emphasize the social, cultural, economic and material conditions shaping communication, circumstances that have changed and transformed over time. Drawing on this impetus, Marie Cronqvist and Christoph Hilgert argue for the importance of *transnational* and *transmedial* approaches in media historical scholarship, emphasizing both cross-border entanglements and the interrelations between media.[20] In the context of this chapter, this entails that analytical weight will be placed on transnational media practices such as media infrastructure development, hands-on everyday work with propaganda and media circulation, rather than an emphasis on propaganda content or representations. Moreover, drawing on the broad media concept discussed above, the analysis will not centre solely on films, but also the broader media ensemble that the British Legation used to communicate with local audiences, including events, newspapers, invitation cards, letters and posters.

Empirically, the analysis in this chapter relies on archival research in two archives: the archive of Sweden's Civilian Security Service [Allmänna säkerhetstjänstens arkiv, ASA] deposited at the National Archives of Sweden [Riksarkivet, RA] and the British Foreign Office archives at the UK's National Archives at Kew. The material deposited in the Civilian Security Service's archive includes monitored correspondence, transcriptions of wiretapped phone calls, film distribution lists and invitation cards. In the British Foreign Office archives, the material collected includes policy documents, correspondence, internal notes on strategy and several reports on the propaganda situation on the ground in neutral Sweden. Also, the Civilian Security Service's 200-page personal file on James Knapp-Fischer, the film attaché of the British Legation and a key figure in British film propaganda, has been utilized as a source. This material includes surveillance of Knapp-Fischer and other personnel from the British and the American Legations, as well as reports on his and the British Legation's activities in Sweden. Notably, the Civilian Security Service's archives were systematically dismantled following the end of the war.[21] From a methodological point of view, this means that it is difficult for today's scholars to know what has been included and what has been excluded in the surveillance collections, regarding the material both on British propaganda in general and on specific individuals. Similarly, scholars have argued that the British Foreign Office archives present a curated image of British foreign policy, organized around foreign policy issues rather than practices and everyday life, something which also needs to be taken into account when assessing the collections on British propaganda in Sweden.[22] Lastly, to contextualize some of the findings in the archival material, searches have been made in the National Library of Sweden's repository for digitized newspapers.

Establishing an infrastructure for film propaganda

British film propaganda in Sweden comprised three key elements: commercial feature films, newsreels and short documentary films. As mentioned, Swedish film censorship was strict when it came to commercial distribution of films with a potentially propagandistic message. Among the fifty-nine films banned by the National Board of Film Censors during the Second World War, listed in Svensson's volume, twenty-nine were of American origin, twenty were of British origin, five were of German origin, three were of Soviet origin, one was of Finnish origin and one was of Australian origin. This reflects Hollywood's major influence on the Swedish film market, which grew during the war.[23] It is noteworthy that British films were the second most banned films during the war. While little systematic research has been done on British film distribution in Scandinavia during the Second World War, and the exact market share of British films on the Swedish market remains unknown, this indicates British film distributors' high level of activity in Sweden at the time. Meanwhile, German films constituted less than 10 per cent of the total supply in Sweden, as noted by Roel Vande Winkel et al., and approximately 8 per cent of the banned films.[24]

The strict censorship regulations meant that the British Legation's Press Office needed to devise means to circumvent them. As Peter Tennant noted in a letter to the Ministry of Information in September 1939, 'Stockholm is reported to have more cinema seats per head of the population than any town in the world', and he added that the medium's wide popular appeal made it key for propaganda purposes.[25] In terms of infrastructure, British and American films arrived in Sweden primarily through air freight.[26] During the first half of the war, commercial films that could not pass the censor were widely distributed in private shows taking place in hired commercial cinemas. However, in January 1943, Sweden's Association of Cinema Owners [Sveriges Biografägarförbund] made the decision that private shows would no longer be accepted in their member cinemas.[27] Following this, non-theatrical screenings gained importance, as well as cooperation with local institutions such as workers' clubs, unions and friendship societies. Around this time, the Press Office developed a collaboration with the production company Filmo, which was established by the Swedish Labour Movement and had ties with the Social Democratic Party,[28] to assist in the circulation of British films in non-theatrical settings such as the People's House and other arenas associated with the labour movement.[29]

Given the clandestine nature of private screenings beyond the censor's watchful eye, reliable audience figures are usually scarce. In the case of Britain, Peter Tennant sent reports to London on the circulation of different types of propaganda in Sweden – from press material to film – on a regular basis. For example, as noted in a 37-page report from November 1944, the Press Office spent £14,837 on films, photographs and publications in the financial year 1943–4 (£669,500 in today's currency), approximately 17 per cent of the total budget. This report also highlights how widespread the British film propaganda had become towards the latter half of the war:

> In the month of April 1944, seven commercial features reached an audience of 9,160. Filmo started to show our films to audiences of workers in December 1942, and films shown in this way reach a large audience. . . . In the period from January to April 1944, 4,112 shows of Ministry of Information shorts and commercial feature films were given to audiences totalling 877,945. May, June and July are slack months in the cinema world and during that period the number of showings fell to 538, reaching an audience of 104,320.[30]

These impressive audience figures likely include both commercial screenings approved by the censors and non-theatrical private shows of feature films, newsreels and short films organized by Filmo and the British Legation itself. Moreover, the latter two categories – newsreels and short films – were important means of mass media propaganda. Since Swedish censorship regulations required that no narration should be added outside of Sweden, newsreels, shorts and documentaries were sent to Sweden without them and instead commentary or intertitles were added locally.[31] The weekly *Paramountjournalen* ['Paramount Journals'] included both British and American newsreels and was under the direction of the British and the American Press Offices.[32]

The newsreel would screen in conjunction with feature films in commercial cinemas, as well as in Svensk Filmindustri's weekly newsreel programme *Dagens spegelbilder* ['Today's Mirror Images'], which typically also included Swedish and German newsreels.[33] Besides this, the Gaumont British newsreel was imported to Sweden and segments were sold and distributed widely through dominant film company Svensk Filmindustri's newsreel *SF-journalen*. In addition, the Press Office produced and circulated other types of visual propaganda beyond film, such as posters and photographs for display in shop windows.

James Knapp-Fischer, a secret service officer and the official film officer at the Press Office, was a pivotal figure in the organization of private film screenings in Sweden.[34] With a background in book publishing, Knapp-Fischer arrived in Stockholm in February 1942 and took over the official duty as film officer from C. Montagu Evans.[35] The fact that Swedish counter-espionage launched close personal surveillance immediately upon his arrival serves as an indication of his status at the legation. For example, one note in his personal file describes how Knapp-Fischer, together with Roger Hinks, an art historian turned diplomat who used to work at the British Museum, 'spends extraordinary sums' and how he would 'throw grand dinners in their joint apartment on Strandvägen 25', the most fashionable street in the Swedish capital.[36] Monitoring such occasions, the Civilian Security Service would track Knapp-Fischer's extensive social network, including individuals from the leading Swedish publishing family Bonnier and the author and public intellectual Amelie Posse.[37] The avowed anti-fascist Posse was a member of the anti-Nazi discussion club Tisdagsklubben [the Tuesday Club] and often spoke out against Nazism in the press.[38] Posse's close connection with Peter Tennant has been well documented.[39] However, records show that she was also engaged in the British film propaganda and the organization of private shows, including the screening of British anti-Nazi thriller *Pimpernel Smith* (Leslie Howard, 1941) for an audience of four hundred[40] and the organization of an exclusive private screening of the British-American prestige picture *Forever and a Day* (1943) with the Swedish royals Prince Eugen and Prince Wilhelm as honorary guests.[41] As Edward Corse points out, the targeting of pro-British elites was a key propaganda strategy for the British Council in neutral territories during the war.[42] Similarly, the British Legation's film events, which were often followed by drinks and mingling, offered ample opportunities for direct contact and word-of-mouth propaganda. In fact, for such occasions, suitable talking points – for example about the Allies' imminent victory over Germany or Sweden's well-placed geography for trade with the United Nations – were distributed among the legation's personnel in Stockholm to be utilized in conversation with Swedes.[43]

Circulation and disruption

The British Legation's private film screenings targeted several different audience groups. Besides pro-British elites, as discussed previously, other common audiences were members of friendship societies, members of workers' unions and diasporic refugee communities. Due to the risk of increased German pressure on Swedish authorities, Montagu Evans noted in a phone call to Tennant that the British Legation should never disclose the official organizer of the private screenings on the invitation cards.[44] Instead, proxies such as the Anglo-Swedish friendship society or the British Colony Committee served as the official sponsors. Given that the sponsor was not correctly identified, this practice corresponds with what Jowett and O'Donnell label as grey propaganda.[45] Records in the Civilian Security Service's archive show that the infrastructure behind the distribution of British films around the country was advanced. For example, an intricate schedule notes when films, such as the British war film *The Silver Fleet* (Vernon Sewell and Gordon Wellesley, 1943), the Nazi resistance film *Underground* (Vincent Sherman, 1941), the war film *The Flemish Farm* (Jeffrey Dell, 1943) and the famous re-edit of footage of Hitler and German soldiers in *The Lambeth Walk – Nazi Style* (Charles A. Ridley, 1942), should be exchanged between twenty-seven different smaller and larger Swedish cities.[46]

Although these types of screenings were private, they were far from secret. For example, a screening of *Pimpernel Smith* in Helsingborg in the south of Sweden reached five hundred people: 'All comments that have come in since have been good. For Helsingborg the applause was quite good, and there was a good deal of laughter at the Germans', the British Vice-Consulate in the city noted.[47] A letter from the Anglo-Swedish society in Malmö concerning their screening of *Pimpernel Smith* shines further light on the practical organization of such events:

> We first send our usual cards informing our members that a film will be shown, and that they may bring friends, but that their names must be handed to me so that a special invitation can be written out for them. Besides these I issue invitations to numerous officials, and business people in the town. We do not charge any entrance fee. On one occasion I had a collection made for British prisoners of war in Germany.[48]

As Arne Svensson notes, the Board of Film Censors, the Swedish Ministry of Foreign Affairs and the Board of Information – as well as local police authorities – made occasional attempts to stop private screenings. With regard to *Pimpernel Smith*, for example, the Swedish Ministry of Foreign Affairs went as far as contacting the British Legation to clarify the meaning of a private screening as 'at most a couple of screenings in front of friends or members of an association', also warning that the Germans could expand their film propaganda if they caught wind of the British activities.[49]

Other private film screenings targeted niche audiences such as anti-fascist groups or diasporic refugee communities. With regard to the former, the Fighting for Democracy Union [Förbundet kämpande demokrati], which had been formed with the explicit aim of influencing public opinion in an anti-Nazi direction and was headed by renowned anti-fascist Ture Nerman,[50] frequently borrowed films for 'agitation meetings', Christmas parties and other gatherings.[51] Similarly, the feature-length propaganda film *Freedom Radio* (Anthony Asquith, 1941) – later banned by the Swedish censors – was loaned out to the Swedish Communist Party.[52] Another key demographic for private film screenings was local refugee communities in Sweden, and the Civilian Security Service's archive includes many examples of such events.

For example, a letter to Knapp-Fischer from a prospective private film screener described how the writer is 'arranging quartering and entertainment for a large group of escaped Norwegians', and how he would like to show them a British film on Christmas or Boxing day.[53] One supervised letter to London describes a Norwegian 'refugee evening' [*flyktingafton*] with music, a speech on the situation in Britain and lastly a screening of *Pimpernel Smith*.[54] Similar events were organized by other refugee communities, such as the Polish one. One transcribed phone call described such a screening in Malmö in the south of Sweden where 'the hall was decorated with English and Polish flags', and a member of the British Legation held an introductory speech.[55] Describing a private show in Metro-Goldwyn-Mayer's private thirty-seat cinema for a group of Polish refugees, Knapp-Fischer noted that 'we are doing these types of shows every night nowadays. I have already organized 30 this month'.[56] These activities arranged for refugee communities highlight how film screenings were often part of a broader communicative ensemble that also included speeches, flags, decorations and so on.

On the ground in Stockholm, Swedish surveillance records show that members of the British Legation's Press Office recurringly met with members of the American Legation's press division.[57] Furthermore, counter-espionage files show that the Allied Press Offices exerted coordinated pressure on British and American film companies operating in Sweden. For example, Knapp-Fischer contacted the American film company Columbia Film's Swedish CEO Oscar Björkman and asked for cuts to be made in Humphrey Bogart's action film *Sahara* (Zoltán Korda, 1943) 'in the interest of Allied propaganda'.[58] In doing so, Knapp-Fischer proposed to cut 'some of the embarrassing back-chat when the Americans first meet the British. This talk would give the impression to the average Swede that the British and the Americans do not get on together very well' as well as '[t]he third-degree methods used against German prisoners, in which they are tempted to answer questions we want to know by withholding water from them'.[59] A carbon copy of this letter was sent to the head of the American Legation, Karl Jensen.

Besides this, the British Legation also coordinated propaganda efforts with the Russian Legation in Stockholm. In this context, Sweden's historical distrust and fear of Russia constituted a challenge for the MoI and the British Legation. For example, in February 1943, the Overseas Planning Committee, the Foreign Office and the MoI started working on a revised version of its *Plan of Propaganda for Sweden*. Besides advocating for an impending Allied victory and the stop of Swedish concessions to Germany, a key aim of the British propaganda was to decrease, or deflect, Swedish fear of the Soviet Union.[60] After the Battle of Stalingrad, German propaganda exploited Sweden's animosity towards Russia, which the country shared with its war-torn neighbour Finland,[61] a propaganda theme labelled by the British as 'The Bolshevik Bogey'. 'It has been constantly emphasised by our Press Office in Stockholm that Swedish fears of Russian predominance in the Baltics and Scandinavia are much greater than is believed in London', the propaganda plan reports. On the ground, the two Allied Legations exchanged experiences and know-how; for example, the British Legation borrowed Soviet propaganda films and offered the Russians advice on how to avoid trouble with the Stockholm police authorities.[62] Moreover, to display a sense of Allied unity, the British and the Russian Legations co-organized a joint private screening of the film *Desert Victory* (Roy Boulting, 1943), an MoI film on the Allies' North African campaign, and the Soviet documentary film *Stalingrad* (Leonid Varlamov, 1943), an unorthodox event which underlines Stockholm's status as a transnational, entangled propaganda hub during the war.[63]

Conclusion

British cultural propaganda had long-term goals in swaying Sweden to see its future as part of the United Nations and in close cooperation with the Anglo-Saxon world, for example, in terms of trade and cultural exchange. From this perspective, British film propaganda was merely part of a broader and much more complex media ensemble including a wide variety of media ranging from print publication *Nyheter från Storbritannien* to displays in shop windows, from the BBC's radio broadcasts to pamphlets and brochures. At the same time, as this chapter highlights, the infrastructure behind the production and circulation of British film propaganda was advanced – and the issue of film propaganda was highly prioritized by both the Swedish authorities and the British Legation. Swedish film censorship strived for neutrality in an effort not to offend the opposing sides in the war. Together with the Ministry of Foreign Affairs and the Government Board of Information, the Swedish film censors monitored the development of film propaganda closely, while simultaneously enacting different regulatory measures such as prohibiting the import of foreign language newsreels.

Moreover, a large portion of the material in the Civilian Security Service's archive on British propaganda during the Second World War centres on film propaganda, further indicating that the authorities monitored the developments within this field closely. As shown in this chapter, the British Legation prioritized film propaganda and invested considerable resources to boost the circulation of such films among different types of audiences, from pro-British elites to businessmen, from political groups to diasporic refugee communities. C. Montagu Evans and James Knapp-Fischer were important figures in British film propaganda, and the latter in particular was the subject of much interest from the Civilian Security Service on account of his extensive social network. Due to media regulation and pushback from Swedish authorities, both local and national, this study shows that the British Legation's film organization constantly needed to adapt to disruptions and breakdown of existing infrastructures and material conditions. This complex cat-and-mouse game further indicates that Stockholm was a transnational hub where competing propaganda interests were negotiated and brought to the fore, a topic in need of further research from the perspective of entangled media history.

Notes

1 Simon MacKenzie, 'On Target: The Air Ministry, RAF Bomber Command and Feature Film Propaganda, 1941–1942', *War & Society* 15, no. 2 (1997): 43–59.

2 Arne Svensson, *Den politiska saxen: En studie i Statens biografbyrås tillämpning av den utrikespolitiska censurnormen sedan 1914* (Stockholm: Stockholms universitet, 1976), 141.
3 Riksarkivet (hereafter RA), Allmänna säkerhetstjänstens arkiv (hereafter ASA), F8EB:4, Letter from Jostein Nyhamar (Det norske selskap i Uppsala) to James Knapp-Fischer (British Legation), 19 December 1942, F8EB:4; RA, ASA, F8EB:4 Letter from Per Wickenberg to Ursula Robertson, 4 March 1943.
4 Jan Olsson, *Svensk spelfilm under andra världskriget* (Lund: Liber läromedel, 1979); Mats Jönsson, *Visuell fostran: Film- och bildverksamheten i Sverige under andra världskriget* (Lund: Sekel, 2011); Emil Stjernholm, *Gösta Werner och filmen som konst och propaganda* (Lund: Mediehistoriskt arkiv, 2018).
5 Jussi Parikka, *What Is Media Archaeology?* (Cambridge: Polity, 2013), 167.
6 The UK National Archives (hereafter TNA), Foreign Office files (hereafter FO) 930/9 'Memorandum', The Press Department, British Legation Stockholm, 31 October 1939.
7 John Gilmour, *Sweden, the Swastika and Stalin: The Swedish Experience in the Second World War* (Edinburgh: Edinburgh University Press, 2010), 169.
8 TNA, FO 930/9, Letter from British Legation Stockholm to Foreign Secretary Lord Halifax, 24 July 1939.
9 Gilmour, *Sweden, the Swastika and Stalin*, 168–9.
10 See Chapter 14 of this volume for a more general analysis of the German magazine *Signal*.
11 See, for example, Åke Thulstrup, *Med lock och pock: Tyska försök att påverka svensk opinion 1933–45* (Stockholm: Bonnier, 1962); Klaus-Richard Böhme, *Signal: Nazitysklands propaganda i Sverige 1941–1945* (Stockholm: Bokförlaget DN, 2005); Jönsson, *Visuell fostran*; Stjernholm, *Gösta Werner och filmen som konst och propaganda*; Birgitta Almgren, *Drömmen om Norden: Nazistisk infiltration i Sverige 1933–1945* (Stockholm: Carlsson, 2005); Maria Björkman, Patrik Lundell and Sven Widmalm (eds), *Intellectual Collaboration with the Third Reich: Treason or Reason?* (Abingdon: Routledge, 2019). For a government report on the German propaganda, see Statens offentliga utredningar, Socialdepartementet, *Den tyska propagandan i Sverige under krigsåren 1939–1945* (SOU 1946:86) (Stockholm: Statens offentliga utredningar (SOU), 1946).
12 TNA, FO 371/43490, Letter from unknown (British Legation) to Reginald Leeper (Foreign Office), 24 July 1939.
13 TNA, FO 930/9, 'Memorandum', 31 October 1939.
14 Ibid. See also Edward Corse, *A Battle for Neutral Europe: British Cultural Propaganda during the Second World War* (London: Bloomsbury, 2013), 113.
15 Gilmour, *Sweden, the Swastika and Stalin*, 173.
16 TNA, FO 930/9, 'Memorandum', 31 October 1939.
17 Gilmour, *Sweden, the Swastika and Stalin*, 172.
18 Ibid., 174.
19 Lisa Gitelman, *Always Already New: Media, History and the Data of Culture* (Cambridge, MA: MIT Press, 2006), 8.
20 Marie Cronqvist and Christoph Hilgert, 'Entangled Media Histories', *Media History* 23, no. 1 (2017): 130–4.
21 Wilhelm Agrell, 'Inre spaning – Att forska i och kring underrättelsearkiv', *Statsvetenskaplig tidskrift* 122, no. 3 (2020): 316.

22 Jason Dittmer, 'Geopolitical Assemblages and Everyday Diplomacy', in Jason Dittmer, *Diplomatic Material: Affect, Assemblage, and Foreign Policy* (Durham: Duke University Press, 2017), 22–3.
23 Olsson, *Svensk spelfilm*, 214.
24 Roel Vande Winkel, Mats Jönsson, Lars-Martin Sørensen and Bjørn Sørenssen, 'German Film Distribution in Scandinavia during World War II', *Journal of Scandinavian Cinema* 2, no. 3 (2012): 273.
25 TNA, FO 930/9, Letter from Peter Tennant to the Ministry of Information, 2 September 1939.
26 TNA, FO 371/43490, Overseas Planning Committee, 'Plan of Propaganda for Sweden: 1st Revision of Channels', 7 November 1944, 1.
27 RA, ASA, F8EB:4, Message from Sweden's Association of Cinema Owners to the German Legation, 30 January 1943.
28 Erik Florin Persson, 'Useful Cinema and the Dynamic Film History beyond the National Archive: Locating Municipally Sponsored Swedish City Films in Local Archives', *Journal of Scandinavian Cinema* 7, no. 2 (2017): 127.
29 RA, ASA, Note in James Knapp-Fischer's personal file no. 3490, 22 March 1943.
30 TNA, FO 371/43490, Overseas Planning Committee, 7 November 1944, 7.
31 Svensson, *Den politiska saxen*, 76.
32 TNA, FO 371/43490, Overseas Planning Committee, 7 November 1944, 8.
33 Emil Stjernholm, 'German Surveillance of the Swedish Film Market during World War II', *Journal of Scandinavian Cinema* 9, no. 2 (2019): 353.
34 Klemens von Klemperer, *German Resistance against Hitler: The Search for Allies Abroad, 1938–1945* (Oxford: Clarendon, 1992), 334.
35 RA, ASA, Note in James Knapp-Fischer's personal file no. 3490, 1 November 1943.
36 RA, ASA, Note in James Knapp-Fischer's personal file no. 3490, 27 June 1942. Translation from Swedish here and for other quotations by the author.
37 RA, ASA, Note in James Knapp-Fischer's personal file no. 3490, 31 October 1942.
38 Rune Bokholm, *Tisdagsklubben: Om glömda antinazistiska sanningssägare i svenskt 30- och 40-tal* (Stockholm: Atlantis, 2001).
39 Victor Lundberg, '"Karlsson", The Amiable Spy: Swedish Experiences of Allied Espionage and Sabotage during World War II', *Diacronie* 4, no. 28 (2016): 9.
40 RA, ASA, F8EB:4 Transcript of phone conversation between Amelie Posse and James Knapp-Fischer's secretary (British Legation), 8 November 1943.
41 RA, ASA, F8EB:4 Transcript of phone conversation between Amelie Posse and Gustav Hellström, 16 June 1943.
42 Corse, *A Battle for Neutral Europe*, 6–7.
43 TNA, FO 371/37075, Ministry of Information, Propaganda to Combat Germany's Bolshevik Bogey – Special Directive for Sweden, 5 March 1943.
44 RA, ASA, F8EB:4, Transcript of phone conversation between C. Montagu Evans and Peter Tennant, 7 May 1942.
45 Garth Jowett and Victoria O'Donnell, *Propaganda and Persuasion* (Los Angeles: Sage, 2019), 20.
46 RA, ASA, F8EB:4, 'Filmprogrammet 10 april – 21 maj 1944'.
47 RA, ASA, F8EB:4, Letter from British Vice-Consulate in Helsingborg to James Knapp-Fischer, 26 January 1943.
48 RA, ASA, F8EB:4, Letter from the Anglo-Swedish Society in Malmö to James Knapp-Fischer, 29 December 1942.
49 Svensson, *Den politiska saxen*, 149.

50 Louise Drangel, *Den kämpande demokratin: En studie i antinazistisk opinionsrörelse 1933–1945* (Stockholm: Sverige under andra världskriget, 1976), 47.
51 RA, ASA, F8EB:4 Letter from Gösta Pettersson (Förbundet kämpande demokrati) to the Press Department at the British Legation, 4 November 1942; Letter from Gösta Pettersson (Förbundet kämpande demokrati) to the Press Department at the British Legation, 28 December 1942; Letter from Gösta Pettersson (Förbundet kämpande demokrati) to the Press Department at the British Legation, 31 January 1943.
52 RA, ASA, F8EB:4 Letter from James Knapp-Fischer to Mr Sjöberg, 29 September 1943.
53 RA, ASA, F8EB:4 Letter from A. Kvist to James Knapp-Fischer, 21 December 1942.
54 RA, ASA, F8EB:4 Letter from Poul to Miss Anna de Meck (Norwegian Ministry of Foreign Affairs, London), 12 February 1943.
55 RA, ASA, F8EB:4 Transcript of phone conversation between Consul Wintermark and the British Legation, 18 August 1941.
56 RA, ASA, F8EB:4 Transcript of phone conversation between Miss Hübinette and James Knapp-Fischer, 17 May 1943.
57 RA, ASA, James Knapp-Fischer's personal file no. 3490.
58 RA, ASA, F8EB:4 Letter from James Knapp-Fischer (British Legation) to Oscar Björkman (AB Columbia Film), 2 February 1944.
59 Ibid.
60 TNA, FO 188/402, Ministry of Information, Overseas Planning Committee, *Draft Plan of Propaganda for Sweden*, paper no. 338, 25 February 1943.
61 On the historical relationship between Sweden and Russia, see, for instance, Kari Tarkiainen, *Moskoviten: Sverige och Ryssland 1478–1721* (Helsingfors: Svenska litteratursällskapet i Finland, 2017). On the theme of anti-Bolshevik concept in Nazi propaganda, see David Welch, *The Third Reich, Politics and Propaganda* (London: Routledge, 2002), 129–30.
62 RA, ASA, F8EB:4, Transcript of phone conversation between the British Legation and the Russian Legation, 4 June 1942; Letter from James Knapp-Fischer to Igor Sprichkin (Russian Legation), 10 April 1943.
63 RA, ASA, F8EB:4, Letter from James Knapp-Fischer (British Legation) to A. Iartseva (Russian Legation), 5 May 1943.

13

Neutrality and (anti-)Imperialism

Multinational propaganda competition in neutral Macau

Helena F. S. Lopes

This chapter focuses on multinational propaganda competition in Macau, a small colonial territory in South China. This case attests to the importance of neutrality in understanding the Second World War as a truly global event, drawing attention to overlooked connections between Asia and Europe. The Portuguese-administered enclave was a commercial hub and refugee haven at the intersection of different imperial and nationalist interests. Chinese, Japanese and British representatives mobilized an intense propaganda campaign that aroused the complaints of the adversaries, while Portuguese authorities used neutrality to promote their colonial rule. This chapter considers practices of propaganda in neutral Macau during the Second World War in Asia (1937–45), with a particular focus on the use of rumours and printed media. Threats to the territory's neutral status were often a topic of propaganda activities, with different sides accusing their opponents of disrespecting neutrality, when the very existence of those activities – including on the part of Portuguese authorities – suggests that neutrality was far from strictly enforced. Overall, the chapter argues that imperialism and anti-imperialism are essential elements to understand practices of propaganda in neutral Macau and its limitations.

The propaganda apparatus of the Portuguese dictatorship of António de Oliveira Salazar and the twists and turns of its neutrality policy in Europe during the Second World War have merited considerable scholarly attention.[1] However, how people of different nationalities experienced Portuguese neutrality and how international propaganda operated in Portuguese colonial territories in Asia and Africa remain understudied.[2] Although there have been a few studies on wartime propaganda in East Asia, they did not delve into neutral colonial territories, apart from the International Settlement and the French Concession in Shanghai between the start of an all-out war between China and Japan in 1937 and the Japanese takeover of those territories starting in late 1941.[3] Likewise, studies of neutrality in the Second World War tend to focus overwhelmingly on Europe. Attempts to consider practices of neutrality beyond it are relatively scarce and have mostly centred on Japanese diplomatic relations with

Spain, Sweden and Switzerland.[4] Here, the focus will be on Portuguese-ruled Macau. The territory had been one of the smallest colonial outposts of the Portuguese Empire since the sixteenth century but sovereignty over it had been contested by successive Chinese authorities.

Macau's position in the Second World War

During the Second World War, Macau comprised a peninsula and two islands, with a total area of around 15 square kilometres; its economic and political relevance in Sino-foreign relations dwarfed by Hong Kong and several Chinese treaty ports since the nineteenth century (Figure 13.1). The occupation of the neighbouring British colony in December 1941 led to a temporary reversal of fortune. As the only foreign-ruled territory in China not occupied by Japan, Macau gained a fresh importance as the last neutral node connecting occupied and unoccupied areas in East Asia. It enabled the flow of people, information, currency and commodities not only between parts of China subject to different wartime jurisdictions but also permitting communications between Asia and Europe.

Despite being under Portuguese rule, different imperial and anti-imperialist interests framed Macau's experience of neutrality: it had strong connections to the British Empire, namely to Hong Kong, and to the Japanese Empire, expanding in South China and Southeast Asia at the time. It was also at the crossroads of competing Chinese forces: the Chinese Nationalists of Chiang Kai-shek, leading the country's resistance against Japan; the Chinese Communist Party that had advocated a resistance policy even before Chiang; a number of Chinese guerrillas resisting Japan not firmly

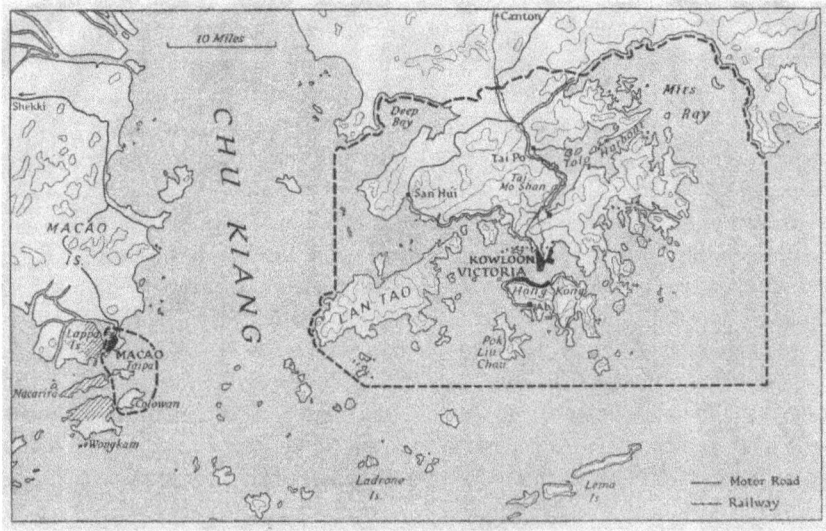

Figure 13.1 Macau and Hong Kong. Royal Navy Intelligence Map, 1945. Courtesy Alamy.

affiliated with any of those parties and a myriad of collaborationist authorities. The most important of the latter was the Reorganized National Government (RNG) led by Wang Jingwei, a prominent Nationalist figure who defected from Chiang's wartime capital in 1938 to settle for peace with Japan.

As Jo Fox noted, in the Second World War, 'state propaganda circulated in a complex and unpredictable environment, alongside rumours, gossip, informal news networks and enemy propaganda, all of which affected the reception of particular appeals'.[5] The examples from Macau addressed in this chapter concern propaganda of specific states but they were often ad hoc efforts, not necessarily centrally directed by major government institutions, and several of them can indeed be seen as relying on 'rumours, gossip and informal news networks'.

Like many other port cities in Asia, Macau had been a haven for diverse communities prior to the Second World War but the number of people arriving during the conflict was unprecedented. Macau's population almost trebled, rising to around half a million people. The multinational refugee influx intersected with propaganda activities: they were both participants and targets of Chinese, Japanese, British and Portuguese propaganda. Accusing adversaries of spreading propaganda in Macau was a common move by both Chinese and Japanese representatives who questioned the practice of neutrality in and around the territory to force the Portuguese colonial authorities into a collaborative position on their side, with varying degrees of success. The Portuguese authorities were not, however, the sole or even the primary target of propaganda activities by China and Japan in regard to Macau. Propaganda was mostly deployed by the belligerents to gather the support of Macau's wartime residents, the great majority of whom were Chinese.

During the Second World War, the Chinese Nationalists and Communists were, at least in theory, working together in the so-called Second United Front against Japan. In Macau both parties tapped into a popular sentiment against Japanese aggression that prevailed among the majority of the population – unsurprisingly, given that many were fleeing the violence of the Japanese invasion. Since the early stages of the war, Macau was a site of Chinese resistance activities, including fund-raising campaigns that involved associations of people from all walks of life, including women; different religious groups and commercial, artistic and educational circles.[6] Activities in Macau were part of regional and transnational efforts to support Chinese resistance. That global reach was sustained by migratory circuits, not only of communities long established overseas but also of people recently displaced by the war.

In tandem with practices in mainland China, visual and performative arts were used as propaganda in Macau to rally support for Chinese resistance. These included motion pictures such as *Kangzhan teji* [War of Resistance Special, 1938]; art exhibitions, namely those of the refugee painter Gao Jianfu; and theatre performances like the famous resistance play *Fangxia nide bianzi* [Put Down Your Whip], among others.[7] The two most important Chinese daily newspapers in wartime Macau, the *Dazhongbao* (*Tai Chong Po*/*Diário para Todos*) [translating as 'Popular Newspaper'] and the *Huaqiao ribao* (*Wah Kiou Po*/*Jornal Va Kio*) ['Overseas Chinese Daily'], which remain in print to this day, began publication in 1933 (two years after the Japanese invasion of Manchuria) and November 1937, respectively, and had a pro-resistance stance.[8]

Public expressions of Chinese support for resistance were not, however, totally unrestricted. Japanese pressure to curb what they saw as Chinese propaganda that violated official neutrality was constant. Japanese representatives frequently admonished the Portuguese authorities for allowing such activities and demanded that they put an end to them. Chinese newspapers initially defied censorship by printing blank squares or an 'X' where characters of sensitive passages would have stood, making it clear to readers that their message was being silenced.[9] As the Japanese invasion of China progressed with speed and brutality, it became increasingly difficult for Chinese pro-resistance activities to take place in the open, though they continued underground or within relatively safe spaces such as schools – dozens of which had relocated from mainland China to Macau during the war. There, visual propaganda was combined with sonic one, such as by singing songs supporting the resistance.[10]

Foreign propaganda, invasion rumours and newspapers

Japanese agents attempted to woo the Portuguese authorities to their side with promises of favouring them against the British in Hong Kong and of turning the territory into a major commercial hub for Japanese and Portuguese products. They sought to attract local colonial officials' compliance by teasing them with suggestions that projects that had been considered before the war, such as a railway linking Macau and Guangzhou (Canton), might now go ahead.[11] Japanese pressure over Portuguese authorities in Macau grew as the war years moved on, anchored in supply blockades, demands for permitting the operation of Japanese agents in Macau and ceding vessels and other materials. Artur Tamagnini de Barbosa, governor of Macau during the first years of the war, was relatively more open to Japanese pressures, sending the police to search Chinese offices, schools and companies which Japanese agents believed were being used by the Chinese resistance, as well to censor the Chinese press to remove articles critical of Japan.[12] Barbosa's successor was Gabriel Maurício Teixeira, who had a more complex interaction with Japan. Although he also bowed to Japanese demands to avoid a formal occupation, he ended up subtly allowing some Allied resistance activities in the territory.[13]

Japanese agents also used tactics that Allied powers deployed with authorities in Lisbon,[14] including flattering officials with invitations for special events and awarding decorations. A particularly high-profile case pertained Captain Carlos Gorgulho, the Macau police commander, who was invited to go to Japan in February 1939. Accompanied by a Japanese intelligence agent, Gorgulho visited ministries and received a decoration, an Order of the Rising Sun – 5th Class.[15] The Macau authorities had their own objectives for the trip, but this chapter will concentrate on its propaganda value for Japan.

Gorgulho's fifteen-day trip, which enjoyed extensive press coverage in different languages, was accompanied by false news, originating in the Japanese press, that Portugal would make a series of concessions to and sign agreements with Japan. These concessions included recognizing Manchukuo, the Japanese-controlled colony-like 'state' that had been established on the site of three occupied Chinese Northeastern provinces in 1932.¹⁶ Gorgulho had no authority to agree to such things, and virtually none of them materialized, but the controversial trip harnessed international attention, drawing concern among Chinese, British and French observers about the potential dangers of a pro-Japanese Portuguese neutrality. The Portuguese government denied the existence of such negotiations, and, interestingly, the Japanese Ministry of Foreign Affairs also distanced itself from these reports, suggesting that Gorgulho's trip had been the sole responsibility of military circles,¹⁷ which hints at the existence of competing civilian and military forces within Japan.

Portuguese neutrality was far from a stable guarantee. Japanese forces had few qualms in occupying the then Portuguese colony of Timor (now East Timor), following an Allied landing in the territory that had itself not had the prior authorization by the Portuguese authorities, during the assault on European colonial territories in Southeast Asia. The Timor case was perceived by contemporary observers as a warning to what could happen to Macau if resistance to Japan became too daring, an outcome that neither the Allied powers nor the Portuguese wanted.¹⁸

Thus, the threat of a Japanese occupation of Macau was ever present during the war years and invasion rumours from unclear sources emerged several times.¹⁹ To those living in the enclave or following events there from afar, a formal invasion by Japan seemed a very likely possibility, particularly after the occupation, from late 1941, of other colonial territories in Asia that had had stronger defence capabilities, such as Hong Kong and Singapore. In Portugal, foreign reports of these rumours were monitored and censored.²⁰

Invasion rumours exploiting Portuguese colonial anxieties illustrate how anti-imperialism was an important dimension of wartime propaganda. For pro-resistance Chinese, noting how easily Portuguese neutrality could be overrun exposed the fragility of colonial rule. In the 1940s, news reports from unoccupied China occasionally mentioned the risk of an imminent invasion of Macau and at one time even announced Teixeira's death – that had not actually happened.²¹ Some of these Chinese reports had a global circulation, from Michigan to Vichy France.²²

After the fall of Hong Kong in December 1941, the British Consulate in Macau also became active in propaganda, prompting more complaints by Japanese and their Chinese collaborators against Allied – namely Chinese and British – activities in the enclave. The British Consul, John Reeves, oversaw a numerous and multinational community of refugees, and he was engaged in intelligence gathering, as well as pro-Allied propaganda. This included the founding of the *Macau Tribune*, an English-language newspaper that, in Reeves' words, 'was an attempt to get the Allied point of view more prominently placed before the public'.²³ Although support for Allied resistance was significant in Macau, there were limits to its expression. During the fall of Hong Kong, the Governor suspended three Chinese newspapers for publishing anti-Japanese news and fired the Chinese censor who had let them pass.²⁴ When Macau was bombed by Allied planes in 1945 – allegedly by mistake – the supportive tone of newspaper reports was so obvious that the local Portuguese authorities, acting without Lisbon's prior approval, forced the *Macau Tribune* to shut down, although a replacement with the same editorial team was later created.²⁵ Censorship of pro-Allied reports – both in Chinese and English – demonstrates a degree of collaboration with Japan.

There are a few interesting mentions of Asia in joint Axis propaganda aimed at readers of Portuguese outside of Macau, such as an article about China and Hong Kong published in the Portuguese-language version of the German illustrated magazine *Signal*.[26] This piece praised the assistance that Japan had given to supposedly bring order to China, critiquing the negative influence of Western imperialism in both mainland China and Hong Kong and representing the Japanese occupation as a force for good. But given that colonial rule was precisely what Portuguese authorities desired to see maintained in Macau, it is unlikely that this was regarded very favourably by Portuguese metropolitan policymakers for whom Japan's pan-Asian propaganda was not welcome. The maintenance of Macau under Portuguese rule had the potential to become an embarrassment for Japanese pan-Asian propaganda, making a mockery of Japan's claims to be helping fellow Asians free themselves from European and American rule. Therefore, Japanese propaganda that mentioned Portugal emphasized not its status as a European imperial power but Japan's supposed respect for Macau's neutrality, chastising Chinese and British elements for imperilling that status quo.[27] A more immediate objective was to sway the Chinese population in favour of Wang Jingwei's RNG.

Unlike Lisbon, Macau was not of major concern to Germany or Italy, and the only Axis power with a consulate in Macau was Japan. Axis propaganda in Macau essentially meant Japanese propaganda or activities by the Chinese collaborationist authorities of the RNG. A wartime propaganda endeavour that served both was another fresh newspaper, the *Xi'nan ribao* (*See Nan Jeh Pao*) ['Southwest Daily'], a pro-Japanese Chinese-language newspaper published in Macau from 1942 until the end of the war. Copies of pro-Wang Jingwei or pro-Japanese propaganda newspapers from Hong Kong, such as the Chinese-language *Nanhua ribao* (*South China Daily News*), the Japanese-language *Honkon Nippō* ['Hong Kong Daily'] or the English-language *Hongkong News*, would have also reached Macau, although their effectiveness was likely as weak there as it was in Hong Kong.[28]

The *Hongkong News* was, in fact, a vehicle for Japanese propaganda targeting Macau. In February 1941, the newspaper sponsored an event at the Japanese Consulate to 'promot[e] more friendly relations between Japan and Macao, or Portugal'.[29] The gathering started with an address by the manager of the *Honkon Nippō* and among its participants was the influential head of the Macau Economic Services, Pedro José Lobo. After the occupation of the British colony, the *Hongkong News* set up a Macau branch at 101–103 Praia Grande and featured a regular section entitled 'News from Macao' that covered social events and living conditions in the neutral enclave.[30] Especially from 1943 onwards, its Macau reports often cited the *Xi'nan ribao*. One of them shows how this newspaper linked its pro-Japanese and pro-RNG propagandistic aims with relief activities, themselves an arena for competition between opposing sides. One telling example of the desperate lengths to which the *Xi'nan ribao* went to increase its circulation was in early August 1943 when it gave two thousand copies to children who, for three days, were able to sell them for charity. The hope was that in the future, 'the public would buy their daily paper from these children' so they could make a living this way.[31] In an environment of increasing material scarcity, the fact that this propaganda newspaper had thousands of copies to spare suggests it was hardly a sought-after publication. At the same time, portraying child labour as a 'positive' charitable activity exposes the level of poverty experienced in Macau in the early 1940s and how those wretched conditions could themselves be exploited for certain propaganda activities. Like in Hong Kong, there were also modest efforts to expand Japanese-language learning in Macau during the early 1940s, including rewarding attendance of a local Japanese school with food.[32]

As the wartime newspapers such as the *Macau Tribune* or the *Xi'nan ribao* attest, the press was a key medium for propaganda in Macau. However, like many other aspects in the territory, it was marked by a strange combination of colonial control and unregulated freedom. On the one hand, newspapers were subject to censorship, which was quite heavy-handed against anti-Japanese reports; on the other hand, coverage could be quite eclectic as newspapers seemingly drew a lot of their content not directly from press agencies – nor even from Lisbon – but from listening to news on private radios.[33] For example, readers of *A Voz de Macau* ['The Voice of Macau'], the main Portuguese-language daily in Macau, could consume unlicensed news from both sides. In the final year of the conflict, news on the Allied victories against Japan appeared next to Japanese reports saying the opposite.

The importance of the press for propaganda activities in Macau was likely due to three factors. One was the relatively high rate of basic literacy when compared to other Portuguese-ruled territories.[34] Another was the centrality of the press for Chinese international propaganda efforts, and the culture of using the press naturally spilled over into Macau. In fact, the architect of Chiang Kai-shek's English-language propaganda system was a journalist, Hollington Tong (Dong Xianguang).[35] A third factor was the technical know-how behind printed media, with Macanese typographical expertise having long been prominent in Macau and other colonial port cities in Asia.[36]

The press played an important role in Chinese propaganda around one of the most daring challenges to Macau's neutrality, the *Sai-On* incident. In August 1943, the *Sai-On*, a British steamer full of refugees (including many Allied civilians) that had been moored in the enclave since the fall of Hong Kong, was hijacked by a group of collaborators working with support from Japanese naval forces. Despite the interesting coincidence that this attack happened in the same month that the Portuguese government agreed to cede basing rights in the Azores to the British – considered a decisive turning point towards a more pro-Allied neutrality – the attack on the *Sai-On* had the hallmarks of other ad hoc maverick actions launched in and around Macau during the war years by members of the Japanese military and their Chinese collaborators.

Chinese Nationalist authorities were quick to capitalize on the propaganda value of the incident, which exposed Japanese disregard for a neutral territory as well as Portuguese impotence to challenge such abuse. Chinese reports on the dramatic event inflated the number of people aboard the ship and reported casualties among Portuguese police that had not actually occurred.[37] The Chinese Central News Agency report was reproduced in other parts of the world, in news items that repeated its exaggerated data (Figure 13.2).[38] This did not strike outside observers as amiss: after all, very un-neutral things had been happening in Macau since the start of the war. Pro-Japanese media also used news channels to get its narrative on the *Sai-On* case and

Figure 13.2 The *Dundee Courier* report on the *Sai-On* case, reproducing the exaggerated information from the Chinese Central News Agency in Chongqing, 30 August 1943. Used with kind permission by DC Thomson & Co. Ltd.

events in Timor across, defending Japan's role in 'rescuing' the victims from the 'pirates' and 'bandits' and taking the opportunity to denounce Allied reports as propaganda and to portray the Azores agreement as a violation of Portuguese neutrality by the United Kingdom and the United States.[39]

Portuguese colonial propaganda

The major belligerents operating in South China questioned Portuguese neutrality by insisting that enemy propaganda activities were taking place in Macau, which, of course, was largely true. Certainly, propaganda was not a monopoly of the belligerents. The Portuguese authorities repeated their mantra of 'strict neutrality' – when the realities on the ground were far from it – which can be seen as a form of propaganda used to dispel accusations of collaboration with Japan. The ultimate goal of this was the continuation of Portuguese colonial rule over Macau. This was a hard balancing act when China was one of the major Allies, especially after the Nationalists had won a major victory in the 1943 treaties with Britain and the United States that negotiated the end of extraterritoriality and the abolition of foreign concessions, including the Shanghai International Settlement.[40]

The Portuguese-language press in Macau, as in Portugal, was subject to a tight censorship regime. It rarely published any meaningful news about Portugal's relations with Japan or with China, nor indeed anything substantial about Macau's situation beyond pieces on festive events, refugee relief or local government edicts. The limited amount of information allowed to be released to the general public had clear propagandistic undertones. *A Voz de Macau* included its fair share of colonial propaganda, particularly evident on occasions such as national holidays or on anniversaries of the rule of Salazar or of the Governor of Macau, culminating in an overblown piece on Macau's collective 'debt' to the latter published in the immediate aftermath of the war.[41]

Salazar's Estado Novo (New State) regime capitalized on neutrality to affirm its imperial project, as the monumental propaganda event that was the Portuguese World Exhibition in 1940 so patently illustrates.[42] In Macau, colonial propaganda could also take on a significant scale, namely the erection of two large bronze statues to two controversial nineteenth-century figures associated with the consolidation of Portuguese rule, Governor João Maria Ferreira do Amaral and Colonel Vicente Nicolau de Mesquita, who were regarded by local Chinese as imperialist aggressors (see Figure 13.3). One scholar interpreted the placing of these statues in central locations as a way 'to secure the territory's neutrality through the means of re-affirming a Portuguese identity'.[43] However, the line between affirming neutrality and affirming colonial rule was a blurred one. During the war, with Chinese anti-imperialist energies concentrated on resisting Japan, such public displays of Portuguese colonial might could unfold virtually unchallenged, even if they were not welcomed.[44]

In Portuguese propaganda in and about Macau, neutrality and colonialism were entangled as if one justified the other. The fact that Macau became a haven for

Figure 13.3 The Ferreira do Amaral statue in Macau, undated. Courtesy Alamy.

hundreds of thousands of refugees was used by the local authorities to promote their supposedly benevolent colonial rule, even if the refugees' experience in Macau was far more complex. For example, among many refugees that came to Macau during the war were Chinese school teachers and students, many of whom were supporters of Chinese resistance efforts. Despite not interfering much with their activities, the Macau authorities sought to force Chinese schools (mostly private) to adopt a series of school workbooks whose bilingual covers celebrated Macau heritage sites and images of 'Sino-Portuguese friendship'.[45] These were vague enough to be palatable to both Chinese resistance and to the collaborationist authorities controlling areas around Macau; for instance, using the figure of Sun Yat-sen, who was venerated as 'founding father' of the Chinese Republic in areas under Chiang and those under Wang, and who had briefly lived in Macau. Still, those workbooks were not welcomed by all, and schools remained important sites for nurturing support for the Chinese resistance, something that could also be subtly expressed in exercise books – as evidenced by surviving examples.[46] Material expressions publicizing Sino-Portuguese harmony such as the planned school workbooks should not obscure the fact that Portugal and China had very different aims for the war and for the future of Macau. In the post-war period, the abuses of Portuguese neutrality in Macau would be used by Chinese critics to call for the return of the territory to Chinese sovereignty.

Conclusion

During the war years, and especially so after the Japanese occupation of Hong Kong, Macau's status as a neutral colonial territory offered opportunities for different propaganda activities. In these, imperialist and anti-imperialist motivations intersected in complex ways. For the Chinese Nationalists and Communists fighting against Japan, their struggle was one against imperial aggression and for national liberation, but their target was then Japan, not European powers. The rhetoric of Asian liberation was also central to Japanese propaganda during the war, but in Macau, pan-Asian ideals clashed with the reality that Japanese forces were comfortable with Portuguese neutrality, providing that it did not interfere with their activities. Hence, Axis propaganda in Macau focused not on Portuguese colonialism, but mostly on trying to curb Allied resistance among the local population and harness support for the RNG.

As this chapter has shown, frequent invasion rumours reflect the uncertainty of Macau's neutral status, complaints against and exposés of un-neutral actions illustrate how that status was frequently challenged by opposing belligerents, but also how it was creatively used by different actors for their own aims. The active engagement with the press – be it through newly founded newspapers, reports in pre-existing publications or the use of censorship – demonstrates how a global propaganda war in Asia could be fought in the multilingual media pages of a small colonial territory and even spillover to the propaganda media distributed further afield. The maintenance of neutrality in Macau mattered to several different constituencies, from governments of opposing powers to family members of refugees living in different parts of the world.

The case of Macau, a small enclave that drew the attention of different belligerents, attests to the importance of imperialism and anti-imperialism when considering propaganda practices in neutral territories in Asia. It also demonstrates how assessing the opportunities and challenges of neutrality beyond Europe is essential to understanding the Second World War from a global perspective, as well as the enduring appeal of policies of neutrality by some colonial powers in the post-war period of emerging Cold War and decolonization.

Notes

Research for this chapter was funded by a Leverhulme Trust Early Career Fellowship.

1 António José Telo, *Portugal na Segunda Guerra: 1941–1945* (Lisbon: Vega, 1991); Fernando Rosas, 'Portuguese Neutrality in the Second World War', in *European Neutrals and Non-Belligerents during the Second World War*, ed. Neville Wylie (Cambridge: Cambridge University, 2001), 268–83; Irene Flunser Pimentel, *Espiões em Portugal durante a II Guerra Mundial* (Lisbon: Esfera dos Livros, 2013); Cláudia Ninhos, *Portugal e os Nazis: Histórias e Segredos de uma Aliança* (Lisbon: Esfera dos Livros, 2017). On propaganda, see, for example: António José Telo, *Propaganda e Guerra Secreta Em Portugal, 1939–1945* (Lisbon: Perspectivas e Realidades, 1990); Luís Reis Torgal (ed.), *O Cinema sob o Olhar de Salazar* (Lisbon: Temas & Debates, 2001); José Luís Garcia, Tânia Alves and Yves Léonard (ed.), *Salazar, o Estado Novo e os* Media (Lisbon: Edições 70, 2017); Edward Corse, *A Battle for Neutral Europe: British Cultural Propaganda during the Second World War* (London: Bloomsbury, 2013), which covers Portugal as well as Spain, Sweden and Turkey.

2 It would be interesting to assess the extent to which the overlap of Allied, Axis and Portuguese colonial propaganda dynamics in the case of Macau bears any similarities to what happened in Goa or Mozambique, places that were also significantly shaped by British interests.

3 Barak Kushner, *The Thought War: Japanese Imperial Propaganda* (Honolulu: Hawaii University Press, 2006); Shuge Wei, *News under Fire: China's Propaganda against Japan in the English-Language Press, 1928–1941* (Hong Kong: Hong Kong University Press, 2017); on Shanghai, see, for example: Wen-hsin Yeh (ed.), *Wartime Shanghai* (London: Routledge, 1998). See also Chapter 8 of this volume, which considers propaganda relating to the French Empire by the Vichy regime.

4 Florentino Rodao, *Franco y el imperio japonés: Imágenes y propaganda en tiempos de guerra* (Barcelona: Plaza y Janés, 2002); Pascal Lottaz, 'Neutral States and Wartime Japan: The Diplomacy of Sweden, Spain, and Switzerland toward the Empire', Doctoral thesis (National Graduate Institute for Policy Studies, Tokyo, 2018); Pascal Lottaz and Ingemar Ottosson, *Sweden, Japan, and the Long Second World War, 1931–1945* (London: Routledge, 2021).

5 Jo Fox, 'The Propaganda War', in *The Cambridge History of the Second World War, Volume II: Politics and Ideology*, ed. Richard J. B. Bosworth and Joseph A. Maiolo (Cambridge: Cambridge University Press, 2015), 92.

6 Fei Chengkang, *Aomen sibai nian* (Shanghai: Shanghai renmin chubanshe, 1988), 417–20; Iok Lan Fu Barreto (ed.), *Macau during the Sino-Japanese War* (Macau: Cultural Institute and Museum of Macao, 2002), 98–137.

7   Lin Faqin and Wang Xi (eds), *Gudao yingxiang: Aomen yu kangRi zhanzheng tuzhi* (Guangzhou: Guangdong jiaoyu chubanshe, 2015), 99; Barreto, *Macau*, 92–7; Ralph Croizier, *Art and Revolution in Modern China: The Lingnan (Cantonese) School of Painting, 1906–1951* (Berkeley: University of California Press, 1988), 153; Helena F. S. Lopes, 'Wartime Education at the Crossroads of Empires: The Relocation of Schools to Macao during the Second World War, 1937–1945', *Twentieth-Century China* 46, no. 2 (2021): 135.
8   Hong Kong University Library (HKUL), PR82/068 Personal Papers of Sir Lindsay Tasman Ride MF230701 (Roll 18), Kweilin Intelligence Summary no. 69, 6 October 1944, Section III (Miscellaneous), sheet 19, Macao Press (hereafter referred to as 'Kweilin Intelligence Summary'); Barreto, *Macau*, 86–7.
9   Barreto, *Macau*, 84–5; Henrique Rola da Silva, *A Imprensa Chinesa de Macau* (Macau: Gabinete de Comunicação Social do Governo de Macau, 1991), 69. Similar practices occurred in British-ruled Hong Kong. On this, see Michael Ng, *Political Censorship in British Hong Kong: Freedom of Expression and the Law (1842–1997)* (Cambridge: Cambridge University Press, 2022), chapter 2.
10 Barreto, *Macau*, 75.
11 Arquivo Nacional Torre do Tombo, Portugal (hereafter ANTT), Arquivo Oliveira Salazar (hereafter AOS), UL-10A1, cx. 767, Artur Tamagnini de Barbosa to Francisco José Vieira Machado, 16 December 1938.
12 ANTT, AOS, UL-10A1, cx. 767, Barbosa to Machado, 13 September 1939; Lopes, 'Wartime Education', 146.
13 ANTT, AOS, UL-10A1, cx. 767, Gabriel Maurício Teixeira, governor of Macau, to Machado, 10 December 1941; Helena F. S. Lopes, *Neutrality and Collaboration in South China: Macau during the Second World War* (Cambridge: Cambridge University Press, 2023), chapter 5.
14 Alexandre Moreli, 'The War of Seduction: The Anglo-American Struggle to Engage with the Portuguese Ruling Elite (1943–1948)', *The International History Review* 40, no. 3 (2018): 654–82.
15 Archives of Macau, MO/AH/AC/SA/01/17164, Condecoração concedida por Sua Majestade o Imperador do Japão, ao capitão Carlos de Sousa Gorgulho, 1939.
16 'Makao seichō waga ho ni kyōryoku–Nippo teikei no ryōkai naru–Konshū made ni jitsugen sen', *Asahi Shimbun*, 1 March 1939 and 'Co-Operation of Japan and Portugal Seen', *The Shanghai Times*, 2 March 1939, clippings in Arquivo Histórico Diplomático (hereafter AHD), 2P, A48, M217; 'Japan and Macao–Understanding Reached in Tokyo', *The South China Morning Post*, 2 March 1939, 13; 'Un journal japonais annonce la conclusion d'un accord nippo-portugais', *Le Journal de Shanghai*, 2 March 1939, 6.
17 AHD, 2P, A48, M217, Antero Carreiro de Freitas, Chargé d'Affaires in Tokyo, to Salazar, Minister of Foreign Affairs, 3 and 4 March 1939; Salazar to Portuguese legation in Shanghai, 6 March 1939; Salazar to Portuguese legation in London, 13 March 1939.
18 The UK National Archives (hereafter TNA), Foreign Office files (hereafter FO) 371/46199, 'Portuguese Possessions in Asia and Oceania', 5 June 1944, 12; ANTT, AOS, NE-10A2, cx. 768. Teixeira to Machado, 7 June 1944; Telo, *Portugal na Segunda Guerra*, vol. 1, 61 and vol. 2, 209.
19 'Macao Rumours', *The South China Morning Post*, 3 April 1940, 12; 'O desmentido oficial dos rumores de ocupação de Macau', *A Voz de Macau*, 26 December 1941, 5; 'Macao Governor's Views', *The South China Morning Post*, 21 October 1945, 3.

20 See files in ANTT, AOS, UL-10A1, cx. 767.
21 ANTT AOS, NE-10A2, cx. 768, Teixeira to Machado, 14 October 1943.
22 'Débarquement japonais près de Macao', *Le Petit Journal*, 24 March 1942, 3; TNA, WO 208/730, 'Portuguese Take a Back Seat in Macao', 21 April 1942; 'Portuguese Disarmed', *San Francisco Chronicle*, 6 July 1943, 14; 'Jap Threat to Portuguese', *Derby Evening Telegraph*, 8 September 1943, 8; 'Flashes of Late News', *The Ypsilanti Daily Press*, 8 September 1943, 1; 'Japan and Macao-Reported Threat to Portugal', *The Times*, 9 September 1943, 3; 'New Jap Threat', *San Francisco Chronicle*, 9 September 1943, 5; clippings from Brazilian press reports sent with dispatch from the Portuguese ambassador in Rio de Janeiro to Salazar, 20 September 1943, available in AHD, 2P, A48, M221.
23 John Pownall Reeves, *The Lone Flag: Memoir of the British Consul in Macao during World War II* (Hong Kong: Hong Kong University Press, 2014), 38.
24 ANTT, AOS, UL-10A1, cx. 767, Teixeira to Machado, 26 December 1941.
25 TNA, FO 371/46199, Ronald Campbell, Ambassador in Lisbon, to Anthony Eden, Foreign Secretary, 14 March 1945, and Campbell to Winston Churchill, 30 June 1945.
26 'Filhos do Céu: A China Espera Gosar de Ordem', *Sinal* 3, no. 5 (March 1942): 27–30. For a more general review of *Signal*, see Chapter 14 of this volume by João Arthur Ciciliato Franzolin.
27 'Aomen dangju sang xinbinkuang bi rang kangRi fenzi Rifang yanzhong kangyi fenkai yichang', *Guangdong xunbao*, 13 September 1939, available in AHD, 3P, A9, M128-129; ANTT, AOS, NE-7B, Pt. 40, Note on conversation with the Japanese minister, 23 March 1945.
28 On the *Nanhua ribao*, see Lawrence M. W. Chiu, 'The "South China Daily News" and Wang Jingwei's Peace Movement, 1939–41', *Journal of the Royal Asiatic Society Hong Kong Branch* 50 (2010): 343–70; on the *Honkon Nippō*, see Wilson Wai Shing Lee, '*Honkon Nippō* and Hong Kong-Japan Relations: Re-examining the Geopolitical Position of Colonial Hong Kong in East Asia before the End of World War II', in *Asian Cities: Colonial to Global*, ed. Gregory Bracken (Amsterdam: Amsterdam University Press, 2015), 125–42. According to Philip Snow, the *Hongkong News* 'became the [occupation] regime's leading vehicle for appealing to the English-speaking Asians, from the Anglicized Chinese and Eurasian gentry to the ordinary Eurasians and Indians' in Hong Kong. See Philip Snow, *The Fall of Hong Kong: Britain, China and the Japanese Occupation* (New Haven: Yale University Press, 2003), 97.
29 AHD, 2P, A48, M221, 'Talks on Japan and Macao sponsored by H.K. News', *The Hongkong News*, 26 January 1941, 1, 6, clipping sent with dispatch from Francisco Paulo de Vasconcellos Soares, Chargé of the Portuguese Consulate in Hong Kong to Salazar, 1 February 1941.
30 See, for example, *The Hongkong News*, 19 February 1943, 2.
31 'News from Macao', *The Hongkong News*, 3 August 1943, 3.
32 Lopes, 'Wartime Education', 147–8.
33 HKUL, Kweilin Intelligence Summary.
34 In 1929, then governor of Macau Artur Tamagnini de Barbosa stated that 'Macau is perhaps the only Portuguese land where one can say there are no illiterates'. See Barbosa, 'O Govêrno de Macau', *Boletim da Agência Geral das Colónias* 5, no. 53 (1929): 17. This achievement was certainly not due to Portuguese rule, whose state-funded schools mainly catered for the Portuguese and Macanese residents, not the majority Chinese population.

35 Shuge Wei, 'News as a Weapon: Hollington Tong and the Formation of the Guomindang Centralized Foreign Propaganda System, 1937–1938', *Twentieth-Century China* 39, no. 2 (2014): 118–43.
36 Hoi-to Wong, 'Interport Printing Enterprise: Macanese Printing Networks in Chinese Treaty Ports', in *Treaty Ports in Modern China: Law, Land and Power*, ed. Robert Bickers and Isabella Jackson (London: Routledge, 2016), 139–57.
37 Guoshiguan (Academia Historica, Taiwan), Waijiaobu, 020000023906A, Putaoya za juan, Central News Agency, 'Japanese Forcibly Seize British Ship in Macao', 29 August 1943. Portuguese policemen had actually stood by while the ship was taken away.
38 'Japs Shoot Portuguese: British Steamer Seized at Macao', *Dundee Courier*, 30 August 1943, 2; 'Japs Take Small Ship From Portuguese Force', *Wilmington Morning Star*, 30 August 1943, 8.
39 'Murder of Portuguese in Timor', *The Hongkong News*, 3 December 1943, 3; 'Portuguese Denial', *The Hongkong News*, 5 December 1943, 2.
40 On the diplomatic successes of Nationalist China as a member of the Allies, see Hans van de Ven, *China at War: Triumph and Tragedy in the Emergence of the New China, 1937–1952* (London: Profile Books, 2017), 172–8.
41 'Uma dívida a pagar', *Renascimento*, 21 August 1945, 1, 4.
42 David Corkill and José Carlos Pina Almeida, 'Commemoration and Propaganda in Salazar's Portugal: The Mundo Português Exposition of 1940', *Journal of Contemporary History* 44, no. 3 (2009): 381–99.
43 Paula Morais, 'Macau's Urban Transformation 1927–1949: The Significance of Sino-Portuguese Foreign Relations in the Urban Form', in *Constructing the Colonized Land: Entwined Perspectives of East Asia Around WWII*, ed. Izumi Kuroishi (Surrey: Ashgate, 2014), 155.
44 João de Pina-Cabral, *Between China and Europe: Person, Culture and Emotion in Macao* (London: Continuum, 2002), 68–70. Chinese opposition to these statues is well illustrated by what happened to them in later decades: one was forcibly removed by a crowd of demonstrators in December 1966 during events connected, in part, to the Chinese Cultural Revolution; the other was dismantled and shipped back to Portugal in the 1990s, before Macau's handover, at the request of the director of Hong Kong and Macao Affairs Office of the State Council of the People's Republic of China.
45 Maria José Peixoto Braga, *Macau Durante a II Guerra Mundial: Sociedade, Educação Física e Desporto* (Macau: Centro de Publicações Universidade de Macau, 2003), 258–62.
46 See school notebooks with resistance iconography on their covers in Lin and Wang, *Gudao yingxiang*, 97.

14

Magazine propaganda

Influencing readership in neutral and occupied countries

João Arthur Ciciliato Franzolin

The belligerent powers of the Second World War created magazines as prominent instruments of war propaganda to try to capture the attention of the target audiences in their daily lives. Indeed, magazines on sale in neutral cities were often the most visual representation that a war was taking place elsewhere. The magazines offered readers an idealized and harmonious world, suggesting that the war was already decided in favour of one or another belligerent. Ana Luiza Martins has stated that magazines were often 'irresistible' to readers as a physical document. Magazines brought 'together text, images, technique, worldviews and collective imaginaries' and are also helpful to historians through providing 'multiple records' which help us to understand both the owners' and the readers' points of view.[1] Magazine production, therefore, was important as it created perceptions to which both belligerents and their audiences were very sensitive. As Nicholas O'Shaughnessy has stated, by creating magazines such as *Signal* the Nazi regime was able to present its 'murderous subtext . . . rinsed in emollient language and imagery' using 'a rhetoric that was allusive and elusive'.[2] The belligerents clearly wanted to show their 'good side' to neutrals, and magazines were attractive to audiences who did not necessarily know any better than to believe the image being presented in the absence of other information.

Both sides invested huge sums of money in the production of these types of magazines. They aimed for the highest quality available at the time through designing attractive layouts and utilizing the most advanced production and printing methods. For example, they used high-quality paper; published colour photos, paintings and drawings; and a range of maps, photomontages and caricatures.

On the Axis side, it was the Germans and the Japanese who were most committed to the production of these illustrated magazines. *Die Wehrmacht* (Berlin, 1936–44) and *Der Adler* (Berlin, 1939–44) were some of the most important, along with *Signal* (Berlin, 1940–5), which was the leading publication in this genre.[3] In the Far East, Japan published *Front* (Tokyo, 1942–5), *Nippon* (Tokyo, 1934–44), *Home Life* (Osaka/Tokyo, 1939–42), later reorganized into *Sakura* (Osaka/Tokyo, 1942–5) and even the pioneering *International Graphic* (Tokyo, 1922–68). Japan began to circulate texts in English, Chinese and German during the war and these were distributed in territories under Japanese control.[4] These magazines were intended to demonstrate to the populations of Southeast Asia the military and economic strength of the Japanese Empire. Italy printed *Tempo* (Milan, 1939–43) in seven different languages which circulated in Germany, France, the Iberian Peninsula and Eastern Europe.[5]

On the other side, the Allies went on the counterattack with their own magazines. Britain distributed *Neptune* (London, 1940–5) for merchant seamen, while *War in Pictures* (London, 1940–5) was sold throughout most neutral countries like Spain, Portugal, Sweden and Switzerland and also in liberated countries like France in 1944. Both were printed in several languages.[6] The United States produced *Em Guarda* (Washington, 1941–5)[7] in three languages: Portuguese, Spanish (as *En Guardia*) and French (as *En Garde*)[8] [all translating as 'On Guard'] and *Victory* (1942–5, published in Portuguese, English, Spanish, French and Italian),[9] which were distributed in Europe and, in the case of the former, also in Latin America. *Victory* was published primarily for liberated countries such as France and Italy. Following Germany's invasion of the Soviet Union, the Soviets distributed by air the famous *Front-Illustrierte* (Moscow, 1941–5), aimed at German soldiers.[10] For soldiers of other nationalities they had a range of other magazines: for the Italians there was *Il Fronte Illustrato*, for the Finns there was *Kuvia Rintamalta*, for the Romanians there was *Frontul Illustrat* and for the Hungarians there was *Képes Frontujsag*.[11]

This chapter focuses on an analysis of three magazines primarily in the context of neutral countries during the Second World War. These were *Signal* – produced by the Wehrmacht Propaganda Department (WPr.), *Victory* – created by the Office of War Information (OWI) and *Em Guarda/En Guardia/En Garde* – published by the Office of the Coordinator of Inter-American Affairs (OCIAA). Unlike previous studies cited, which emphasized the creation and development of each of these magazines separately, the objective here is to undertake a comparative analysis. These magazines were conceived as tools to confront other productions of a similar nature and with similar objectives. At stake was the idea of obtaining political support, whether for fascist or democratic regimes. Therefore, comparing them side by side provides insights into how the audiences in neutral countries, who had access to publications from both sides in the war, would have received the messaging contained within them. Consequently, all the magazines in this chapter are being analysed to understand their general form, in order to find out their most important characteristics but also, through utilizing examples of themes and reports, to demonstrate the propaganda present in these publications.

From a theoretical point of view, this chapter is inspired by three historiographical perspectives. The first of these is the notion of connected history, discussed recently by historians such as Serge Gruzinski and Sanjay Subrahmanyam. Gruzinski has suggested that 'stories are bonded, connected and that they communicate with each other' and historians need to find ways to 're-establish the international and intercontinental connections' which overcome barriers created by borders.[12] The propaganda created by Germany and the United States was not carried out in isolation from each other. They went beyond their respective national borders and involved several others in an effort to promote their view of the world to a wider audience. Such a clash, which took place through the medium of illustrated magazines, can be understood, in the words of Sandra Ficker, as a 'transnational phenomenon, intrinsically characterized by the movement, the flow, the circulation'.[13]

The second perspective relates to 'mediascapes', a term coined by the anthropologist Arjun Appadurai which relates to the flow of images and information. In his works on globalization, Appadurai draws attention to the construction of extensive 'iconographic landscapes' around the world, and the images produced by the warring states during the Second World War invite us to reflect on this concept's potential. In Appadurai's words mediascapes 'tend to be image-centered, narrative-based accounts of strips of reality, and what they offer to those who experience and transform them is a series of elements (such as characters, plots, and textual forms) out of which scripts can be formed of imagined lives, their own as well as those of others living in other places'.[14] It seems clear that the vast iconographic material present in these publications can be seen as mediascapes. They were created and controlled by external producers (i.e. German and US propagandists), who conveyed to potential readers from different countries a particular narrative about the ongoing conflict, as well as how those nations should relate to them more generally. As Appadurai suggests, these were complex relationships and the propagandists focused on the creation of narratives which helped to create 'imagined lives' beyond neutral citizens' day-to-day existence.

The third perspective is the concept of propaganda itself. As the introduction to this book outlines there are a number of different definitions available. However, the definition of Garth Jowett and Victoria O'Donnell is useful in this context, as they consider it to be 'the deliberate, systematic attempt to shape perceptions, manipulate cognitions, and direct behavior to achieve a response that furthers the desired intent of the propagandist'.[15] Propagandists struggled to influence readers domestically, both in fascist and democratic countries, as well as internationally. They tried to create and shape a favourable opinion about themselves and the policies implemented by their regimes in order to gain support for a democratic world view of the future, expressed by the Atlantic Charter (in the case of the United States and Britain) or for a New Order to be consolidated in Europe (in the case of Germany, Italy and other fascist countries) if they won the confrontation.

Signal, Victory and *Em Guarda*: Creation, development and objectives

The origins of *Signal* magazine can be traced back to prior to the beginning of the war, in 1939, when specialists in the Wehrmacht began to research how they could improve German magazine propaganda in Europe. The magazine was conceived inside the WPr. in collaboration with the German Foreign Ministry.[16] It was also composed of propagandistic material of the Propagandakompanien (PK – the Propaganda Companies of the German Armed Forces).[17]

In late 1938 and early 1939, a cooperation agreement was signed between Joseph Goebbels' Reichsministerium für Volksaufklärung und Propaganda (or RMVP) ['Reich Ministry for Public Enlightenment and Propaganda'] and the Oberkommando der Wehrmacht ['Upper Command of the Armed Forces'], which regulated the 'Conduct of Propaganda in the war', ending their previous rivalry and arguments. This agreement resulted in the PK being created, with military training offered by the Wehrmacht, while following instructions and directives sent by the RMVP.[18] The PK was responsible for creating all the journalistic and propagandistic material from 1939 to 1945 (such as combat drawings and caricatures, reports, photos, films and paintings) which supplied the content of German publications, including *Signal*. The German magazine had exclusive material, supplied by a special PK unit called the 'Correspondent Squad for Special Use by the High Command of the Army' (*Berichterstaffel z.b.V. ObdH.*). The unit was used for activities of propaganda in specific regions of the various battlefronts and was the 'Crème of the PK-soldiers', because it created propaganda materials only for magazines published by the WPr. Department.[19]

According to Rainer Rutz, *Signal* was inspired by the model of *Life*, the famous American illustrated publication reorganized and relaunched by Henry Luce in 1936. *Em Guarda* and *Victory* were also heavily influenced by the American magazine, given its role in the improvement of use of the photographic essay. In *Life*, just like in *Signal*, *Em Guarda* and *Victory*,[20] the pictures were not trying to depict reality, but were representations that brought the style of the photographers in them.[21] Furthermore, *Life* and its propaganda successors in Germany and America had a variety of contents to attract large readerships and also brought together both advertising and articles.[22]

Signal was created in 1940 to counteract British and French hegemony in the European magazine market. A group of specialists and technicians from the Wehrmacht Propaganda Department, led by Lieutenant Fritz Solm, created and issued its first edition in April 1940, launched by the Deutscher Verlag (formerly Ullstein Verlag). The involvement of Deutscher Verlag was important as the publisher was considered 'neutral', and therefore this meant, particularly for international audiences, the magazine was seen as less propagandistic. This was unlike the Eher Verlag which was known for disseminating journalistic material linked to the Nazi Party. However, as Rutz points out, it did not take long for the magazine to be recognized as a propaganda organ, as Deutscher Verlag belonged to the central publishing house of the Nazi Party.[23] Even so, *Signal* quickly became a publishing success, reaching a circulation of 2.5 million copies in the years 1942–3, a best-seller across neutral and occupied Europe. The magazine contained an average of 40–50 pages, of which between eight and twelve were in colour. In 1942, editions were available in more than twenty different languages.[24]

Victory is the least-known magazine among those selected for the analysis. There is no previous research that has analysed its history nor is there much information about its creation within the Foreign Information Service, the predecessor of the Office of War Information[25] or about its contents. The OWI was a US government agency headed by journalist and CBS newsman Elmer Davis and was created to boost support on the home front and also to gain overseas backing for the American war effort and propaganda activities abroad. The organ had two branches, the Domestic Branch and Overseas Branch. The first was mainly concerned with film and radio activities in the

United States, while the second dealt with leaflet warfare and the production of two magazines abroad, *U.S.A.* and *Victory*.²⁶ The last one has been referenced by researchers since the 1960s, but this is usually in relation to the same criticisms by Republican congressmen: that the image of Roosevelt present in the publication was supposedly aimed to garner support for his fourth re-election. This was despite the magazine being published for foreign audiences. At the time, there was also a certain unwillingness of US politicians to support the magazine. They thought that the physical space the magazine occupied on ships was not justified and that space would be better used for sending ammunition to US soldiers. In addition, the colour photos, portraying the American abundance and plenty, were seen as capable of compromising US relations with the poorest countries in Latin America. In response to these criticisms, the director of the OWI, journalist Elmer Davis, asserted that the publication was intended for readers abroad and, therefore, should contain information about Roosevelt and the United States. To this little amount of existing information about *Victory*, there is also a bit more data about its materiality, which was made public in the autumn of 1942. In its first issue, it had a circulation of 450,000 copies and, from the second onwards 540,000, with distribution in Europe, Asia and Africa,²⁷ which made the magazine a publishing success. *Victory* was bimonthly and printed on high-quality paper, with extensive colour photo reports. It was published in English, Portuguese, Spanish, French, Italian and Polish.²⁸ However, in 1943, the magazine was accused by *Life* itself of being a 'pallid imitation of *Signal*', because it had 'less than half the circulation' and also had 'no terrific propaganda sock' like the German magazine.²⁹

Em Guarda was a product of the Office of the Coordinator of Inter-American Affairs, a US government agency headed by Nelson Rockefeller – owner of Standard Oil, who visited Latin America frequently and had good relations with the countries in the region. Established in 1940, the main objective of the OCIAA was to expand the American zone of influence and counterattack any Axis advances in the Americas. From 1940 to 1946, it operated with a $140 million budget, with 1,100 employees and 300 technicians in all Latin American countries. It operated in four main areas: public relations, health, commercial/finance and communications. This last division handled radio, film, sport and press activities, and it was consequently responsible for the production of *Em Guarda*.³⁰

Em Guarda was conceived by a former director of the United Press, Karl A. Bickel and, like the others, thanks to an agreement between the OCIAA and Business Publishers International Corporation, a subsidiary of McGraw-Hill Publishing Company. The editor was J. C. Stark, and in charge of the project were Francis S. Jamieson, chief of the OCIAA's information department, along with Michael J. McDermott, spokesman for the State Department. The success of *Em Guarda* can be seen in its circulation, at around 550,000 copies in 1943, the same time when *Signal* reached its peak in terms of sales. *Em Guarda* tried to create a positive image of the United States abroad, while fighting the vision designed by Germany and thus preventing the war from reaching the American continent. Idyllic images of American families and workers shared space with military machinery and equipment, to which were added articles about Latin American nations, all filled with colour photographs, as in the German publication.³¹

Belligerents not only spent time creating the magazines to promote certain images but also needed to ensure they were distributed widely in neutral, occupied and liberated countries to give an impression of power. As well as being sold, magazines were widely distributed by hand or distributed clandestinely. Some of the copies were even miniaturized and dropped on the war fronts, through bombing planes[32] and rockets – like the German V-1.[33] Even if neutral audiences did not purchase or open the magazines and read their content, just their very presence (or absence), the quality (or not) of the paper and covers resulted in different perceptions being created of the belligerent powers. For example, the British Ministry of Information (MoI) received reports from visitors to Turkey in the summer of 1940 that 'the bookstalls and kiosks are hung with German publications of which "Signal" is the most in evidence. . . . I have failed to discover any single British periodical even one or two months old'.[34] In response, the MoI worked throughout the war to produce and import its own periodicals of *Réalité* and *Cephe* ['Vanguard'] to Turkey, as well as subsidizing local Turkish-produced magazines of *Demokrat Politika* and *Foto Magazin* with varying degrees of success.[35] American magazines were also distributed widely in the Iberian Peninsula, using the US embassies in Madrid and Lisbon as redistribution centres to the rest of the mainland and archipelagos.[36] In Spain, Allied magazines were especially distributed via diplomatic bag in order to avoid the restrictions imposed by the Spanish authorities and the postal services, who dedicated part of their effort to seize and destroy Allied propaganda material – especially the most visual – while favouring the distribution and sale of German magazines.[37] According to Pizarroso Quintero, the Spanish edition of *Signal* was so distributed that, in the eyes of many Spaniards, this was often considered a local publication.[38]

The projection of the 'other' in magazine propaganda: Some examples from 1942 to 1944

The three magazines used the most advanced technology available at the time in printing not only to glorify and extol themselves – or even just show that life continued as normal at home despite the war – but also to harshly attack their enemies. The belligerents projected the justice of their war causes, their warlike potential and the benefits of their inevitable victory. Nevertheless, magazines also projected the way of life of the nations, their sociocultural traits and personal characteristics through episodes such as sports, fashion, the working class, the daily life in the front, the rural environment and the political practices.

There were differences, but also similarities in the propaganda of both countries. *Signal* showed the United States, in the words from Rainer Rutz, as 'the playground of an elite hungry for world domination, a paradise for the *Rockefellers* and *Al Capones*, a haven of brutality, blackmail, neglected youth, and lack of culture'.[39] A good example of this line of argument was a report on America's youth through the so-called Americana series of various reports that handled domestic 'problems' in the United States. One of the texts from the series, named 'From "Victory Girl" and what *Collier's* Magazine say about it', used a report from 13 March 1943 in *Collier's* magazine[40] about juvenile delinquency in the United States during the war. Altering the original context of the American report and using examples like the 'Victory Girls' – who offered sex to American soldiers – *Signal* showed its readers how American youth experienced rapid decay. The text goes further by citing other excerpts from *Collier's* report – translated to German and taken out of context – which show how New York and Detroit had become centres of juvenile delinquency and race struggles, which leads the anonymous author of the text to make the following remarks along it:

> Sometimes it would be good if the European public could judge for themselves the same United States that claims to be the most progressive country in the world ... so even the unbiased observer must get a downright horrific picture of the moral decay in which a certain part of the population of the USA finds itself. The war there has completely destroyed the low personal, manners and moral ties that existed before! ... In that essay in which Henry Luce claims our century is American, he wrote that the USA was already a leader in all trivial things in life. It is not the trivial ones alone, but also the criminal ones.[41]

The magazine presented itself as the representative of Europe and Europeans, in an attempt to convey a narrative of widespread support across the continent for German rule (the so-called *Neuordnung* or 'New Order'), which was contrasted against a British historical lack of interest in Europe, and Soviet Bolshevism being a threat.[42] This was a theme that was present in the magazine since its establishment, and it painted a grim scenario of what a possible Allied victory would mean: the supposed lack of morality in US culture would spread to Europe via the American soldiers who 'shared' the same lack of morality with delinquents in New York and Detroit outlined in the *Collier's* report. Europe would experience the same decadence that America was, in the view of the publication, already living. The article also cast doubt about the wisdom of US leadership after the war, since the United States could not seemingly solve the racial and social issues of their own country.

Not only was the nation of the United States heavily criticized, but US soldiers were also considered not to be a worthy enemy for the Germans, as they could be defeated easily. One example to demonstrate this was an image of a captured, saddened and injured American soldier with an eye bandage. The text accompanying the photo showed that he was no match for the German soldiers he confronted:

> I've always had bad luck. When we landed in Sicily, I was a corporal, but I had a stupid affair with a woman and was demoted; ... Of course I wanted to get on again and was very busy with raiding troops and business like that, which fall sour. One night I was lying in a mountain position ... I was posted as a sentinel; ... How your people manage to sneak up on the darkest night like panther cats without making a sound, I don't know. ... My people were gutted, and before I could pull the trigger on my machine pistol, someone slammed a thing on my head that made me feel like a soft melon. It wasn't until the next morning that I realized that I had hit German paratroopers of all people.[43]

The text offers a contrast between the German paratroopers, presented as efficient, professional and highly trained, and the American soldier, seen as a demoralized womanizer who was disorganized in combat – and who had been captured exactly because of these reasons. The Nazis' Allies, the Italians (for the first part of the war) and Japanese, were also highlighted as having 'close ties' and an efficient 'military spirit' which avoided 'individualism', unlike their British and American foes.[44] Just like Rainer Rutz suggested, when the American forces made territorial gains in Africa or in Italy after 1943, these victories were played down, as if they were not decisive in precipitating the downfall of the German war machine.[45]

Sebastien Saur has described *Signal* as misunderstood as a 'sweet' version of Nazi propaganda, without its racism and anti-Semitism. While he says that a 'cursory glance' might give that impression, a closer examination shows that *Signal* was as 'strongly tinted by racism' particularly towards the end of the war. Although the Americans may have been portrayed as disorganized, Saur states that the Soviets were particularly denigrated as 'subhuman'.[46]

Em Guarda, published in the Americas before the United States' entry into the war, condemned the Nazi activities in Europe right from the outset. The most interesting example of this nature was the report 'The Free World or Enslaved', which showed pictures (see Figures 14.1 and 14.2) comparing life in the United States and in Nazi-occupied Europe. For the United States, there were images symbolizing the Four Freedoms (of Speech, of Worship, from Want and from Fear) expressed by Roosevelt – and these were juxtaposed with images of destroyed churches, hunger and brutality towards other peoples in the Nazi-occupied territories.[47] The idea was to portray a fight between 'Good' versus 'Evil', a Manichean format used throughout its existence to create support for the American forces among the readership in Central and South America.

But there were also similarities in the three magazines on certain issues. *Victory* and *Em Guarda* also used the same strategy of *Signal* in ridiculing war prisoners and contrasting differences between different nations. In a text from *Victory*:

> The Germans were never tired of proclaiming their 'racial superiority' [. . . Yet] when fortune was bad for them, thousands of Germans and Italians surrendered. They did not fight like the Russians, until their last breath. At Cape Bon, they did not behave like the English at Dunkirk. The German 'Superman' was not even the one who resisted the most. The last to surrender were the Italians.[48]

Just like the Nazi propagandists undermined the American soldier in *Signal*, the German soldiers were ridiculed in *Victory* and presented as hypocrites owing to the contrast between their proclaimed superiority differed heavily from their actions taken in battle. This ridiculing of the enemy was also present in *Em Guarda*, with an image of a German general guarded by American soldiers (see Figure 14.3). Unlike the wounded US soldier depicted in the pages of *Signal*, the saddened general is not injured but looks disappointedly into the distance. At the same time, he is depicted as a laughing stock for the US soldiers that watch him. The image caption also corroborates this intention: 'Captured by the Americans, this German general contemplates his miserable future,

Figure 14.1 '*O mundo livre*' [The Free World], *Em Guarda*, Ano 1, No. 8 (1942), page 24. Rockefeller Archive Center, New York.

completely empty of great conquests.'⁴⁹ The criticism in the text has parallels with the German text from *Signal*: the general was defeated by a far superior American force that would not allow any more Nazi conquests in Europe. The rank of this prisoner of war would also show the readers how powerful the US Army was. The Germans might be able to capture ordinary American soldiers in 1944, but only the United States could

Figure 14.2 '*O mundo escravizado*' [The Enslaved World], *Em Guarda*, Ano 1, No. 8 (1942), page 25. Rockefeller Archive Center, New York.

Figure 14.3 '*Capturado pelos americanos, esse general alemão contempla o seu mísero futuro, completamente vazio des grandes conquistas*' [Captured by the Americans, this German general contemplates his miserable future, completely empty of great conquests], *Em Guarda*, Ano 4, No. 1 (1944/5), page 6. Rockefeller Archive Centre, New York.

capture officers and generals, showing the disintegration of the Wehrmacht at the end of the war, and ultimately the defeat of Nazi Germany.

Conclusion: A paper's war

The analysis presented in this chapter showed that from the beginning of the Second World War, all the belligerents engaged in a power struggle not only in the battlefields but also on the magazine markets, particularly in neutral countries. Through this medium, the belligerents felt it was necessary to indoctrinate populations in other countries in order to gain support for new ideals that they had, regardless of whether those audiences were in favour of the Axis or Allied forces or more strictly neutral.

The analysis in this chapter has shown that *Em Guarda*, *Victory* and *Signal* constitute mediascapes that tried to bring to different peoples in neutral and occupied countries narratives, images and ideas to generate support and/or acceptance for US and German plans for a new state of affairs in an eventual post-war world. In addition, the fight between the Axis and Allied forces in the magazine market formed a 'connected history' because there was an interrelationship between those real battles and the battles taking place in relation to the content of these magazines. The propaganda departments responsible for their production tried constantly to improve the quality of the publications in order to keep up with the competition, sometimes using innovations presented by enemy magazines. Although all three of them were modelled after *Life*, it can be said that *Victory* was inspired by the success of *Signal*, and *Signal*, in turn, probably introduced colour covers in early 1944 to counter *Victory* and *Em Guarda*.

Given that magazines were produced with different values – democratic and authoritarian – the contents of the publications had some perhaps surprising similarities, and the propagandists were clearly fighting on similar territory to gain the attention of neutral audiences. Both sought to demonize the other: *Signal*, for example, demonized life in America, while the American magazines demonized the already known German atrocities in occupied countries. Members of both armies were presented as demoralized, saddened and already effectively defeated. The only difference was that the US Army could capture officers, while the Wehrmacht could only capture soldiers at the end of the war, perhaps showing the reality of their respective strengths.

Notes

1. Ana Luiza Martins, 'Da fantasia à História: folheando páginas revisteiras', *História e Outras Linguagens* 22, no. 1 (2003): 60–1.
2. Nicholas O'Shaughnessy, *Marketing the Third Reich: Persuasion, Packaging and Propaganda* (London: Routledge, 2018), 81.
3. For more information about the three magazines, see Rainer Rutz, *Signal. Eine deutsche Auslandsillustrierte als Propagandainstrument im Zweiten Weltkrieg* (Essen:

Klartext Verlag, 2007); Jeremy Harwood, *Hitler's War: World War II as Portrayed by Signal, the International Nazi Propaganda Magazine* (Minneapolis: Zenith Press, 2014); João Arthur Ciciliato Franzolin, '"Die Wehrmacht". Die offizielle illustrierte Propagandazeitschrift der deutschen Wehrmacht für das In- und Ausland (1936–1944)', Doctoral thesis (Europa-Universität Flensburg, Flensburg, 2017); Jordan Henry, '"We Europeans": Signal Magazine and Political Collaboration in German-occupied Europe, 1940–1945', Undergraduate Research Thesis (The Ohio State University, 2017); Masami Tokoi and Sydney L. Mayer, *Der Adler: The Official Nazi Luftwaffe Magazine* (Berlin: T.Y. Crowell, 1977).

4 For references on the Japanese publications, see Gennifer Weisenfeld, 'Touring Japan-as-Museum: *NIPPON* and Other Japanese Imperialist Travelogues', *Positions* 8, no. 3 (2000): 747–93; Andrea Germer, 'Adapting Russian Constructivism and Socialist Realism. The Japanese Overseas Photo Magazine "Front" (1942–1945)', *Zeithistorische Forschungen/Studies in Contemporary History* 12, no. 2 (2015): 236–63 and Yūko Inoue, *Senji gurafu zasshi no sendensen*: jūgonen sensōka no Nihon imēji (Tokyo: Seikyūsha, 2009).

5 Anna Antonello, 'The Milan-Hamburg Axis: Italy for German Readers (1940–1944)', *Modern Italy* 21, no. special 2 (2016): 125–38.

6 Archivo Fernández-Xesta, 'War in Pictures'. n.d. Available online: http://fernandez-xesta.es/PRENSA/REVISTAS/REVISTAS%20REINO%20UNIDO/WAR%20IN%20PICTURES.html (accessed 31 January 2022) and Archivo Fernández-Xesta, 'Neptune'. n.d. Available online: http://fernandez-xesta.es/PRENSA/REVISTAS/REVISTAS%20REINO%20UNIDO/NEPTUNE.html (accessed 31 January 2022). Original versions of *War in Pictures* and *Neptune* can be found at the UK National Archives (TNA) in the following files: INF 2/1 to INF 2/50.

7 There are some important studies regarding *Em Guarda* such as Monica A. Rankin, *México, la patria! Propaganda and Production during World War II* (London: University of Nebraska Press, 2009) and Julio Cesar dos Santos Silva, *A construção do pan-americanismo na revista Em Guarda: o olhar americano pela defesa das Américas (1941–1946)*, Master Dissertation (Universidade Estadual Paulista, 2009).

8 The Portuguese and Spanish versions of *Em Guarda* have basically the same contents, with some extra reports about Brazil in the Portuguese version, with the French version having a different numbering.

9 *Victory* is often cited without deep analysis. See, for example, John Morton Blum, *V was for Victory* (New York: Harvest, 1976), 37–40, 43; Allan M. Winkler, *The Politics of Propaganda. The Office of War Information 1942–1945* (New Haven: Yale University Press, 1978), 66–7, 79, 154–6; Clayton D. Laurie, *The Propaganda Warriors. America's Crusade against Nazi Germany* (Lawrence: University Press of Kansas, 1996), 172–3 and Marja Roholl, 'Preparing for Victory. The U.S. Office of War Information Overseas Branch's Illustrated Magazines in the Netherlands and the Foundations for the American Century, 1944–1945', *European Journal of American Studies* 7, no. 2 (2012). Available online: https://journals.openedition.org/ejas/9629 (accessed 31 January 2022).

10 Erika Wolf, *Aleksandr Zhitomirsky – Photomontage as a Weapon of World War II and the Cold War* (Chicago: The Art Institute of Chicago, 2016). Also see Archivo Fernández-Xesta 'Front-Illustrierte'. n.d. Available online: http://fernandez-xesta.es/PRENSA/REVISTAS/REVISTAS%20URSS/FRONT%20ILLUSTRIERTE.html (accessed 31 January 2022).

11 Archivo Fernández-Xesta '"Front-Illustrierte": Other editions'. n.d. Available online: http://www.fernandez-xesta.com/PRENSA/PASQUINES/REVISTAS/FRONT%20ILLUSTRIERTE%20OE-i.html (accessed 17 February 2022).
12 Serge Gruzinski, 'Os mundos misturados da monarquia católica e outras connected histories', *Topoi* 2, no. 2 (2001): 176.
13 Sandra Kuntz Ficker, 'Mundial, trasnacional, global: Un ejercicio de clarificación conceptual de los estudios globales', *Nuevo Mundo Mundos Nuevos Debates* (2014): 6. Available online: https://journals.openedition.org/nuevomundo/66524 (accessed 17 February 2022).
14 Arjun Appadurai, *Modernity at Large: Cultural Dimensions of Globalization* (Minneapolis: University of Minnesota Press, 1996), 35.
15 Garth S. Jowett and Victoria O'Donnell, *Propaganda and Persuasion* (Los Angeles: Sage, 2019), 7.
16 Rutz, *Signal*, 25–52.
17 Ibid., 157.
18 Daniel Uziel, *The Propaganda Warriors: The Wehrmacht and the Consolidation of the German Home Front* (Bern: Peter Lang, 2008), 85–8.
19 Rutz, *Signal*, 157.
20 Caroline Angle, 'The New Ju-Ju: Ijo Masquerades and the Office of War Information in Second World War Nigeria', *Journal of Contemporary History* 56, no. 2 (2021): 20.
21 About the importance of *Life*, see Thierry Gervais and Gaëlle Morel, *The Making of Visual News. A History of Photography in the Press* (London: Bloomsbury, 2017), 131.
22 Ibid., 112.
23 Ibid., 55.
24 Rainer Rutz, 'Die netten Deutschen und das "Neue Europa". Sympathiewerbung für die Wehrmacht, den Krieg und die Besatzung in der NS-Auslandsillustrierten *Signal*', in *Die Kamera als Waffe. Propagandabilder des Zweiten Weltkrieges*, ed. Rainer Rother and Judith Prokasky (Munich: Edition Text, 2010), 196. See also Claire Aslangul-Rallo, 'Signal (1940–1945): propagande «universelle» ou adaptation à des publics hétérogènes?', *Matériaux pour l'histoire de notre temps* 135-6, no. 1–2 (2020): 56–67.
25 Roholl, 'Preparing for Victory'.
26 Winkler, *The Politics of Propaganda* and Laurie, *The Propaganda Warriors*.
27 'Pictorial "Victory" for Foreign Readers', *Victory. Official Weekly Bulletin of the Office of War Information* 4, no. 6 (1943): 186.
28 Archivo Fernández-Xesta 'Victory'. n.d. Available online: http://fernandez-xesta.es/PRENSA/REVISTAS/REVISTAS%20USA/VICTORY.html (accessed 6 December 2021).
29 'U.S. is Losing the War of Words', *Life*, March 1943, 11.
30 Aline Vanessa Locastre, *Seduções impressas: a veiculação do paradigma estadunidense no Brasil em tempo de Segunda Guerra Mundial* (Curitiba: CRV, 2017). See also Aline Vanessa Locastre, 'As promessas da revista "Em Guarda" para o Brasil no pós-guerra (1941–1945)', *Antíteses* 8, no. 15 (2015): 488–519.
31 Carlos Roberto de Souza, 'Para la defensa de las Américas: The Pictorial Magazine En Guardia in Nelson A. Rockefeller's Propaganda Campaign for Latin America during World War II', Rockefeller Archive Center Online (November 2012). Available online: https://scholarworks.utrgv.edu/cgi/viewcontent.cgi?article=1002&context=art_fac (accessed 21 February 2022).

32 Konstantin Akinsha, 'The Second Life of Soviet Photomontage, 1935–1980s', Doctoral thesis (University of Edinburgh, Edinburgh, 2012), 253.
33 Herbert A. Friedman, 'The German V1 Rocket Leaflet Campaign', *Psywarrior*, 19 December 2003. Available online: http://www.psywarrior.com/V1RocketLeaf.html; and Archivo Fernández-Xesta. n.d. 'Signal, Ausgabe V1 (E)'. Available online: http://fernandez-xesta.es/PRENSA/REVISTAS/REVISTAS%20ALEMANIA/SIGNAL%20%20Ausgabe%20V-1.html (accessed 6 December 2021).
34 Edward Corse, '"To accustom Turkish minds to a state of belligerency": The Delicate Balance of British Propaganda in Turkey during the Second World War', *Journal of Balkan and Near Eastern Studies* 23, no. 6 (2021): 898.
35 Ibid., 906.
36 Alejandro Pizarroso Quintero, *Diplomáticos, propagandistas y espías: Estados Unidos y España en la Segunda Guerra Mundial: información y propaganda* (Madrid: CSIC Press, 2009), 147.
37 Ingrid Schulze Schneider, 'La propaganda alemana en España: 1942–1944', *Espacio Tiempo y Forma. Serie V, Historia Contemporánea* 7 (1994): 371–86.
38 Pizarroso Quintero, *Diplomáticos, propagandistas y espías*, 148.
39 Rutz, *Signal*, 223.
40 Ella Winter, 'Are Children Worse in Wartime?' *Collier's*, March 1943, 52–5.
41 '"Americana". Vom "Victory-girl" und was "Collier's Magazine" dazu sagt', *Signal* 3, no. 16 (August 1943): 38. Translation from the German here and in later quotations by the author.
42 'Aujourd'hui, L'Europe Unifiee', ne peut être que le résultat d'une Victoire allemande', *Signal* (French version) 4, no. 2 (January 1943): 8.
43 Kriegsberichter Wundshammer, 'Er sah die "Grünen Teufel" . . .', *Signal* 5, no. 13 D (1944): 5.
44 Delio Vecchi, 'Sur le sable et dans la steppe, sur la mer et dans les airs: l'Italie en Guerre', *Signal* (French version), no. 2 (January 1942): 11; Etu Endo, 'Soldats Japonais: Formation, spirit et tradition de l'armée japonaise', *Signal* (French version), no. 2 (January 1943): 8. Translation from the French by the editor.
45 Rutz, *Signal*, 229–30.
46 Sebastien Saur, 'The Soviet Union in *Signal*', *Histoire de Guerre* 38 (2003): 9. See also O'Shaughnessy, *Marketing the Third Reich*, 81.
47 'O mundo livre ou escravizado', *Em Guarda*, 1 no. 8 (1942): 24–5.
48 'Los Aliados capturan más y más prisioneiros', *Victory* 1, no. 3 (1943): 19. Translation from the Portuguese by the author.
49 'Desmorona-se a "Nova Ordem" de Hitler', *Em Guarda* 4, no. 1 (1944): 6.

Part III

Propaganda and neutrality in the Cold War and beyond

15

'Operation Mrs Partington'

The British Council and the emergence of the Non-Aligned Movement

Edward Corse

The British Council had been established in 1934 by the British government in recognition that Britain's culture and way of life were not well known in some parts of the world, and an organization was required to promote Britain's thinking and values. In 1938, the Council had established its first institutes abroad and continued to expand during the Second World War in places not occupied by the enemy. Promoting culture has generally been termed 'cultural propaganda', although the Council often shied away from the word 'propaganda' because of its perceived negative and political connotations.[1]

After borrowing and spending so much money to fight the war, British government budget cuts were inevitable. The British Prime Minister, Winston Churchill, had already concluded in November 1944 that the Council was 'certainly one of the objects ripe for retrenchment when the war comes to an end'.[2] Indeed, various criticisms were levelled at the Council around inefficiency and its inability to control its enormous wartime expansion, and financial constraints were imposed on its activities by the incoming Labour administration. Between the financial years 1948–9 and 1953–4, the total reduction in Foreign Office funding to the Council was 42.4 per cent.[3] The Council survived but clearly could no longer operate in the way that it had during the war.[4]

The independence of India in August 1947 also heralded the beginning of the end of the British Empire and retrenchment in a broader sense of direct British influence in the world. The world was becoming increasingly polarized between the two superpowers, the United States and the Soviet Union, in what was becoming known as the Cold War – and Britain's influence and power was not what it once had been. The irony was that at a time when more of the world was available to accommodate a British Council presence, and there was perhaps more need for its softer activities as the empire shrunk in size, less money was available to service the Council.

The Council and its activities were subject to several reviews in this period. One such review was commissioned in July 1953 with the Earl of Drogheda being asked to chair a committee to examine British overseas information services. This was arguably in recognition that, in the absence of the empire, there was an increasing need for Britain to project itself in other ways. The British government endorsed the report which outlined specific recommendations on the future of the British Council. The Drogheda Report suggested that the Council needed to change emphasis from cultural to educational activities and move away from the developed world to concentrate more on the less developed parts of the world.[5] Indeed, places where a new neutralist movement was forming.

The emergence of the Non-Aligned Movement (NAM)

Several countries in this new post-war world did not see their interests best served by being drawn into the spheres of influence of the two superpowers. Instead, they sought a third way through engaging closely with other like-minded states. This work would, over the next decade, lead to the establishment of the Non-Aligned Movement. The NAM was essentially an initiative established by three men: Jawaharlal Nehru of India, Gamal Abdel Nasser of Egypt and Josip Broz Tito of Yugoslavia, and as Dietmar Rothermund has stated, the NAM 'owed a great deal to the charisma and vision of its three co-founders'.[6] This chapter, therefore, concentrates on the British Council's efforts in those three countries, although the NAM grew to encompass a wider group of countries over time.

The movement is generally recognized to have started formally at the Belgrade Summit hosted by Tito in September 1961, which was attended by all three leaders. However, the idea of non-alignment in the post-war context had been emerging slowly following the conclusion of hostilities.[7] For example, even before formal independence, Nehru had hosted the Asian Relations Conference in March 1947 in New Delhi, which was followed by the Bandung Conference in April 1955 in Indonesia which gathered Asian, Arab and African states. Bandung has been described as a 'beacon of hope' for decolonization, and indeed NAM's origins were very much drawn from the decolonization agenda.[8]

With Indian independence secured, Nehru was in a strong position to play a leading role in this growing movement. India had had a long colonial relationship with Britain, with many challenges, but also multiple links through the two world wars as well as through family ties that continued to be forged after independence. The partition of British India, and the lack of settlement over Kashmir between Pakistan and Nehru's India, however, continued to make Indian–British relations difficult. There also remained several non-British, but European-administered enclaves still in existence after 1947 – notably French Mahé and Pondicherry (until 1954) and Portuguese Goa (until 1961), which made Indians still feel, understandably, that they were not yet free from European influence despite independence. Nehru was keen also to promote Hindi as *the* Indian language instead of English, something clearly symbolic in relation to independence, but caused many internal political challenges given the linguistic diversity of the country. Nehru sought friends in Moscow and

Beijing as well as the West, including Britain, and walked a tightrope between these different interests.⁹

Nasser's view of the world in some ways was very different. This centred on the creation and impact of the state of Israel and reaching a resolution on who controlled the Suez Canal. Even before Nasser had seized power in 1952, Egypt had already been a leading nation of the new Arab League taking an active role in the first Arab–Israeli war in 1948. In addition, the Great Cairo Fire in January 1952, sparked by the continued British presence and actions at Suez, had destroyed many symbols of British influence including the British Council offices. However, following the revolution in July 1952, Nasser's charisma and foreign policy agenda made him a leading light for those wanting to throw off the influence of the Western imperialists more fully. He was not popular everywhere – many in the Arab world itself, notably Saudi Arabia and conservative Arab regimes, saw him as a dangerous force. As Anthony McDermott has observed, 'Egypt was simultaneously admired, feared and hated in the region'.¹⁰ It was the Suez Crisis in November 1956, however, that cemented Nasser's reputation for dealing with foreign imperialism after the botched invasion of Egypt as a result of British–French–Israeli collusion to seize back control of the Egyptian-nationalized Suez Canal.

Tito's involvement in this growing movement shifted the emphasis from decolonization (and its Asian and African focus) to non-alignment in a more general sense. Tito ruled the only major country in Eastern Europe that was not under Soviet domination, despite Yugoslavia being a communist country. This stemmed from the fact that Tito had fought the Nazis without the military assistance of the Soviets, and so no Soviet forces were situated on Yugoslav soil at the end of hostilities. Stalin and Tito also did not agree on ideological matters. Although Tito had benefited from assistance from the United States through the Marshall Plan, he was not immune from events that took place in the Soviet-dominated bloc. This particularly manifested itself in the events in Budapest in November 1956, and he had a complicated relationship with Stalin's successor, Nikita Khrushchev. Nora Beloff noted in her book, *Tito's Flawed Legacy*, that she was sceptical of the reasons behind Tito's involvement in the NAM, believing it to be merely 'an epithet suggesting neutrality' whereas in reality Tito 'directed his foreign policy primarily towards propping up his political structure'.¹¹

This emerging neutralist movement was, therefore, representative of a mixture of domestic and foreign policies and interests in these three countries. This included a wish to reject the old imperialists (such as Britain and France) as well as striving for a third way between the two superpowers.

In the aftermath of the Bandung Conference, Tito invited Nehru and Nasser to a summit on the Croatian island of Brioni in July 1956, which has been described as the 'Third World's Yalta'.¹² As Nataša Mišković has noted, at the Brioni summit the three men 'interpreted non-alignment as active neutrality which did not keep quiet and passive in international politics, but strove to interfere and serve as mediators in the service of the UN Charter'.¹³ Just as neutrality had often been positioned as a moral stance in earlier conflicts, non-alignment was again promoted as a way of being above conflict, and a propaganda tool in itself. In September 1961, in the shadow of the building of the Berlin Wall, the NAM was formally inaugurated in Belgrade. Although its size remained modest compared to what it would become

Figure 15.1 Gamal Abdel Nasser of Egypt, Jawaharlal Nehru of India and Josip Broz Tito of Yugoslavia at the Brioni Summit, July 1956. Courtesy Getty Images.

later, Rothermund has noted that 'the atmosphere of this first conference was charged with great enthusiasm' and represented a serious challenge to the positions of both East and West (Figure 15.1).[14].

Risking 'Operation Mrs Partington'

In this context the two superpowers sought to influence the countries of the NAM movement through cultural activities. The United States was active through the work of the United States Information Agency (USIA), which was established in 1945 on 'the idea that America needed a permanent apparatus to explain itself to the post-war world'.[15] Soviet activity was generally organized by the All-Union Society for Cultural Ties (or VOKS by its Russian acronym), established in 1925, and which became the Union of Soviet Societies of Friendship and Cultural Relations with Foreign Countries in 1957.[16]

For both countries there was a heavy emphasis on academic cooperation and student exchanges. For the United States this was facilitated by the Fulbright Program, established in Egypt in 1949 and India in 1950, but only in 1964 in Yugoslavia because of concerns around cooperating with a communist country.[17] As Molly Bettie has observed, there was often a careful balancing act for the Fulbright Program to ensure both the achievement of objectives and avoiding charges of cultural imperialism.[18]

The Americans were able to build upon existing institutions such as the American University in Cairo and the American School in Assiut.[19] The Soviets also arranged visits of Indian professors to Moscow and delegations to the All-India Science Congress as well as opportunities to study in the Soviet Union.[20] Printed material was also important, particularly for the Soviets who flooded the market, often targeting the student population of India with cheap communist textbooks and literature.[21]

Both the USIA and VOKS facilitated the 'cultural manifestation' – in other words, the visit of a generally well-known personality or group, which they hoped would grab the headlines in the local press and radio. For the Soviets this often meant a tour of the Bolshoi Ballet, but also included the violinist David Oistrakh, circuses and football teams, often accompanied by the organization of film festivals.[22] In January 1954, for example, there was a large Soviet Cultural Delegation featuring 'a feast of Russian music, dance and song' which toured many cities in India and 'played to packed houses'.[23] The Indo-Soviet Cultural Society helped ensure Soviet films were seen in remote Indian villages and clubs to enable the study of the Russian language.[24] For the United States, cultural manifestations were made through visits of the Wayne State University Theatre Group and the Dave Brubeck Jazz Quartet to India, and by composers Igor Stravinsky and Aaron Copland to Yugoslavia in 1961, to name just a few.[25]

The British Council's representatives often looked enviously at the resources at the disposal of the USIA, in particular, and observed with some concern the activities of the Soviets.[26] Before the Suez Crisis and even the Egyptian Revolution, the Council's representative there had already noted that the authorities were increasingly turning to the Americans who were 'rapidly taking the lead in cultural and social propaganda'.[27] However, despite this, the Council often regarded the American efforts as 'clumsy' either because of a lack of recognition of local sensitivities or because it was felt that the Americans were more interested in 'propaganda stunts' than the needs of any of the three countries – 'a pitfall into which we must not fall'.[28]

However, both the United States and the Soviet Union were slow to make progress in Yugoslavia. This appeared to be closely connected to politics. For the Soviet Union, cultural activity tended to follow the ebb and flow of diplomatic relations; for the United States, cultural activity in this communist country was limited because of domestic McCarthyism.[29] It is worth stating too, that unlike the significant American presence in Egypt, Soviet activity was not apparent until the summer of 1955 and the lead-up to the Suez Crisis, when a permanent VOKS presence was established in Cairo.[30]

The French (primarily through the Alliance Française), and to a lesser extent a range of other countries, such as Italy, the two Germanies (particularly West Germany through the Goethe-Institut or Max Mueller Bhavan in India), Poland, Czechoslovakia and the People's Republic of China, also made inroads into this 'cultural rat race', as the British Council's Representative in India called it.[31] Added to the state-sponsored cultural activities were a growing range of private educational, cultural and scientific organizations. These included the Ford Foundation,[32] the Rockefeller Foundation[33] and the Nuffield Foundation – all of which were particularly active in India. The Council cooperated with many of these and other multinational organizations, such as the United Nations Educational, Scientific and Cultural Organization (UNESCO) and the Colombo Plan, in some form.[34] For example, the Nuffield Foundation funded the establishment of an English Language Teaching Institute in Allahabad with the cooperation of the Council: a model the Council was keen to see established elsewhere.[35]

Clearly, any British Council activities were far from being in a bubble, and instead would form part of a complex mosaic of cultural diplomacy of varying levels of funding, objectives and quality. Making an impact in these NAM countries would be difficult, particularly with a lack of funding. As the Council's representative in India remarked, the Council needed to avoid spreading itself too thinly and being engaged in 'Operation Mrs Partington', alluding to a nineteenth-century character who was observed in a futile attempt to deal with a tidal surge, with merely a broom to hand.[36]

From Shakespeare to snowballs

Although Britain's role in the world was to diminish during this period, the British Council's activity in all three countries remained significant. Notwithstanding budget constraints and other restrictions such as the availability of foreign exchange and visa issues, the Council was arguably punching above its weight. It was often still able to ride upon Britain's historical influence, the primacy of the English language and consequential demand for its teaching, and also often being seen as less controversial and political than the cultural offerings of either of the two superpowers. As Alice Byrne has observed, the Council was always keen to avoid being seen as anti-communist in an active sense, to avoid any accusation that it was political.[37]

In all three of the leading non-aligned countries, there was a need for the types of services the Council could offer. The Council did try to take a 'one size fits all' approach wherever it could although, as we have seen, these three NAM countries were very different in historical experience and culture. Several touring individuals also visited 'aligned' countries, such as Poland and Pakistan, which were also open to British Council activities. This showed that the interrelationship between neutrality and cultural activity was more complex than it had been during the Second World War.[38] The establishment of libraries, the offering of scholarships and bursaries, performances and readings of the plays of Shakespeare, art exhibitions and, of course, the teaching of English remained important across all of the territories where the Council operated. Technical assistance and medical expertise were also increasing in demand across many countries. Nevertheless, the differences between the NAM countries were more important, however, and therefore required different approaches.

James Lee Taylor has argued that in places such as Yugoslavia 'ancient cultural ties, subsumed national identities, and shared Enlightenment values, pre-dated current Cold War antagonisms'.[39] With Tito keen to distance himself from Moscow, and McCarthyist America still wary about too much cooperation with a communist country, the British Council was able to fill the vacuum and build upon these pre-Cold War links. Indeed, the Council itself had previously existed in Yugoslavia before the Second World War and quickly re-established centres in Belgrade and Zagreb. It was active across all the republics that formed the Yugoslav Federation. The Council was not actually given formal recognition until 1961 with the signing of a Cultural Convention, but it had a generally positive relationship with the Yugoslav authorities, apart from a short period following the decision to return Trieste to Italy rather than Yugoslavia.[40]

Music and theatre were particularly in demand in Yugoslavia which had an active performing arts community. The Yugoslav authorities would only consider visits by individuals and organizations who were already famous or at the top of their professional field. The Council arranged for visits by the orchestral conductors Léon Goossens and Sir Malcolm Sargent, the composer Benjamin Britten and the tenor Peter Pears, film stars Sir Laurence Olivier and Vivien Leigh, who performed Shakespeare's *Titus Andronicus* in June 1957, and the Old Vic with actors John Neville and Judi Dench, starring in a tour of *Hamlet* in March 1959.[41] While there were certainly genuine elements of cultural exchange, the tour of Olivier and Leigh was widely covered in the Yugoslav press with Leigh's stardom from *Gone with the Wind* almost two decades before, 'continu[ing] to be a certain draw for audiences who were largely indifferent to Shakespeare'.[42] In addition, Britten, Pears, Olivier and Leigh all met Tito as part of their visit.[43] Just as Olivier had been able to influence Éamon de Valera, the Irish Taoiseach, in 1943 during his filming of *Henry V* in neutral Eire, the presence of big cultural names in Yugoslavia helped influence Tito, the key decision-maker in Yugoslavia, through the medium of Shakespeare and the arts (Figure 15.2).[44].

Medicine was also a particularly strong area of collaboration for the British Council in Yugoslavia with plastic surgery being one such area of focus with the visits by Sir Harold Gillies and Rainsford Mowlem.[45] There was also a training scheme for

Figure 15.2 Sir Laurence Olivier and Vivien Leigh meeting Josip Broz Tito and Jovanka Broz after a performance of Shakespeare's *Titus Andronicus* at the National Theatre in Belgrade, June 1957. Courtesy Getty Images.

Yugoslav nurses operated by the Council which, by the end of 1957, had led to nearly one hundred nurses having spent a year in British hospitals.[46] It was reported that the British National Health Service and public health services were 'greatly admired' and 'definitely preferred as models for future development to those of Russia and other communist countries'.[47] The Council was also able to facilitate the sending of a large number of medical journals to Yugoslav medical practitioners – British doctors appeared only too glad to help their Yugoslav counterparts and 'increase British prestige', following an appeal in the *British Medical Journal*.[48] The medical exchange relationship in Yugoslavia appears to have been genuinely mutually worthwhile.

By contrast, the Council's position in Egypt was not in a good state in the early 1950s and, as a result of the Suez Crisis in November 1956, came to a complete halt. Donaldson claimed that when the Council restarted its activities in Egypt following the Suez Crisis 'an entirely fresh start had to be made', as the former British Institutes which had existed 'were regarded as sources of propaganda and anti-Government feeling'.[49] While this is true, and the new office in Cairo remained 'without even a brass plate with the words "British Council" on the door', it was actually the Egyptians that made it known that they would welcome assistance from the British Council.[50] The Council's report of 1961–2 suggests that the Egyptian government was worried by the indoctrination of students who had been sent to Eastern Europe, and needed a countermeasure – the services offered by the British Council were an ideal solution.[51] Slowly the Council re-established itself primarily through scientific and medical exchanges which, as in Yugoslavia, were seen as sufficiently non-political, followed by scholarships and English teaching.[52] Not long after the British Council re-established itself in Egypt after the Suez, the Old Vic also made a visit to Cairo.[53]

India also benefited from artistic visits by Britten and Pears, as part of their world tour after their visit to Yugoslavia, as well as Sargent and the actors Sir Lewis Casson and Dame Sybil Thorndike.[54] Just as Britten and Pears had met Tito, the pair also recorded their meeting with Nehru in a letter to Mary Potter in December 1955. They noted how relaxed Nehru appeared to be, but also how the Indian Prime Minister had clearly been courted by the Soviet leaders not long before their meeting (Figure 15.3).

However, India generally presented a different experience for the Council. As Byrne has noted, India was a test case for the role of the British Council in fostering cultural ties during the process of decolonization.[55] Nehru met with Sir Angus Gillan, Director of the Overseas Section of the British Council, in January 1947 where Nehru had 'indicated that he would welcome the early establishment in India of a British Council office under a representative of high academic standing'.[56] While there is no doubt that Nehru was genuine in his desire to see the Council established, his general policy of seeking to replace English with Hindi was seemingly at odds with the British Council's aim to promote and facilitate the teaching of English. India was also a challenge because of its sheer size: India's population in 1951 was 361 million – about twenty times larger than either Yugoslavia or Egypt.[57]

One particular method the Council deployed in India to promote the use and standard of the English language became known as the 'Madras Snowball'. The Snowball was designed to train 27,000 teachers to help them improve the quality of English among students with the idea of a multiplier effect – the Council would train

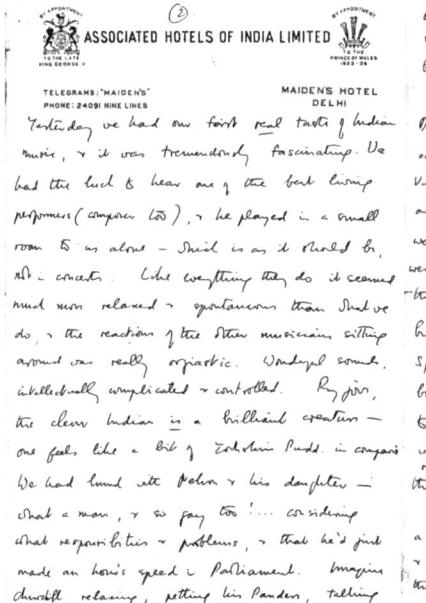

Figure 15.3 An extract from a letter from Benjamin Britten and Peter Pears to Mary Potter, recording their meeting with Nehru in December 1955, in the handwriting of Britten. © Britten-Pears Arts (brittenpearsarts.org), Ref: BBA_Potter_Mary. Reproduced with kind permission.

tutors, who would train other tutors, and then, in time, students.[58] The majority of the cost of the campaign was borne by the Madras Government – and that cost was considerable. The Council recognized the limits of such a campaign and that by the time the campaign filtered through to the classrooms the impact of their efforts would be diluted. However, it was pleased to report 'almost no public criticism. All visitors seem to have been impressed with the pace and efficiency' of the courses.[59] The Council was sure other states in India would adopt the same approach, although the fact that the Madras regional language was Tamil rather than Hindi played an important part.

Not everyone was impressed, however. Some have described the Snowball as a 'most notorious and utterly embarrassing episode in the annals of the British Council in India'.[60] A report commissioned by the Government of India, written by Professor Prabodh Bechardas Pandit at Delhi University, reportedly regarded 'the "Madras Snowball" disaster of having sought to advance a secret agenda of neo-colonial ramifications'.[61] The Council would, of course, deny that this was their aim – however, the effect of the Snowball was limited for other reasons. A more realistic criticism might be that despite the investment, the speed of roll-out meant there was not a depth to the campaign, and it failed to have a lasting impact.[62] One might reasonably argue that the Council had fallen into the very trap of indulging in a propaganda stunt that it had suggested the USIA was guilty of falling into – and it had backfired.

The Council also tried to play the Soviets at their own game in India. Having seen the heavily subsidized communist literature that was available across the country, the Chancellor of the Duchy of Lancaster, Dr Charles Hill, asked the Council to similarly subsidize British publications and expand its budget dramatically. While the Council successfully created twenty-five titles and sold them at speed, the Council was not able to do 'any serious planning' to carry out Hill's recommendations effectively.[63] By the time it was starting to make progress, the Council's budget was again cut, resulting in a frustratingly stop–start approach which threatened to undermine the Council's credibility.

Conclusion

The British Council's cultural propaganda work in the leading NAM countries was in many ways very similar to its work in other countries both neutral and aligned during this and other periods such as the Second World War. In substance its work was perhaps not particularly different to the work of the USIA or VOKS – and indeed there was sometimes a feeling among the Council's representatives that its effective work was being copied by others, and then applied *more* effectively with the help of larger budgets. In my previous analyses of the British Council, I developed a model of cultural propaganda to help frame how the Council operated and what was needed to deploy the propaganda effectively. In that model I outlined three pillars that I considered were necessary in order to make cultural propaganda successful. These pillars were *Perception* (i.e. the way in which cultural propaganda needs to be presented), *Substance* (i.e. the actual content of the cultural propaganda) and *Organization* (i.e. the need for a vehicle to encourage and direct propaganda). I argued that in Spain, Portugal, Turkey and Sweden during the Second World War, and in early Cold War Poland, elements of all of these three pillars existed all of the time, and therefore the Council was able to make headway.[64]

However, in the leading NAM countries, it is not possible to argue that all three pillars existed all of the time. There was clearly no fulfilment of the *Organization* pillar in Egypt following the Suez Crisis where the Council was thrown out of the country, and it had had a declining presence in any case. Even in India, where the Council was expanding, the Council's presence was small for the size of the country and it struggled to compete on the scale as the two superpowers. This affected the way in which the Council's work was perceived. Elements of the *Perception* pillar were fulfilled through the library work, personal contacts, demonstration of cultural intelligence in the science and the arts and through generally taking an incremental approach. However, the Madras Snowball and the general Partingtonesque nature of its operations meant either it was not particularly subtle in trying to make an impact (with its efforts backfiring) or its efforts were sometimes not perhaps even noticed. That is not to say there was no impact at all. The visits of Britten and Pears, Olivier and Leigh, Casson and Thorndike, among many others, were widely reported in the local press and radio, and often brought the work of the Council to a wider audience than could have achieved by solely focusing on the teaching of English or library work.

The Council was also more successful in relation to the *Substance* pillar. It was, as elsewhere, looking to make a genuine connection through the promotion of expertise (particularly in science and medicine), fulfilling the needs of the NAM countries, and generally maintaining a credibility which enabled the Council to punch well above its weight.

Ultimately the Council's activities were, however, not determined by the quality of its work and the effectiveness of its organization, important those though were. The Council's operations were more affected by the budget it received from the British government, which in turn was impacted by political circumstances. Its effectiveness was also heavily influenced by the new environment which the Council, and Britain generally, operated in after the Second World War. This was a world dominated by two superpowers, and which also increasingly wished to become independent from the old colonial ties which Britain and France represented. The fact that the British Council made any impact at all in the alternative battleground of the leading NAM countries is perhaps the most intriguing part of all.

Notes

1. Edward Corse, *A Battle for Neutral Europe: British Cultural Propaganda during the Second World War* (London: Bloomsbury, 2013), 5–7.
2. Frances Donaldson, *The British Council: The First Fifty Years* (London: Jonathan Cape, 1984), 131.
3. Ibid., 176.
4. Ibid., 124–39.
5. Douglas Coombs, *Spreading the Word: The Library Work of the British Council* (London: Mansell Publishing, 1988), 66; Donaldson, *The British Council*, 164, 183.
6. Dietmar Rothermund, 'The Era of Non-alignment', in *The Non-Aligned Movement and the Cold War: Delhi-Bandung-Belgrade*, ed. Nataša Mišković, Harald Fischer-Tiné and Nada Boškovska (London: Routledge, 2014), 22.
7. Nataša Mišković, 'Introduction', in *The Non-Aligned Movement*, ed. Nataša Mišković, Harald Fischer-Tiné and Nada Boškovska (London: Routledge, 2014), 1, 4–8.
8. Rothermund, 'The Era of Non-alignment', 21–2.
9. Ibid., 23. The issue of official languages in India remains to this day – see, for example, Hannah Ellis-Petersen, '"A threat to unity": Anger over Push to Make Hindi National Language of India', *The Guardian*, 25 December 2022. Available online: https://www.theguardian.com/world/2022/dec/25/threat-unity-anger-over-push-make-hindi-national-language-of-india (accessed 28 December 2022).
10. Anthony McDermott, *Egypt from Nasser to Mubarak: A Flawed Revolution* (Abingdon: Routledge, 2013), 15.
11. Nora Beloff, *Tito's Flawed Legacy: Yugoslavia and the West since 1939* (London: Routledge, 2019), 159.
12. Jovan Čavoški, 'Between Great Powers and Third World neutralists: Yugoslavia and the Belgrade Conference of the Non-Aligned Movement, 1961', in *The Non-Aligned Movement*, ed. Nataša Mišković, Harald Fischer-Tiné and Nada Boškovska (London: Routledge, 2014), 190.
13. Mišković, 'Introduction', 7.

14 Rothermund, 'The Era of Non-alignment', 27.
15 Nicholas J. Cull, *The Cold War and the United States Information Agency: American Propaganda and Public Diplomacy, 1945–1989* (Cambridge: Cambridge University Press, 2008), xiii.
16 Severyan Dyakonov, 'Soviet Cultural Diplomacy in India, 1955–1963', MA thesis (Concordia University, Montreal, Canada, 2015), 16–17.
17 'The Mandate', Fulbright Egypt website. Available online: https://fulbright-egypt.org/about-us (accessed 10 February 2022); 'US, India Celebrate 70 yrs of Fulbright Exchange Program', *The Asian Independent*, 3 February 2020. Available online: https://theasianindependent.co.uk/us-india-celebrate-70-yrs-of-fulbright-exchange-program (accessed 10 February 2022); 'Fulbright Student Exchange Pact Signed by U.S. and Yugoslavia', *New York Times*, 9 November 1964, 18.
18 Molly Bettie, 'The Scholar as Diplomat: The Fulbright Program and American's Cultural Engagement with the World', *Caliban*, December 2015, 54.
19 'History', website of The American University in Cairo. Available online: https://www.aucegypt.edu/about/history (accessed 10 February 2022); The UK National Archives (hereafter TNA), British Council files (hereafter BW) 29/46 'The British Council, Egypt: Representative's Report [hereafter 'BCRR, Egypt [or other country/city]'], 1950–51', 4.
20 TNA BW 38/18, BCRR, India, 1951–2, 6; TNA BW 38/18, BCRR, Bombay, 1953–4, 3.
21 See, for example, TNA BW 38/18, BCRR, Calcutta, 1952–3, 2 and TNA BW 38/18, BCRR, Bombay, 1954–5, 3.
22 See references to Bolshoi Ballet at TNA BW 66/13, BCRR, Yugoslavia, 1954–5, 2 and TNA BW 29/75, BCRR, United Arab Republic (hereafter UAR), 1960–1, 7; to David Oistrakh at TNA BW 66/20, BCRR, Yugoslavia, 1961–2, 4; to Soviet cultural delegations, see TNA BW 38/18, BCRR, Bombay, 1954–5, 3, TNA BW 38/18, BCRR, Madras, 1954–5, 3 and Dyakonov, 'Soviet Cultural Diplomacy', 28–30, 49–53.
23 TNA BW 38/18, BCRR, Bombay 1953–4, 3.
24 Frederick C. Barghoorn and Paul W. Friedrich, 'Cultural Relations and Soviet Foreign Policy', *World Politics* 8, no. 3 (1956): 334.
25 TNA BW 38/19, BCRR, Madras, 1958–9, 4–5; TNA BW 66/20, BCRR, Yugoslavia, 1961–2, 4.
26 See, for example, TNA BW 38/18, BCRR, India, 1951–2, 6; TNA BW 38/19, BCRR, India, 1957–8, 7; TNA BW 29/46, BCRR, Egypt, 1953–4, 2.
27 TNA BW 29/46, BCRR, Egypt, 1951–2, 3.
28 There are numerous examples of how the British Council Representatives viewed American efforts. The quotations come from TNA BW 38/18, BCRR, India, 1950–1, 3 and TNA BW 29/46, BCRR, Egypt, 1954–5, 5. See also Robert J. McMahon, 'Food as a Diplomatic Weapon: The India Wheat Loan of 1951', *Pacific Historical Review* 56, no. 3 (1987): 373, 377 for how American aid efforts were received in India.
29 See analysis of Soviet–Yugoslav cultural relations in TNA BW 66/13, BCRR, Yugoslavia 1955–6, 2, TNA BW 66/13, BCRR, Yugoslavia, 1956–7, 1 and TNA BW 66/20, BCRR, Yugoslavia, 1957–8, 1.
30 Barghoorn and Friedrich, 'Cultural Relations', 336, 338.
31 TNA BW 38/19, BCRR, India, 1957–8, 2.
32 There are multiple references to the Ford Foundation such as at TNA BW 38/19, BCRR, India, 1955–6, 3.
33 See reference to Rockefeller Grants in TNA BW 38/22, BCRR, Bombay, 1959–60, 7.

34 See reference to Yugoslav visitors to Britain sponsored by UNESCO at TNA BW 66/13, BCRR, Yugoslavia, 1951–2, 26; see also reference to Colombo Plan trainees in India at TNA BW 39/19, BCRR, Madras, 1956–7, 12.
35 TNA BW 38/19, BCRR, Delhi, 1956–7, 4.
36 TNA BW 38/19, BCRR, India, 1957–8, 2. See B. P. Shillaber, *Life and Savings of Mrs. Partington, and Others of the Family* (New York: J.C. Derby, 1854), vii–viii, with regard to the origins of the character.
37 Alice Byrne, 'The British Council in India, 1945–1955: Preserving "old relationships under new forms"', in *Fins d'empires / Ends of Empires*, ed. Laurent Dornel and Michael Parsons (Pau: Presses de l'Universite de Pau et des pays de l'Adour, 2016), 131.
38 In relation to Poland, see Edward Corse, 'The British Council behind the Iron Curtain: Cultural Propaganda in Early Cold War Poland', in *Propaganda and Conflict: War, Media and Shaping the Twentieth Century*, ed. Mark Connelly, Jo Fox, Stefan Goebel and Ulf Schmidt (London: Bloomsbury, 2019), 237.
39 James Lee Taylor, 'Shakespeare, Decolonisation, and the Cold War', Doctoral thesis (The Open University, 2018), 138.
40 TNA BW 66/13, BCRR, Yugoslavia, 1953–4, 1.
41 Ibid., 4; TNA BW 66/13, BCRR, Yugoslavia, 1955–6, 2; TNA BW 66/20, BCRR, Yugoslavia, 1957–8, 3; TNA BW 66/20, BCRR, Yugoslavia, 1958–9, 3.
42 Taylor, 'Shakespeare', 165.
43 Extracts taken from Philip Reed (ed.), *Peter Pears: Travel Diaries 1936–1978* (Woodbridge: The Boydell Press and The Britten-Pears Library, 1995), 22–4 and 24–31.
44 Edward Corse, '*Henry V* and the Battle of Powerscourt', in *Shakespeare at War: A Material History*, ed. Sonia Massai and Amy Lidster (Cambridge: Cambridge University Press, 2023), 172.
45 Rainsford Mowlem, 'Medicine in Yugoslavia', *British Medical Journal* 1(4661) (6 May 1950): 1072–3; TNA BW 66/13, BCRR, Yugoslavia, 1949–50, 2.
46 TNA BW 66/13, BCRR, Yugoslavia, 1956/57, 17.
47 Ibid., 9.
48 'Bring Out Your Old Journals', *British Medical Journal* 2(4742) (24 November 1951): 1291; D. J. Collihole, 'Journals for Yugoslavia', *British Medical Journal* 1(4766) (10 May 1952): 1030–1.
49 Donaldson, *The British Council*, 343.
50 TNA BW 29/75, BCRR, UAR, 1960–1, 3, 8.
51 TNA BW 29/75, BCRR, UAR, 1961–2, 1.
52 See Ibid., 3–4 and Donaldson, *The British Council*, 343.
53 TNA BW 29/75, BCRR, UAR, 1962–3, 1, 3.
54 TNA BW 38/18, TNA BW 38/19, BCRR, Delhi, 1955–6, 4; TNA BW 38/27, BCRR, India, 1961–2, 3 and BCRR, Delhi, 1954–5, 6.
55 Byrne, 'The British Council in India', 119.
56 National Archives of India, Ministry of Education files, NA F 92/2/47 A.C.B. Symon (Office of the High Commissioner for the UK in India) letter to Sir John Sargent (Secretary, Education Department, Government of India), 17 January 1947.
57 Office of the Registrar General & Census Commissioner, India, 'Variation in Population since 1901'. Data from 1951 Census. Available online: https://censusindia.gov.in/census_data_2001/india_at_glance/variation.aspx (accessed 10 February 2022).

58 D. A. Smith, 'The Madras "Snowball": An Attempt to Retrain 27,000 Teachers of English to Beginners', *ELT Journal* XVII, no. 1 (1962): 3.
59 Ibid., 8.
60 Kanavillil Rajagopalan, 'Down Memory Lane . . . as LAEL Celebrates Its Golden Jubilee', *DELTA* 36, no. 3 (2020): 10–11.
61 Ibid., 13.
62 Ibid., 12.
63 Coombs, *Spreading the Word*, 131.
64 Corse, *A Battle for Neutral Europe*, 183–94; Corse, 'The British Council behind the Iron Curtain', 246.

16

Neutrality and Maoist propaganda in 1960s Switzerland

Cyril Cordoba

On 17 January 1950, Switzerland became one of the first Western countries to recognize the People's Republic of China (PRC).[1] This decision, which was partly motivated by the defence of Swiss commercial interests in China,[2] was in line with Berne's foreign policy principles of neutrality, solidarity and universality. Severely criticized for its role in the Second World War, the Confederation was de facto aligned with the Western bloc during the Cold War and openly anti-communist,[3] but nevertheless wanted to improve its reputation as a neutral country on the international stage.[4] Capitalist and conservative Switzerland, which had just re-established relations with the USSR after almost thirty years, was perceived by Beijing as having no known colonial past or direct link with the imperialism of European powers.[5] Therefore, Switzerland became a central hub for the spread of Maoism, as anti-communist activists abundantly emphasized.[6]

The Chinese regime acquired a certain prestige because of the Korean War (1950–3), through its presence at the Geneva Conference on Indochina (1954) and through the non-aligned summit in Bandung (1955). As tensions with the USSR grew significantly during the 1950s, the PRC gradually attempted to assert itself as an alternative leader of the international communist movement. Then, Chinese propaganda not only inspired people in the West (as the numerous books devoted to European Maoist movements might lead one to believe),[7] but mainly met success in developing countries.[8] After suffering 'a century of humiliation' at the hands of the European powers, China claimed the position of 'natural ally' to colonized countries and positioned itself as an anti-imperialist spearhead.[9] Therefore, the divorce between the PRC and the USSR (known as the Sino-Soviet Split) in the early 1960s marked the blossoming of a global Maoist movement, when pro-Chinese dissidents broke away from communist parties to follow Beijing rather than Moscow.[10]

This chapter, based primarily on research in the Swiss Federal Archives as well as interviews with former Maoist activists, will analyse how Switzerland, a small neutral state at the crossroads of Europe, became a strategic hub for the PRC's propaganda. It will firstly examine the Confederation's reaction to the international diffusion of magazines such as *People's China*, *China Pictorials*, *China Reconstructs* and *Chinese*

Literature, as well as the newspaper *Peking Review* via leftist bookshops.[11] It will then dwell on the activities of the Chinese Embassy in Berne and the surveillance exerted on it by the Swiss Federal Police [Bundespolizei, BUPO].[12] Finally, it will present the role played by a young publisher from Lausanne, who edited and spread Maoist pamphlets in collaboration with the Chinese export service Guoji Shudian [translating as 'International Bookshop'], the organ responsible for the distribution of the regime's foreign language publications.

Political bookshops as intermediaries

In April 1960, as China accused the post-Stalinist USSR of having become revisionist and moving towards a return to capitalism, the publishing house Beijing Foreign Languages Press – a government agency that was the regime's main provider of printed propaganda material such as books, periodicals and pamphlets – circulated a famous column entitled *Long Live Leninism*. The dispute continued in 1963 with polemical articles in the *Renmin Ribao* ['People's Daily'] and *Hongqi* ['Red Flag'] which were later translated and published as pamphlets for foreign readers under the alternative title *Leninism and Modern Revisionism*. Moscow responded to these attacks with an *Open Letter from the Central Committee of the Communist Party of the Soviet Union* before Beijing definitively marked the rupture between the two communist powers in June 1963 with its famous 'Letter in 25 points' (or *Proposals concerning the general line of the international communist movement*) resulting in the Sino-Soviet Split.[13] All these polemical texts gave rise to fierce ideological battles throughout the world, for which some Swiss bookshops provided the weapons.

The first emblematic rallying point of pro-Chinese activists in Switzerland was the Pinkus Buchhandlung ['Pinkus bookstore'] in Zurich. Theo Pinkus (1909–1991), son of German Jewish emigrants, had become a bookseller in Berlin in the late 1920s before returning to his hometown. A known communist, he founded a publishing house and opened his own bookshop in Zurich.[14] In 1949, Theo and his wife Amalie were approached by Guoji Shudian to supply Beijing with foreign literature and to circumvent the US embargo on the PRC.[15] Pinkus also became one of the main distributors of Chinese propaganda in Switzerland (in the late 1960s, he supposedly sold sixty thousand copies of the *Quotations of Chairman Mao*, a compilation which was widely designated as the 'Little Red Book' because of its red vinyl cover).[16] Even though he was monitored by the Swiss intelligence services during his whole life (at the end of the Cold War, his surveillance file was 250 pages long), no legal action was ever taken against him for collaborating with Beijing. As the police explained in another case involving the distribution of Little Red Books: 'The propaganda material [was] not directed against Switzerland and therefore [did] not constitute a punishable offence. For this reason, it [was] not possible for the police to put an end to this activity.'[17] However, such was not the case for other booksellers, which were considered as endangering Swiss neutrality because of their role as intermediaries between China and developing countries.

In French-speaking Switzerland, two important leftist bookshops – the Librairie Nouvelle and the Librairie Rousseau – were situated in Geneva. Both were created in the 1950s and were close to the Swiss Party of Labour.[18] Placed under the surveillance of the BUPO for selling pro-Chinese propaganda material (coming from the PRC but also from ideologically close countries such as North Vietnam and Albania), they were partners of Guoji Shudian, or, as the Federal Police quoted it: 'someone named Gouzi Shudian in Beijing'.[19] The Librairie Rousseau was particularly active in this regard, since it was responsible for forwarding thousands of pamphlets, leaflets and magazines to Africa and Latin America that the Chinese 'International Bookshop' entrusted to it in order to circumvent the measures taken against Chinese propaganda in countries such as the former Belgian Congo, Ghana, Chile or Costa Rica. After discovering the nature of this bookshop's relationship with the PRC, the Swiss government immediately tried to limit its activities.

Political brochures and magazines in various languages such as *China*, *La Chine Populaire* ['People's China'], *Peking Review* and *China revista ilustrada* ['China Illustrated Magazine'] circulated around the globe as a result of being first sent to Switzerland. In order to prevent the country 'from becoming an international centre for receiving and forwarding extremist political propaganda material', the Federal Council confiscated the material sent by Guoji Shudian to the Librairie Rousseau.[20] Berne wanted to avoid offending states with which it had diplomatic relations, since the Chinese propaganda in question called for solidarity with national liberation movements that were hostile to them. As the following quote shows, it was, therefore, primarily the image of Swiss neutrality that motivated the decision of the government to seize the material:

> We have no legal or political obligation towards foreign countries to oppose such shipments. . . . There is nothing in the dispatch of this propaganda material that could lead us into an armed conflict. On the other hand, there is no doubt that Swiss interests are at stake in this case. The fact that Switzerland can serve as a kind of 'relay' for such propaganda is undoubtedly likely to give our country an unfavourable, even false, impression and thus damage its reputation. It may also damage our relations with certain foreign states.[21]

Noting the increasing number of Chinese magazines being sent to Switzerland in the midst of the Sino-Soviet Split, the Federal Council used, at the beginning of 1961, a decree of 29 December 1948 to justify its actions. According to this text, the state was able to take measures against material considered as 'propaganda likely to endanger the internal or external security of the Confederation, in particular its independence, neutrality, relations with foreign countries, political institutions, especially democratic institutions, or the interests of national defence, as well as anti-religious writings or objects'.[22] In his defence, the owner of the Librairie Rousseau – Roland Audéoud – pointed out that the publications of the Moral Rearmament,[23] an important anti-communist organization, were also distributed internationally from Switzerland, without the slightest protest from the Swiss authorities.[24] Despite this, all the packages addressed to foreign countries were seized, while the Chinese propaganda apparatus was

Table 16.1 Chinese Periodicals Seized by Swiss Customs (Number of Copies)

1954	1955	1956	1957	1958	1959	1960	1961	1962	1963
649	754	751	1,166	1,797	6,502	5,167	7,294	2,546	2,026

Source: SFA, E4320C#1994/78#711*: report by the Swiss customs direction, 6 February 1964.

growing in capacity year after year. The sending of Maoist publications to Switzerland did not stop, and in the 1960s, far from running out of steam, the phenomenon entered its most intense phase (Table 16.1).[25]

If leftist bookshops certainly played an important role in the dissemination of Maoist propaganda in the late 1950s and early 1960s, until the recognition of the PRC by several states in the early 1970s, the Chinese Embassy in Berne was the main channel for the funding and distribution of information, instructions and Chinese material in Western Europe.[26] That is why, as former Soviet diplomat Nicolas Polianski explained, Moscow was particularly keen to spy on 'Chinese activities in Switzerland [and primarily] those of the Chinese Embassy in Berne'.[27]

Berne: A Maoist headquarters under surveillance

The Chinese Embassy in Berne (and to a lesser degree the Chinese Consulate General in Geneva) developed a large spectrum of activities – including film screenings – to appeal not only to political sympathizers, but to the wider population. Chinese diplomats regularly imported feature films in Switzerland, even if some of them were banned because they promoted anti-imperialist (i.e. anti-American) movements in Asia and Latin America and were considered as propaganda threatening Switzerland's independence and neutrality. Nevertheless, these reels could be legally shown inside the embassy or consulate, where many spectators were regularly invited to attend screenings of films such as *Chairman Mao Is the Red Sun in Our Hearts*.[28] Most of the time, local cinemas in Geneva or Berne were used by Chinese diplomats to promote their regime on the big screen. In 1969, a production of pure Maoist propaganda even reached an unexpected audience because of the lack of precaution by Swiss public television. Entitled *The Anti-Chinese Atrocities of the New Tsars*, this documentary about the Sino-Soviet border conflict (on the Ussuri River) attacking the USSR was renamed *The Truth about the Border Incidents of the Ussuri* when it was exported to Switzerland.[29] The broadcasting of the film, which presented Sino-Soviet military confrontations from Beijing's point of view, was a victory for the PRC, which triumphantly announced: 'After seeing the film, the Swiss friends were highly indignant at Soviet revisionism's anti-China atrocities and denounced the acts of aggression by Soviet revisionist social-imperialism.'[30] Concerned about potential Soviet protests, the government reprimanded the director of Swiss television Edouard Haas, explaining that his negligence had caused him to commit an infraction against the country's neutrality.[31]

More generally, the activities of the Chinese Embassy in Berne were well known to the Swiss intelligence services, which monitored all comings and goings of Chinese diplomats, as well as those of all their guests. In addition to Maoist activists from Africa and Latin America, nationals from countries bordering Switzerland were the most frequent visitors. In order to identify them, the BUPO kept a close eye on the building. For example, all the registration numbers of vehicles that stopped in front of it were noted. As a result, many guests preferred to go there on foot or by taxi to escape the surveillance of the agents hidden in the vicinity, whose presence was an open secret. As one former Maoist remembered: 'We saw them when we entered the Embassy. We waved at them.'[32] Some activists ironically explain today: 'It was so stupid, so absurd, that it was laughable.... As if we were going to go in ... and come out with a bazooka under our arm.'[33] On the phone, the pro-Chinese activists gave false names and false appointment times to escape the surveillance of the Federal Police, which they knew to be omnipresent. Moreover, all calls to and from the embassy were tapped, recorded and transcribed by a police officer. An interpreter was even hired by the BUPO to translate the conversations of Chinese diplomats, who began recruiting young teachers to work in the PRC to improve the quality of its foreign language propaganda in the early 1960s.

Invited at the Chinese government's expense via the embassy in Berne to work in China for a couple of years, these 'foreign experts' (called wàiguó zhuānjiā) taught French, German or English at university and corrected texts in periodicals such as *Chinese Literature* or *Peking Review* for the Foreign Languages Press,[34] since, following the Sino-Soviet Split, Beijing hired many Westerners to improve the quality of its international propaganda.[35] The Confederation, being very worried about seeing its citizens working for a communist country, quickly tried to prevent the hiring, but without finding a legal basis to act.[36] China's recruitment of foreign experts was a source of deep concern for the Swiss authorities, especially when they noticed that the travellers returned enchanted by their experience. Seduced by their experience within the socialist system, many of these experts sought to praise the PRC by giving lectures, granting interviews to the press or organizing exhibitions on their return. Those most convinced founded or joined friendship associations with China or even Maoist parties and were put under surveillance for decades.[37] However, what bothered Swiss authorities the most was the role of the Chinese Embassy in Berne as a hub for global Maoism.

Even after the recognition of the PRC by several Western European countries, the building continued to represent an important meeting point for Marxist–Leninists throughout the world.[38] Most notably, in June 1965, six French Maoists were arrested on their way out of the embassy with just over $2,000 in their pockets. In addition to providing them with money and materials, Chinese diplomats also gave them guidelines on how to organize their movement. After being questioned at length, these activists were banned from entering Swiss territory 'as representatives of a foreign anti-democratic party [carrying out] illegal political activity'.[39] The Confederation, which was unwilling to damage its diplomatic relations with Beijing that were already weakened by a dispute over the presence of Tibetan refugees in Switzerland, only timidly protested to the Chinese Embassy.[40] However, the Swiss press, largely anti-communist, was very vocal.

Beyond this highly publicized episode, the methods used by China to support its followers were much more discreet.[41] For example, Guoji Shudian sent large quantities of books, pamphlets and magazines to pro-Chinese groups, either with a discount of at least 50 per cent or for free. The activists then sold this material at a price they set freely to fill their coffers, while participating in the regime's propaganda. Maoist groups were also supported by the international bookstore Waiwen Shudian [Foreign Language Bookshop - the service that imported publications from abroad into China], which subscribed to their political newspapers. Beijing's funding of the Maoist groups thus went through the 'back door' and not, as the Swiss intelligence services might have believed, through briefcases full of money, which made it more difficult for the authorities to prevent.[42] However, knowing that their relations with the PRC via Switzerland were under close scrutiny, Maoists used multiple intermediaries in various locations to obtain financial support, such as Albania,[43] where a solidarity fund had been specially created to help the development of Marxist–Leninist groups around the world.[44] Despite these precautions, one key partner of Guoji Shudian in Switzerland (Nils Andersson) became, as the next section outlines, a victim of Berne's intransigence towards Maoism.

Swiss transnational networks

Born on 14 February 1933 in Lausanne, Andersson, a young intellectual who had made a name for himself in the literary circles of French-speaking Switzerland in the 1950s, was labelled 'the champion of Chinese communism' by the Federal Police in the early 1960s.[45] Initially a sympathizer of the Party of Labour, he quickly followed a more anti-colonial path, supporting the cause of the so-called Third World.[46] The publishing house La Cité, which he founded in 1958, became a vast network of support for the Algerian National Liberation Front (FLN), especially after publishing two books about the use of torture in Algeria that were banned in France.[47] In these anti-colonialist circles, Andersson met the lawyer Jacques Vergès (1925–2013), future husband of Djamila Bouhired (an FLN activist who had been sentenced to death for terrorism). In February 1963, Vergès took over the directorship of the Algerian newspaper *Révolution africaine*, just before being received by Mao Zedong and moving closer to the Chinese side of the Sino-Soviet Split. In disagreement with President Ahmed Ben Bella, Vergès left the FLN newspaper in May 1963 and funded his own periodical, now openly pro-Chinese, *Revolution Africa, Latin America, Asia* (or simply *Revolution AAA*), described by the Swiss Federal Police as 'one of the most ambitious adventures of Chinese communist propaganda abroad'.[48]

With only nine issues in English (from May 1963 to February 1964) and then thirteen issues in French (until December 1964), *Revolution AAA* was, nevertheless, short-lived. First printed in Lausanne, it was translated and formatted in the offices of La Cité. With texts by Ernesto 'Che' Guevara, the Argentine Marxist revolutionary, and Nelson Mandela, the South African anti-Apartheid activist, this publication stood out in Marxist–Leninist circles for its accessible language and its quality illustrations. The newspaper, nicknamed the 'Paris Match of revolutionaries', owed its premium style to Chinese support.[49] Ten thousand copies of every issue were purchased by Guoji Shudian;[50] five thousand were sent to London and New York, three thousand to Beijing, another one thousand to Dar es Salaam in Tanzania, five hundred to Lagos in Nigeria, while five hundred remained in Lausanne. As they did with the Librairie Rousseau, the authorities considered it unacceptable for neutral Switzerland to serve as a shipping centre for revolutionary material. Very quickly, the government therefore took measures against this publication, which called for revolution in countries with which Berne had diplomatic relations. Vergès was expelled from Swiss territory on 3 October 1963, and the newspaper was banned a few months later – although *Revolution AAA* had actually already ceased to be published.[51] Yet this unprecedented editorial experience was not the only pro-Chinese activity by La Cité, which also participated in the dissemination of other Chinese propaganda in the midst of the Sino-Soviet Split.

In the early 1960s, when the Swiss Party of Labour (which remained loyal to Moscow rather than Beijing) asked the Librairie Rousseau to get rid of the polemical texts published by Beijing, Andersson approached the Chinese Embassy in Berne to take over their distribution. This was agreed and took place until 1964. In addition, Andersson put Guoji Shudian in touch with Parisian bookshops such as La Joie de Lire ['The Joy of Reading'], which became the first to sell these documents in France.[52] In this way, he established himself as a privileged interlocutor of Guoji Shudian, until China developed a more efficient distribution network worldwide. Under surveillance by the Federal Police since 1953, Andersson was first warned that his political activities were problematic in 1961. Although he had lived in Switzerland his entire life, his Swedish nationality allowed the Federal Department of Justice and Police to order his deportation from Switzerland on 25 October 1966:

> Too deeply involved politically because of his past activities, surrounded exclusively by extremist elements, maintaining numerous relations with European, African and Latin American revolutionary and nationalist circles, linked commercially with foreign publishing companies that cannot publish anything other than literature hostile to Western governments and regimes. . . . His presence in Switzerland is likely to endanger the internal and especially external security of the Confederation.[53]

Under Articles 265 and 266 of the Swiss Penal Code, Andersson was charged with high treason and undermining the independence of the state. He was, consequently, expelled from the country in 1967, despite a major campaign of support from intellectual and activist circles in Switzerland and France. Andersson, who was 'neither a formidable Swiss-Swedish Carlos [the nickname given to the Venezuelan terrorist Ilich Ramírez Sánchez] nor a harmless, naive idealist',[54] moved to Albania for five years, where he worked at the Naim Frashëri publishing house and Radio Tirana to continue supporting the diffusion of pro-Chinese and pro-Albanian propaganda.

Meanwhile, another character, with a much shadier profile, did not arouse the same concerns within the Swiss intelligence services, which were more scrupulous in their investigation about left-wing activism than they were about right-wing extremism. Gérard Bulliard (1926–2009) was one of the first to enjoy the trust of Chinese diplomats in Switzerland. This former boxer, who sought above all to obtain money and power by riding the wave of nascent Maoism,[55] returned from a trip to Tirana and created the 'Communist Party of Switzerland' in September 1963. Although he never attracted more than a dozen sympathizers, his international connections enabled Bulliard to receive, through the Chinese Embassy in Berne and the Albanian Embassy in Paris, tens of thousands of Swiss francs to launch his political formation.[56] However, his unstable personality quickly led the diplomats to break off all contact with him. Riddled with debts, he tried to extort several thousand francs from the Chinese Embassy and from communist activists by threatening to denounce them to the Federal Police. Cast adrift on all sides, Bulliard finally offered his services to anti-communist organizations as an informant.[57]

The Swiss authorities, neglecting Bulliard's increasingly suspicious activities – his newspaper was particularly virulent against Israel and the Jewish community more generally – did not pay him particular attention. Nevertheless, by ignoring his case, the intelligence services completely overlooked his relations with Aginter Press – also known under the name 'Central Order and Tradition' – an international anti-communist organization under the cover of being a press agency established in Lisbon in 1966. Linked to Polícia Internacional e de Defesa do Estado [the International and State Defence Police], the security agency of the Portuguese dictator António Salazar entered the ranks of Bulliard's party (then renamed People's Party of Switzerland, PPS) in the late 1960s.[58] Between June 1968 and October 1969, these extremist activists were able to travel to Mozambique with PPS press cards and spread false information to create rivalries within the FRELIMO (Liberation Front of Mozambique),[59] and carried out operations that may have led to the death of politician, and President of FRELIMO, Eduardo Mondlane.[60] Although Bulliard denied any involvement in this movement, numerous documents have since proven that he played an active, rather than passive, role in these fascist movements.[61]

Conclusion

In the 1960s, and most particularly in the midst of the Sino-Soviet Split, Switzerland functioned as a strategic hub for the diffusion and distribution of Maoist propaganda throughout the world.[62] This situation was a result of the early recognition of the PRC by the Confederation, which tried to restore and preserve its reputation as a neutral country on the international stage. Swiss intelligence services, which closely monitored Chinese and pro-Chinese activities on its territory, regularly alerted the authorities that Maoist actions endangered Switzerland's neutrality. However, Berne's reaction proved largely ineffective against Beijing's transnational networks. No legal basis was found to be able to act against the distribution of Chinese printed material inside the country or against the recruitment of young intellectuals by the PRC's propaganda apparatus. Measures against the newspaper *Revolution AAA* were taken too late, restrictions against the Chinese Embassy's role as an international meeting point were bypassed or even ridiculed by activists and many decisions – such as listing the recipients of Maoist magazines – achieved disappointing results.[63] Until the 1970s, reports about Chinese propaganda in Switzerland multiplied in the domestic and the foreign press, with a growing number of articles mocking the authorities and the BUPO's inaction and lack of responsiveness. That is why, as the American anti-communist columnist Victor Riesel wrote, Swiss counter-intelligence earned the unenviable reputation of being 'as full of holes as its cheese'.[64]

Notes

1. Great Britain, Norway, Denmark, Finland and Sweden recognized China earlier. Other European countries followed years later, such as France (1964), Italy (1970), Austria and Belgium (1971) and West Germany (1972).
2. Michele Coduri, *La Suisse face à la Chine: une continuité impossible? 1946–1955* (Louvain-la-Neuve: Bruylant-Academia, 2004), 202–48; Daniel Trachsler, *Bundesrat Max Petitpierre: Schweizerische Aussenpolitik im Kalten Krieg 1945–1961* (Zürich: NZZ Libro, 2011).
3. Michel Caillat et al. (eds), *Histoire(s) de l'anticommunisme en Suisse* (Zürich: Chronos, 2009); Luc van Dongen et al. (eds), *Transnational Anti-communism and the Cold War: Agents, Activities, and Networks* (Basingstoke: Palgrave Macmillan, 2014); Hadrien Buclin, 'Swiss Intellectuals and the Cold War. Anti-Communist Policies in a Neutral Country', *Journal of Cold War Studies* 19, no. 4 (2017): 137–67.
4. Andreas Wenger and Christian Nuenlist, 'A "Special Case" between Independence and Interdependence: Cold War Studies and Cold War Politics in Post-Cold War Switzerland', *Cold War History* 8, no. 2 (2008): 213–40; Antoine Fleury, 'De la neutralité "fictive" à la politique de neutralité comme atout dans la conduite de la politique étrangère', *Politorbis, Revue de politique étrangère* 1, no. 44 (2008): 5–12; Sandra Bott, Janick Marina Schaufelbuehl and Sacha Zala, 'Die internationale Schweiz in der Zeit des Kalten Krieges', *Itinera* 30 (2011), full volume; Sandra Bott et al., 'Suisse et Guerre froide dans le tiers-monde', *Relations internationals* 3, no. 163 (2015), full volume; Sandra Bott, Jussi M. Hanhimaki, Janick Schaufelbuehl and Marco Wyss (eds), *Neutrality and Neutralism in the Global Cold War: Between or Within the Blocs?* (London: Routledge, 2016); Thomas Fischer and Daniel Möckli, 'The Limits of Compensation: Swiss Neutrality Policy in the Cold War', *Journal of Cold War Studies* 18, no. 4 (2016): 12–35.
5. On this topic, see Patricia Purtschert and Harald Fischer-Tiné (eds), *Colonial Switzerland: Rethinking Colonialism from the Margins* (Basingstoke: Palgrave Macmillan, 2015); Béatrice Veyrassat, *Histoire de la Suisse et des Suisses dans la marche du monde: (XVIIe siècle – Première Guerre mondiale): espaces, circulations, échanges* (Neuchâtel: Alphil, 2018); Sandro Cattacin and Marisa Fois (eds), *Les Colonialismes suisses. Entretiens/Études (Vol. I/II), Sociograph* 49/50 (Genève: Département de sociologie, 2020).
6. Suzanne Labin, *Reconnaissance Chine communiste, ambassades pour subversions* (Paris: Ligue de la liberté, 1964); Friedrich-Wilhelm Schlomann and Paulette Friedlingstein, *Die Maoisten. Pekings Filialen in Westeuropa* (Frankfurt am Main, Societäts-Verlag, 1970).
7. Henning Böke, *Maoismus: China und die Linke – Bilanz und Perspektive* (Stuttgart: Schmetterling, 2007); Sebastian Gehrig, Barbara Mittler and Felix Wemheuer (eds), *Kulturrevolution als Vorbild? Maoismen im deutschsprachigen Raum* (Frankfurt am Main and Bern: Peter Lang, 2008); Richard Wolin, *The Wind from the East: French Intellectuals, the Cultural Revolution, and the Legacy of the 1960s* (Princeton:

Princeton University Press, 2010); Tom Buchanan, *East Wind China and the British Left, 1925–1976* (Oxford: Oxford University Press, 2012); Aaron J. Leonard and Conor A. Gallagher, *Heavy Radicals: The FBI's Secret War on America's Maoists: The Revolutionary Union/Revolutionary Communist Party 1968–1980* (Winchester and Washington DC: Zero Books, 2014); Chi Miao et al. (eds), *La Révolution culturelle en Chine et en France* (Paris: Riveneuve, 2017).

8 Matthew D. Rothwell, *Transpacific Revolutionaries: The Chinese Revolution in Latin America* (New York: Routledge, 2013); Matthew Galway, 'Boundless Revolution: Global Maoism and Communist Movements in Southeast Asia, 1949–1979' (PhD diss., University of British Columbia, 2017).

9 However, Beijing's suppression of the 1959 Tibetan uprising and the Sino-Indian war of 1962 particularly tarnished China's anti-imperialist image. In addition, several pro-PRC groups suffered severe debacles in 1965 in areas such as Indonesia, Algeria and Kashmir. Jeremy Friedman, *Shadow Cold War: The Sino-Soviet Competition for the Third World* (Chapel Hill: University of North Carolina Press, 2015).

10 Julia Lovell, *Maoism. A Global History* (London: The Bodley Head, 2019).

11 Mareike Svea Ohlberg, 'Creating a Favorable International Public Opinion Environment: External Propaganda (Duiwai Xunachuan) as a Global Concept with Chinese Characteristics' (Doctoral thesis, Heidelberg University, 2013).

12 During the Cold War, the BUPO (created in 1935) accumulated an enormous database on anyone who dared to question the country's political and economic order: about 900,000 people were kept on file. Hans-Ulrich Jost et al., *Cent ans de police politique en Suisse: (1889–1989)* (Lausanne: AEHMO, En Bas, 1992).

13 Li Danhui and Xia Yafeng, *Mao and the Sino-Soviet Split, 1959–1973: A New History* (Lanham: Lexington Books, 2018).

14 Elmar Altvater et al. (eds), *Erinnern und Ermutigen: Hommage für Theo Pinkus, 1909–1991* (Zürich: Rotpunktverlag, 1992).

15 This collaboration continued until the mid-1960s. Archives of the Zurich Central Library: Pinkus Family archives (Ar. 07,36): Amalie Pinkus to *Guoji Shudian*, 17 July 1985.

16 Rudolf M. Lüscher et al. (eds), *Amalie und Theo Pinkus-De Sassi: Leben im Widerspruch* (Zürich: Limmat Verlag, 1987).

17 Swiss Federal Archives (SFA), E4320C#1994/78#745*: report by the Berne city police, 5 September 1967.

18 The Communist Party of Switzerland, founded in 1921, was banned in 1940. It was replaced by the Swiss Party of Labour in 1944.

19 SFA, E4320B#1981/141#271*: memo from the BUPO, 29 March 1955.

20 SFA, E4320C#1995/392#146*: Federal Department of Justice and Police (FDJP) press release, 20 January 1961.

21 SFA, E4320C#1994/78#711*: Federal Political Department (FPD) to the Attorney General, 21 November 1960. All translations from German and French are from the author.

22 SFA, E4320C#1994/78#711*: decision from the FDJP, 18 January 1961.

23 In its early days, this American political and spiritual organization based in the canton of Vaud had fought against fascism and Nazism. It later became more clearly anti-communist. Cyril Michaud, 'For God's sake, wake up! Le Réarmement moral sur le sol helvétique (1932–69). Une internationale des croyants face au spectre communiste. Organisation, réseaux et militance' (PhD diss., University of Lausanne, 2021).

24　SFA, E4320C#1994/78#711*: Audéoud to the Attorney General, 19 May 1961.
25　Cagdas Ungor, 'Reaching the Distant Comrade: Chinese Communist Propaganda Abroad (1949–1976)' (PhD diss., State University of New York, 2009).
26　Chinese diplomatic representations in Copenhagen, Stockholm and The Hague, and later in Paris and Rome, were also strategic locations for Beijing. They have become increasingly important as the global reach of Chinese propaganda grew.
27　Nicolas Polianski, *M.I.D: douze ans dans les services diplomatiques du Kremlin* (Paris: Pierre Belfond, 1984), 141.
28　Most of the documentaries and newsreels broadcast illustrated, for example, the national day celebrations or those of May Day in Tiananmen Square. They usually attracted between two hundred and three hundred people to local cinemas, while the audience was usually limited to about one hundred people when the screenings took place inside the embassy.
29　SFA, E4320C#1994/78#748*: memo from BUPO, 24 September 1969.
30　SFA, E4320C#1994/78#748*: *Xinhua* dispatch, 15 September 1969.
31　SFA, E4320C#1994/78#748*: FPD to Edouard Haas, 25 September 1969.
32　Interview with Vincent Errard, 9 February 2016.
33　Interview with Lucien Favre, 13 January 2016.
34　The foreign experts were not hired for their knowledge of Chinese, and only corrected proofs that had been previously translated into their own language, in order to make them grammatically acceptable.
35　Recruitment of Italian speakers only started in 1965 and German speakers in the early 1970s. Subsequently, the Bureau of Foreign Experts increased its working languages (including Polish, Bulgarian, Farsi, Turkish and Greek). The few hundred foreign experts working in the PRC in the mid-1960s were housed in the Friendship Hotel, where they lived in a state of 'privileged segregation', providing free transportation and various services specially reserved for them. On the preferential treatment of foreigners (*yōudài*), see Beverley Hooper, *Foreigners under Mao: Western Lives in China, 1949–1976* (Hong Kong: Hong Kong University Press, 2016).
36　SFA, E2001E#1978/84#2341*: FPD to the Swiss Embassy in China, 16 June 1965.
37　According to Georg Kreis (presumed) pro-Chinese activists accounted for just over 4 per cent of the "extremists" surveilled by the BUPO during the Cold War. Georg Kreis (ed.), *La protection politique de l'État en Suisse: l'évolution de 1935 à 1990* (Bern and Stuttgart: Paul Haupt, 1993), 75.
38　SFA, E4320C#1994/78#765*: report from BUPO, 22 June 1972.
39　SFA, E4320C#1994/76#253*: FDJP to Georges Frêche, 17 May 1966.
40　After the 1959 repression of a Tibetan uprising, Bern agreed to welcome one thousand refugees in 1963, a decision which damaged the Sino-Swiss relations in the following years. Ariane Knüsel, '"Armé de la pensée de Mao Tsé-toung, on peut résoudre tous les problèmes": l'influence de la Révolution culturelle sur les relations entre la Suisse et la République populaire de Chine', *Relations internationales* 3, no. 163 (2015): 29–46.
41　Cyril Cordoba, 'Les maoïstes suisses et 'l'or de Pékin' au cœur de la Guerre froide', *Monde(s)* 19 (2021): 241–55.
42　For example, BUPO believed that the PRC was distributing $1,500 each month to friendship associations and to the Swiss Maoist Party. SFA, E4005#1995/305#607*: memo from the BUPO, 30 July 1975.

43 Albania was a bridgehead for the PRC in Europe between the Sino-Soviet Split of the early 1960s and the Sino-Albanian break of 1977.
44 Ylber Marku, 'Sino-Albanian Relations during the Cold War, 1949–1978: An Albanian Perspective' (Doctoral thesis, Lingnan University of Hong Kong, 2017).
45 SFA, E4320C#1994/78#747*: report by the BUPO, March 1964.
46 Nils Andersson, *Mémoire éclatée: de la décolonisation au déclin de l'Occident* (Lausanne: En Bas, 2016), 299.
47 Damien Carron, 'De La Question au Manuel du militant algérien: Nils Andersson, La Cité: Editeur et la guerre d'indépendance algérienne', in *Livre et militantisme: La Cité Editeur, 1958–1967*, ed. François Vallotton (Lausanne: En Bas, 2007), 29–67.
48 SFA, E4320C#1994/78#709*: report by the BUPO, 16 August 1965.
49 Pierre Jeanneret, 'Les engagements politiques des années 60 et l'expulsion de Nils Andersson', in *Livre et militantisme*, ed. Francois Vallotton et al. (Lausanne: D'en bas Editions), 121.
50 SFA, E4320C#1994/76#252*: hearing of Vergès by the BUPO, 17 January 1964.
51 SFA, E4320C#1994/78#709*: report by the BUPO, 16 August 1965.
52 In order to avoid the seizure of packages from Beijing by French customs, the shipment often passed through Lausanne. See Nils Andersson's personal archives: *La Cité* to *Guoji Shudian*, 19 March 1963.
53 Andersson, *Mémoire éclatée*, 299.
54 Pierre Jeanneret, *Popistes: histoire du Parti ouvrier et populaire vaudois, 1943–2001* (Lausanne: En Bas, 2002), 147.
55 SFA, E4320C#1995/392#60*: report by the BUPO, 20 March 1964.
56 SFA, E4320C#1995/392#60*: memo from the BUPO, 28 February 1964.
57 Luc van Dongen, '"De toute façon la gauche était contrôlée": agents provocateurs, infiltrations et subversion de droite à l'intérieur des mouvements sociaux', in *Mourir en manifestant: répressions en démocratie: le 9 novembre 1932 en perspective*, ed. Charles Heimberg, Stéphanie Prezioso and Marianne Enckell (Lausanne: AEHMO En Bas, 2008), 159–83.
58 Frédéric Laurent, *L'Orchestre noir* (Paris: Stock, 1978), 117.
59 José Manuel Duarte de Jesus, *A guerra secreta de Salazar em África: Aginter Press: uma rede internacional de contra-subversão e espionagem sediada em Lisboa* (Alfragide: Publicações Dom Quixote, 2012), 111.
60 George Roberts, 'The Assassination of Eduardo Mondlane: FRELIMO, Tanzania and the Politics of Exil in Dar es Salaam', *Cold War History* 17, no. 1 (2017): 8.
61 Jeffrey McKenzie Bale, 'The "Black" Terrorist International: Neo-Fascist Paramilitary Networks and the "Strategy of Tension" in Italy, 1968–1974' (Doctoral thesis, University of California in Berkeley, 1994), 230.
62 Ariane Knüsel, *China's European Headquarters. Switzerland and China during the Cold War* (Cambridge: Cambridge University Press, 2022).
63 Considering that enterprises and cultural institutions received such printed material, the intelligence services concluded: 'Most of the people on this list are known by their educational or professional activities [so] the mere fact of receiving the newsletter in question does not allow any conclusion to be drawn.' See SFA, E4320C#1994/78#747*: Neuchâtel cantonal police to the BUPO, 22 January 1964.
64 Victor Riesel, 'Chinese Communists Direct Long Distance Revolutions Out of Advance Mass Base in Switzerland', *Los Angeles Times*, 17 August 1964.

17

Diverging ideas in a tragic effort for the neutrality of Laos

P. Mike Rattanasengchanh

When Laos achieved independence from France in 1954, it sought neutrality as protection amid the Cold War, but divergent ideas propagated about it complicated this process, as did superpowers and regional actors who saw the country as a battleground for hearts and minds. Even more difficult were the competing factions in Laos: communist Pathet Lao (PL)/Neo Lao Hak Xat (NLHX), neutralists and the rightists. Lao cadres, under the influence of the Viet Minh, began operating in Laos in the 1930s, establishing bases in 1953. The neutrality movement grew when Laos gained independence from France, with Prince Souvanna Phouma being one of the biggest proponents. Right-wingers were primarily anti-communist but lacked unity, fracturing first between rival families and later among older and younger military and civilian groups. Previous studies have focused on the instability created by these factions, overlooking the differing definitions of neutrality and ways to achieve it proposed to the international community and Lao people by Souvanna and separately by Bong Souvannavong and his National Union Party (NUP).

Through international and countrywide tours, speeches and mass media, Souvanna and Bong propagated their own versions of neutralism. Souvanna saw neutrality as including all political parties in a coalition government, even the communist NLHX, who he argued were not real communists. Bong, by contrast, promoted neutralism based on a Buddhist-type governance and anti-communism.[1] The different viewpoints on neutralism disseminated by Souvanna and Bong show that the disputes inside the country went beyond the rightist and leftist disagreements: there were more significant difficulties in defining what neutrality was specifically in the Lao context. Souvanna wanted friendly relations with both communist and pro-Western groups, while Bong sought to be free from foreign and right- and left-wing entanglements by following Buddhist teachings of the middle way, avoiding extremes – which he considered true Lao doctrine.

With multiple competing forces in the country, it is no wonder that neutrality and peace were difficult to achieve. This chapter examines the years between 1958 and 1960 and how neutralists Souvanna and Bong, through public events and mass media, tried to convince the superpowers and the Lao people why Laos should remain neutral in the Cold War. This period saw a significant chance of achieving peace in and neutrality for Laos, more than other times.[2] The year 1958 marked one of several major attempts at creating a neutral coalition government, which was ultimately thwarted by Lao rightists supported by the United States. From there to the end of 1960, Souvanna and Bong went on the public relations offensive pleading their cases and often propagandizing opposing ideas. By the early spring of 1961, the superpowers saw the expedience of neutrality and the creation of a fragile coalition government, culminating with the 1962 Geneva Agreement declaring Laos neutral.[3] Unfortunately, the arrangement did not last long as Laos plummeted into civil war when all sides ignored the tenets, ending in 1975 with the triumph of the communist PL takeover.

Much of the scholarship on modern Lao history, specifically on the late 1950s and early 1960s, is written from the American perspective and utilizes US government documents. Works by Seth Jacobs, William J. Rust and Arthur J. Dommen chronicle US foreign relations in Laos, generally arguing that Washington's meddling was a major cause of instability.[4] A few scholars, like Ryan Wolfson-Ford and Sophie Sidwell, have studied these years with Lao sources. Scholars have yet to look at the competing views on neutrality, so there is no previous comparative study of the two leading neutralists. This chapter examines the Lao perspective of neutralism from 1958 to 1960 using Lao-based sources like the *Lao Ruam Samphan* (*LRS*) [translating as 'National Union'] and French *Lao Presse* ['Lao News'] newspapers and radio communiqués. Through an analysis of essays, public speeches and news articles, this chapter considers how Souvanna and Bong articulated their ideas through the use of language, culture and religion.

First, however, it is important to note the background of the key players. Son of a prince, Souvanna was born in 1901. He received his education in France and became a major figure in Lao politics after the Second World War. Souvanna was well known among elites and respected as a capable statesman. He was willing to compromise to build a coalition government with all sides, even the communist PL/NLHX. Rust stated that some saw Souvanna as weak but in reality, he stood his ground against the Americans and later the communists.[5] Born in 1906, Bong was not of royal lineage but came from a loyalist family. After receiving his education in Hanoi, Bong served the Royal Lao Government (RLG) in several capacities, notably as Governor of Luang Prabang province and as a Lao Assembly member. In 1946, he helped form the NUP, the first Lao political party.[6] Wolfson-Ford argued that they were anti-communists but perplexingly, both Souvanna and Bong called themselves neutralists, even though they differed on its definition.[7] This chapter does not seek to settle this debate, yet looking at their diverging views on neutralism demonstrates the complexity of Laos' involvement in a rapidly developing Cold War.

Additionally, an explanation of Southeast Asian viewpoints on political power and propaganda, or the projection of power, sheds further light on the period. Local traditions like Buddhism and ideas on political authority and language played a key role in politics. Scholarship on public diplomacy/propaganda overwhelmingly examines Western institutions; non-Western societies, however, had alternate forms of propagating ideas and thoughts on power. Clifford Geertz has examined the *negara*, or theatre state, based in Bali, where rulers attained power because of fate – that is, the gods/spirits approved –

and legitimized through elaborate processions and ceremonies.[8] Similarly as Souvanna was a member of the royal family, Lao saw kings as having connections with the supernatural, his authority was derived from his perceived fate – that he was just meant to rule. Bong, though not royalty, was also in a position of power as a politician. Lao viewed political leaders similarly, they received their offices because of good karma. Public events were opportunities for the audience to engage with politicians and reinforce their perceived legitimacy. In their speeches and print communications, Souvanna and Bong weaved foreign ideas like democracy or communism with Lao culture and Buddhist doctrine. Bong published his teachings in a book titled *Latthi Lao phua sang santhiphap* [Lao Doctrine for Building Unity], where he gave Buddhism a modern tint by showing its congruence with democracy and neutralism.[9] Any patronage of Buddhism brought blessings to the patron and the people, which looked good in the public's eyes.

In the mid-twentieth century, radio and print were mechanisms for conveying ideas and information to the masses. In *Imagined Communities*, Benedict Anderson coined the phrase 'print capitalism' to suggest that printed materials, proliferated by market capitalism, helped unify different peoples of a nation under a set of government ideologies.[10] In this way, both Souvanna and Bong utilized mass media to reach the attention of the international community and Lao people towards their version of neutralism.

Historically, the kingdom of Laos was a small player among larger principalities. Siam, Dai Viet and Khmer empires intervened in Lao affairs making the kingdom a tributary state. In 1893, France turned Laos into a protectorate as part of the wider French Indo-China colony. Eventually, Laos gained its independence from France in 1954. At the Geneva peace conference in 1954, ending French colonization of Indo-China, the communist PL/NLHX gained political authority over two provinces near North Vietnam, namely Sam Neua and Phong Saly. The United States moved to contain communism in Laos by working with the RLG, led by Souvanna at the time. However, his goals were to unify the country through a coalition government with the communists and declaring neutrality. Washington feared that these policies would lead to a communist takeover. By 1958, it appeared that Souvanna's plans were about to be realized as the country prepared for an election in the spring.

Projecting Lao's politics and neutrality

Neutralism faced opposition among some in the international community and Laos, so much so that Souvanna engaged in a public relations offensive to promote his hue of the policy and goals for the country. Souvanna began an international tour to convince the world, especially the United States, that neutralism was the right path for Laos. Other groups engaged in this type of activity like the National Liberation Front (NLF/Viet Cong) during the Vietnam War. *Guerrilla Diplomacy*, by Robert K. Brigham, examines the NLF's international diplomatic strategy trying to win support for Vietnam's war against the United States and was successful in stirring public opinion in favour of Hanoi.[11]

In early 1958, Souvanna visited France, Canada and the United States. He met with leaders, the public and the press advocating the need for unity with the communist NLHX. One of Souvanna's notable visits was to France, where he promoted reconciliation with the communists. Souvanna declared that although he viewed communism as dangerous and that its threat should not be minimized, 'Laos is not communist and will not become any time soon'.[12] Part of the criticism of the PL/NLHX was that one of its leaders, Souvanna's half-brother Prince Souphanouvong, was a member of the party. Souvanna viewed Souphanouvong as not a real communist.[13] In regard to the communist-controlled provinces of Sam Neua and Phong Saly, Souvanna compared them to Alsace–Lorraine, territories taken by the Germans in 1871. He emphasized that he wanted to reintegrate the two provinces back into the nation through a coalition government with the NLHX, not conflict. This would be the only path to peace and unity. Some French welcomed Souvanna's visit and saw his plan as a way to improve the political situation.[14]

In an interview, Souvanna continued disavowing concerns about the NLHX. He emphasized that much of Laos was 'concerned with subversive movements from exterior' and that many believed in democracy.[15] Most importantly, people need not fear the communist PL. Souvanna argued, 'Members of the Pathet Lao are all Laotian'. Further, 'they [the communist world] have had contacts with the Pathet Lao and they have received aid, but to conclude that they are communists is jumping to conclusions'.[16] In another setting in France, Souvanna talked about his visit to China, illustrating that he 'respected their ideology and does not seek to introduce communism in Laos' because the Lao people, including the NLHX, 'respected the king and religion [Buddhism] and are not communists'.[17] This would be one of many times when Souvanna would make a similar argument.

After France, Souvanna went to the United States, his toughest audience. This visit was much different, as Dwight D. Eisenhower's administration opposed neutralism. Further, many US policymakers looked down on the Lao and Souvanna and as historian Jacobs argued, this negative sentiment was based on racist views about non-Whites.[18] One member of the staff expressed concern about the inclusion of the NLHX in the upcoming spring 1958 election and in the government, citing 'danger in the present situation and that the new elements participating for the first time in the political life of Laos might be so astute as to end up taking over the government'.[19] The United States ignored Souvanna's argument that 'neutrality is for us a vital necessity' to reunify the nation and bring peace and safety.[20] After failing to sway Souvanna, the administration threatened to cut aid while simultaneously supporting non-communist groups for the 1958 elections, seeing neutralism as synonymous with communism.

While Souvanna toured propagating what he believed was neutralism for Laos, Bong used his newspaper, the *LRS*, to get his point of view to the international and Lao communities. Sophie Sidwell described Bong's and the NUP's tenets, specifically the connection between Buddhism and neutralism.[21] The *LRS* was the voice of Bong's political party since the late 1940s. It targeted the general public, with the party's core themes usually printed on its front page, consisting of Buddhist governance and the Buddhist middle way to neutrality. Although some of these ideas will be discussed hereafter, his anti-communist views have been underexamined.[22] In 1958, the NUP protested arguing that the NLHX was not neutral, only pretending to be.²³ Most issues included criticism of communism and the NLHX, with Bong seeing both as incongruent with Lao traditions and Buddhism.

In the lead up to the spring 1958 elections, Bong advocated that Laos needed to follow Buddhist teachings to remain free from foreign intervention. The party invoked Buddhist language by saying, '[w]e have ideals that will keep us in the middle path between two parties of the world'.²⁴ The 'middle path' sought to stay away from extremes in all aspects of life, including politics. To stay neutral, Lao should follow the five main Buddhist precepts and eightfold path of Buddhism. Any acceptance of foreign aid from non-Buddhist countries would bring outside powers and ideas in, resulting in a loss of sovereignty.²⁵ The NUP saw Laos as a nation that could be modern and democratic while also holding to traditional values. Buddhism helped distinguish the party from the rightist and leftist factions. Though Souvanna also understood Buddhism to be an important part of the RLG's policies, Bong articulated how it could be applied to a modern context, specifically with neutralism.

In May 1958, the NLHX won thirteen of the twenty-one seats in the election. Souvanna formed a short-lived government until right-wing Phoui Sananikone orchestrated a coup in August 1958. The new government was pro-American and anti-communist, overturning NLHX gains from the election. Neutrality had been averted, the outcome the United States wanted.

Bong joined the Phoui government as Minister of Education, Public Health and Cults and continued to spread his ideas against communism. In many issues of the *LRS* there was at least one article warning the Lao people of the dangers of communism with titles like, 'How Is There Proof That Laos Might Have International Communist Ideals' or 'Incite Is the Method of the Red Principles'.²⁶ Bong and the NUP argued that communism was the opposite of democracy and no one would have a voice politically.²⁷ Wolfson-Ford cited a special issue of the *LRS*, where Bong 'unmasks the communists before the National Assembly', suggesting that the NLHX was a threat to Laos.²⁸ In addition, it would not promote unity as the communists only sought to divide the people through breaking the law, working underground and using violence.²⁹ Specifically, the *LRS* condemned the NLHX. One issue reported that a Lao cadre leader had committed suicide. Apparently, he had hopes of becoming a village headman in order to spread communist teachings. The *LRS* asserted, with no evidence, that the cause of death was depression from having to work for 'the upper echelons of the party'.³⁰ Suicide was the only way to 'release himself from the affliction' of serving the communists. If the party took over, Lao would kill each other. The article ended by stating that the NLHX was the main opposition to the NUP.

Despite Bong's anti-communist postulates, the *LRS* articulated a neutral space between capitalism and communism. Bong's neutrality excluded alignment with any side.³¹ According to one article, 'Both sides are searching for members' and many small nations were being swept up. Bong argued that both sought to use Laos for its resources and economic value and pit 'Lao against Lao'.³² The *LRS* declared that NUP doctrine was 'to build Laos for Laos'. This theme became a catchphrase in the newspaper.

What further distinguished NUP's neutralism was the Lao philosophy of Buddhist authority. Several issues of *LRS* had an illustration with an explanation of how Laos could uphold its traditions and neutrality through 'Lao ideology' or Lao Doctrine, *Latthi Lao*.[33] This, Bong explained, was dhammic governance, or rule of law through Buddhism. As Lao people and politicians lived according to the teachings of Buddha, the nation would be blessed. To achieve this, one core teaching was 'we should be in the middle line, living and working to have peace'.[34] Laos would be true to itself and neutral by upholding Buddhism's middle path.

The difficult road towards neutrality in 1960

Eventually in March 1960, Souvanna presented himself as a political candidate in the upcoming April election. He continued espousing neutrality through a coalition government with the communist NLHX. At the National Assembly he proclaimed, 'The only reasonable policy for Laos, which is currently under various foreign pressures, is neutrality and peaceful coexistence'.[35] At an interview with the *Lao Presse*, Souvanna defended the PL/NLHX saying that the members were not traitors to Laos.[36] Much to the chagrin of the US and NUP, he did not waver from his desire for a neutral coalition government with the communists.

Friction arose after non-communist groups won a majority of the seats in the election on 24 April 1960. As a result of a lack of unity, on 25 May, Souvanna became President of the National Assembly and Tiao Somsanith as Prime Minister, both being seen as good figures to bring stability. This new government declared neutrality, but there was still a debate whether it was more pro-West or strictly neutral. Right-wing groups disliked the new political arrangement and threatened a coup.

Then seemingly out of nowhere, a mid-level army officer named Kongle orchestrated another coup on 9 August 1960, also declaring neutrality. A captain in the paratroopers from a rural poor tribe, Kongle had grown dissatisfied with government and military corruption. Sidwell suggests that Kongle's ideas of neutrality had aligned with Bong's. For example, through the Lao national radio he stated he wanted to 'bring peace and to stop killing Lao by Lao'.[37] Kongle went on to say, '[w]e wish for the government to carry out its national policies in a strictly neutral fashion. We must maintain control of our country through neutrality, siding neither with the Free World nor with the communists'.[38] Sidwell said that Kongle's goals 'expounded to the citizenry followed closely the specifics of the Peace Through Neutrality move' advocated by the NUP.[39] Although this might be true, the captain had few links to Bong. In fact, Kongle invoked a message of unity through neutrality with Souvanna as the leader. The captain relinquished power to Souvanna and promoted that the prince would be the best and true path to neutrality, unity and peace.[40]

Souvanna formed a government and the National Assembly unanimously legitimized it. He made a plea to the Lao people and international audience on behalf of the NLHX, saying that neutrality included the communist party, calling them 'brothers'.[41] Later Souvanna said, 'I ask you, my dear compatriots who are members of the NLHX party', to rejoin the nation and government. He promised to apply the agreement made previously to form a government together.[42] The *Lao Presse* newspaper was joyful about the return of Souvanna saying that he would bring reconciliation and his name was 'now engraved with a hot iron on the heart of all the Lao to whom he restored peace and confidence in the future'. Reunification with the NLHX seemed to be the sentiment of some Lao when a spontaneous protest took place in Vientiane. According to the *Lao Presse*, the demonstrators contended the division of the country's territories, specifically Sam Neua and Phong Saly not being united with the rest of Laos.[43] Souvanna spoke to the gathering reassuring them that his goal was to bring unity by working with the NLHX, having already communicated with the party. He was positive that a peaceful arrangement would take place soon.

In September, Thai leaders issued a statement declaring that Laos had turned communist because of Kongle's coup and the establishment of Souvanna's government. Souvanna, again, had to defend his policy and version of neutrality, as he 'repeated that Laos is not and will not become communist'.[44] He argued instead that the policy of 'rapprochement with communist countries [was] for the benefit of the nation'. He ended his response to the opposition by stating, 'Lao customs and religion were the furthest from the communist ideology'. In essence, he argued, Lao turning communist would never happen.

Bong devoted much of the first *LRS* issue after Kongle's coup to warning the Lao people of the dangers the country was in. One article stated that Laos had been in almost constant chaos because of the infiltration of what Bong termed red (communism) and white (capitalism) ideologies. Both superpowers had the same goal of seeking their own profits. 'All benefits go to the state', he said and all people would fall under the power of the leaders of these superpowers, and become 'water buffaloes', driven as slaves.[45] Specifically, the free world or 'white ideology' 'made people depressed through an immoral way of life and only sought for wealth'.[46] On the other side, communists stymied free thinking and exploited the people. The *LRS* published an essay reminding and clarifying what the NUP meant by neutrality. The title read, 'Proclamation for Those Who Do Not Yet Understand Us'. It was important to propagate and emphasize a different form of neutralism to distinguish the NUP from Souvanna, especially on the heels of Kongle's coup. 'Our policy', the writer began, 'opposes other ideological groups that seek to intervene in Laos'.[47] Free world and communist ideologies – the forces interfering – were waging war on the third way, the *Latthi Lao* path of staying neutral.[48] The way to be a 'true Lao' was the middle path, which was Buddha's way.

On the front page of one issue of *LRS* there was a column titled, 'Communists Beginning a New Big Plan'. According to the NUP, communism was already spreading through channels such as NLHX radio and print materials. For some time, the communists had used the northern parts of Laos to win converts to their cause 'behind the scenes'.[49] In another example from the NLHX-held Sam Neua province, the *LRS* reported 'our brothers', meaning the Lao communists, were stealing from the people and sending rice to Vietnam.[50] In addition, they had taken children away to join the revolution. However, there was no corroboration of the news. The paper questioned whether the Lao Communist Party could abide by the constitution. Bong did not see the NLHX as 'brothers' like Souvanna had.

Bong went further, again pitting communism in opposition to Lao traditions. People from one district told the newspaper that leftists were trying to push their ideology on them. In one example, communists discouraged villagers from listening to the teachings and advice of the monks. Instead, they were to 'be like slaves' and follow leftist doctrine.[51] The communists did not want the people to use the formal polite word for 'yes', *dooy*. One would say *dooy* to monks, elders and people of a higher status. Ostensibly, they promoted the abolition of drugs and prostitution, but in reality, perpetuated it in a different form.

More importantly, Bong's argument was that communism sought to destroy Buddhism. In one issue the *LRS* asked, 'Does Communism Destroy Religion?' It answered the question with two others, 'Why did the Dali Lama flee to India' from Tibet after the communist Chinese takeover? 'Has communism brought sin and no benefits to the people?' Lao cadres, on the surface, presented themselves as pure, but did 'not let the people see their evil sins'.[52] Communism, in essence, was the opposite of all aspects of Lao, its traditions, culture and language.

Bong published a letter calling out the communists for threatening the NUP. He criticized the new government created from the Kongle coup, saying that few have benefited and 'our brothers', the NLHX, have been taking advantage of the people.[53] Mocking Souvanna's use of 'our brothers', he argued that these Lao were not 'our brothers'. Bong pointed out that the communists have established its 'front' organization seeking to overthrow the peace of the country. This would be the first of several instances where the *LRS* published examples of communists threatening or hoping to silence Bong and the party.[54] When the PL eventually took over the country in 1975, the party arrested Bong and he died shortly thereafter.

Rushing to a false sense of neutrality

On 13 December 1960, US-backed right-wing Phoumi Nosavan attacked Vientiane and drove Kongle and the Souvanna government out of power, causing a civil war. Souvanna joined forces with the NLHX in opposition to the right and the United States. The *LRS* blamed Souvanna for the cause of the chaos by arguing that he had not been centre or neutral enough but in fact was 'leaning too much to the left'.[55] At the same time, the NUP asserted that the NLHX had lied to the people about wanting neutrality and to instil democracy. 'The world', one article stated, 'has seen enough of neutrality playing off as communism. Thus, be careful to stay away from this type of neutrality', including Souvanna's version of neutralism.[56]

After the Lao right wing suffered military setbacks, President John F. Kennedy, the international community and Lao rival groups began talking to stop the civil war from expanding. Laos turned neutral as a result of the 1962 Geneva Agreement. The new government was a coalition of right-wingers, neutralists and communists. Unfortunately, neither pro-American or pro-communist groups intended to uphold the tenets. Eventually, neutralists were 'absorbed into' the rightist and leftist armies.[57] In 1964, the coalition government collapsed, leading to civil war again, until 1975 when the communists took over.

Historians have placed more attention on US involvement in the country or the civil war between the right wing and communists. However, the disagreements between neutralists add an important perspective in the Cold War in Asia and Lao history. Souvanna promoted a foreign policy of being friendly with the communist bloc. Bong saw any foreign entanglements as dangerous, especially affiliating with the NLHX. Through speeches, language, public events, newspapers and the use of cultural ideas, we see the complexity of the Cold War in a small country like Laos. Mass media helped Souvanna and Bong reach a wider audience and engage in debates about the meaning of neutralism and how it applied to the local circumstances. In some ways, the NUP had a distinct view on neutralism by showing how Buddhist teachings of the 'middle way' was the correct path for Laos and by arguing that Buddhism was part of Lao identity and it was only natural to adhere to it. Unfortunately, the US, North Vietnam, Lao right-wingers and the NLHX disagreed with the two neutralist leaders, leading to another civil war. Laos demonstrates the ambiguity of neutralism and how ideological and propaganda battles over its interpretation can impact small powers wanting peace.

Notes

1. Bong did support the NLHX in the 1958 spring supplementary elections but it was only temporary. See Ryan Wolfson-Ford, 'Ideology in the Royal Lao Government-era (1945–1975): A Thematic Approach' (Dissertation, University of Wisconsin, 2018), 184.
2. Seth Jacobs, *The Universe Unraveling: American Foreign Policy in Cold War Laos* (Ithaca: Cornell University Press, 2012); William J. Rust, *Before the Quagmire: American Intervention in Laos, 1954–1961* (Lexington: University of Kentucky Press, 2021); Arthur J. Dommen, *The Indochinese Experience of the French and the Americans: Nationalism and Communism in Cambodia, Laos, and Vietnam* (Bloomington: Indiana University Press, 2001); Bernard B. Fall, *Anatomy of a Crisis: The Laotian Crisis of 1960–1961* (Garden City: Doubleday, 1969).
3. Declaration on the Neutrality of Laos, 23 July 1962. Available online: https://treaties.un.org/doc/publication/unts/volume%20456/volume-456-i-6564-english.pdf (accessed 21 February 2022). Lao neutralist Souvanna Phouma and the Pathet Lao met several times in 1961, trying to negotiate a separate deal until John F. Kennedy, according to Jacobs and Rust, saw neutrality as the best option as he wanted to focus more on South Vietnam. Laos was not the best place for a war. See Jacobs, *The Universe Unraveling* and Rust, *Before the Quagmire*.
4. Jacobs, *The Universe Unraveling*; Rust, *Before the Quagmire*; Dommen, *The Indochinese Experience of the French and the Americans*; Fall, *Anatomy of a Crisis*; Timothy N. Castle, *At War in the Shadow of Vietnam: US Military Aid to the Royal Government, 1955–1975* (New York: Columbia University Press, 1993).
5. Rust, *Before the Quagmire*, 17–18.
6. Wolfson-Ford, 'Ideology in the Royal Lao Government-era', 36.
7. Ibid.
8. Clifford Geertz, *Negara: The Theatre State in Nineteenth-Century Bali* (Princeton: Princeton University Press, 1980).
9. Lao Ruam Samphan, *Latthi Lao phua sang santhiphap* (Vientiane: Lao Mai, 1960).
10. Benedict Anderson, *Imagined Communities: Reflections on the Origin and Spread of Nationalism* (London: Verso, 1991), 41–2.

11. Robert K. Brigham, *Guerrilla Diplomacy: The NLR's Foreign Relations and the Vietnam War* (New York: Cornell University Press, 1998).
12. 'Declaration of Tiao Souvanna Phouma', *Lao Presse*, 11 January 1958, D and 'The Reunification of Laos and Western Opinion', *Lao Presse*, 13 January 1958, D-E. See also 'The Government of Souvanna Phouma is Not and Never Communist', *Lao Presse*, 14 September 1960, A-3 and A-4. Translations from Lao and French into English by the author.
13. Grant Evans, *The Last Century of Lao Royalty: A Documentary History* (Chiang Mai: Silkworm Press, 2009), 190.
14. 'The Reunification of Laos and Western Opinion', *Lao Presse*, 13 January 1958, D.
15. 'The Paris Interview', *Lao Presse*, 16 January 1958, C.
16. Ibid.
17. 'Relations with Communist Countries', *Lao Presse*, 16 January 1958, H.
18. Jacobs, *The Universe Unraveling*, 9.
19. 'Memorandum of a Conversation', 13 January 1958, *Foreign Relations of the United States, 1958–1960, East Asia-Pacific Region; Cambodia; Laos*, Vol. XVI, Document 159. Available online: https://history.state.gov/historicaldocuments/frus1958-60v16/d159 (accessed 9 December 2021).
20. D. R. SarDesai, *Indian Foreign Policy in Cambodia, Laos and Vietnam, 1947–1964* (Berkeley: University of California Press, 1968), 180. The meeting took place in January 1958.
21. Sophie Sidwell, 'A New Interpretation of Kongle's Neutralist Coup in Laos, August 1960', *Sojourn: Journal of Social Issues in Southeast Asia* 35, no. 1 (2020): 1–30.
22. Ryan Wolfson-Ford's dissertation gives a brief discussion on Bong's anti-communist ideas, 'Ideology in the Royal Lao Government-era', 184–5.
23. 'Lao Ruam Samphan Announcement', *Lao Ruam Samphan*, 25 February 1958, 3.
24. 'Lao Ruam Samphan Announcement', *Lao Ruam Samphan*, 2 February 1958, 7; see also 'Buddha's 5 *Sinh* Leads Us to be Neutral', *Lao Ruam Samphan*, 8, 15, 22 April 1959, 1.
25. 'Defending the Country', *Lao Ruam Samphan*, 8, 15, 22 April 1959, 4.
26. *Lao Ruam Samphan*, 6 August 1958, 4. See also issues 27 August 1958, 3 September 1958, 10 September 1958, 5 November 1958 and 19 November 1958.
27. 'News from the National Assembly', *Lao Ruam Samphan*, 2 June 1958, 2.
28. Wolfson-Ford, 'Ideology in the Royal Lao Government-era', 184. See also 'His Excellency Bong Souvannavong Warns the Deputies of the Danger of Communism in Laos', *Lao Ruam Samphan*, September 1958, 3.
29. 'News from the National Assembly', *Lao Ruam Samphan*, 23 June 1958, 1 and 4; see also 'Where the Communists? Who are Communists?', *Lao Ruam Samphan*, 5 November 1958, 2, 'How Can Red Expand so Quickly?', *Lao Ruam Samphan*, 19 November 1958, 1, 'Official Letter', *Lao Ruam Samphan*, 31 December 1958, 2; 'Official Letter', *Lao Ruam Samphan*, 14 January 1959, 1.
30. 'Head of the NLHX Party', *Lao Ruam Samphan*, 14 January 1959, 1.
31. 'The Way Out is Lao for Lao', *Lao Ruam Samphan*, 17–24 February 1960, 1; see also 'An Image Explaining the Way Out for Laos or for Nations to be Their Own Nations to Lead to True Peace Permanently', *Lao Ruam Samphan*, 2 March 1960, 2. See also issues 9 March 1960, 16–23 March 1960, 30 March 1960.
32. 'Eat the Money of the Free World, Work for the Communist World', *Lao Ruam Samphan*, 27 January 1960, 2.
33. 'An Image Explaining the Way out for Laos or for Nations to be their Own Nations to Lead to True Peace Permanently', 2.

34 'Laws Treatise on Laws and Customs . . .', *Lao Ruam Samphan*, 2 March 1960, 2.
35 'First Session of the National Assembly', *Lao Presse*, 13 May 1960, A-2.
36 'Souvanna Interview', *Lao Presse*, 20 May 1960, A-2.
37 'Speech Delivered by the Revolutionary Group', *Lao National Radio*, 11 August 1960, 2.
38 Ibid.
39 Sidwell, 'A New Interpretation of Kongle's Neutralist Coup in Laos', 19.
40 'Mimeographed Leaflet #10', *Kong Le's Radio Communique*, 17 August 1960, 23.
41 'Speech of Chao Souvanna Phouma', *Radio Vientiane, Kong Le's Radio Communique*, 17 August 1960, 26. See also *Radio Vientiane*, 17 August 1960, 29.
42 'Souvanna's Appeal', *Lao Presse*, 25 August 1960, A-2. See also 'Souvanna's Appeal', *Lao Presse*, 31 August 1960 and 'Kongle's Appeal', *Lao Presse*, 31 August 1960, A-3 and 'Souvanna's Appeal', *Lao Presse*, 1 September 1960, A-7.
43 'The Population Protests against the Secession of the Kingdom', *Lao Presse*, 14 September 1960, A-7.
44 'Let's Repeat it Once Again: Le Laos', *Lao Presse*, 22 September 1960, A-5. See also 'The PM Defines Laos' Position Following the Radio Speech by Marshal Sarit', *Lao Presse*, 4 October 1960, A-1.
45 'To All and All the Nation Who Love Peace, I Invite you to Know', *Lao Ruam Samphan*, 14 September 1960, 4.
46 Ibid.
47 'Proclamation for Those Who Do not Yet Understand Us', *Lao Ruam Samphan*, 22 November 1960, 1.
48 'Communist Ideology, the Way to Divide', *Lao Ruam Samphan*, 22 November 1960, 2.
49 'Communists Beginning a New Big Plan', *Lao Ruam Samphan*, 21 November 1960, 1.
50 'New from Sam Neua', *Lao Ruam Samphan*, 24 November 1960, 1.
51 'Lao Culture Changed', *Lao Ruam Samphan*, 26 November 1960, 1.
52 'Why Have Communists made Lao Kill Lao?', *Lao Ruam Samphan*, 1 December 1960, 2.
53 'Communists Threaten Our Party', *Lao Ruam Samphan*, 22 November 1960, 1. For other instances of the *LRS* using 'brothers' in quotations when describing the Pathet Lao/NHLX, 'News from Sam Neua', 24 November 1960, 1, 'Lao Culture Changed', 1–2 and 5 and 'Why Have Communists made Lao Kill Lao', 3. Souvanna referred to the communist Pathet Lao/NLHX as brothers during Kongle's coup, 'Speech of Chao Souvanna Phouma', *Radio Vientiane, Kong Le's Radio Communique*, 17 August 1960, 26. See also *Radio Vientiane*, 17 August 1960, 29.
54 'Communists Threaten Us Again', *Lao Ruam Samphan*, 2 December 1960, 1.
55 *Lao Ruam Samphan*, 12 December 1960, 1 and 6.
56 'Being Center/Neutral is Ordinarily Red', *Lao Ruam Samphan*, 24 December 1960, 1. See also 'NLHX Proclamation is an Example Revealing that it is Communist', *Lao Ruam Samphan*, 26 December 1960, 1.
57 C. J. Christie, 'Marxism and the History of the Nationalist Movement in Laos', *Journal of Southeast Asian Studies* 10, no. 1 (1979): 152.

18

The global anti-Apartheid campaign as counter-neutrality propaganda

The US and the UK cases compared

Nicholas J. Cull

In the spring of 1948, a general election in South Africa delivered a shock result. After a hard-fought campaign, the National Party, representing the country's White Afrikaans-speaking minority, took control of the legislature and formed a government. The new regime promised to ensure White security and supremacy for the future by extending the network of laws governing residence and employment of non-White South Africans. They dubbed this interlocking system 'Apartheid', using the Afrikaans word for separateness.[1] From its first articulation, activists inside South Africa mobilized against Apartheid under the banner of the African National Congress (ANC) and other groups. International sympathizers took up the cause abroad, more especially after the Sharpeville Massacre of 21 March 1960 when South African police opened fire on a group of peaceful protestors from the Pan Africanist Congress (PAC), killing sixty-nine.

When the United Nations (UN) attempted to sanction the Apartheid state, a number of Western countries blocked the toughest moves. The governments of both Britain and the United States limited responses to events in South Africa and worked to maintain an officially neutral position. The opponents of Apartheid therefore found themselves facing an uphill battle to erode Anglo-American neutrality. While the story of the campaign against Apartheid is most often recalled as pressure exerted on the government of South Africa, the parallel campaigns to spur action from the bystander governments are also instructive, more especially as most observers would see the ultimate decision of those governments to sanction South Africa as critical to the end of Apartheid. The frame of anti-neutrality propaganda opens helpful perspectives on the story and contributes to the overall explanation of why and how the global anti-Apartheid campaign was successful. It also helps connect the more familiar historiography of US and British foreign policy with the emerging discourse around non-state campaigns and transnational activism.

The anti-neutrality paradigm

As this book has demonstrated, propaganda campaigns to counter neutrality were a common occurrence in the twentieth century. They figured in both world wars and other conflicts too, with prime examples being the powerful campaigns twice waged by Britain in the United States. Explanations of why countries shift policy as a result of campaigns typically emphasize the context of the campaign as well as the techniques and themes of the messages used. Comparing cases, five broad contextual factors plainly contribute to a shift in attitudes. The first is the existence of moral arbiters in the culture of the neutral state to which the opponents of neutrality can appeal. Does their appeal resonate with established values or even values shared and endangered in the conflict concerned? The second is the existence of diasporic links that make the population concerned feel connected to the specific situation and to one side in particular. The third is a set of economic links connecting the neutral country with the place where the problem is. Do the economic ties pull in one direction? The fourth is the way in which the local mass media depict the problem. What frames are the media using? The fifth is the local political context. These factors taken together can account for whether a neutral society is moved to act or remains aloof. The international campaign to draw the US and UK governments to act over Apartheid worked with all five of these factors. In fact, the range and depth of these connections suggests that South Africa was a uniquely significant case. The leverage deployed to undermine official neutrality would be difficult to reproduce in other situations.[2]

Moral arbiters

The first arguments to respond to the situation in South Africa came in the early 1950s from moral arbiters working at the overlap of South African and Anglo-American values. Specifically, the protestant church took the lead, especially figures interested in the issue of race. The first generation of British voices decrying the immorality of Apartheid were missionaries who had seen Apartheid and its antecedents at close quarters and who acted as rapporteurs or even spokesmen for the indigenous anti-Apartheid campaign in South Africa. The pioneer was a churchman called Rev Michael Scott. His advocacy succeeded in impressing the newspaper proprietor and philanthropist David Astor, who bankrolled a think tank called the Africa Bureau as a platform for Scott's advocacy against Apartheid and for decolonization in general. Scott was closely followed by Father Trevor Huddleston who wrote a best-selling account of repression in South Africa entitled *Naught for Your Comfort* in 1956.[3] Huddleston called for a cultural boycott of South Africa as early as 1954.[4]

UK-based clerical activists who turned their attention to South Africa included Canon John Collins, who raised money to fund legal defence for ANC activists in South Africa. Similar figures in the United States included a White Methodist minister called George Houser, who had been connected to the Congress on Racial Equality during the Second World War. Houser established the American Committee on Africa which lobbied the US government to action, initially with little traction.[5] Interestingly, breakthrough critiques of Apartheid in fiction also proceeded from a foundation of shared religious values. Alan Paton's seminal novel *Cry, the Beloved Country* (1948) only came to publication because members of a religious, anti-racist network in the United States, who Paton chanced to meet during a sabbatical trip, learned of the book as a unpublished manuscript. Its publication in the United States led to subsequent global availability including in South Africa.[6]

The first generation of moral arbiters appealed to the emerging ideas about universal human rights articulated at and by the UN. One of Michael Scott's earliest activities was his appeal to the UN on behalf of the Herero people in South African-occupied South West Africa (now Namibia).[7] Ideas of racial justice were central. It helped the early anti-Apartheid campaigners that the events of the Second World War had challenged the West's complacency over race. Adolf Hitler had given racism a bad name – and the new National Party government of South Africa was not helped by some members' wartime sympathies for Nazi Germany. The anti-Apartheid press in the UK especially regularly reminded audiences that key architects of Apartheid had served time in jail during the war because of their Nazi sympathies.[8]

While arguments couched in religious terms presented by people with religious credentials or evoking the anti-Nazi struggle of the Second World War were directed at Anglo-American audiences, appeals couched in other terms came from South Africa to other key audiences. Anti-imperialism had its own morality and this was combined with arguments expressed in Marxist terms about social and economic justice. Such arguments found a receptive audience about the newly decolonized African states, and Eastern bloc nations seeking strategic advantage even as they embraced a chance to be on the right side of history. The African states and Eastern bloc became enduring opponents of Apartheid.[9] Their position undercut the religious case, giving a power politics and Cold War logic for the United States and the United Kingdom to maintain a relationship with South Africa, which delivered on the role, sending its airforce to the Korean War, offering hospitality to the naval forces of the West and referring to itself as the 'Bastion of the South'.[10]

Diasporic links

The second factor in play in the anti-Apartheid campaign was diasporic links. The first foreign government to protest against racial abuse in South Africa was that of India which even before its own independence raised concerns about anti-Indian laws in South Africa at the UN. In the United States, pan-African organizations and leading Black Americans like Paul Robeson and W. E. B. Du Bois spoke of a duty to help. Campaigns began in the 1930s and at the end of the Second World War they seemed poised to be drivers of public pressure for the United States to respond to settler abuse in Southern Africa. The Red Scare disrupted such work. Du Bois and Robeson were ostracized for their left-wing politics and the movement split with some anti-communist African Americans (most famously Max Yergan) serving as apologists for the Apartheid government in Pretoria.[11] The diasporic link (or perceived diasporic link) between African American Civil Rights and South African anti-Apartheid re-emerged strongly in the later 1960s. By the 1970s and throughout the 1980s, mobilizing the US government against Apartheid was a major concern for the Congressional Black Caucus, playing a key role in the watershed moment of the US government's enactment of comprehensive economic sanctions against South Africa in 1986.[12]

In the UK the connection was not about shared race, but shared empire and the way in which the bonds of that empire played out in the lives of individual people. In the 1950s young people, who had grown up in the British Empire as South Africans, moved to the UK for education. They became the initial core of people who were interested in South African affairs and their activism was the foundations of British anti-Apartheid activity. The struggle began with a boycott campaign launched in 1959. In some ways, their endorsement of a boycott was a reversal of British Empire propaganda from a generation earlier, urging citizens to help the empire by buying its exports.[13] Now the exile community in the UK flipped the script and looked to correct the errors of policy in South Africa by refusing to buy its products.[14] In time, the British anti-Apartheid movement outgrew its roots in the expat community. By the 1970s, members were mostly British born and the issue a mainstream element of British politics. The issue became the cause of a generation rather like opposition to the Vietnam War in the United States. While some leaders – like student leader Peter Hain – were South African born, many others like Mike Terry – the secretary of the anti-Apartheid movement – or its president Bob Hughes were home-grown.[15]

Britain had another link to South Africa that if not strictly diasporic was certainly historical which provided a vector for persuasion. The existence of the Commonwealth organization ensured an ongoing elite interest in the welfare of former countries of the British Empire. Queen Elizabeth II remained concerned about South Africa, and even though the country had pulled out of the Commonwealth in 1961, Commonwealth countries maintained pressure on successive London governments against UK neutrality.[16]

Economic links

The third set of factors which came into play in the struggle against neutrality in the face of Apartheid flowed from economic links. For the UK, the trading relationship which gave the diaspora the leverage of a boycott also gave the UK government the vested interest of preserving relations with the Apartheid state. Even Labour governments formed by politicians associated with the anti-Apartheid campaign found that it was impossible to walk away from economic links with South Africa entirely. Harold Wilson's government honoured its pre-existing defence contracts with the Apartheid state. In the United States, the absence of pre-existing substantial economic ties initially limited the scope of the boycott. George Houser noted that he could achieve little traction by calling on Americans to stop eating frozen lobster tails.[17] Yet the relative absence of US pressure over economic links to Apartheid enabled a rapid acceleration of those links. By the 1970s, the United States had developed a massive stake in the South African economy and the US-based anti-Apartheid movement had a viable vector for leverage. Particular issues included the behaviour of US and British corporations with subsidiaries in South Africa. Campaigns like the 'starvation wages' campaign run by Britain's *Guardian* newspaper in the early 1970s showed how British corporations were benefiting from their South African operations by exploiting Black labour corralled under the Apartheid system. Such campaigns brought Apartheid home. It was not just South African brands like Cape apples or Outspan oranges that were the problem but British household staples like Tate & Lyle sugar or Hovis bread, Leyland vehicles and Bowater paper all doing business in South Africa. Apartheid was part of the British kitchen, living room, garage and bathroom.[18]

In the United States, the lightning conductor corporations were Polaroid – which assisted in the creation of Apartheid's identity documents – and General Motors (GM). In 1977, GM board member and preacher Leon Sullivan successfully persuaded the corporation to insist on certain non-racial principles as a condition of remaining in South Africa. Many American companies operating in the country followed suit to diffuse public criticism. In later years, Sullivan conceded that the principles were not enough to prompt real change. By the mid-1980s, pressure on the corporations had reached such a pitch that they finally pressed for political reform. South African business negotiation with the ANC preceded talks between the liberation movement and the Pretoria government.[19]

Media

One of the advantages enjoyed by the South African government in the early decades of Apartheid was their ability to dominate media coverage of the country. Censorship was always part of Pretoria's propaganda strategy and this ratcheted up dramatically in the 1960s, as the ANC and PAC shifted into an armed struggle against Apartheid. The outside world saw more of the gilding than the cage. South Africa's information ministry and tourist board spent lavishly to promote an image of the country as a tourist destination, and with censorship of criticism of the system, a distorted view prevailed. Windfalls to enhance the image of South Africa included the news of the first human heart transplant accomplished by Christiaan Barnard in Cape Town in December 1967. South African spending was such that Anglo-American media outlets had every interest in keeping on good terms with Pretoria. When the anti-Apartheid movement attempted to purchase their own advertising space to contest South Africa's claims, they found newspapers unwilling to jeopardize a proven revenue stream.[20] One way in which images of Apartheid did get out from South Africa was through secret filming and smuggling. Significant films made undercover in South Africa included *Come Back, Africa* (1959), by American Lionel Rogosin; *Dilemma* (1962), an adaptation of a Nadine Gordimer short story by Danish director Henning Carlsen; and, after the South African authorities clamped down, two remarkable documentaries made by British students working with the Pan Africanist Congress: *Phela Endaba/ End of the Dialogue* (1970) and *Last Grave at Dimbaza* (1974). The South African government archives reveal that these last two films were particularly impactful, perhaps because they juxtaposed the luxuries of White life with the deprivations of

Black and had secured substantial mainstream TV audiences, while the previous films had been limited to the art house circuit. The rising in Soweto in 1976 transformed the media landscape and ended the era of the hidden camera. The images of South Africa police shooting school children destroyed any pretence that Apartheid was somehow altruistic. It also made Apartheid into an international news story. The eruption of violence in Soweto and across the country thereafter was on such a scale that the US TV news organizations who had given little attention to South Africa previously now opened their own bureaux in Johannesburg and kept Apartheid on the new agenda while other stories faded.[21]

One crucial player in the media landscape of Apartheid was the output of the UN's Centre Against Apartheid – a hub for anti-Apartheid communication established by the General Assembly at the end of the 1960s and run by a deeply committed Indian diplomat named E. S. Reddy. The UN Centre took materials from the liberation movement and from various civil society organizations opposing Apartheid around the world and published them with the imprint of the UN, giving them all of that institution's credibility, and distancing them from the potentially divisive connections between the chief opposition group – the ANC (now reconstituted in exile) and the Eastern bloc. Reports, studies and hearings abounded and circulated in multiple languages as a result of the UN's efforts. The Centre Against Apartheid even commissioned its own documentary films. The UN organized special anti-Apartheid days and even designated an international anti-Apartheid year (1978) as a focus for activism.[22] The South African government was not particularly worried by the ANC in the early 1970s as they saw it as a spent force. They were, however, worried by the UN.[23] In the face of a global wave of anti-Apartheid campaigning, the Minister of Information in Pretoria – Connie Mulder – initiated an ill-advised secret propaganda campaign. This campaign involved lavish spending to get South African materials into Western media, including creating and fully funding magazines – particularly conservative magazines – in the United States, the United Kingdom and right across Europe. Mulder's team even attempted to purchase the ailing newspaper *The Washington Star* as a friendly voice in the United States. Within South Africa they created an English-language newspaper called *The Citizen* to drive some of the critical local English media out of business. The official dishonesty about the propaganda campaign exploded into what became known as the 'Muldergate scandal', which ended the career of Prime Minister B. J. Vorster and enabled the ascent of an uncompromising strong man, P. W. Botha.[24]

Pretoria's alarm over the UN was well placed. The United Nations Centre Against Apartheid had a hand in two of the most successful communication gambits levelled against the presence of Western neutrality over Apartheid: the cultural and sporting boycott, and the elevation of Nelson Mandela as an icon of the movement. In the case of the cultural and sporting boycott, the move began with a UN General Assembly resolution in 1968. Thereafter the UN Centre provided a logistical core for the enterprise by maintaining a register of violators to hold those who played with or in South Africa to account. The tactic was especially interesting from the point of view of a counter-neutrality strategy, as it implicitly problematized all contact with Apartheid South Africa and presented an argument in which to be neutral was to be supportive of the regime.[25]

The UN's role in the refocusing of anti-Apartheid work on Mandela came as a result of a meeting in 1977 between the UN's Centre director E. S. Reddy and a newly released political prisoner from Robben Island, Mac Maharaj, who had been a close confidante of the jailed leader behind bars, and brought out a first draft of Mandela's memoirs when he left prison. Meeting Reddy at a conference in Accra (Ghana), Maharaj mentioned that Mandela was approaching his sixtieth birthday and the veterans on Robben Island were eager to see the occasion marked. Reddy recognized an opportunity to publicize the entire issue of Apartheid by focusing on the case of just one man. The idea had its problems. Mandela had been out of the public eye since the Rivonia trial in 1964 and had not been part of recent developments in the ANC leadership. Communication between the prisoners and the movement was minimal. He was, moreover, outranked in the ANC hierarchy by the organization's president Oliver Tambo, and some in the organization felt that it was Tambo – also approaching sixty – who should be publicized. Others wanted all political prisoners to be celebrated. Some even worried that Mandela had somehow already sold out and was secretly negotiating with Pretoria. Tambo for his part encouraged Reddy to act, feeling that such a move was better made by an outside organization. The ANC agreed to a compromise campaign with the slogan 'Free Nelson Mandela and All Political Prisoners'. The extent to which Mandela had hitherto not been front and centre of anti-Apartheid messaging was underlined by the difficulty that Reddy had in establishing the exact date of Mandela's birthday. He discovered that Mandela had a habit of cheating and announcing it was his birthday when it actually wasn't. Reddy sent a series of letters to people who might know the correct date, including Mandela's wife Winnie. He received no response until March 1978, when the ANC's HQ in Lusaka, Zambia, cabled to confirm the correct date for the sixtieth birthday would be 18 July that year. At this point, Reddy alerted his network of government and activist contacts that they had an opportunity to celebrate. The refocus worked. While it had been hard for a neutral world to understand the suffering of an entire nation, the fate of a single individual was miraculously comprehensible. Evidence of the effectiveness of the strategy included a celebration of Mandela's birthday in a committee room at the House of Commons in London with members of the Labour government and a birthday cake. India awarded Mandela the Nehru Prize for International Understanding: the first of many international honours awarded to the jailed leader. A ball had begun to roll.[26]

The Free Nelson Mandela campaign gained momentum in 1980 when the Black press in South Africa began focusing on the demand. It spiked around his sixty-fifth birthday in 1983. A celebratory concert in south London underlined the potential for culture to be actively harnessed on behalf of the anti-Apartheid cause. This had been a regular practice in the 1960s but had not been seen in the interim. The British musician Jerry Dammers was inspired to create the pop anthem *Free Nelson Mandela*. By Mandela's seventieth birthday in 1988, it was possible to book Wembley Stadium and line up eleven hours of world-class musicians from both sides of the Atlantic and South Africa to pay tribute to Mandela and call for his release. ANC insiders worried that people would attend or tune in because of the music rather than the politics, but were eventually convinced that the regime in Pretoria would assume the worst and be further compelled towards compromise.[27]

The British political context

The final element in the stance of the United States and the United Kingdom on the situation in South Africa was – of course – the political context. In the UK, the core context of the stance on Apartheid was decolonization. The issue was often conflated with the challenge of Rhodesia where in 1965 a White colonial government unilaterally declared its independence from Britain and resisted calls for a democratic constitution. The British anti-Apartheid movement campaigned on both South Africa and Rhodesia until a settlement was reached for the creation of Zimbabwe in 1980. Equally the defence of South Africa within UK political circles was focused on broader pro-colonial issues. South Africa's key Allies in British politics were members of an organization called the Conservative Monday Club, created as a reaction against Prime Minister Harold Macmillan's famous endorsement of decolonization in 1960 – his 'Wind of Change' speech – delivered to the South African parliament on Monday, 3 February of that year.[28] While the Conservative Party found itself split over South Africa, the Liberal Party in the UK was consistently supportive of anti-Apartheid positions, as was the Labour Party, most especially when out of government. British anti-Apartheid feeling peaked during periods of Conservative government: the premierships of Alec Douglas-Home in the 1960s, Edward Heath in the early 1970s and, above all, Margaret Thatcher in the later 1970s and throughout the 1980s. Thatcher was especially closely identified with maintaining relations with South Africa and encouraging small steps towards reform. Family members had known business links in the country. Thatcher's position added a domestic relevance to the Apartheid issue.

Opposing Apartheid became another way to defy Thatcher and assert local sovereignty. British Local Authorities had a long history of speaking out on Apartheid and participating in the boycott, but during the Thatcher years an anti-Apartheid stance became a key vector to perform local political identity and distinguish oneself from a deeply disliked national government. Activities included widespread renaming of streets to celebrate Mandela and other anti-Apartheid figures. It is notable that British anti-Apartheid politics had only a loose connection to racial issues at home. Black British voices were a relatively late addition to the campaign, figuring only in the 1980s, and were closely related to the anti-Apartheid movement's overlapping with local authority politics. Local councils and city governments were more likely to include politicians with Black backgrounds than the less porous, ethnically ossified national line up of Members of Parliament. All these factors converged to undermine the Conservative government's resistance towards sanctions against South Africa in favour of what was termed 'constructive engagement' encouraging reform. Thatcher accepted limited sanctions in 1985 and a stiffer programme in the summer of 1986. The exact balance of influences on her decision to abandon rigid neutrality remains unclear but private pressure from other Commonwealth countries and the Queen seem to have pushed her along. In later years, Mandela – ever emollient – stated that this, and later pressures from Thatcher on the South African government to compromise, had helped to end Apartheid.[29]

The US political context

If the foundation of Britain's response to Apartheid was decolonization, the foundation of the US response was the Cold War. The US government was alarmed by the leading role of the South African Communist Party in the struggle against Apartheid and tended to accept Pretoria's frame that the ANC was compromised by its connections to the communist world. Significantly, Mandela's famous Rivonia trial speech in 1964 devotes considerable space to linking his own politics to icons of Western democracy such as Magna Carta.[30] This Cold War frame was challenged in time by a second frame casting the situation in terms of human rights. As this perspective grew in the 1970s, it seemed increasingly hard to accept that the United States could have integrity in its foreign policy and be neutral on the issue of Apartheid.

As in the UK, the issue of Apartheid became linked to domestic political identities. It was a priority issue for the Congressional Black Caucus. It was a way for young Americans to hold the older generation to account as pressure for divestment from South Africa became a major campus issue in the early 1980s. Conversely, as in the UK, American conservatives also saw the defence of links to South Africa as a priority. In the end, mass participation pushed businesses to change sides and Congress passed comprehensive sanctions over US President Ronald Reagan's veto in 1986. Although Pretoria found ways to lobby their way into opening enough loop holes to avoid a total severing of economic ties with the United States, the heightened pressure was sufficient to push the South African government to the negotiating table with the ANC and moved Apartheid into its final phase. The end was much helped by the simultaneous end of the Cold War. The liberation movements could see a horizon on their hitherto generous support and the South African government had a chance to tell its own people that it was safe to compromise now that the 'Red Peril' had passed. Both Britain and the United States were glad to play an active role in the last act, shepherding South Africa to its first democratic election in 1994.

Conclusion

What are the lessons from this story? There are many reasons why the governments of the United States and the United Kingdom ended their neutrality over South Africa, but plainly the leverage from anti-Apartheid propaganda directly and indirectly from publics inspired by their own exposure to that material helped. The opposition and liberation movements in South Africa and their Allies at the UN successfully developed links with sympathetic civil society organizations in the United Kingdom, the United States and elsewhere and placed their cause higher on the agenda than comparable issues of the time, such as the struggle for democracy and human rights in South America or issues between the Israelis and Palestinians in the Middle East. Of particular gambits, plainly there was tremendous value in personalizing the entire story of Apartheid around Nelson Mandela. It also helped the movement to frame contact with South Africa in the broadest possible way. The

The Global Anti-Apartheid Campaign 259

Figure 18.1 Anti-Apartheid demonstrators picketing Barclays Bank near Trafalgar Square in London, March 1978. Courtesy Getty Images.

anti-Apartheid movement ensured that small personal acts like the purchase of a South African orange, banking at Barclays (see Figure 18.1) or buying gasoline from Shell, a company with well-known links to South Africa, were problematized.

The convergence of factors mitigating against British and American neutrality can seem so overwhelming as to make the eventual support for reform seem inevitable. It is important to recall that it did not seem so at the time. Pretoria's initial defence of Apartheid was made easier by the alignment of the liberation movements with the Eastern bloc, but by the 1970s that alignment had matured from welcome rhetorical backing into essential sustaining support though training, funding and arms supplies. The Eastern bloc helped the ANC maintain a global profile of what amounted to a government in waiting. Help included printing the movement's journal and supporting its radio station. The end of Apartheid deserves to be seen as one of the strategic foreign policy successes of the Soviet Union and its Allies. Despite the material support from the East, it was equally valuable that the campaign against Apartheid was coordinated through the offices of the UN. The UN lent coherence to a campaign that might otherwise have been subdivided. It is an important lesson that networked actions like cultural and sporting boycotts work best when there is someone clearly in charge. There are a number of human rights campaigns in the twenty-first century that would benefit from a similar level of coordination. Arguably, the anti-Apartheid campaign happened at a time when the UN was uniquely positioned to take a lead. Perhaps, today the UN lacks the credibility with many audiences to play such a role.

Not all the communication gambits employed by the anti-Apartheid movement landed well. Some, in retrospect, seem counterproductive. Gandhi – responding to his own experience of racism in South Africa – stressed the importance of the maxim 'Hate the sin and not the sinner'.[31] Anti-Apartheid communication often failed to include this kind of distinction and slipped into a vilification of White South Africans in general and Afrikaners in particular. The demonization encouraged a sense in Afrikaner circles that no one understood them and that they had to protect their own way of life, above everything else.

Seen through the lens of anti-neutrality campaigns the success of international propaganda against Apartheid seems explicable but dependent on specific factors of history, geography, economics and timing that make it hard to reproduce. Post-Apartheid governments in South Africa have sometimes recalled the international interest in their country during the struggle as if it were a resource that could be tapped once again. The historical specificity of the campaign argues against this. The campaign was tied to its times, from its relationship to decolonization to the generational aspect of a specific age group in the United Kingdom and the United States embracing anti-Apartheid as an issue in their wider battles against the outlook of Thatcher and Reagan. Other times and other generations will favour other places and issues. From the point of view of global activism, the traction achieved by the anti-Apartheid movement seems hard to match. In a new century in which a new generation of politicians is showing an ability to remain aloof from a fresh set of human rights outrages, today's advocates for human rights face up an uphill struggle in their own battles against governmental neutrality. It is sadly not enough simply to pick up the same tools of boycotts and demands for sanctions used by the campaign against Apartheid and assume that success will follow.

Notes

This chapter is based on research conducted in the British anti-Apartheid movement archive at the Bodleian Library in Oxford, the UN archive in New York, the ANC archive at Fort Hare in South Africa and the South African foreign ministry archive, which is still held internally in Pretoria. The author has also benefited from extensive interviews with participants in the events described, especially the late E. S. Reddy.

1. On election, see Martin Meredith, *In the Name of Apartheid: South Africa in the Postwar Period* (New York: Harper & Row, 1988).
2. Justus Drew Doenecke remains the leading historian of US neutrality. His works include *Nothing Less Than War: A New History of America's Entry into World War I* (Lexington: University Press of Kentucky, 2011) and *From Isolation to War, 1931–1941* (New York: Thomas Y. Crowell Co., 1968). The neutrality paradigm is drawn from the analysis of US entry into the First World War and such books as H. C. Peterson, *Propaganda for War: The Campaign against American Neutrality, 1914–1917* (Norman: University of Oklahoma Press, 1939) also the literature on the end of US neutrality in the Second World War to which the author contributed Nicholas J. Cull, *Selling War: The British Propaganda Campaign against American 'Neutrality' in World War II* (New York: Oxford University Press, 1995).

3   For an overview, see Rob Skinner, *The Foundations of Anti-Apartheid: Liberal Humanitarians and Transnational Activists in Britain and the United States, c.1919–64* (London: Palgrave, 2010) and Robin Denniston, *Trevor Huddleston: A Life* (London: Macmillan, 1999).
4   Trevor Huddleston, 'The Church Sleeps On', *Observer*, 10 October 1954, 6. Italics in original.
5   Denis Herbstein, *White Lies: Canon Collins and the Secret War against Apartheid* (Oxford: James Currey, 2004); on Houser, see George M. Houser, *No One Can Stop the Rain: Glimpses of Africa's Liberation Struggle* (Cleveland: Pilgrim Press, 1989).
6   Alan Paton, *Cry, the Beloved Country* (New York: Scribner/London: Jonathan Cape, 1948). For context, see Peter F. Alexander, *Alan Paton: A Biography* (Oxford: Oxford University Press, 1994).
7   Anne Yates and Lewis Chester, *The Troublemaker: Michael Scott and His Lonely Struggle Against Injustice* (London: Aurum, 2006).
8   For examples of British anti-Apartheid comment on links between Nazis and Apartheid, see 'South Africa's Nazis Come into the Open', *Anti-Apartheid News*, November 1966, 1 and 'In Nazi Memory', *Anti-Apartheid News*, November 1967, 4.
9   For an overview of international solidarity including the Eastern bloc, see Ronnie Kasrils (ed.), *International Brigade against Apartheid* (Johannesburg: Jacana Media, 2021).
10 The South African government used the title *Bastion of the South* for a propaganda short film regularly shown by embassies in the 1960s.
11 On Yergan, see David Henry Anthony, *Max Yergan: Race Man, Internationalist, Cold Warrior* (New York: New York University Press, 2006).
12 On Black American reaction for Apartheid, see Nicholas Grant, *Winning Our Freedoms Together: African Americans and Apartheid, 1945–1960* (Chapel Hill: University of North Carolina Press, 2017) also Robert Trent Vinson, 'Up from Slavery and Down with Apartheid! African Americans and Black South Africans against the Global Color Line', *Journal of American Studies* 52, no. 2 (2018): 297–329.
13 On the EMB, see Philip M. Taylor, *The Projection of Britain: British Overseas Publicity and Propaganda, 1919–1939* (Cambridge: Cambridge University Press, 1981), also Stephen Constantine, *Buy and Build: The Advertising Posters of the Empire Marketing Board* (London: HMSO, 1986) and Melanie Horton, *Empire Marketing Board Posters* (Manchester: Scala, 2010).
14 For a survey of exile politics, see Mark Israel, *South African Political Exile in the United Kingdom* (London: Macmillan, 1999). On the early days of the AAM, see Christabel Gurney, 'A Great Cause: The Origins of the Anti-Apartheid Movement, June 1959–March 1960', *Journal of Southern African Studies* 26, no. 1 (2000): 123–44.
15 Hain's activism is documented in Peter Hain, *Outside In* (London: Biteback, 2012). On Terry, see Denis Herbstein, 'Mike Terry: Obituary', *Guardian*, 7 December 2008. On Hughes, see Brian Wilson, 'Lord Hughes of Woodside: Obituary', *Guardian*, 14 January 2022.
16 On the Commonwealth and Apartheid, see Richard Bourne, *Shridath Ramphal: The Commonwealth and the World* (Hertford: Hansib, 2009).
17 Donald R. Culverson, *Contesting Apartheid: US Activism 1960–1987* (London: Taylor & Francis, 2019).
18 For a study created by the movement, see Ruth First, Jonathan Steele and Christabel Gurney, *The South African Connection: Western Investment in Apartheid* (London:

Temple Smith, 1972/London: Penguin, 1973). On the starvation wages campaign, see Adam Raphael, 'The Company We Keep ... Britain's Shame in Africa', *Guardian*, 12 March 1973, 11. For follow-up pieces, see 'South Africa: Does British Money Bolster Apartheid?' *Guardian*, 3 April 1973, 14 and 'Award', *Guardian*, 18 January 1974, 1.

19 On the Sullivan principles, see Zeb Larson, 'The Sullivan Principles: South Africa, Apartheid, and Globalization', *Diplomatic History* 44, no. 3 (2020): 479–503.

20 For correspondence between British activists and newspapers, see Bodleian Library, Oxford, AAM 2298, 'Press advertisements' especially Hoyle (*Times* of London) to de Keyser, 13 October 1970.

21 For an overview of film and the representation of Apartheid, see Peter Davis, *In Darkest Hollywood: Exploring the Jungles of Cinema's South Africa* (Athens: Ohio University Press, 1996).

22 For a summary of UN work, see E. S. Reddy, 'Behind the Scenes at the UN', in *No Easy Victories: African Liberation and American Activists over a Half Century, 1950–2000*, ed. William Minter, Gail Hovey and Charles Cobb Jr (Trenton: Africa World Press, 2007), 74–7.

23 High-level meetings reflecting a deep concern over UN communication activity in the archives of the South African foreign ministry (currently held at the Department of International Relations and Cooperation) include DIRCO 152/1 'Inter-Departementele vergadering . . ', 29 June 1972. For a South African government survey of UN activity, see DIRCO 152/2 'Political Info. and Related . . ', Perm. Rep. C. F. G. Von Hirschberg (UN) to Sec. for Foreign Affairs, Information Campaign at the United Nations, confidential, 12 March 1974.

24 On South African propaganda, see Mervyn Rees and Chris Day, *Muldergate: The Story of the Info Scandal* (Johannesburg: Macmillan, 1980).

25 United Nations, *The United Nations and Apartheid, 1948–1994* (New York: UN Department of Public Information, 1994).

26 This paragraph is based on author interviews with E. S. Reddy (New York, 23 February 2014) and Mac Maharaj (via Zoom, 24 August 2021).

27 Author interviews with organizers: Palo Jordan (Cape Town, 17 April 2014); Dali Tambo (Johannesburg, 14 November 2014); Taren Brokenshire (Cambridge, 9 May 2019); Peter Watrous, 'Pop Music's Homage to Mandela', *New York Times*, 13 June 1988, C18.

28 For an overview of the Monday Club, see Robert Copping, *The Story of The Monday Club: The First Decade* (London: Current Affairs Information Unit, 1972).

29 Nicholas J. Cull, 'British Cities versus Apartheid: UK Local Authority Activism as City Diplomacy', *Diplomatica* 2, no. 1 (2021): 187–99.

30 Nelson Mandela, *The Struggle is My Life* (London: International Defence and Aid Fund, 1986), 176.

31 M. K. Gandhi, *An Autobiography or the Story of My Experiments with Truth* (Ahmedabad: Navajivan Publishing House, 1927 and 1929; London: Penguin, 2001), chapter 86.

Epilogue

The Russo-Ukrainian war, propaganda and the end of neutrality?

Pascal Lottaz

Writing an epilogue to a book on propaganda and neutrality in spring 2022 has a strange feel to it. Only a few months ago, this would have been a relatively abstract affair, but since Russia's invasion of Ukraine on 24 February, the debate about neutrality has suddenly re-entered public perception – and with that the realm of propaganda. Newspapers, magazines and TV shows are discussing neutrality in its various complexities, from foreign policy to international law, impartiality, humanitarianism, the sanction question, the discourse of non-alignment and even neocolonialism. In this context, the chapter uses 'propaganda' as an analytical concept, close to its religious meaning of 'that which is ought to be spread (by us) and believed (by others)'. Avoiding a lengthy definition, the premise is that certain beliefs about perceived reality are so important to nation states and their affiliates that they try to convince their citizenry (and sometimes attempt to convince the citizenry of other states) of the validity of their interpretation – or the falsehoods of rivalling narratives, which are often denounced as 'lies'.[1] David Welch probably put it best in 2019: 'Whatever definition of propaganda we choose to use or, indeed, whether we need more or less propaganda – we have been living through *the* age of propaganda.'[2] This has only become worse. Recently we have seen state attempts for narrative control over the Covid-19 pandemic and now the war in Ukraine. This chapter will reflect on how modern propagandistic trends are trying to shape the perception about the Russo-Ukrainian war and whether this closes or opens spaces for 'neutrality'.

Propaganda and the battle for *Deutungshoheit* over the Russo-Ukrainian war

First a word of caution: an analysis of international politics in 2022 might turn out to be as ephemeral as those in the springs of 1989, 1939 or 1914. There are moments when world order shifts, when global systems break and when new fundamentals are born. Even if this year does not become such a moment, it certainly *feels* as if it would.

Something broke in 2022. Even though this new war is for now still incomparably smaller than the decade-old conflicts and proxy wars in places like Afghanistan, Iraq, Syria, Libya or Yemen, this war is being reported differently – at least in the West. As a colleague recently observed: today every child in Europe can draw a Ukrainian flag but their parents would hardly recognize even one flag of a country in a Middle Eastern war. The shock about the Russo-Ukrainian tragedy seems less about the fact that there is a war *again* than that there is a war again *in Europe*. After all, was it not the promise of the end of the Cold War that the days of classic interstate conflicts on the continent were over? Had we not reached 'the end of history?'[3] Would not the 'liberal international order' prevail indefinitely? In this believe-shattering sense, not even the Yugoslav wars of the 1990s felt as epoch-making – at least that is the impression emerging from the headlines and newsfeeds of Western media. But why that discrepancy to the other wars since 1991?

One part of the answer might just have to do with racism. In the days after the invasion of Ukraine, when the first refugees crossed the border into the European Union (EU), video compilations spread on social media of Western correspondents expressing shock not about people fleeing this conflict but that they were *White*. CBS reporter, Charlie D'Agata, commented on air: 'This isn't a place, with all due respect, you know, like Iraq or Afghanistan that has seen conflict raging for decades. You know, this is a relatively civilized, relatively European – I have to choose those words carefully, too – city where you wouldn't expect that or hope that it's going to happen.'[4] Shortly thereafter it transpired that Black and Arab people fleeing the war – students and other immigrants who had been living legally in Ukraine – were subjected to entirely different and stricter refugee processes in EU countries than White Ukrainians.[5]

Nevertheless, even considering the racist elements of the European discourse, it is hard to overlook its ideological component and the battle for what German speakers call *Deutungshoheit* – the sovereignty over interpretation (of what we perceive as reality). This power to define what events and actions mean is naturally the goal of propaganda, which, in extreme cases, can go all the way to include propaganda about a *casus belli* for a war of aggression, like the 2002–3 propaganda stunt of the George W. Bush administration asserting Iraq possessed 'Weapons of Mass Destruction' (WMDs) and therefore needed to be attacked to prevent Saddam Hussein from attacking the United States and Europe. With twenty years of hindsight, the arguments and mechanisms of this propaganda were conclusively dismantled by academics and even government-commissioned reports like the Iraq Inquiry (the 'Chilcot Inquiry') in the UK.[6] The imaginary WMDs were never more than a convenient excuse to bring about regime change in Iraq – at the cost of an estimated 600,000 to 1 million Iraqi lives.[7] No persecution of the perpetrators ever occurred.

The Russo-Ukrainian war is still much too fresh to distinguish fact from fiction, calls for war crime tribunals have already been made on the highest Western levels, including US President Joe Biden.[8] When it comes to the reasons given by Russia for its invasion, unsurprisingly, Moscow, too, cited the right to (collective) self-defence, even invoking Article 51 of the UN Charter, about the Donbas republics.[9] Tellingly, however, when Russian President Vladimir Putin announced the invasion, he dwelt for the major part on the threat the expansion of the North Atlantic Treaty Organization (NATO) posed to Russia, not on the concrete *casus belli* – the humanitarian situation in the Donbas.[10] The discrepancy is a reminder that while this war might be between Russia and Ukraine, the root conflict is between Russia and the United States.

Yet, propaganda is not the only way to realize *Deutungshoheit*. The other important mechanism is the suppression of counter-narratives (or counter-propaganda). In most Western European countries and the United States, the news stations *Russia Today* and *Sputnik* have been banned from the air and are being repressed even on the internet, where search giants like Google have removed all links to the outlets. Josep Borrell, the EU's High Representative of Foreign Affairs, justified the move with the words 'we are not trying to decide what is true and what is false. We don't have ministers of the Truth. But we have to focus on foreign actors who intentionally, in a coordinated manner, try to manipulate our information environment'.[11] Social media platforms, too, are banning certain interpretations of the war in Ukraine, even when they come from experienced specialists, like Scott Ritter, a former US Marine Corps intelligence officer and UN arms control officer. He was banned from Twitter for posting dissenting views about the 'Bucha Massacre' that took place in late March during Russia's withdrawal from the greater Kyiv region.[12] While many creators on social media platforms like YouTube, Facebook and Twitter have complained for years about the increasing trend towards censorship and the impossibility of expressing certain opinions without being banned (as had happened even to Donald Trump, a sitting US president), the debate has been taken up a notch since Elon Musk, the business maverick, decided to buy Twitter with the stated goal of defending free speech on the platform. What this will lead to is anyone's guess but the question of information control in the West has certainly reached the top levels, including the very recent decision by the US administration to establish a 'Disinformation Governance Board' (to be part of the Department of Homeland Security), which even the *Wall Street Journal* has already dubbed a partisan instrument and dystopian 'Ministry of Truth'.[13] At the same time, the Russian side, too, is engaging in restricting free speech even threatening its news networks with legal punishment for using the word 'war' when describing what the Kremlin has deemed to be a 'special military operation' in Ukraine, and forcing many Western media outlets out of the country.[14]

After narrative battles about the Covid-19 pandemic, it is now the Russo-Ukrainian war that lays bare how much nation states still care about what their citizens believe. There have even been skilful attempts at changing the beliefs of foreign social media consumers. The best example was an emotional (but professional) appeal by Arnold Schwarzenegger, the world-famous movie star and former Republican Governor of California talking directly to his 'dear Russian friends', trying to convince them to oppose the war. Within a few days the video had already been watched on Twitter over thirty-seven million times and many more times via other channels.[15] In short, the beliefs of the masses is a highly contested space. The developments around free speech on social media platforms are part of that. Welch identified this trend already in 2019, observing that since private social media posts are more important than classic media in shaping public opinion, 'we are all propagandists now'.[16] In other words, attempts at gaining *Deutungshoheit* over the current war at home – and challenging the narratives that are believed abroad – are in full swing.

Propaganda and the conceptual space for neutrality

The trend leaves a mixed outlook for 'neutrals'. We shall see below who is currently considered neutral in what sense of the word. In any event, it is important to appreciate that while neutrals might be able to stay out of third-party conflicts, they are always part of the larger conflict dynamics. This includes the propaganda environment as they are often not only the battleground of clandestine activities by belligerents but also the targets of information competition to sway them to one side or the other.[17] That is no surprise as conflicts – and even more so wars – polarize. After all, both sides in a war are willing to use ultimate means to realize their political goals. That must go hand in hand with ever stronger beliefs about the 'justice' of the own cause. The framing of the 'War on Terror' as a struggle against the 'Axis of Evil' is a perfect example of how the moralization of a violent intervention under Just War Theory (JWT – a political doctrine that experienced a revival during the Iraq War) led to a shrinking of the conceptual space for neutrality. As George W. Bush put before Congress, 'either you are with us, or you are with the terrorists'.[18] The JWT premise is that not supporting the just side of a war is equivalent to supporting the unjust one. Such framing makes it difficult – if not impossible – for countries not wanting to support either side to explain their position. Although in the Russo-Ukrainian war JWT has not emerged (yet) as a theoretical pillar, the arguments especially for economic sanctions are the same. While some media outlets in the West have relatively sober views on why a large part of the (non-Western) world is not joining the sanctions against Russia, more ideological (propaganda) outlets like the German *Deutsche Welle* are portraying that decision as implicitly supporting Moscow and standing 'on the wrong side of history'.[19] Unsurprisingly, it tends to be the side with the better propaganda in its sphere of influence that carries the day. Although traditional European neutrals did not join the war in Iraq, they also did not impose sanctions on the United States during any of its violent interventions in the Middle East – something swiftly achieved after Russia's intervention in Ukraine.

Whenever wars are imagined as a contest of good against evil, the moral justification to remain neutral approaches zero, especially if *both sides* frame their actions as the only moral thing to do. The conceptual space for neutrality is by far bigger under the Clausewitzian paradigm. Although (military) realists might disagree about the wisdom of not joining alliances, they usually accept that the choice for neutrality is based on self-interest, not morality. If war is, as Clausewitz holds, 'the continuation of politics by other means', then neutrality is the continuation of politics by the same means. This is what the JWT framing makes impossible, since 'business as usual' with the guilty side of a Just War becomes itself a moral crime. The debate about third parties in the Russo-Ukrainian war is currently raging within this opinion spectrum.

Neutral towards the war? Neutral towards the conflict?

To understand where this situation leaves neutrality, it is crucial to differentiate between two distinct conflict phenomena. There is a 'hot' shooting war, raging between Russia and Ukraine (although Russia denies this is a war), and, on the other hand, we have got a 'cold' structural conflict between Russia and the United States/ NATO, in which both sides perceive each other as threats (although NATO denies that it is a threat to Russia). There are four levels of analysis that matter concerning neutrality and propaganda: international law, international politics, national politics and national discourse.[20] The first, international law, is a technical aspect, concerning only the shooting war but it cannot be overlooked since 'neutrality' in the classic sense is a legal concept which many states – especially the European neutrals – still cling to. Unfortunately, this is not a particularly helpful level of analysis. First, under a strict reading, international law does not even provide for a neutrality debate because neither Russia nor Ukraine have officially declared war, hence there might be a question if the law of neutrality even applies. Assuming that the world community deems the hostilities a war (which is enough for neutrality law to apply), this automatically transforms any state not part of the hostilities into a neutral power. Meaning, in this case, all states except for Russia or Ukraine would 'count' as neutral – technically.[21] This is hardly helpful, nor does it correspond to the public signalling of the actors. Furthermore, contrary to popular opinion, international law does not prohibit neutral states from exporting weapons to belligerents – the V. Hague Convention explicitly allows it – meaning that international law is not even a useful way to evaluate if weapon exports by neutrals like Sweden and Finland constitute a legal breach of neutrality.[22]

International politics is a more fruitful place for analysis. While, so far, all third parties have refrained from actively joining the battle – except for mercenaries fighting unofficially – all countries had to position themselves in the greater conflict as expressed in their voting behaviour on UN resolutions about the shooting war and the question of imposing sanctions on Russia. At the UN General Assembly meeting on 24 March, 140 countries decided to vote for a draft resolution putting the blame for the war squarely at the feet of Russia. Only five countries voted against the resolution – Russia itself and its close political Allies: Belarus, North Korea, Syria and Eritrea. However, thirty-eight countries chose to abstain from voting at all, including the geopolitical giants, China and India.[23] Furthermore, the United States and NATO have called for tough economic sanctions to punish and ultimately dissuade Russian actions. While all traditional European neutrals have heeded the call and levied sanctions, including closing their airspaces to Russian commercial aviation, banking and other restrictions on the import and export of goods to the Russian Federation, the list excludes nearly all Latin American, African, Middle Eastern, Central Asian and Southeast Asian countries. In Europe, Serbia and Bosnia and Herzegovina have refrained from joining the sanctions, while Turkey has adopted only relatively light sanctions and even tried to broker negotiations between Russia and Ukraine, despite being a NATO member. Although the condemnations and sanctions have no direct bearing on the international law of neutrality, they have produced much political analysis about countries that chose not to side with either camp. Good examples are some of the media reactions to Switzerland copying the EU sanction system which has widely been reported in Western media as Switzerland 'giving up' its neutrality – albeit the Swiss defend the view that sanctions are not a violation of their *legal* (military) neutrality towards the shooting war.[24] On the other side, the Chinese and Indian refusal to take sides has led to perceptions about Beijing and New Delhi following a 'neutral' foreign policy, or, less benignly, as 'sitting on the fence'.[25]

Beijing's approach, aptly referred to as 'China's Neutrality in a Grave New World' by Yu Bin, is not unexpected since the Russo-Ukrainian war produces a dilemma for China. It has been emphasizing for decades non-intervention as a pillar of its foreign policy and it has nothing to gain from this conflict.[26] However, joining the US-led initiative to punish Russia, which bears undeniable similarities to the way the United States is treating China, is also not acceptable to Beijing. In addition, the memories of a near-catastrophic confrontation with the Soviet Union during the intra-communist Cold War when the two superpowers got close to a nuclear exchange are relatively fresh.[27] Beijing has no appetite to antagonize Russia. On the contrary, the sanctions seem to be pushing China and Russia closer together as Chinese companies are stepping up in various fields where the United States and its Western Allies are leaving.[28] However, it is also relatively clear that Russo-Chinese relations have undergone cyclical up and downturns, providing a good reason for Beijing not to tie itself irreversibly to Moscow.

The Indian reaction – also largely perceived as 'neutral' in Western media – was more of a surprise. Despite being one of the founding members of the Non-Aligned Movement in the 1950s and 1960s, India has recently started collaborating in security affairs, primarily with the United States, Japan and Australia in the Indo-Pacific through the 'Quadrilateral Security Dialogue'.[29] This, coupled with the fact that India is a democracy, led to the perception New Delhi was edging closer to a formal alliance. However, the refusal to let its good relationship with Russia turn sour shows that India's strategic interest lies in the Indo-Pacific only where it is caught in security competition with China. There is no incentive for India to pick a side in Europe.

Similar dynamics are taking place in other formerly colonized parts of the world. South America, Africa and Southeast Asia are mostly refraining from following Western sanctions. The Association of Southeast Asian Nations (ASEAN) is particularly interesting regarding neutrality developments. Among its ten members, only Singapore has levied sanctions on Russia. Singapore is also the strongest US security cooperation partner in ASEAN, which includes large-scale weapons purchase.[30] In contrast, Myanmar, receiving weapons from Russia, has rhetorically come out in support of Russian actions.[31] The other members fall somewhere in between the two extremes, for which there are various economic, geostrategic and institutional reasons.[32]

In Europe, the war has first and foremost opened new national debates (discourse level) in traditional neutrals about their security arrangements. First, political consequences are unfolding for the two Nordic neutrals, Sweden and Finland, whose leaders have publicly shifted their stance on NATO membership and lethal military aid for one side of the war (national politics level). They have both supported Ukraine directly with weapons, something other neutrals like Ireland, Austria and Switzerland have so far ruled out – Switzerland even forbade Germany to re-export its weapons to Ukraine.[33] Although Sweden and Finland had both been on a pro-NATO course for two decades, including dropping the label 'neutrality' for 'non-alignment', the war in Ukraine has pushed the opinions of policymakers and the public towards seeking security in an alliance instead of neutrality.[34] Finland and Sweden are both likely to join NATO. In Austria, too, despite the Nehammer government standing firmly behind the country's neutrality policy, newspaper articles calling for the country to join NATO have appeared in large numbers after Russia's invasion.[35] Even in Switzerland, a public debate has ensued about 'the right way' of being neutral, including calls for closer collaboration with NATO.[36] Protestors in Berne have advocated for a stronger Swiss stance against Russian aggression (see Figure 19.1). The Swiss Parliament requested the federal government to formulate a new white paper on neutrality and, in reaction to any perceived loss of neutrality, the country's right-wing conservative party is contemplating launching a neutrality referendum to prevent the government in the future from copying EU sanctions.[37]

Much research will be needed to better understand the individual national positions, but it seems for now (by way of a hypothesis) that populations in India, China, Southeast Asia and other formerly colonized states are more prone to perceive the Russo-Ukrainian war under the lens of the larger Russo-US/NATO conflict. In contrast, the debate in Europe – including the question of what still

Figure 19.1 Protestors outside the Swiss Parliament in Berne, demonstrating against the Russian invasion of Ukraine, March 2022. Courtesy Getty Images.

counts as 'neutral' and what not – focuses strongly on the illegality of the shooting war. This situation has striking similarities to the Cold War, where traditional neutrals like Switzerland, Austria and Ireland were on a legal level committed to their neutralities, while on a political and economic level they remained firmly embedded in the Western camp.[38] Simultaneously, a block of non-aligned countries that were not formally neutral adopted policies that did not clearly support either side in the larger Cold War.

Who wants neutrality for Ukraine?

There is one more element, namely Russia's demand that Ukraine abandons its aspiration to join NATO and officially become neutral, that is, an imposed neutralization. This has sparked another neutrality debate, albeit one that is much older than the shooting war. A plethora of Western realists, diplomats, politicians and academics argued for a long time that the United States and Russia would fall into a new great power conflict if NATO expanded eastward. For decades, they were strong proponents of a neutral Ukraine (and Georgia). George Kennan, Jack Matlock, Henry Kissinger, Stephen Walt, John Mearsheimer, Anatol Lieven, Michael O'Hanlon and Heinz Gärtner have all spoken in favour of neutralized buffer states between Russia and NATO, which they argued were in the interest of all parties and beneficial to the security architecture of Europe.[39] Even after the outbreak of the war, a neutralization of Ukraine together with a federalization of its political structure seemed to realist thinkers the only way to avoid a drawn-out war or permanent division.[40]

Opposition to a neutral solution comes from thinkers who perceive the war not in the first place as a great power competition, but as the aggression of a dictatorial state (Russia) that wants to stop the democratic tendencies of its neighbours. They interpret Vladimir Putin as implementing a malevolent policy of a revisionist and power-hungry Russia, wishing to occupy and destroy Ukraine for the sake of resurrecting the 'glory' of the former Soviet Union. To this school of thought, a neutral Ukraine would signify a Russian victory and lay the groundwork for more aggression. They portray a neutral Ukraine as being a defeat of the country and if NATO did not stop this outcome (directly or indirectly), it would mean consent to a Europe dominated by Russia. A perfect example of this view is Natia Seskuria, who argues neutrality for Ukraine was a 'trap' because 'Putin's goal isn't halting NATO enlargement – it's destroying Ukraine's sovereignty and democratic future'.[41] Unsurprisingly, the battle for *Deutungshoheit* is raging fireclay on this front with thinkers like Noam Chomsky or the former US Ambassador Chas Freeman openly supporting the realist school.[42] Concerning military support, Freeman most memorably coined the phrase that the United States was willing to 'fight to the last Ukrainian' in its conflict with Russia – a view repeated by Chomsky.[43] This produced fierce counter reactions with Polish writer Szczepan Twardoch accusing them of grossly misunderstanding Russian intentions. In his view, only eastern Europeans who had endured the Soviet yoke before could accurately understand the situation.[44]

Conclusion

In all three instances, the foreign policy of neutral countries towards the shooting war, the policy of non-aligned states towards the greater conflict and the policy preferences about a neutralized Ukraine, a key factor seems to be the perception of the underlying causes of the war and the great power conflict. The situation is by far too dynamic and too young to attempt a proper analysis of the information environment. However, it seems evident from the examples on corporate and state censorship, media control, and what Herman and Chomsky identified as the mechanisms of 'manufacturing consent', that it is not only autocracies caring a great deal about the information flowing to their citizens.[45] Concerning the West's curtailing of freedom of expression, and propaganda, the 79-year-old ambassador Freeman said: 'I lived through, as a Child, the McCarthy Era in the United States. I saw its aftermath when I joined the diplomatic services because I was working on China, which was a major focus of the insanity, basically. But this is worse than anything that we have seen.'[46]

In brief, neutrality, non-alignment and neutralization as a solution to the war and its conflict are currently the subject of intense debate, wrapped up in propaganda battles. Much research is needed in the coming years over the propagandistic battle for *Deutungshoheit* in the shooting war and the great power conflict. Although there is no definite telling where this dynamic will lead, it is quite certain that it is a cataclysmic moment for neutrality in Eurasia. For now, it seems likely that some traditional neutrals in Europe may give up their signature foreign policy, while others will keep clinging to the legal understanding of neutrality – even while politically joining one camp of this great power conflict. There is an open question about some of the 'border lands', like Serbia, Bosnia, Moldova, Georgia, Turkmenistan and Mongolia.[47] Perhaps some or all might try to remain neutral towards the shooting war and the larger conflict (as they are doing for now), but that might prove impossible in the long run if the conflict and the propaganda surrounding it leads to an even stronger JWT framing of the global contest for power. Should Russia – and eventually China – also change position from seeking neutral buffers (as is Moscow's stated goal for Ukraine) to seeking Allies, and if the moralization of the positions increases, the conceptual spaces for the neutrals will further shrink. However, there may be a 'New Non-Aligned' movement emerging. Even if the traditional neutrals in Europe were to completely disappear, it is unlikely that the non-alignment sentiment of the formerly colonized world will vanish – be it for geopolitical, economic or institutional reasons. As long as war and conflict remain part of international politics, neutrality will remain, too. Propaganda surrounding neutrality, be that its promotion or denigration, or debates around what neutrality really means, is also likely to stay with us.

Notes

1 In this sense, 'propaganda' focuses on the nexus between government interests and the beliefs of the public. Of course, the term 'propaganda' is fraught with moralistic

undertones. For a discussion, see Erwin W. Fellows, '"Propaganda": History of a Word', *American Speech* 34, no. 3 (1959).

2   David Welch, '"We Are All Propagandists Now": Propaganda in the Twenty-First Century', in *Propaganda and Conflict: War Media and Shaping the Twentieth Century*, ed. Mark Connelly et al. (London: Bloomsbury Academic, 2019), 322. Emphasis in original.
3   Francis Fukuyama, 'The End of History?', *The National Interest*, no. 16 (1989): 3.
4   Josephine Harvey, 'CBS Journalist Apologizes for Saying Ukraine more "civilized" than Iraq, Afghanistan', *Yahoo! News,* 28 February 2022. https://news.yahoo.com/cbs-journalist-apologizes-saying-ukraine-024714455.html (accessed 23 May 2022).
5   'Ukraine Refugee Crisis Exposes Racism and Contradictions in the Definition of Human', *The Conversation*, 22 March 2022. https://theconversation.com/ukraine-refugee-crisis-exposes-racism-and-contradictions-in-the-definition-of-human-179150 (accessed 23 May 2022).
6   Larry Hartenian, *George W Bush Administration Propaganda for an Invasion of Iraq* (New York: Routledge, 2021); Report of a Committee of Privy Counsellors, *The Report of the Iraq Inquiry*, vol. I–XII (London: House of Commons, 2016). Available online: https://www.gov.uk/government/publications/the-report-of-the-iraq-inquiry (accessed 23 May 2022).
7   Gilbert Burnham et al., 'Mortality after the 2003 Invasion of Iraq: A Cross-Sectional Cluster Sample Survey', *The Lancet* 368, no. 9545 (2006): 1427. See also the Opinion Research Business survey as reported in 'Poll: Civilian Death Toll in Iraq May Top 1 Million', *The Los Angeles Times*, 14 September 2007.
8   Dan Mangan, 'Biden Calls to Put Putin on Trial for War Crimes over Russia Killings in Ukraine', *CNBC*, 5 April 2022. https://www.cnbc.com/2022/04/04/biden-calls-to-put-putin-on-trial-for-war-crimes-over-russias-actions-in-ukraine.html (accessed 23 May 2022).
9   Vladimir Putin, 'Address by the President of the Russian Federation', *The Ministry of Foreign Affairs of the Russian Federation*, 24 February 2022. http://en.kremlin.ru/events/president/news/67843 (accessed 23 May 2022).
10 Ibid. On the humanitarian situation of the Donbas and the military conflict since 2014, see Jacques Baud, 'The Military Situation in the Ukraine', *The Postil Magazine*, 1 April 2022. https://www.thepostil.com/the-military-situation-in-the-ukraine (accessed 23 May 2022).
11 'EU Officials Defend Move to Ban RT and Sputnik Amid Censorship Claims', *euronews*, 8 March 2022. https://www.euronews.com/my-europe/2022/03/08/eu-officials-defend-move-to-ban-rt-and-sputnik-amid-censorship-claims (accessed 23 May 2022).
12 Scott Ritter, 'Twitter Wars—My Personal Experience in Twitter's Ongoing Assault on Free Speech', *Scheerpost*, 14 April 2022. https://scheerpost.com/2022/04/14/scott-ritter-twitter-wars-my-personal-experience-in-twitters-ongoing-assault-on-free-speech (accessed 23 May 2022).
13 Roger Koppl and Abigail Devereaux, 'Biden Establishes a Ministry of Truth', *Wall Street Journal*, 1 May 2022. https://www.wsj.com/articles/biden-establishes-a-ministry-of-truth-disinformation-governance-board-partisan-11651432312 (accessed 23 May 2022).
14 'Russia bans Words "invasion" and "assault" in Media, Warns Several Outlets', *The Times of Israel*, 26 February 2022. https://www.timesofisrael.com/russia-bans-words-invasion-and-assault-in-media-warns-several-outlets (accessed 23 May 2022); 'RFE/RL Suspends Operations In Russia Following Kremlin Attacks', RadioFreeEurope, 6

March 2022. https://www.rferl.org/a/rferl-suspends-russia-operations/31738541.html (accessed 23 May 2022).

15 Arnold Schwarzenegger (@Schwarzenegger), 'I Love the Russian People. That is Why I have to Tell You the Truth', *Twitter*, 17 March 2022. https://twitter.com/schwarzenegger/status/1504426844199669762?s=21&t=JpN0EsYPB8eQ90f5ycfaQQ (accessed 23 May 2022).

16 Welch, '"We Are All Propagandists Now"', 311.

17 André Gerolymatos, Denis Smyth and James Horncastle (eds), *Neutral Countries as Clandestine Battlegrounds, 1939–1968: Between Two Fires* (Lanham: Lexington Books, 2020); Edward Corse, *A Battle for Neutral Europe: British Cultural Propaganda During the Second World War* (London: Bloomsbury, 2013).

18 George W. Bush, 'Address to a Joint Session of Congress and the American People', *The White House*, 20 September 2001. https://georgewbush-whitehouse.archives.gov/news/releases/2001/09/20010920-8.html (accessed 23 May 2022).

19 Jen Kirby, 'Why India isn't Denouncing Russia's Ukraine War', *Vox*, 18 March 2022. https://www.vox.com/22982698/india-russia-ukraine-war-putin-modi (accessed 23 May 2022); Antonio Cascais, 'Russia's Reengagement with Africa Pays Off', *Deutsche Welle*, 9 March 2022. https://www.dw.com/en/russias-reengagement-with-africa-pays-off/a-61064011 (accessed 23 May 2022).

20 The four levels are causally related. Without going into any details shall it suffice to say that national discourse impacts national politics, especially in democracies but also in autocratic systems. National politics – that is, the way national parties and political stake holders interact – impact the foreign policy of a country which, when interacting with foreign policies of other countries, constitute 'international politics' and those movements can, if they lead to legal proceedings and norm building, impact international law. Naturally, this is a bidirectional process on all levels.

21 This follows from general practice, see Lassa F. L. Oppenheim, *International Law: A Treatise—War and Neutrality*, vol. II (London: Longmans, Green, 1912), 307. It also follows directly from Article 16 of the V Hague Convention of 1907, https://ihl-databases.icrc.org/applic/ihl/ihl.nsf/ART/200-220017?OpenDocument (accessed 23 May 2022).

22 Ibid. Article 7, https://ihl-databases.icrc.org/applic/ihl/ihl.nsf/ART/200-220017?OpenDocument (accessed 23 May 2022).

23 United Nations, 'General Assembly Adopts Text Recognizing Scale of Humanitarian Woes Arising from Russian Federation's Ukraine Offensive as Unseen in Many Decades', *Meeting Coverage and Press Releases*, 24 March 2022. https://www.un.org/press/en/2022/ga12411.doc.htm (accessed 23 May 2022).

24 See, for example, 'Neutral Switzerland Join EU Sanctions against Russia in Break with Past', *Reuters*, 28 February 2022. https://www.reuters.com/world/europe/neutral-swiss-adopt-sanctions-against-russia-2022-02-28 (accessed 23 May 2022); Schweizerische Eidgenossenschaft, *Die Neutralität Der Schweiz* (Berne: Eidgenössisches Departement für auswärtige Angelegenheiten EDA, 2022).

25 See, for example, Yu Bin, 'China's Neutrality in a Grave New World', Russia in Global Affairs, 11 April 2022. https://eng.globalaffairs.ru/articles/chinas-neutrality (accessed 23 May 2022); Stanly Johny, 'Ukraine and the Anatomy of India's Neutrality', *The Hindu*, 8 April 2022. https://www.thehindu.com/opinion/lead/ukraine-and-the-anatomy-of-indias-neutrality/article65300245.ece (accessed 23 May 2022). Also see, for example, the *Wall Street Journal*'s use of the word 'neutral' as pertaining to countries that did not levy sanctions against Russia, like China: Andrew Duehren,

'Yellen Warns Nations Staying Neutral in Russia's War With Ukraine', *Wall Street Journal*, 13 April 2022. https://www.wsj.com/articles/yellen-warns-nations-staying-neutral-in-russias-war-with-ukraine-11649879113 (accessed 23 May 2022).
26 Bin, 'China's Neutrality in a Grave New World'.
27 Lorenz M. Lüthi, *The Sino-Soviet Split: Cold War in the Communist World* (Princeton: Princeton University Press, 2008).
28 Trym Eiterjord, 'What Does Russia's Invasion Mean for China in the Arctic?', *The Diplomat*, 25 March 2022. https://thediplomat.com/2022/03/what-does-russias-invasion-of-ukraine-mean-for-china-in-the-arctic (accessed 23 May 2022).
29 On the portrayal of India in Western media, see, for example, 'India's Neutrality on Ukraine Tops Agenda as Modi Heads to Europe', *France 24*, 2 May 2022. https://www.france24.com/en/europe/20220502-india-s-neutrality-on-ukraine-tops-agenda-as-modi-heads-to-europe (accessed 23 May 2022).
30 US Department of State, 'U.S. Security Cooperation with Singapore', *Fact Sheet of the Bureau of Political-Military Affairs*, 20 April 2021. https://www.state.gov/u-s-security-cooperation-with-singapore (accessed 23 May 2022).
31 Lukas Singarimbun, 'ASEAN Members' Responses to the Invasion of Ukraine', *Asia & The Pacific Policy Society*, 6 April 2022. https://www.policyforum.net/asean-members-responses-to-the-invasion-of-ukraine (accessed 23 May 2022).
32 Charis Si En Tay, 'Neutrality in International Organizations Ii: ASEAN', in *Neutral Beyond the Cold: Neutral States and the Post-Cold War International System*, ed. Pascal Lottaz, Heinz Gärtner and Herbert Reginbogin (Lanham: Lexington Books, 2022); Laura Southgate, 'ASEAN: Still the Zone of Peace, Freedom and Neutrality?', *Political Science* 73 (2021): 31–47.
33 For an overview of arms support going to Ukraine, see the UK research briefing by John Curtis and Claire Mills, *Military Assistance to Ukraine since the Russian Invasion* (London: House of Commons Library, 2022). See also 'Neutral Swiss Rule Out Arms Deliveries to Poland', *Reuters*, 22 March 2022. https://www.reuters.com/world/europe/neutral-swiss-rule-out-arms-deliveries-poland-2022-03-21 (accessed 23 May 2022); 'Schweiz verbietet Deutschland Munitionslieferung an Ukraine', *t-online*, 24 April 2022. https://www.t-online.de/nachrichten/ausland/id_92066020/ukraine-krieg-schweiz-verbietet-deutschland-munitionslieferung.html (accessed 23 May 2022).
34 'Majority of Finns Now Want to Join NATO–Poll', *Reuters*, 1 March 2022. https://www.reuters.com/world/europe/majority-finns-now-want-join-nato-poll-2022-02-28 (accessed 23 May 2022); 'New Poll Finds Majority of Swedes in Favour of Joining Nato', *The Local*, 4 March 2022. https://www.thelocal.se/20220304/new-poll-finds-majority-of-swedes-in-favour-of-joining-nato (accessed 23 May 2022).
35 Liam Hoare, 'As Finland and Sweden Consider Nato Membership, Austria Clings to Neutrality', *The New Statesman*, 22 March 2022. https://www.newstatesman.com/international-politics/geopolitics/2022/03/as-finland-and-sweden-consider-nato-membership-austria-clings-to-neutrality (accessed 23 May 2022); 'Debatte über NATO-Beitritt Österreichs: "Neutraler Staat bleibt bei Angriff alleine"', *Vienna Online*, 6 March 2022. https://www.vienna.at/debatte-ueber-nato-beitritt-oesterreichs-neutraler-staat-bleibt-bei-angriff-alleine/7317500 (accessed 23 May 2022).
36 See, for instance, the interview with the president of the Switzerland's liberal party, Thierry Burkart, 'Wir müssen änger mit der NATO zusammenarbeiten', *Tagesanzeiger*, 8 April 2022. And his essay on the same issue: Thierry Burkart, 'Ende

der Igel-Schweiz: Zusammenarbeit mit der NATO verstärken', *Neue Zürcher Zeitung*, 8 April 2022.

37. Foreign Policy Commission of the State Council, 'Kommission verlangt aktualisierten Neutralitätsbericht', *Swiss Parliament*, 12 April 2022. https://www.parlament.ch/press-releases/Pages/mm-apk-s-2022-04-12.aspx?lang=1031 (accessed 23 May 2022); Christoph Blocher, 'Neutralität—Höchstes Gebot der Stunde', *Der Züricher Bote*, 11 March 2022.
38. Sandra Bott, Jussi M. Hanhimaki, Janick Schaufelbuehl and Marco Wyss (eds), *Neutrality and Neutralism in the Global Cold War between or within the Blocs?* (London: Routledge, 2017).
39. On George Kennan, see James M. Goldgeier, 'The US Decision to Enlarge NATO', *Brookings Review* (Summer 1999): 18–21. https://www.brookings.edu/wp-content/uploads/2016/06/goldgeier.pdf (accessed 23 May 2022); on Jack Matlock, see Interview by the author: 'Last US Ambassador to the USSR, Jack Matlock, on Ukraine, Russia, and the West's Mistakes', *Neutrality Studies* (YouTube), 4 February 2022. https://www.youtube.com/watch?v=pPuIfiAeXsw (accessed 23 May 2022); on Henry Kissinger, see Henry A. Kissinger, 'To Settle the Ukraine Crisis, Start at the End', *Washington Post*, 5 March 2014; on Stephen Walt, see Stephen Walt, 'Liberal Illusions Caused the Ukraine Crisis', *Foreign Policy*, 19 January 2022. https://foreignpolicy.com/2022/01/19/ukraine-russia-nato-crisis-liberal-illusions (accessed 23 May 2022); on John Mearsheimer, see John J. Mearsheimer, 'Why the Ukraine Crisis Is the West's Fault: The Liberal Delusions That Provoked Putin', *Foreign Affairs*, September 2014; on Anatol Lieven, see Interview by the author: 'Solving Ukraine: Federalization and Permanent Neutrality can End the Conflict – Dr. Anatol Lieven', *Neutrality Studies* (YouTube), 22 February 2022. https://www.youtube.com/watch?v=9XyQw6CGpdo (accessed 23 May 2022); on Michael O'Hanlon, see Michael O'Hanlon, *Beyond NATO: A New Security Architecture for Eastern Europe* (Washington DC: Brookings Institution Press, 2017) and on Heinz Gärtner, see Heinz Gärtner, 'Neutrality for Ukraine according to the Austrian Model', *Österreichisches Institut für Internationale Politik*, March 2014.
40. See, for example, Michael Jonas, 'Dauerhaft neutral oder geteilt', *Frankfurter Allgemeine Zeitung*, 5 April 2022.
41. Natia Seskuria, 'Why Neutrality is a Trap for Ukraine', *Foreign Policy*, 22 April 2022. https://foreignpolicy.com/2022/04/22/ukraine-russia-putin-nato-neutrality-trap (accessed 23 May 2022).
42. On Noam Chomsky, see C. J. Polychroniou, 'Chomsky: Our Priority on Ukraine Should Be Saving Lives, Not Punishing Russia', *Truthout*, 20 April 2022. https://truthout.org/articles/chomsky-our-priority-on-ukraine-should-be-saving-lives-not-punishing-russia (accessed 23 May 2022); and on Chas Freeman, see Interview by the author: 'Chas Freeman: On Propaganda, the Resurrection of Spheres of Influence, and Peace Failing', *Neutrality Studies* (YouTube), 21 April 2022. https://www.youtube.com/watch?v=E0n6v5SHqpI (accessed 23 May 2022).
43. On Freeman, see 'US Fighting Russia "to the last Ukrainian": Veteran US Diplomat', *The Grayzone* (YouTube), 23 March 2022. https://www.youtube.com/watch?v=0vxufUeqnuc (accessed 23 May 2022); on Chomsky, see transcript of interview conducted by C. J. Polychroniou. Available in Tom Kirk, 'Chomsky: Our Priority on Ukraine Should Be Saving Lives, Not Punishing Russia', *Global Policy*, 28 April 2022. https://www.globalpolicyjournal.com/blog/28/04/2022/chomsky-our-priority-ukraine-should-be-saving-lives-not-punishing-russia (accessed 23 May 2022).

44 Szczepan Twardoch, 'Ihr habt keine Ahnung von Russland', *Neue Zürcher Zeitung*, 9 April 2022.
45 Edward S. Herman and Noam Chomsky, *Manufacturing Consent: The Political Economy of Mass Media* (New York: Pantheon Books, 1988).
46 Freeman Interview (minute 0:00–0:52).
47 See also Pascal Lottaz, Heinz Gaertner and Herbert Reginbogin (eds), *Neutral Beyond the Cold: Neutral States and the Post-Cold War International System* (Lanham: Lexington Books, 2022).

Select Bibliography

Abbenhuis, Maartje, *An Age of Neutrals: Great Power Politics, 1815–1914*. Cambridge: Cambridge University Press, 2014.
Agius, Christine and Karen Devine, 'Neutrality: A Really Dead Concept? A Reprise', *Cooperation and Conflict* 46, no. 3 (2011): 265–84.
Alkan, Resul, 'Die "Türkische Post": Türkiye'de Bir Nazi-Propaganda Gazetesi ve Matbuat Umum Müdürlüğü [The "Türkische Post": A Nazi-Propaganda Newspaper in Turkey and General Directorate of Press]', *SUSBED* 42, no. 1 (2019): 200–8.
Altvater, Elmar et al. (eds), *Erinnern und Ermutigen: Hommage für Theo Pinkus* [*Remembering and Encouraging: A Tribute to Theo Pinkus*], *1909–1991*. Zürich: Rotpunktverlag, 1992.
Amaury, Philippe, *Les Deux Premières Expériences d'un Ministère de l'Information en France* [*The First Two Experiences of a Ministry of Information in France*]. Paris: Librairie Générale de Droit et de Jurisprudence, 1969.
Anabtawi, Samir N., 'Neutralists and Neutralism', *The Journal of Politics* 27, no. 2 (1965): 351–61.
Andisha, Nasir Ahmad, *Neutrality and Vulnerable States: An Analysis of Afghanistan's Permanent Neutrality*. London: Routledge, 2020.
Axelrod, Alan, *Selling the Great War: The Making of American Propaganda*. New York: Palgrave Macmillan, 2009.
Azéma, Jean-Pierre and François Bédarida (eds), *Le Régime de Vichy et les Français* [*The Vichy Regime and the French*]. Paris: Fayard, 1992.
Badsey, Stephen, *The German Corpse Factory: A Study in First World War Propaganda*. Warwick: Helion, 2019.
Bağce, H. Emre, 'Milli Şef Döneminde İktidar-Basın İlişkisi [Power-Press Relations During the National Chief Era]', in *Medya ve Siyaset 2: 1923–1946 Tek Partili Dönem* [*Media and Politics 2: 1923–1946 One-party Rule Era*], edited by Tolga Yazıcı, 87–126. Kocaeli: Volga Yayıncılık, 2016.
Balcells, Albert, *El pistolerisme, Barcelona* [*The Pistolerismo. Barcelona*] *(1917–1923)*, 167–84. Barcelona: Pòrtic, 2009.
Bannister, Christopher, 'Diverging Neutrality in Iberia: The British Ministry of Information in Spain and Portugal During the Second World War', in *Allied Communication to the Public during the Second World War*, edited by Simon Elliot and Marc Wiggam. London: Bloomsbury, 2020.
Barreiro Gordillo, Cristina, 'España y la Gran Guerra a través de la prensa [Spain and the Great War in the Press]', *Aportes* [Contributions] 29, no. 84 (2014): 161–82.
Boghardt, Thomas, *The Zimmermann Telegram: Intelligence, Diplomacy, and America's Entry into World War I*. Annapolis: Naval Institute Press, 2012.
Böhme, Klaus-Richard, *Signal: Nazitysklands propaganda i Sverige* [*'Signal': Nazi Germany's propaganda in Sweden*] *1941–1945*. Stockholm: Bokförlaget DN, 2005.

Bott, Sandra, Jussi M. Hanhimäki, Janick Marina Schaufelbuehl and Marco Wyss (eds), 'Suisse et Guerre froide dans le tiers-monde [Switzerland and the Cold War in the Third World]', *Relations internationales* [*International Relations*], no. 163 (2015), full volume.

Bott, Sandra, Janick Marina Schaufelbuehl and Sacha Zala, 'Die internationale Schweiz in der Zeit des Kalten Krieges [International Switzerland during the Cold War]', *Itinera* 30 (2011), full volume.

Bott, Sandra, Jussi M. Hanhimaki, Janick Schaufelbuehl and Marco Wyss (eds), *Neutrality and Neutralism in the Global Cold War: Between or within the Blocs?*. London: Routledge, 2017.

Brewer, Susan A., *Why America Fights: Patriotism and Propaganda from the Philippines to Iraq*. Oxford: Oxford University Press, 2009.

Briffa, Hillary, 'Neutrality and Shelter Seeking: The Case of Malta', in *Small States and the New Security Environment. The World of Small States*, edited by A. M. Brady and B. Thorhallsson, 135–51. Cham: Springer International Publishing, 2021.

Buclin, Hadrien, 'Swiss Intellectuals and the Cold War. Anti-Communist Policies in a Neutral Country', *Journal of Cold War Studies* 19, no. 4 (2017): 137–67.

Burns, Jimmy, *Papa Spy: Love, Faith and Betrayal in Wartime Spain*. London: Bloomsbury, 2009.

Byrne, Alice, 'The British Council in India, 1945–1955: Preserving "old relationships under new forms"', in *Fins d'empires / Ends of Empires*, edited by Laurent Dornel and Michael Parsons, 119–35. Pau: Presses de l'Universite de Pau et des pays de l'Adour, 2016.

Carswell, Richard, *The Fall of France in the Second World War: History and Memory*. London: Palgrave, 2019.

Cavarocchi, Francesca, *Avanguardie dello spirito. Il fascismo e la propaganda culturale all'estero* [*Vanguards of the spirit: Fascism and cultural propaganda abroad*]. Rome: Carocci, 2010.

Chadwick, Kay, 'Radio Propaganda and Public Opinion under Endgame Vichy: The Impact of Philippe Henriot', *French History* 25, no. 2 (2011): 232–52.

Chalmers Mitchell, Peter, 'Propaganda', in *The Encyclopaedia Britannica 12th Edition*, edited by Hugh Chisholm, 176–85. London: The Encyclopaedia Britannica Company, 1922.

Coldwell Adams, John, *Seated with the Mighty: A Biography of Sir Gilbert Parker*. Ottawa: Borealis Press, 1979.

Cole, Robert, *Britain and the War of Words in Neutral Europe, 1939–1945: The Art of the Possible*. New York: Macmillan, 1990.

Cole, Robert, *Propaganda, Censorship and Irish Neutrality in the Second World War*. Edinburgh: Edinburgh University Press, 2006.

Compagnon, Olivier, 'Entrer en guerre? Neutralité et engagement de l'Amérique latine entre 1914 et 1918 [To go to war? Neutrality and commitment in Latin America between 1914 and 1918]', *Relations Internationales* [*International Relations*] 1, no. 137 (2009): 31–43.

Connelly, Mark, Jo Fox, Stefan Goebel and Ulf Schmidt (eds), *Propaganda and Conflict: War, Media and the Shaping of the Twentieth Century*. London: Bloomsbury, 2019.

Cordoba, Cyril, *China-Swiss Relations during the Cold War, 1949–1989: Between Soft Power and Propaganda*. Abingdon and New York: Routledge, 2022.

Cordoba, Cyril, 'Les maoïstes suisses et l'or de Pékin' au cœur de la Guerre froide [Swiss Maoists and "Beijing Gold" at the heart of the Cold War]', *Monde(s)* [*World(s)*] 19 (2021): 241–55.

Corkill, David and José Carlos Pina Almeida, 'Commemoration and Propaganda in Salazar's Portugal: The Mundo Português Exposition of 1940', *Journal of Contemporary History* 44, no. 3 (2009): 381–99.

Correa Martín Arroyo, Pedro, 'Propaganda Wars in Wartime Spain: Sir Samuel Hoare, the British Embassy, and the British Propaganda Campaign for "Neutral" Spain', MA Dissertation, Leiden University, 2014.

Corse, Edward, *A Battle for Neutral Europe: British Cultural Propaganda during the Second World War*. London: Bloomsbury, 2013.

Corse, Edward, 'British Propaganda in Neutral Eire after the Fall of France, 1940', *Contemporary British History* 22, no. 2 (2008): 163–80.

Corse, Edward, '*Henry V* and the Battle of Powerscourt', in *Shakespeare at War: A Material History*, edited by Sonia Massai and Amy Lidster, 164–73. Cambridge: Cambridge University Press, 2023.

Corse, Edward, '"To accustom Turkish minds to a state of belligerency": The Delicate Balance of British Propaganda in Turkey during the Second World War', *Journal of Balkan and Near Eastern Studies* 23, no. 6 (2021): 896–913.

Cottey, Andrew (ed.), *The European Neutrals and NATO*. London: Palgrave Macmillan, 2018.

Cull, Nicholas J., 'British Cities versus Apartheid: UK Local Authority Activism as City Diplomacy', *Diplomatica* 2, no. 1 (2021): 187–99.

Cull, Nicholas J., *The Cold War and the United States Information Agency: American Propaganda and Public Diplomacy, 1945–1989*. Cambridge: Cambridge University Press, 2008.

Cull, Nicholas J., *Selling War: The British Propaganda Campaign against American 'Neutrality' in World War II*. New York: Oxford University Press, 1995.

Cull, Nicholas J., David Culbert and David Welch (eds), *Propaganda and Mass Persuasion: A Historical Encyclopedia, 1500 to the Present*. Santa Barbara: ABC-CLIO, 2003.

da Costa Leite, Joaquim, 'Neutrality by Agreement: Portugal and the British Alliance in World War II', *American University International Law Review* 14, no. 1 (1998): 185–99.

Delporte, Christian, *Philippe Henriot: la résistible ascension d'un provocateur* [*Philippe Henriot: The Resistible Rise of a Provocateur*]. Paris: Flammarion, 2018.

Demm, Eberhard, *Censorship and Propaganda in World War I: A Comprehensive History*. London: Bloomsbury Academic, 2019.

Deringil, Selim, *Denge Oyunu* [*Balance Game*]. Istanbul: Tarih Vakfı Yurt Yayınları, 2009.

Díaz Plaja, Fernando, *Francófilos y Germanófilos. Los Españoles en la guerra Europea* [*Francofilos and Germanófilos. Spanish Society in the European War*]. Barcelona: Dopesa, 1973.

Doğaner, Yasemin, 'İkinci Dünya Savaşı Yıllarında Türkiye'de Nazi Propagandası (Emniyet Genel Müdürlüğü Raporlarına Göre) [Nazi Propaganda in Turkey during the Second World War (According to the Reports of the General Directorate of Security)]', *Türkiyat Araştırmaları* [*Turkish Studies*], no. 17 (2012): 65–81.

Donaldson, Frances, *The British Council: The First Fifty Years*. London: Jonathan Cape, 1984.

Dordanas, Stratos, *'Argyronitoi'. He Germaneke Propaganda stin Ellada kata ton A Pagkosmio Polemo* [*'Venal'. German Propaganda in Greece during WWI*]. Athens: Alexandreia, 2020.

Drangel, Louise, *Den kämpande demokratin: En studie i antinazistisk opinionsrörelse* [*The Struggling Democracy: A Study in the Anti-Nazi Opinion Movement*] *1933–1945*. Stockholm: Sverige under andra världskriget, 1976.

Dwyer, T. Ryle, *Irish Neutrality and the USA, 1939–47*. Dublin: Gill & Macmillan, 1977.
Dyakonov, Severyan, 'Soviet Cultural Diplomacy in India, 1955–1963', MA dissertation. Concordia University of Montreal, 2015.
Fall, Bernard B., *Anatomy of a Crisis: The Laotian Crisis of 1960–1961*. Garden City: Doubleday, 1969.
Field, Geoffrey, 'Elizabeth Wiskemann, Scholar-Journalist, and the Study of International Relations', in *Women's International Thought: A New History*, edited by Patricia Owens and Katharina Rietzler, 198–220. Cambridge: Cambridge University Press, 2021.
Fields, Marek, 'Balancing between Neutral Country Promotion and Cold War Propaganda: British and American Informational and Cultural Operations in Finland', in *Regime Changes in 20th Century Europe: Reassessed, Anticipated and in the Making*, edited by Marja Vuorinen et al., 200–33. Cambridge: Cambridge Scholars Publishing, 2016.
Fischer, Thomas and Daniel Möckli, 'The Limits of Compensation: Swiss Neutrality Policy in the Cold War', *Journal of Cold War Studies* 18, no. 4 (2016): 12–35.
Fisk, Robert, *In Time of War: Ireland, Ulster and the Price of Neutrality, 1939–1945*. London: Andre Deutsch Ltd, 1983.
Fox, Jo, 'The Propaganda War', in *The Cambridge History of the Second World War, Volume II: Politics and Ideology*, edited by Richard J. B. Bosworth and Joseph A. Maiolo, 91–116. Cambridge: Cambridge University Press, 2015.
Franzolin, João Arthur Ciciliato, '"Die Wehrmacht". Die offizielle illustrierte Propagandazeitschrift der deutschen Wehrmacht für das In- und Ausland ['Die Wehrmacht': The official illustrated propaganda magazine of the German Army for home and abroad] (1936–1944)', doctoral thesis. Europa-Universität Flensburg, 2017.
Fuentes Codera, Maximiliano, *España en la Primera Guerra Mundial: una movilización cultural* [*Spain in the First World War: A Cultural Mobilization*]. Madrid: Akal, 2014.
Fuentes Codera, Maximiliano, *España y Argentina en la Primera Guerra Mundial. Neutralidades transnacionales* [*Spain and Argentina in the First World War. Transnational Neutralities*]. Madrid: Marcial Pons Historia, 2022.
Fulwider, Chad R., *German Propaganda and U.S. Neutrality in World War I*. Missouri: University of Missouri Press, 2017.
García Cabrera, Marta, *Bajo las zarpas del león: La persuasión británica en España durante las guerras mundiales* [*Under the Lion's Paws: British Persuasion in Spain during the World Wars*]. Madrid: Marcial Pons, 2022.
García Cabrera, Marta, 'Filias y fobias en acción: propaganda británica en España durante la Primera y la Segunda Guerra Mundial [Fondness and phobias in action: British propaganda in Spain during the First and the Second World War]', doctoral thesis. University of Las Palmas de Gran Canaria, 2021.
García Sanz, Fernando, *España en la Gran Guerra. Espías, diplomáticos y traficantes* [*Spain and the Great War. Spies, Diplomats and Salesmen*]. Barcelona: Galaxia Gutenberg, 2014.
Garner, Karen, *Friends and Enemies: The Allies and Neutral Ireland in the Second World War*. Manchester: Manchester University Press, 2021.
Garnett, David, *The Secret History of PWE: The Political Warfare Executive 1939–1945*. London: St Ermin's Press, 2002.
Gerolymatos, André, Denis Smyth and James Horncastle (eds), *Neutral Countries as Clandestine Battlegrounds, 1939–1968: Between Two Fires*. Lanham: Lexington Books, 2020.

Gienow-Hecht, Jessica and Mark Donfried (eds), *Searching for Cultural Diplomacy*. New York: Berghahn Books, 2010.

Gilmour, John, *Sweden, the Swastika and Stalin: The Swedish Experience in the Second World War*. Edinburgh: Edinburgh University Press, 2010.

Girvin, Brian, *The Emergency: Neutral Ireland 1939-45*. London: Pan Macmillan, 2007.

Glasneck, Johannes, *Türkiye'de Faşist Alman Propagandası* [*Fascist German Propaganda in Turkey*]. Ankara: Onur Yayınları, n.d.

González Calleja, Eduardo and Paul Aubert, *Nidos de Espías: España, Francia y la Primera Guerra Mundial 1914-1919* [Nest of Spies. Spain, France and the First World War]. Madrid: Alianza Editorial, 2014.

Gordon, Robert S. C., 'An Intellectual at Mauthausen: Aldo Bizzarri between Essay, Fiction (and Cinema)', *Laboratoire italien* 24 (2020).

Gori, Annarita and Rita Almeida de Carvalho, 'Italian Fascism and the Portuguese Estado Novo: International Claims and National Resistance', *Intellectual History Review* 30, no. 2 (2019): 295-319.

Green, Leanne, 'Advertising War: Picturing Belgium in First World War Publicity', *Media, War and Conflict* 7, no. 3 (2014): 309-25.

Greenburg, Melanie C., John H. Barton and Margaret E. McGuinness, *Words over War: Mediation and Arbitration to Prevent Deadly Conflict*. New York: Carnegie Corporation of New York, 2000.

Gregory, Ross, *The Origins of American Intervention in the First World War*. New York: Norton, 1971.

Halsey Ross, Stewart, *Propaganda for War: How the United States was Conditioned to Fight the Great War of 1914-1918*. Joshua Tree: Progressive, 2009.

Hartenian, Larry, *George W. Bush Administration Propaganda for an Invasion of Iraq*. New York: Routledge, 2021.

Harwood, Jeremy, *Hitler's War: World War II as Portrayed by Signal, the International Nazi Propaganda Magazine*. Minneapolis: Zenith Press, 2014.

Herbstein, Denis, *White Lies: Canon Collins and the Secret War against Apartheid*. Oxford: James Currey, 2004.

Herman, Edward S. and Noam Chomsky, *Manufacturing Consent: The Political Economy of Mass Media*. New York: Pantheon Books, 1988.

Horne, John and Alan Kramer, *German Atrocities 1914: A History of Denial*. New York: Yale University Press, 2001.

Hull, Isabel V., *A Scrap of Paper: Breaking and Making International Law during the Great War*. New York: Cornell University Press, 2014.

Ivani, Mario, *Esportare il fascismo. Collaborazione di polizia e diplomazia culturale tra Italia Fascista e Portogallo di Salazar* [*Exporting Fascism: Collaboration of the police and cultural diplomacy between Fascist Italy and Salazar's Portugal] (1928-1945)*]. Bologna: CLUEB, 2008.

Jacobs, Seth, *The Universe Unraveling: American Foreign Policy in Cold War Laos*. Ithaca: Cornell University Press, 2012.

Jeanneret, Pierre, 'Les engagements politiques des années 60 et l'expulsion de Nils Andersson [The Political Commitments of the 1960s and the Expulsion of Nils Andersson]' in *Livre et militantisme* [*Books and activism*], edited by François Valloton, Pierre Jeanneret, Damien Carron and Léonard Burnand, 109-59. Lausanne: D'en bas Editions, 2007.

Jönsson, Mats, *Visuell fostran: Film- och bildverksamheten i Sverige under andra världskriget* [*Visual education: Film and image activities in Sweden during the Second World War*]. Lund: Sekel, 2011.

Jowett, Garth and Victoria O'Donnell, *Propaganda and Persuasion*. Los Angeles: Sage, 2019.

Karagöz Kızılca, Gül, '1942 Yılında Mihver ve Müttefik Devletlerce Düzenlenen Türk Basın Gezileri [Turkish Press Trips Organized by the Axis and Allied Powers in 1942]', *Kebikeç*, no. 14 (2002): 5–27.

Karsh, Efraim, 'Geographical Determinism: Finnish Neutrality Revisited. Cooperation and Conflict', *Cooperation and Conflict* 21, no. 1 (1986): 43–57.

Karsh, Efraim, *Neutrality and Small States*. London: Routledge, 1988, reprinted 2012.

Kılıç, Sezen, *Türk-Alman İlişkileri ve Türkiye'deki Alman Okulları (1852'den 1945'e kadar)* [*Turkish-German Relations and the German Schools in Turkey (From 1852 to 1945)*]. Ankara: Atatürk Araştırma Merkezi, 2005.

Knightley, Philip, *The First Casualty: From the Crimea to Vietnam – The War Correspondent as Hero, Propagandist, and Myth Maker*. London: Harcourt, 1975.

Knüsel, Ariane, *China's European Headquarters. Switzerland and China during the Cold War*. Cambridge: Cambridge University Press, 2022.

Laborie, Pierre, *L'opinion française sous Vichy: les Français et la crise d'identité nationale* [*French Opinion under Vichy: The French and the Crisis of National Identity*] *1936–1944*. Paris: Éditions du Seuil, 2001.

Lackerstein, Debbie, *National Regeneration in Vichy France: Ideas and Policies 1930–1944*. London: Routledge, 2012.

Larsen, Daniel, *Plotting for Peace: American Peacemakers, British Codebreakers, and Britain at War, 1914–1917*. Cambridge: Cambridge University Press, 2021.

Lasswell, Harold D., *Propaganda Technique in the World War*. New York: Alfred Knopf, 1927.

Laurie, Clayton D., *The Propaganda Warriors. America's Crusade Against Nazi Germany*. Lawrence: University Press of Kansas, 1996.

Lemonidou, Elli, 'La Grèce vue de France pendant la Première guerre mondiale; entre censure et propagandes [Greece seen from France during the First World War: between censorship and propaganda]', doctoral thesis. Universite Paris IV, Sorbonne, 2007.

Leon, George B., *Greece and the Great Powers 1914–1917*. Thessaloniki: Institute for Balkan Studies, 1974.

Leontaritis, Georgios B., *He Ellada ston A Pagkosmio Polemo* [*Greece in the First World War 1917–1918*]. Athens: National Bank of Greece Cultural Foundation, 2005.

Lima, Helena and Jorge Pedro Sousa, 'A Ilustração Portuguesa e Cobertura da Primeira Guerra Mundial (1914–1918): Imagens da guerra em contextos de censura e propaganda [The Portuguese Illustration and Coverage of the First World War (1914–1918): images of the war in contexts of censorship and propaganda]', in *A Grande Guerra (1914–1918): Problemáticas e Representações* [*The Great War (1914–1918): Problems and Representations*], edited by Gaspar Martins Pereira, Jorge Fernandes Alves, Luís Alberto Alves and Maria Conceição Meireles, 283–98. Porto: CITCEM, 2015.

Locastre, Aline Vanessa, 'As promessas da revista "Em Guarda" para o Brasil no pós-guerra [The promises of the magazine "Em Guarda" for post-war Brazil] (1941–1945)', *Antíteses* [*Antithesis*] 8, no. 15 (2015): 488–519.

Lopes, Helena F. S., *Neutrality and Collaboration in South China: Macau during the Second World War*. Cambridge: Cambridge University Press, 2023.

Lopes, Helena F. S., 'Questioning Neutrality: Sino-Portuguese Relations during the War and the Post-war Periods, 1937–1949', doctoral thesis. University of Oxford, 2018.

Lopes, Helena F. S., 'Wartime Education at the Crossroads of Empires: The Relocation of Schools to Macao during the Second World War, 1937–1945', *Twentieth-Century China* 46, no. 2 (2021): 130–52.

Lottaz, Pascal, 'Neutral States and Wartime Japan: The Diplomacy of Sweden, Spain, and Switzerland toward the Empire', doctoral thesis. National Graduate Institute for Policy Studies of Tokyo, 2018.

Lottaz, Pascal, Heinz Gaertner and Herbert Reginbogin (eds), *Neutral Beyond the Cold: Neutral States and the Post-Cold War International System*. Lanham: Lexington Books, 2022.

Lottaz, Pascal and Herbert R. Reginbogin, *Notions of Neutralities*. London: Lexington Books, 2018.

Lottaz, Pascal and Ingemar Ottosson, *Sweden, Japan, and the Long Second World War, 1931–1945*. London: Routledge, 2021.

Lüscher, Rudolf M. and Werner Schweizer (eds), *Amalie und Theo Pinkus-De Sassi: Leben im Widerspruch* [*Amalie and Theo Pinkus-De Sassi: Life in contradiction*]. Zürich: Limmat Verlag, 1987.

Lutz, Martin Andreas, 'Britische Propaganda in der Schweiz während des Zweiten Weltkriegs [British propaganda in Switzerland during the Second World War] 1939–1945', doctoral thesis. Luzern University, 2019.

Lyon, Peter, 'Neutrality and Emergence of the Concept of Neutralism', *The Review of Politics* 22, no. 2 (1960): 255–68.

Maxwell Hamilton, John, *Manipulating the Masses: Woodrow Wilson and the Birth of American Propaganda*. Baton Rouge: Louisiana State University Press, 2020.

Meaker, Gerald, 'A Civil War of Words. The Ideological Impact of the First World War on Spain, 1914–1918', in *Neutral Europe between War and Revolution, 1917–1923*, edited by Hans Schmitt, 1–65. Charlottesville: The University Press of Virginia, 1988.

Mišković, Nataša, Harald Fischer-Tiné and Nada Boškovska (eds), *The Non-Aligned Movement and the Cold War: Delhi-Bandung-Belgrade*. London: Routledge, 2014.

Müller, Leos, *Neutrality in World History*. New York and London: Routledge, 2019.

Neiberg, Michael S., *The Path to War: How the First World War Created Modern America*. Oxford: Oxford University Press, 2016.

Niyazioğlu, M. Sinan, *İroni ve Gerilim: İkinci Dünya Savaşı Yıllarında İstanbul'da ve Ankara'da Savaş Algısı* [*Irony and tension: Perception of War in İstanbul and Ankara During the Second World War Years*]. Ankara: Koç University VEKAM, 2016.

Norén, Fredrik, Emil Stjernholm and C. Claire Thomson (eds). *Nordic Media Histories of Propaganda and Persuasion*. Basingstoke: Palgrave, 2022.

Novais, Noémia Malva, *Imprensa e I Guerra Mundial: Censura e Propaganda* [*Press and World War I: Censorship and Propaganda*] *1914–1918*. Lisboa: Caleidoscópio, 2016.

Ohlberg, Mareike Svea, 'Creating a Favorable International Public Opinion Environment: External Propaganda (Duiwai Xunachuan) as a Global Concept with Chinese Characteristics', PhD dissertation. Heidelberg University, 2013.

Olson, Lynne, *Those Angry Days: Roosevelt, Lindbergh, and America's Fight Over World War II, 1939–1941*. New York: Random House, 2013.

Olsson, Jan, *Svensk spelfilm under andra världskriget* [*Swedish feature films during the Second World War*]. Lund: Liber läromedel, 1979.

Oppenheim, Lassa F. L., *International Law: A Treatise—War and Neutrality*, vol. II. London: Longmans, Green, 1912.

Paddock, Troy (ed.), *Propaganda and the First World War*. Leiden: Brill, 2014.

Papadimitiou, Despina, 'O Typos ke o Dichasmos 1914-1917 [The Press and the National Schism 1914-1917]', doctoral thesis. National and Kapodistrian University of Athens, 1990.
Parker, Sir Gilbert, 'The United States and the War', *Harper's Monthly Magazine* CXXXVI, no. 814 (March 1918): 521-31.
Paz Rebollo, María Antonia, 'La propaganda francesa en España 1940-1944 [French propaganda in Spain 1940-1944]', *Mélanges de la Casa de Velázquez* XXXI, no. 3 (1995): 219-47.
Peñalba-Sotorrío, Mercedes, 'Beyond the War: Nazi Propaganda Aims in Spain during the Second World War', *Journal of Contemporary History* 54, no. 4 (2019): 902-26.
Peterson, H. C., *Propaganda for War: The Campaign against American Neutrality, 1914-1917*. Norman: University of Oklahoma Press, 1939.
Pich Mitjana, Josep and David Martínez Fiol, 'Manuel Brabo Portillo. Policía, espía y pistolero [Manuel Brabo Portillo. Policemen, Spy and Gunman] (1876-1919)', *Vínculos de Historia [Historical Links]* 8 (2019): 387-408.
Pires, Ana Paula, 'The Iberian Peninsula and the First World War: Between neutrality and non-belligerency (1914-1916)', *War in History* 28, no. 3 (2021): 544-61.
Pires, Ana Paula, 'Portugal, África e a Grande Guerra: entre a neutralidade e a não beligerância [Portugal, Africa and the Great War: between neutrality and non-belligerence] (1914-1916)', *Storicamente.Org - Laboratorio di Historia* 12 (2016): 1-24.
Pizarroso Quintero, Alejandro, *Diplomáticos, propagandistas y espías: Estados Unidos y España en la Segunda Guerra Mundial: información y propaganda* [*Diplomats, Propagandists, and Spies: The United States and Spain in the Second World War: Information and Propaganda*]. Madrid: CSIC Press, 2009.
Ponce Marrero, Javier, 'La neutralidad española durante la Primera Guerra Mundial: nuevas perspectivas [The neutrality of Spain during the First World War: New perspectives]', in *Ayeres en discusión: temas clave de Historia Contemporánea hoy* [*Yesterdays in Discussion: Key Issues in Contemporary History Today*], edited by María Encarna Nicolás Marín and Carmen González Martínez, 159-70. Murcia: Servicio de Publicaciones de la Universidad de Murcia, 2008.
Ponsonby, Arthur, *Falsehood in War-Time: Containing an Assortment of Lies Circulated Throughout the Nations During the Great War*. London: George Allen and Unwin, 1928.
Quinn Olmstead, Justin, *The United States' Entry Into the First World War: The Role of British and German Diplomacy*. Woodbridge: Boydell, 2018.
Read, J. M., *Atrocity Propaganda 1914-1919*. New Haven: Yale University Press.
Rees, Mervyn and Chris Day, *Muldergate: The Story of the Info Scandal*. Johannesburg: Macmillan, 1980.
Rinke, Stefan, *Latin America and the First World War*. Cambridge: Cambridge University Press, 2017.
Rizas, Sotiris, *Venizelismos ke antivenizelismos* [*Venizelism and Anti-Venizelism*]. Athens: Psychogios, 2019.
Rodrigues da Silva, Júlio Joaquim, 'A Ilustração Portuguesa [The Portuguese Illustration]', in *Portugal na 1.ª Guerra Mundial* [*Portugal in the First World War*], edited by Abílio Pires Lousada and Jorge Silva Rocha, 697-710. Lisboa: Comissão Portuguesa de História Militar, 2018.
Roholl, Marja, 'Preparing for Victory. The U.S. Office of War Information Overseas Branch's Illustrated Magazines in the Netherlands and the Foundations for the American Century, 1944-1945', *European Journal of American studies* 7, no. 2 (2012).

Rola da Silva, Henrique, *A Imprensa Chinesa de Macau* [Macau's Chinese Press]. Macau: Gabinete de Comunicação Social do Governo de Macau, 1991.

Rollo, María Fernanda, Ana Paula Pires and Noémia Malva Novais (eds), *War and Propaganda in the XXth Century*. Lisboa: Universidad Nova de Lisboa, 2013.

Romero Salvadó, Francisco, *Spain 1914–1918. Between War and Revolution*. London and New York: Routledge, 1999.

Rossignol, Dominique, *Histoire de la Propagande en France de 1940 à 1944: l'utopie Pétain* [*The History of Propaganda in France from 1940 to 1944: The Pétain utopia*]. Paris: Presses Universitaires de France, 1991.

Rust, William J., *Before the Quagmire: American Intervention in Laos, 1954–1961*. Lexington: University of Kentucky Press, 2021.

Rutz, Rainer, *Signal. Eine deutsche Auslandsillustrierte als Propagandainstrument im Zweiten Weltkrieg* [*'Signal': A German foreign-magazine as a propaganda tool in the Second World War*]. Essen: Klartext Verlag, 2007.

Sanders, Michael, 'Official British Propaganda in Allied and Neutral Countries during the First World War, with Particular Reference to Organization and METHODS', doctoral thesis. London School of Economics and Political Science, 1972.

Sanders, Michael and Philip M. Taylor, *British Propaganda during the First World War, 1914–1918*. London: Macmillan, 1982.

Santoro, Stefano, *L'Italia e l'Europa orientale. Diplomazia culturale e propaganda* [*Italy and Eastern Europe: Cultural Diplomacy and Propaganda*] *1918–1943*. Milan: Franco Angeli, 2005.

Schlomann, Friedrich-Wilhelm and Paulette Friedlingstein, *Die Maoisten. Pekings Filialen in Westeuropa* [*The Maoists: Beijing's branches in Western Europe*]. Frankfurt am Main: Societäts-Verlag, 1970.

Schulze Schneider, Ingrid, 'La propaganda alemana en España [German propaganda in Spain] 1942–1944', *Espacio, Tiempo y Forma. Serie V, Historia Contemporánea* [*Space, Time and Form. Series V, Contemporary History*], no. 7 (1994): 371–86.

Seydi, Süleyman, *1939–1945 Zor Yıllar! 2.Dünya Savaşı'nda Türkiye'de İngiliz-Alman Propaganda ve İstihbarat Savaşı* [*1939–1945 Difficult Years! The British and German Propaganda and Intelligence War in Turkey during the Second World War*]. Ankara: Asil Yayın, 2006.

Sidwell, Sophie, 'A New Interpretation of Kongle's Neutralist Coup in Laos, August 1960', *Sojourn: Journal of Social Issues in Southeast Asia* 35, no. 1 (2020): 1–30.

Smyth, Denis, *Diplomacy and Strategy of Survival: British Policy and Franco's Spain, 1940–41*. Cambridge: Cambridge University Press, 1986.

Southgate, Laura, 'ASEAN: Still the Zone of Peace, Freedom and Neutrality?', *Political Science* 73, no. 1 (2021): 31–47.

Squires, James Duane, *British Propaganda at Home and in the United States from 1914 to 1917*. Cambridge, MA: Harvard University Press, 1935.

Stjernholm, Emil, 'German Surveillance of the Swedish Film Market during World War II', *Journal of Scandinavian Cinema* 9, no. 2 (2019): 349–64.

Stjernholm, Emil, *Gösta Werner och filmen som konst och propaganda* [*Gösta Werner and Film as Art and Propaganda*]. Lund: Mediehistoriskt arkiv, 2018.

Stuart, Campbell, *Secrets of Crewe House: The Story of a Famous Campaign*. London: Hodder & Stoughton, 1920.

Svensson, Isak, 'Who Brings Which Peace?: Neutral versus Biased Mediation and Institutional Peace Arrangements in Civil Wars', *Journal of Conflict Resolution* 53, no. 3 (2009): 446–69.

Tato, María Inés, 'Fighting for a Lost Cause? The Germanophile Newspaper *La Unión* in Neutral Argentina, 1914–1918', *War in History* 25, no. 4 (2018): 464–84.

Tato, María Inés, 'La cuestión Malvinas y las batallas por la neutralidad argentina durante la Gran Guerra [The Malvinas question and the battles for Argentine neutrality during the Great War]', in *La cuestión Malvinas en la Argentina del siglo XX. Una historia social y cultural [The Malvinas question in Argentina in the 20th century. A social and cultural history]*, edited by María Inés Tato and Luis Esteban Dalla Fontana, 17–38. Rosario: Prohistoria Ediciones, 2020.

Tato, María Inés, *La trinchera austral. La sociedad argentina ante la Primera Guerra Mundial [The Southern Trench. Argentine Society before the First World War]*. Rosario: Prohistoria Ediciones, 2017.

Tato, María Inés, 'Propaganda de guerra para el Nuevo Mundo. El caso de la revista *América-Latina* [War propaganda for the New World: the case of the América-Latina magazine] (1915–1918)', *Revista Historia y Comunicación Social [Journal of History and Social Communication]* 18 (2013): 63–74.

Taylor, James Lee, 'Shakespeare, Decolonisation, and the Cold War', doctoral thesis. The Open University, 2018.

Taylor, Philip M., *Munitions of the Mind: A History of Propaganda from the Ancient World to the Present Day*. Manchester: Manchester University Press, 2003.

Taylor, Philip M., *The Projection of Britain: British Overseas Publicity and Propaganda, 1919–1939*. Cambridge: Cambridge University Press, 1981.

Telo, António José, *Portugal na Segunda Guerra [Portugal in the Second World War] 1941–1945*, 2 vols. Lisbon: Vega, 1991.

Telo, António José, *Propaganda e Guerra Secreta Em Portugal [Propaganda and Secret War in Portugal] 1939–45*. Lisboa: Perspectivas e realidades, 1990.

Thulstrup, Åke, *Med lock och pock: Tyska försök att påverka svensk opinion [By Allurements and Force: German Attempts to Influence Swedish Opinion] 1933–45*. Stockholm: Bonnier, 1962.

Türk, Fahri and Servet Çınar, 'Türkiye ile Almanya Arasındaki Bilimsel İlişkiler: Türk-Alman Üniversiteleri [Scientific Relations Between Turkey and Germany: Turkish-German Universities]', *Gazi Akademik Bakış [Veteran Academic Perspective]* 7, no. 13 (2013): 45–65.

Vande Winkel, Roel, Mats Jönsson, Lars-Martin Sørensen and Bjørn Sørenssen, 'German Film Distribution in Scandinavia during World War II', *Journal of Scandinavian Cinema* 2, no. 3 (2012): 263–80.

Vaz, Nuno Mira, 'Opiniões Públicas [Public Opinions]' in *Portugal na 1.ª Guerra Mundial. Uma História Militar Concisa [Portugal in the First World War. A Brief Military History]*, edited by Jorge Silva Rocha. Lisboa: Comissão Portuguesa de História Militar, 2018.

Viereck, George Sylvester, *Spreading Germs of Hate*. London: Duckworth, 1931.

Viñas, Ángel, *Sobornos: De cómo Churchill y March compraron a los generales de Franco [Bribery: How Churchill and March bought Franco's Generals]*. Barcelona: Crítica, 2016.

Weinmann, Ricardo, *Argentina en la Primera Guerra Mundial: Neutralidad, transición política y continuismo económico [Argentina in the First World War: Neutrality, political transition and economic continuity]*. Buenos Aires: Biblos, 1994.

Welch, David, *Germany and Propaganda in World War I: Pacifism, Mobilization and Total War*. London: I.B. Tauris, 2014.

Welch, David, 'Powers of Persuasion', *History Today* 49, no. 8 (1999): 24–6.

Welch, David, *Propaganda: Power and Persuasion*. London: British Library, 2013.

Welch, David (ed.), *Propaganda, Power and Persuasion: From World War I to Wikileaks*. London: IB Tauris, 2013.

Welch, David, *World War II Propaganda: Analysing the Art of Persuasion during Wartime*. Santa Barbara: ABC-CLIO, 2017.

Westlake, Steve, 'Building the BBC-branded NGO: Overseas Development, the World Service, and the Marshall Plan of the Mind, c.1965–99', *Twentieth Century British History* 33, no. 1 (2022): 29–51.

Whelan, Bernadette, 'Biography of David Gray', in *A Yankee in De Valera's Ireland: The Memoir of David Gray*, edited by Paul Bew. Dublin: Royal Irish Academy, 2012.

Wills, Clair, *That Neutral Island: A Cultural History of Ireland during the Second World War*. London: Faber and Faber Ltd, 2007.

Wilson, Robert R., '"Non-Belligerency" in Relation to the Terminology of Neutrality', *American Journal of International Law* 35, no. 1 (1941): 121–3.

Winkler, Allan M., *The Politics of Propaganda. The Office of War Information 1942–1945*. New Haven: Yale University Press, 1978.

Wiskemann, Elizabeth, *The Europe I Saw*. New York: St. Martin's Press, 1968.

Wolfson-Ford, Ryan, 'Ideology in the Royal Lao Government-Era (1945–1975): A Thematic Approach', MA Dissertation. University of Wisconsin, 2018.

Wylie, Neville, *Britain, Switzerland, and the Second World War*. Oxford: Oxford University Press, 2003.

Wylie, Neville (ed.), *European Neutrals and Non-Belligerents during the Second World War*. Cambridge: Cambridge University Press, 2001.

Young, Robert, *Marketing Marianne: French Propaganda in America 1900–1940*. New Brunswick: Rutgers, 2004.

Zuckerman, Larry, *The Rape of Belgium: The Untold Story of World War I*. New York: New York University Press, 2004.

Index

Abyssinian war (1935–1936) 145
Accra, Ghana 256
Adams, Walter 108, 111
Adana Conference (1943) 134
Afghanistan 264
Africa 11, 14, 15, 63–4, 66–7, 71–2, 93, 98, 117, 120, 122, 126, 162–3, 177, 181, 199, 202, 214, 215, 229, 231–3, 252, 267, 268
African National Congress (ANC) 250–1, 254–6, 258–9
Aiken, Frank 92, 94, 96–8
Albania 133, 229, 232–4
Alexander, King of Greece 51
Alexandria, Egypt 120
Algeria 120, 232
Alliance Française 217
Allies (often referred to as The Allies, Western Allies, the Entente)
 and Argentina (First World War) 35–8, 40–1, 44
 and atrocity propaganda 25, 40, 94
 and Belgium (First World War) 4
 and Greece (First World War) 10, 48–57
 and Ireland (Second World War) 91, 94
 and Italy (Second World War) 7, 149, 151
 and magazines 196
 and naval blockades and war at sea 23, 64, 67, 71
 and Portugal (First World War) 63, 67, 71
 and Portugal (Second World War) xv, 152, 188
 and Spain (First World War) 75, 76, 78, 81
 and Spain (Second World War) 157–9, 161
 and Sweden (Second World War) 13, 170, 174, 177
 and Syria (Second World War) 117, 122
 and Turkey (Second World War) 13, 133–4
 and United States (First World War) 23, 25, 28, 36–7
 and United States (Second World War) 91
 and Vichy France (Second World War) 117, 118, 122, 126
 and Yugoslavia (Second World War) 107–8
Almafuerte (Pedro Bonifacio Palacios) 41
Almandos Almonacid, Vicente 38
Almeida, António José de 66
Alsace-Lorraine, France 116, 242
American Friends of Irish Neutrality (AFIN) 96
Andersson, Nils 6, 232–3
Andrade, Freire de 63
Anglo-Portuguese alliance xv, 11, 62–4, 144–5
Angola 63–4, 66, 69
Ankara, Turkey 134, 135, 137, 138, 140
anti-Semitism. See racism
Apartheid (and anti-Apartheid) 8, 14–15, 232, 250–60
Arab-Israeli conflict 215, 258
Arab League 215
Argentina 6, 9, 35–44, 146
Armengol, Bernardo 82
armistices 116–17, 120, 122–4, 127, 151–2
Asia 13, 14, 93, 181–3, 185–7, 190–1, 196, 199, 214–15, 230, 232, 240, 247, 267–9
Asian Relations Conference 214
Association of Southeast Asian Nations (ASEAN) 268
Astor, David 251
Atatürk, Mustafa Kemal 132, 138

Index

Athens, Greece   50, 52, 55–6
Atlantic Charter   96, 197
Audéoud, Roland   229
Auslands-Organization (Nazi Party)   135–6
Australia   172, 268
Austria   14, 105, 107, 136, 138, 269, 270
Austria-Hungary   23, 30, 35, 53–5
Azores, Portugal   xv, 187–8

Badoglio, Pietro   151–2
Baker White, John   109
Balearic Islands, Spain   157, 163
Balfour, Michael   106–9
Bali, Indonesia   240
Balkans   48–50, 110, 133, 148
Banda Negra (Black Gang)   81–3
Bandung Conference, Indonesia (1955)   214–15, 227
Barbosa, Artur Tamagnini de   184
Barcelona, Spain   6, 8, 75–84, 161, 163, 165
Barman, Thomas   106
Barnard, Christiaan   254
Barret, Josep Albert   79–81, 83–4
Barroetaveña, Francisco   6, 39–40
Bartlett, Vernon   104
Basque Country, Spain   75, 77–8, 82
Beaverbrook, Max (Lord)   26
Beijing, People's Republic of China   14, 215, 227–34, 268
Belarus   267
Belgium   xvi, 4, 9–10, 29, 38, 40, 43, 116, 149, 166. *See also* Low Countries
Belgrade, Serbia (formerly within Yugoslavia)   218–19
   Summit (1961)   214–15
Bella, Ahmed Ben   232
Bellés Moliner, Guillermo   80–1
Beltrame, Alfredo Luis   42
Benoliel, Joshua   67, 71
Berlin, Germany   24, 63, 64, 69, 71, 80, 82, 97, 103, 104, 107, 109, 138, 139, 149, 195, 215, 228
Berne, Switzerland   14, 103, 105–7, 110–12, 227–34, 269
Bethmann Hollweg, Theobald von   xvi
Betjeman, John   xvi
Bickel, Karl A.   199

Biden, Joe   264
Bilbao, Spain   163
Bizzarri, Aldo   146–9
Björkman, Oscar   176
Bong Souvannavong   239–47
books, bookstores and libraries   5, 9, 28–30, 38–40, 42, 43, 62, 137–9, 146, 150, 171, 190, 200, 217–18, 222, 227–30, 232–3, 241, 252
Bosnia and Herzegovina   267, 271
Botha, P. W.   255
Bouhired, Djamila   232
boycotts   251, 253, 255, 257, 259–60
Bracken, Brendan   111
Bravo Portillo, Manuel   79–83
Brell, Walter   136, 140
Brennan, Robert   96
Brioni Summit (1956)   215–16
Britain (Great Britain/United Kingdom (UK))
   and Argentina (First World War)   35, 37–42, 44
   and Belgium (First World War)   10
   cultural propaganda of   xv, 7, 14, 145, 146, 171, 213–23
   and decolonization   3
   and Egypt   214, 215, 217, 220, 222
   and films   169–77
   before First World War   3
   and Greece (First World War)   48–57
   and India   213–15, 217–18, 220–2
   and Iraq   264
   and Ireland (Second World War)   4, 91–9
   and Macau (Second World War)   13, 181–6, 188
   and magazines   196–8, 200–2
   and the Non-Aligned Movement   13, 213–23
   and Portugal (First World War)   11, 62–5, 67, 69, 71
   and Portugal (Second World War)   144–6, 152
   and South Africa   8, 15, 250–60
   and Spain (Second World War)   157–66
   subversive propaganda of   xv, 5, 103–12
   and Sweden (Second World War)   13, 169–77

and Switzerland (Second World War)   103–12
and Turkey (Second World War)   133–5, 139, 200
and the United States (First World War)   6, 24–31
and the United States (Second World War)   4, 91–9
and Vichy France (Second World War)   116, 117, 120, 122–4, 126–7
and Yugoslavia   214, 215, 217–20
British Archaeological School (Greece)   50
British Broadcasting Corporation (BBC)   3, 106, 108–9, 117, 126, 161, 171, 177
British Colony Committee (Sweden)   169, 175
British Council (including individual institutes)   xv, 7, 14, 145–6, 171, 174, 213–15, 217–23
British Patriotic Committee (Argentina)   39
British Society (association)   39–40
Britten, Benjamin   219–22
Brogan, Denis   128
Brooks, Dallas   109
Brubeck, Dave   217
Bruce Lockhart, R. H.   106, 109–11
Brüning, Heinrich   104
Buckhardt, Carl   107
Budapest, Hungary   148, 215
Buddhism. *See* religion
Buenos Aires, Argentina   6, 38–40, 64
Bulgaria   48–50, 54, 103
Bulliard, Gérard   233–4
Bundespolizei (BUPO, Swiss Federal Police)   228–35
Burns, Thomas Ferrier   161
Burrows, Ronald   50
Bush, George W.   264, 266

Cairo, Egypt   215, 217, 220
   Conference (1943)   134
Calder, Peter Ritchie   109
Cameroun   122
Canada   11–12, 27, 117, 242
Canary Islands, Spain   157, 159, 162

Cape Town, South Africa   254
capitalism   14, 28, 37, 127, 227, 228, 241, 243, 245
Carbonell, Ramón   81
Caribbean   120, 122
Carnegie, Lancelot   64
Carrico, Néstor   40
cartoons   12, 69, 76–7, 139
Casablanca Conference (1943)   134
Casadevall, Jaume   80
Casson, Lewis   220, 222
Catalonia, Spain   8, 11, 75–83
Catholicism. *See* religion
censorship and other restrictions   xv, 4–5, 7, 11, 24, 25, 27, 30, 37, 65–6, 69, 71, 94, 97, 99, 118, 120, 126, 139, 144–5, 161, 165, 169–77, 184–5, 187–8, 190, 254, 265, 271
Chagas, João   62
Chalmers Mitchell, Peter   24, 29
Chamberlain, Neville   120
Chatham House. *See* Royal Institute of International Affairs
Chiang Kai-shek   182–3, 187, 190
Child, Clifton   110
Chile   43, 146, 229
China (including People's Republic of China (PRC))   6, 7, 13, 181–90, 196, 217, 227–34, 242, 246, 267–9, 271
Chomsky, Noam   270–1
Churchill, Winston   xv, 91, 93–6, 98, 122, 134, 213
Ciano, Galeazzo   147
Cicco, Attilio de   148
cinema and films (including TV)   2, 5, 13, 38, 55–7, 118, 120, 161, 165, 169–77, 198, 199, 217, 219, 230, 254–5, 263
civil rights   14, 253
Cold War   3–8, 14–15, 213–23, 227–35, 239–47, 252, 258, 264, 268, 270
Colombo Plan   217
Commonwealth   253, 257
communism (sometimes referred to as bolshevism) and anti-communism   4, 11, 14, 107, 108, 118, 124–7, 139, 147, 149, 157, 159, 175, 182–3, 190, 201,

215–18, 220, 222, 227–9, 231–2, 234–5, 239–47, 252, 258, 268
Red Peril or Red Scare 252, 258
Confederación Nacional del Trabajo (Spain) (CNT) 79, 82–3
Congo (formerly Belgian) 229
connected history 196, 206
Constantine, King of Greece 48–51
Copland, Aaron 217
Cordier, Daniel 128
Costa, Alfonso 66, 69
Costa Rica 229
Covid-19 263, 265
Cowan, Denys 160
Creel Committee 30
Creyssel, Paul 118
Crossman, Richard 109
cultural propaganda (also referred to as cultural diplomacy) xiv–xvi, 2, 5, 7, 13, 14, 25, 37, 43–4, 53, 135, 144–53, 165, 166, 171, 177, 213–14, 216–23
Cysne 6, 62, 67–9, 71
Czechoslovakia 104, 106, 217

Dachau 104
D'Agata, Charlie 264
Dai Viet empire 241
Dakar, Senegal 121–2
Dali Lama 246
Dalton, Hugh 104
Dammers, Jerry 256
Dansey, Claude 106
Danzig (previously Germany, now Gdańsk, Poland) 104
Dar es Salaam, Tanzania 233
Darlan, François 123, 128
Dato, Eduardo 75–6
Davis, Elmer 198–9
decolonization. *See* imperialism (including anti-imperialism)
Delmer, Sefton 110
Demartial, Georges 25
democracy (and anti-democracy) 11, 12, 31, 37, 65, 92, 94, 95, 118, 126, 147, 157, 159, 175, 196, 197, 206, 229, 231, 241–3, 246, 257, 258, 268, 270
Deutsche Nachrichtenbüro (DNB) 136, 138

Deutungshoheit (concept of sovereignty over interpretation) 263–6, 270–1
Diamantopoulos, George 54–5
digital propaganda (social media) xvi, 2, 264, 265
Dillon, James 96
diplomacy and propaganda xvi, 1, 2, 4–6, 9, 12–14, 24, 36, 39, 42, 50, 54–6, 62, 63, 71, 91–2, 97, 104, 106, 111, 112, 137, 145–8, 151, 153, 157–62, 165, 166, 170, 177, 185, 200, 217, 230–1, 233–4, 255, 270, 271
disinformation and fake news xv, 83, 112, 184, 265
Disinformation Governance Board 265
Dodecanese Islands, Greece (formerly within Italy) 133
Dolchstosslegende (German 'stab-in-the-back myth') 23–4, 30
Donbas, Ukraine 264–5
Dorchy, Paul 161
Douro 6, 62, 67, 69–71
Drogheda, Earl of (Henry Charles Ponsonby Moore) 213–14
Dublin, Ireland 91–2, 94–8
Du Bois, W. E. B. 252
Dulles, Allen 108
Dunkirk, Battle of (1940) 202

education (including schools and student exchanges) 133–8, 146–7, 150–1, 183–4, 190, 214, 216–18, 220–2, 231, 243, 246, 253
Egypt 14, 120, 135, 214–17, 220, 222
Electra House (EH) 103, 105
Eliers, Wilhelm 135
Eliot, T. S. 171
Elizabeth II, Queen of United Kingdom 253, 257
empires
    British 3, 14, 42, 92–3, 182, 213–14, 253
    French 7, 14, 116, 118, 120–3, 126, 127
    German 42, 48, 52, 54
    Italian 146

Japanese   182, 196
Ottoman   53–4, 132
Portuguese   62–4, 66, 71–2, 182
Spanish   80
English language   185–7, 196, 199, 214, 218, 220, 222, 232, 255
Eritrea   267
espionage and other clandestine activities   xiv, 5, 13, 42, 54, 76, 78, 80–3, 97, 98, 103, 106, 110, 136, 140, 144, 158–61, 163, 169–70, 173, 174, 176, 200, 230, 266
European Union (EU)   264, 268–9
exhibitions   38, 56, 146, 171, 183, 189, 218, 231
Ezratty, Isaac   81

Facebook   265
Falange   163–4
Falke, Friedrich   137
Falklands/Malvinas Islands   42
falsehood as propaganda   2, 26, 29, 52, 97, 164, 184, 231, 234, 263, 265
Fascist National Party   146–7
Fay, Sidney Bradshaw   30–1
Federación Patronal (Spain)   81–3
Federzoni, Luigi   148
Felici, Luigi   150
Ferreira do Amaral, João Maria   189
Filmo (Sweden)   173
Finland   4, 14–15, 176, 267–9
flags as a form of propaganda   138, 176, 264
Foeyer, Herman   137
Foreign Information Service   198
France
    and Alliance Française   217
    and Argentina (First World War)   37–40, 43–4
    and China   181, 232–3
    decolonization   3, 14, 223, 239–41
    and Egypt   215
    fall of (1940)   116–17, 144–5, 159–60
    and the First World War   24, 25, 29, 31, 35
    Free French   111, 117–18, 122, 126
    and Greece (First World War)   48–51, 53, 55, 56
    and India   214
    and Italy (Second World War)   149
    and Laos   239–42
    and magazines   196, 198
    and Operation Overlord   98, 127
    and Portugal (First World War)   64–5, 67, 69
    and Portugal (Second World War)   144–6
    and Spain (First World War)   75–8, 81–3
    and Spain (Second World War)   159, 162
    study of propaganda in   24
    and Turkey (Second World War)   133–4, 136, 139
    and the United States (First World War)   25
    Vichy France   7–8, 12–13, 103, 105, 107–9, 111, 116–28, 185
Franco, Francisco   7, 13, 144, 149, 157–60, 162–3, 165–6
Freeman, Chas   270–1
FRELIMO (Liberation Front of Mozambique)   234
French-Argentine Committee   38
French Equatorial Africa   120, 122

Galicia, Spain   78
Gallagher, Frank   97
Gandhi, Mahatma   259–60
Gao Jianfu   183
Garcez, Arnaldo   71
Garnett, David   104, 108, 112
Gärtner, Heinz   270
Gaulle, Charles de   117–18, 127
Gaunt, Guy   27
Gautier, Raymond   107
gender   54, 91–4, 111, 112
Geneva, Switzerland   107, 229–30
    Agreement (1962)   240, 241, 246
    Conference on Indochina (1954)   227
Gennadius, Joannes   50
Gentile, Giovanni   152
Georgia   270–1
Gerchunoff, Alberto   39
Germany
    and Argentina (First World War)   9, 35–44

and Belgium (First World War)   xvi,
    9, 29
Elizabeth Wiskemann in and
    connections to   104, 107
and France (Second World War)   12–
    13, 116–18, 120, 122–4, 126–8
and Greece (First World War)   48–56
and Ireland (Second World War)   93–8
and Italy (Second World War)   7, 151
and Macau   186
and magazines   195–206
and Portugal (First World War)   11,
    63, 64, 66, 67, 69, 71
and Portugal (Second World War)   xv,
    144–5, 149, 152
and South Africa   252
and Spain (First World War)   75–6,
    79–84
and Spain (Second World War)   13,
    157–66
and Sweden (Second World
    War)   169–70, 172, 174–6
and Switzerland (Second World
    War)   103, 105, 106, 108–10
and Turkey (Second World
    War)   133–40
and Ukraine   266, 269
and the United States (First World
    War)   4, 25, 28, 30–1
West Germany   217
Gestapo   83, 104, 108, 163
Ghana   229, 256
Gibraltar   63, 120, 157, 159, 161
Gillan, Angus   220
Gillie, Darsie   104
Gillies, Harold   219
Goa, India (formerly Portuguese)   214
Goebbels, Joseph   104, 109, 198
Goethe-Institut   217
Goltz, Colmar Freiherr von der   137
Google   265
Goossens, Léon   219
Gore, Arthur 'Boofy' (Lord Arran)   111
Gorgulho, Carlos   184–5
Gothenburg, Sweden   169
Graupera, Félix   81–3
Gray, David   6, 91–2, 94–8
Great Britain. *See* Britain (Great Britain/
    United Kingdom (UK))

Greece   2, 6, 8–10, 48–57, 133
Greene, Hugh Carleton   104
Grosse Plan (Great Plan)   160, 165
Gual Villalbí, Pedro   77
Guangzhou, China   184
Guevara, Ernesto 'Che'   232
Guoji Shudian (International
    Bookshop)   228–9, 231–3

Haas, Edouard   230
Hague Convention and conferences   xiv,
    3, 267
Hain, Peter   253
Halifax, Edward (Lord)   170
Hall, Reginald 'Blinker'   27
Hanfstaengl, Ernst   104
Hanoi, Vietnam (formerly North
    Vietnam)   240, 241
Hansen, Klaus   69
Hardinge, Arthur Henry   63
Helsingborg, Sweden   175
Henriot, Philippe   118, 126–7
Hetzer, Walther   137
Heuvel, Vanden   106
Hill, Charles   222
Himmler, Heinrich   109
Hindi   214, 220–1
Hinks, Roger   174
Hintze, Otto   42
Hitler, Adolf   104, 105, 107–9, 116, 118,
    122–4, 128, 136, 138, 145, 149,
    160, 175, 252
Hoare, Samuel   160
Hollywood   172
Homet, Juan B.   42
Hong Kong, China (formerly
    British Empire)   182, 184–7,
    190
Honnermann, Albert   81
Houser, George   251, 253
Huddleston, Trevor   251
Hughes, Bob   253
Hungary   103, 148. *See also* Austria-
    Hungary
Hussein, Saddam   264

Iberian Peninsula   7, 10–11, 77, 144,
    149, 158, 160, 196, 200. *See also*
    Portugal; Spain

imperialism (including anti-imperialism)   3, 7, 9, 13, 14, 30, 40–4, 63, 66, 75, 92, 95, 120–3, 149, 163, 181–91, 214–16, 220, 227, 230, 251–2, 257–8, 260. *See also* empires
India   5, 14–15, 120, 213–14, 216–18, 220–2, 246, 252, 255, 256, 267–9
Indo-China   120, 122, 227, 241
Indonesia   214
Indo-Soviet Cultural Society   217
İnönü, İsmet   132, 134, 140
intelligence   12, 13, 27, 36, 50, 52–7, 81, 83, 92, 93, 97, 103–12, 133, 135–40, 144, 152, 159, 162, 163, 170, 184, 185, 228, 230, 232–5
International Committee of the Red Cross   3, 107
International news agencies   37–8, 44, 118, 136, 138, 187–8, 234
Ioannina (Epirus), Greece   55
Iran   134
Iraq   124, 137, 264, 266
 Iraq Inquiry (Chilcot Inquiry)   264
Ireland (sometimes Eire, usually referring to the southern countries not constituting the Republic of Ireland, but sometimes the whole island)   xiv, xvi, 1, 4, 6, 7, 11, 12, 15, 91–9, 219, 269, 270
 Northern Ireland   93, 96–9
 partition of   93–4, 98–9
Irish Republican Army (IRA)   93, 95, 97
Israel   215, 234, 258
Istanbul, Turkey   105, 135–9
Italian Institute of Culture (the Istituto Italiano di Cultura)   145–53
Italian Social Republic (the Repubblica Sociale Italiana, RSI)   151–2
Italy   5, 7, 51, 55, 81, 98, 103, 106, 107, 110, 116, 122, 133, 135, 136, 138, 144–53, 186, 196, 197, 199, 202, 217, 219
Izmir, Turkey   135, 137
 Fair   138

Japan   7, 11, 13, 98, 122, 181–90, 195–6, 202, 268
Jellicoe, Admiral (John)   61

Jensen, Karl   176
Joaquín Mumbrú   80–1
Joffre, Joseph   78
Johannesburg, South Africa   255
Joint Intelligence Division (British)   163
Jullemier, Henri   39
Just War Theory   266, 271

Kashmir (disputed region between India and Pakistan)   214
Kelly, David   105, 111
Kennan, George   270
Kennedy, John F.   246
Khmer empire, Cambodia   241
Khrushchev, Nikita   7, 215
Kipling, Rudyard   26
Kirkpatrick, Helen   92, 97–8
Kirkpatrick, Ivone   104, 109
Kissinger, Henry   270
Knapp-Fischer, James   172, 174, 176, 177
Koch, Ottaviano   147
Koenig, Baron von. *See* Stallmann, Fritz (alias Baron von Koenig)
Koestler, Arthur   104
Köhler, Kurt   135
Korea, North   167
Korean War (1950–1953)   227, 252
Krukmann, Oluf   135

Lagos, Nigeria   233
Lao Doctrine (Latthi Lao)   239, 241, 244
Lao Ruam Samphan (LRS)   240, 242–3, 245–6
Laos   5, 7–8, 14, 239–47
Larissa (Thessaly), Greece   55
Lasswell, Harold   28–9
Latin America   9, 36–8, 41–3, 196, 199, 229–33, 267. *See also* South America
Latinity   7, 37, 147, 149, 163
Lausanne, Switzerland   228, 232–3
 Peace Treaty (1923)   132
Laval, Pierre   118, 123–4
Lazar, Hans   160
Lebensraum (Nazi concept of further 'living space')   135
Leeper, Rex   104–6, 112
Leigh, Vivien   219, 222
Lend-Lease aid   95–6

Lerroux, Alejandro   81
libraries. *See* books, bookstores and libraries
Libya   264
Lieven, Anatol   270
Lisbon, Portugal   6, 62–7, 71, 105, 111, 144–53, 184–7, 200, 234
Lloyd George, David   27–8, 52–3
Lobo, Pedro José   186
London, United Kingdom   26, 27, 52, 62, 63, 69, 91–2, 97, 103–8, 111, 112, 117, 120, 126, 160, 161, 173, 176, 196, 232, 253, 256, 259
   Naval Declaration of (1909)   69
   Treaty of (1839)   xvi
Low Countries   105, 116. *See also* Belgium; Luxembourg
Luang Prabang, Laos   240
Luce, Henry   198, 201
Ludendorff, Erich   23, 30
Lugano, Switzerland   107
Lugones, Leopoldo   39, 41
Lusaka, Zambia   256
Lusitania, RMS   28, 69
Luxburg affair. *See* Von Luxburg, Karl
Luxembourg   116. *See also* Low Countries

McCann, William (Billy)   160
McCarthyism   217–18, 271
Macau, China (formerly Portuguese)   7, 13, 181–91
Machado, Bernardino   62–3, 65, 66
Machiavelli, Niccolò   2
Mackenzie, Compton   50
Macmillan, Harold   257
McDermott, Michael J.   199
Madagascar   122
Madras Snowball   220–2
Madrid, Spain   75, 78, 80–1, 83, 105, 160, 163, 165, 200
Maffey, John   92, 98
magazines and journals   5, 9, 13, 27, 38, 40, 41, 43, 62, 65–71, 136, 138–9, 146, 150, 161, 170, 173, 186, 195–206, 220, 227, 229, 232, 234, 255, 263
Mahé, India (formerly French)   214
Malmö, Sweden   175–6

Manchuria/Manchukuo, Japanese Empire   183–4
Mandela, Nelson   232, 255–8
Manila, Philippines   64, 80
Manuel II, King of Portugal   63
Maoism   14, 227–35
Mao Zedong   232
Maribor, Slovenia   107
Marion, Paul   118
Marshall Plan   215
Martorell, Francisco   81
Masterman, Charles   26–8
Matlock, Jack   270
Mearsheimer, John   270
mediascapes   197, 206
Meinecke, Friedrich   42
Mendoza, Eduardo   83
Menemencioğlu, Numan   134
Mers el-Kébir, Algeria (also known as Oran)   119–22
Meves, Kresten   137
Middle East   4, 135, 258, 264, 266, 267
Mihailović, Draža   107–8
Milli Emniyet Hizmetleri Riyaseti (MEH) (the Presidency of National Security Services), Turkey   136, 139
Ministry of Information (MoI)
   British (First World War)   26, 28
   British (Second World War)   106, 111, 112, 160, 161, 165, 169–70, 173, 176–7, 200
   French (Second World War)   118, 126
   German (Second World War) (*see* Reichsministerium für Volksaufklärung und Propaganda (RMVP))
   South African   254
Moldova   271
Mondlane, Eduardo   234
Mongolia   271
Montagu Evans, C.   174–5, 177
Montoire, France   122–3
Montreux Convention (1936)   133
Moral Rearmament (organization)   229
Morocco   75, 163
Moscow, Russia (formerly Soviet Union)   134, 196, 214, 217, 218, 227–8, 230, 233, 264, 266, 268, 271

Mowlem, Rainsford 219
Mozambique 63–4, 69, 234
Mulder, Connie (and Muldergate scandal) 255
Müller, Emma 54, 56
Musk, Elon 265
Mussolini, Benito 11, 138, 145–51, 153
Myanmar 268

Namibia. *See* South West Africa
Nasser, Gamal Abdel 214–16
national languages, use as propaganda tool and/or form of national identity 7, 37, 150, 151, 187, 214, 217–18, 220–1, 240, 246, 247
National Liberation Front (NLF/Viet Cong) 241
National Schism, Greece 8, 10, 48–57
National Union Party (NUP), Laos 239, 240, 242–7
navies and navalism 26, 27, 61–72, 116, 118, 120, 159
  French Navy 116, 118, 120
  Portuguese Navy 65–7, 71
  Royal Navy (British) 26, 27, 61, 63–4, 120, 182
  Spanish merchant navy 159
Nedić, Milan 110
Nehru, Jawaharlal 214–16, 220–1, 256
Neo Lao Hak Xat (NLHX) 239–47
Neutralism 3, 14, 214, 239–41, 247
Neutrality
  and anti-neutrality 91, 250–1, 260
  changing nature to fit circumstances 134, 151, 158–9, 165
  debate around definition and importance xiv, 2, 48, 49, 117, 118, 159–60, 239–40, 263 (*see also* non-alignment; non-belligerency)
  debate around morality of 2–3, 8, 91, 93, 95, 98, 215, 251–2, 266
  debate on the future of 271
  declaration and non-declarations of 62, 64, 159, 241, 244

  importance of individuals and personalities in maintaining 91–2, 94, 214–15
  as part of national identity 2, 3, 8–10, 49–50, 57, 227
  reasons for (potentially) ending/violation of 4, 11, 15, 31, 41, 64, 76, 134–5, 157, 163–4, 229, 240, 257, 258
  and relationship with friendships, treaties and alliances xv, xvi, 75, 95, 132–4, 136, 144, 159, 188, 269
  in relation to mediation 4, 8, 75, 215
  in relation to trade and economic links 3, 5, 7–9, 35, 36, 38, 52–4, 63, 77, 96, 107, 124, 126, 134, 138, 160–1, 172–4, 177, 181, 183, 184, 227, 233, 251, 253–4, 258–9, 267
  and the role of collaboration 62, 63, 118, 122–4, 127, 133, 157, 159, 183, 185, 187, 188, 190, 268, 269
  role of neutrals as buffer states 4, 270, 271
  as a tool of propaganda 1, 8–10, 166, 215
  as a way of avoiding internal civil unrest 36, 75, 93, 118, 124, 132
  as a way of balancing belligerent powers 3, 36–7, 75, 83, 133–5, 139, 157, 162, 188
Neville, John 219
New Delhi, India 214, 268
newspapers. *See* press
New York, United States of America 27, 64, 81, 201, 232
Nicolau de Mesquita, Vicente 189
Nigeria 233
Non-Aligned Movement (NAM) 7, 14, 213–15, 218, 222, 268
non-alignment 3, 8, 14, 263, 269–71
non-belligerency 4, 7, 13, 63, 66–7, 69, 158–9, 162, 165
North Atlantic Treaty Organization (NATO) 15, 99, 265, 267, 269, 270

Northcliffe, Lord (Alfred Harmsworth) 26–9
Norway (and Norwegians-in-exile) 54, 169, 176

O'Hanlon, Michael 270
Office of Strategic Services (OSS) 108
Office of the Coordinator of Inter American Affairs (OCIAA) 196, 199
Office of War Information (OWI) 112, 163, 196, 198–9
Oistrakh, David 217
Old Vic 219–20
Olivier, Laurence 219, 222
Overlord (Operation) 98

Pais, Sidónio 63
Pakistan 214, 218
pan-Africanism 252
Pan Africanist Congress (PAC) 254
pan-Americanism 7, 36, 41, 43
pan-Asian 186, 190
pan-Germanism 40
pan-Hispanism 36, 164. *See also* Latinity
Paniguian, H. A. 111
pan-Turkism (Turan) 134, 139
Papen, Franz von 137, 140
Paris, France 62, 105, 108, 109, 126, 232–4
Parker, Gilbert 26–9
Pathet Lao (PL) 239–47
Paton, Alan 252
Patras, Greece 6, 51–2, 54–7
Pearl Harbor, Hawaii, United States of America 11
Pears, Peter 219–22
Pears, Thomas 160
Peloponnese, Greece 51–3, 55
People's Party of Switzerland (PPS) 234
Pestaña, Ángel 80
Pétain, Marshal Philippe 8, 108, 116–18, 122–4, 128
Peterson, H. C. 29
Phong Saly, Laos 241–2, 245
photographs/photography 2, 5, 38, 66, 67, 69, 71, 171, 173, 174, 195, 198–9, 201, 203–5
Phoui Sananikone 243

Phoumi Nosavan 246
Pinkus, Theo 6, 228
Pistolerismo 8, 11, 75–84
Plaza, Victorino de la 36
Poland 106, 176, 217–18, 222
Polianski, Nicolas 230
Political Warfare Executive (PWE) xv, 5, 12–13, 103–12, 158, 162–5
Pondicherry, India (formerly French) 214
Ponsonby, Arthur 29–30
Poppa, Lorenzo di 150
Porto, Portugal 62, 69, 148, 151
Portugal xiv–xv, 5–7, 11, 13, 61–72, 81, 105, 128, 144–53, 160, 181–91, 196, 214, 222, 234
Posse, Amelie 174
posters 5, 9, 10, 38, 117–19, 121–3, 125, 126, 172, 174
Potter, Mary 220–1
press 2, 5, 13, 26–7, 29, 30, 38–9, 44, 48–50, 52–4, 61–2, 64–7, 69, 71, 75, 76, 79–84, 94, 97–8, 104–5, 111–12, 118, 126, 127, 132, 136, 138–40, 144–5, 150, 160, 161, 165, 170–4, 176, 183–90, 199, 217, 219, 222, 228, 231–4, 240, 242–5, 247, 251, 252, 254–6, 263, 265–6, 269
Pretoria, South Africa 252, 254–6, 258, 259
printed publications (including leaflets, brochures, pamphlets, etc.) 2, 5, 9, 38–40, 43, 62, 71, 111, 136, 138–9, 152, 161, 163, 177, 199, 217, 228, 229, 232. *See also* magazines and journals; posters; press
Prisoners of War (PoWs) 42, 53, 56, 116, 123–4, 126, 175, 176, 202, 203, 205
propaganda
    through academic and student exchanges 135, 216–17, 220–1
    aiming to break neutrality 6–7, 11, 31, 41, 91, 250, 255, 257
    atrocities 6, 9, 11, 25, 29, 31, 40–3, 53, 94, 108, 110, 164, 206, 230, 250, 265

black propaganda   xv, 2, 103, 108–10, 112
challenges around coordination and execution   148, 157–8, 160, 173, 218, 222
changing of messages to circumstances   124, 218
connection to personal visits and personalities   2, 171, 184, 217–20, 222, 242, 256
debate around meaning   xiv–xv, 1–2, 51, 197, 213, 263
depictions of 'the other'   6, 42, 52, 54, 56, 91, 94, 118, 124, 126, 136–8, 140, 200–2, 206, 255, 260
grey propaganda   2, 175
importance of cross-border connections (including migration)   35–6, 38, 39, 43, 53, 93, 96, 151, 171, 174–7, 183, 214, 251–3, 257
importance of local circumstances   xiv, 5, 6, 35–40, 43, 48, 50, 52, 54, 55, 173, 200, 217, 240, 247, 251, 257, 260
for justifying war   2, 4, 6, 7, 35, 69, 93, 99, 164, 166, 264–6
and national identities and history   8, 10–11, 49, 56, 117, 145, 162, 201, 218, 254
objectives (especially in neutral countries)   1, 2, 6–7, 13, 26, 99, 160–2, 164, 196–8, 216–18
operational   6, 13, 158, 161–2, 165, 166
role of intellectuals   5–6, 35, 38–9, 41–3, 50, 76, 103–12, 137, 147, 148, 151, 171, 174, 222, 232–4
through speech acts   5, 27, 38–9, 52–3, 94, 96, 136, 176, 239–41, 247, 258
theme of empire/imperialism   7, 40, 42, 44, 120–2, 163
white propaganda   xv, 2
Propagandakompanien (PK-the Propaganda Companies of the German Armed Forces)   197
psychological warfare   xiv, xvi, 162
Pueyrredón, Honorio   36
Putin, Vladimir   265, 270

Quennell, Hugh   161
Quesada, Ernesto   6, 39, 42

racism   149, 202, 242, 252, 260, 264. *See also* propaganda, depictions of 'the other'
anti-Semitism   118, 124, 127, 137, 138, 228, 234
radio   2, 5, 62, 95, 108, 109, 117, 118, 123, 124, 127, 144, 163, 170, 171, 177, 187, 198, 199, 217, 222, 233, 240, 241, 244, 245, 259
Ramírez Sánchez, Ilich   233
Ramos, Juan P.   39–40, 42
Reagan, Ronald   258, 260
Red Cross. *See* International Committee of the Red Cross
Reddy, E. S.   255–6
Reeves, John   185
refugees   9, 174–7, 181–3, 185, 187, 189, 190, 231, 264
Rego, Leote do   71
Reichsministerium für Volksaufklärung und Propaganda (RMVP) (German propaganda ministry)   138–9, 198
religion
Anglicanism   159
Buddhism   239–44, 246–7
Catholicism   1, 7, 75, 92–3, 107, 127, 149, 160–1
Protestantism   93, 251
Relvas, José   66
Renault   109, 126
Reorganized National Government (RNG), China   183, 186, 190
Reparaz, Gonzalo de   43
Reservists (*Epistratoi*) Greece   52, 55
resistance (clandestine groups within occupied countries)   6, 103, 107, 110, 126, 127, 162–4, 169, 182–5, 190
Ribbentrop, Joachim von   109
Riesel, Victor   235
Robeson, Paul   252
Rockefeller, Nelson   199
Rockefeller Foundation   217
Rojas, Ricardo   39, 41
Romania   48, 50, 103, 149, 196

Romanones, Count of (Álvaro de Figueroa)   75–7
Rome, Italy   41, 110, 151
Roosevelt, Franklin Delano   91, 93–6, 98, 134, 199, 202
Rossi, Giuseppe Carlo   150
Royal Air Force (British)   109, 126, 169
Royal Institute of International Affairs (also known as 'Chatham House')   104, 106
Royal Lao Government (RLG)   240–1, 243
Ruben, Walter   137
Rueggeberg, Frederick   81
rumour-spreading, gossip, word-of-mouth propaganda   2, 5, 13, 54, 76, 78–9, 81, 84, 97, 105, 108–9, 112, 123, 161, 165, 174, 181, 183–5, 190
Russia   1, 4, 8, 15, 83, 93, 134, 176, 202, 216–17, 220, 263–71. *See also* Soviet Union
Russian Revolution   11, 76, 83
Russo-Ukrainian war (2022-)   263–71

Sachs, Eric   109–10
Sai-On   187–8
Salazar, António de Oliveira   xv, 144–5, 148–50, 153, 181, 189, 234
Sam Neua, Laos   241–2, 245
sanctions   15, 250, 253, 257, 258, 260, 263, 266–9
San Fulgencio   76
Sans Pau, Mariano   82
Sargent, Malcolm   219–20
Sarper, Selim   139
Saviotti, Gino   6, 148–53
Schafer, Eduard   137
Schenck, Karl Freiherr von   50
Schmidt, Hans-Thilo   83
Schmidt-Dumont, Franz Frederik   135–6, 140
Schwarzenegger, Arnold   265
Scoppa, Renato Bova   149
Scott, Michael   251–2
'Scrap of paper' (reference to violation of Belgian neutrality, 1914)   xvi, 40
Second United Front, China   183
Secret Intelligence Service (SIS/MI6)   103, 106

Senegal (formerly French West Africa)   122
Serbia   49, 110, 267, 271. *See also* Yugoslavia
Seskuria, Natia   270
Seton-Watson, R. W.   104
Seville, Spain   163
Shakespeare, William   218–19
Shanghai (now People's Republic of China)   181, 188
Sharpeville massacre (1960)   15, 250
shipping
  blockades   7, 9, 23, 43, 50–1, 120, 126–7, 184
  general interest in, and the importance of   65–7, 81, 95, 134, 159, 187, 199
  sinking of   6, 36, 62, 67, 69–71, 76, 80, 81, 120
  submarine warfare   7, 9, 28, 31, 36, 41, 53, 61, 64, 67, 69, 71, 76, 80–1, 96, 159
  warships   61, 66
Sicily, Italy   201
Singapore   185, 268
Sino-Soviet Split   7, 14, 227–34, 268
Slovenia   107, 110. *See also* Yugoslavia
social media. *See* digital propaganda
soft power   xiv–xv, xvi, 13, 14, 165, 213
Solm, Fritz   198
South Africa   8, 14, 232, 250–60
South America   7, 35–44, 146, 164, 202, 258, 268. *See also* Latin America
South West Africa (Namibia)   252
Souvanna Phouma   239–47
Soviet Union (sometimes referred to as USSR)   3, 14, 93, 96, 117, 124, 126, 128, 133–5, 159, 166, 172, 176–7, 196, 201, 202, 213, 215–17, 220, 222, 227–30, 259, 268, 270. *See also* Russia
Soweto, South Africa   255
Spain   xiv, 6–8, 11, 13, 36, 40, 75–84, 105, 120, 122, 144, 149, 157–66, 182, 196, 200, 222
Spanish Civil War   11, 13, 76, 144, 149, 157, 159, 163

Special Operations Executive (SOE) (also SO1)   103, 105–6, 111, 161, 170
Sprigge, Cecil   104
Squires, James Duane   30
Stalingrad, Battle of   126, 176, 177
Stallmann, Fritz (alias Baron von Koenig)   79, 82–4
Stark, J. C.   199
Stavropoulos, Aristides   54
Stewart, Michael   160
Stockholm, Sweden   13, 105, 169, 170, 173, 174, 176–7
Stohrer, Eberhard von   160
Stoltenhoff, Herman   54
Straits (Turkish) of the Dardanelles and Bosphorus   133–4
Streit, Georgios   48
Stuart, Campbell   29, 105–6
Stummvoll, Alber   137
Suez Canal, Egypt (including Suez Crisis (1956))   7, 215, 217, 220, 222
Sullivan, Leon   254
Sun Yat-sen   190
surveillance (and counter-surveillance)   110, 132, 136, 140, 169, 172, 174, 176, 228–33
Sutton, Nigel   108–9
Sweden   11, 13, 15, 127, 169–77, 182, 196, 222, 233, 267–9
    Swedish Civilian Security Service   170, 172, 174–5, 177
Swiss Party of Labour   229, 232–3
Switzerland   2–3, 6–7, 9, 11–12, 14–15, 51, 54, 65, 103–12, 120, 182, 196, 227–35, 268–70
Syria (including former French mandate of)   117, 122, 124, 264, 267

Tambo, Oliver   256
Tannenberg, Otto Richard   40
Tanzania   233
Tarragona, Spain   83
Tehran Conference (1943)   134
Teixeira, Gabriel Maurício   184–5
Tennant, Peter   170–1, 173–5
Terragni, Vittorio   152
Terry, Mike   253
Teutonia Club, Turkey   136

Thailand (previously Siam)   241
Thatcher, Margaret   257, 260
Thessaloniki, Greece   49–50
Thorndike, Sybil   220, 222
Tiao Somsanith   244
Tibet   231, 246
Ticino/Tessin, Switzerland (with Italian enclave)   110
Timor, Portuguese (now East Timor)   185, 188
Tirana, Albania   233
Tito, Josip Broz   107–8, 214–16, 218–20
Tong, Hollington (Dong Xianguang)   187
Torch (Operation)   126
Toulouse, France   108
Tower, Reginald   39
Toydemir, Ahmet Muzaffer   139
Toynbee, Arnold   104
treaties   xv, xvi, 30, 76, 99, 116, 118, 122, 132–4, 144, 188, 265
Trieste, Italy   55, 219
Trinchet, Avelino   80
Troeltsch, Ernst   42
Turkey   6, 13, 132–40, 200, 222, 267
Turkmenistan   271
Twardoch, Szczepan   270
Twitter   265

Ukraine   1, 8, 15, 263–71
Union of Soviet Societies of Friendship and Cultural Relations with Foreign Countries   216
United Kingdom. *See* Britain (Great Britain/United Kingdom (UK))
United Nations (during Second World War, often meaning Great Britain, the United States of America and the Soviet Union)   98, 159, 162–6, 174, 177
United Nations (post-war organization)   99, 135, 215, 217, 250, 252, 255–6, 258–9, 265, 267
United Nations Educational, Scientific and Cultural Organization (UNESCO)   217
United States
    and Argentina (First World War)   35–7, 41, 43–4

and Britain (First World War)   6, 9, 23–31
and Britain (Second World War)   4
and China   188
and Cold War   3, 14, 213, 215, 216, 240–3, 246–7
and Egypt   217
and Germany (First World War)   4
and Iraq   264
and Ireland (Second World War)   91–9
and Laos   240–3, 246–7
and magazines   13, 196–205
and Pearl Harbor (1941)   11
and South Africa   14–15, 250–60
and Spain (First World War)   76
and Spain (Second World War)   159, 162
and Sweden (Second World War)   176
and Turkey (Second World War)   139
and Ukraine   15, 264–71
and Vichy France   117, 124, 126
and 'War on Terror'   266
and Yugoslavia   215–17
United States Information Agency (USIA)   216–17, 221–2
Uppsala, Sweden   169
USSR. *See* Soviet Union

Valera, Éamon de   12, 91–8, 219
Vatican   117
Venizelos, Eleftherios   48–52, 54, 55, 57
Vergès, Jacques   232–3
Versailles (Peace Conference, and Treaty of, (1919))   30, 69
Vichy France. *See* France
Vienna, Austria   2, 8, 30, 105, 107, 136
Vientiane, Laos   245, 246
Viereck, George Sylvester   29
Viet Minh   239
Vietnam (including North Vietnam and Vietnam War)   7, 229, 241, 245, 247, 253
Visser t'Hooft, Willem   107
visual and performative arts (including music and theatre)   xvi, 2, 13, 62, 67, 152, 174, 176, 183, 184, 195, 200, 217–19, 222, 256

Voigt, Frederick   104
VOKS (All-Union Society for Cultural Ties)   216–17, 222
Volos, Greece   55
Volpel, Alfons   137
Volpen, Bavarian   137
Von Luxburg, Karl   36, 41
Vorster, B. J.   255

Walshe, Joseph   92, 94, 96–8
Walt, Stephen   270
Wang Jingwei   183, 186, 190
Washington, George   96
Washington DC, United States of America   25, 27, 91, 96, 196, 240, 241
Weapons of Mass Destruction (WMDs)   264
Wehrmacht Propaganda Department (WPr.)   196–8
Wehrmachtsender Nord ('Wehrmacht Transmitter North'-PWE black radio station)   109
Wellington House   26–8
Weyler, Valeriano   80
Wilhelm II, Kaiser of Germany   30, 41, 49, 68
Wilson, Harold   253
Wilson, Woodrow   28, 30–1, 53, 78–9
Winant, John   97
Winsor, Rita   106
Wiskemann, Elizabeth   6, 12, 103–12
Wutöschingen, Germany   108

Yemen   264
Yergan, Max   252
YouTube   265
Yrigoyen, Hipólito   36
Yugoslavia   5, 14, 103, 106, 107, 110–11, 214–20, 264. *See also* Serbia; Slovenia
Zagreb, Croatia (formerly within Yugoslavia)   218
Zaharoff, Basil   50
Zambia   256
Zimbabwe   257
Zimmermann Telegram   28, 31
Zurich, Switzerland   105, 228

www.ingramcontent.com/pod-product-compliance
Lightning Source LLC
Chambersburg PA
CBHW071802300426
44116CB00009B/1178